Mayhem in the Morra!

By

Marc Esserman

Quality Chess
www.qualitychess.co.uk

First edition 2012 by Quality Chess UK Ltd
Fourth print 2021

Mayhem in the Morra!

Paperback ISBN 978-1-907982-20-0
Hardcover ISBN 978-1-907982-21-7

All sales or enquiries should be directed to Quality Chess UK Ltd,
Suite 247, Central Chambers, 11 Bothwell Street,
Glasgow G2 6LY, United Kingdom
Phone +44 141 204 2073
e-mail: info@qualitychess.co.uk
website: www.qualitychess.co.uk

Distributed in North and South America by National Book Network

Distributed in Rest of the World by Quality Chess UK Ltd through
Sunrise Handicrafts, ul. Szarugi 59a, 21-002 Marysin, Poland

Typeset by Jacob Aagaard
Proofreading by Andrew Greet & John Shaw
Edited by Colin McNab
Cover design by Jason Mathis
Printed in Estonia by Tallinna Raamatutrükikoja LLC

Contents

Foreword

"It's not business Larry, it's strictly personal." So said International Master Marc Esserman when I asked him why he planned to write a book on the Morra Gambit. His massive treasury of Morra files will be unlocked and the secrets and ideas he has accumulated over the years will be revealed in this book.

Marc adopted the Morra Gambit in his youth and soon weaponized the quaint, tame house pet into a snarling, vicious pitbull of an opening. Esserman has convinced hardcore skeptics. He has refuted many a "refutation". He has forced many opponents to spend countless hours preparing for the dreaded thing. Many formerly proud acceptors have become meek, sniveling decliners when faced with Esserman's dreaded 3.c3. Essermania has spawned Esserphobia. Answering 1.e4 c5 2.d4 cxd4 3.c3 with the "beta" replies 3...♘f6 and 3...g6 is a significant psychological victory for White by move 3.

In 2011, when preparing for the US Championship, I decided to employ the Morra Gambit as a surprise weapon if given the chance. Marc supplied me with a vast amount of analysis and novelties for that tournament and I became convinced that the gambit was not only dangerous, but perfectly sound. There is no greater authority in the world on this line than Marc Esserman and he lays it all out there in this book.

"It's not business, it's strictly personal."

Grandmaster Larry Christiansen
Three-time US Champion

Foreword

The first time I met Marc was at the Foxwoods Open in 2009. Friends had warned me about him. After the game, which I won, it became clear to me that Marc is a passionate lover of chess who likely dedicates more time to analyzing the game than many top GMs.

Our rematch took place at the 2011 US Open in Orlando. Marc played the Morra Gambit! What !#%?@?$!%! I had just recently visited Boston, where Marc resides. There I played some blitz games in Harvard Square versus his friend, Jorge Sammour-Hasbun, who also used this "weapon". When Marc ventured 1.e4 c5 2.d4, I thought, "Is he serious? Are we going to play coffeehouse today?" Now I know the answer, and the answer is *yes*! I got crushed in an impressive way, leaving me both groggy and completely mad, forcing me to consider the Morra seriously for the first time in my life. After the tournament, Marc and I had a thematic blitz match to test our ideas.

I must admit, life still isn't easy against the Morra. I am sure that in this book, Marc will provide you with many interesting ideas and analysis. I am also convinced that you will have some enjoyable attacking games, at the cost of *only* one pawn!

Grandmaster Loek van Wely
Winner of countless tournaments and former top 10 player

Key to symbols used

±	White is slightly better
∓	Black is slightly better
±	White is better
∓	Black is better
+−	White has a decisive advantage
−+	Black has a decisive advantage
=	equality
∞	with compensation
⇄	with counterplay
∞	unclear
→	with an attack
↑	with initiative
?	a weak move
??	a blunder
!	a good move
!!	an excellent move
!?	a move worth considering
?!	a move of doubtful value
#	mate
□	the only move
N	a new move

Dedication

To my professional coaches throughout the years – GM Anatoly Lein, GM William Lombardy, and IM Calvin Blocker. Without them, this book would not be possible.

Preface

By the author

At 16, I found myself in the bookstore innocently browsing before the 2000 US Masters, my first ever invitational event. Suddenly, a title struck my eye. Leafing through, some words popped out of the pages and became etched in my memory forever:

> "Why did you elect to take up the Smith-Morra Gambit in the first place? The gambit is a good weapon for blitz chess, useful in teaching tactics to a young player, and fun to play. But if you expect to get a good result with it at the higher levels of serious tournament competition, and think the logical outcome of a game after using it is only a draw for Black with perfect play, we express our condolences. It is difficult to have a serious discourse with someone who insists the earth is flat."[1]

As a teenager all I knew were the games of Paul Morphy, the leader of the Romantic generation. Pawns were sacrificed as the pieces came to the fore with stunning speed, sweeping away all in their path until the king himself succumbed to their power. Whereas now the Berlin and Petroff steal the show, then the Evans and King's gambits governed the landscape. Occasionally the gambiteer would flounder as the defender grabbed all material in sight and lived to tell the tale. But far more inspiring were those cases when two plus two did not equal four,[2] and our royal game revealed far greater depth than mere greed and number-crunching extra pawns to bland victory. Perhaps the author meant simply to attack only the Morra Gambit, but in my young mind he was desecrating the great Morphy and the entire Romantic chess era. I would not let such dogma stand; it could not stand.

A few hours later the Morra appeared on my board, but my opponent was not in the least perturbed. He blitzed out the opening with an aura of confidence bordering on arrogance that I had never encountered, until we reached the very starting position of the book I had just been reading, "Smith-Morra Gambit, Finegold Defense". Quite odd, I mused, but plowed forward nonetheless, thinking for over an hour on move 11. Eventually my opponent too slowed down, I drummed up a decisive attack, tragically missed a mate in two, and lost.

Only afterwards did I receive the shock that my adversary, National Master Bob Ciaffone, co-authored the "Finegold Defense". In the post-mortem, the masters surmised that I fought valiantly and showed some imagination, but ultimately the Morra Gambit remained unsound and I should just learn a new opening. But every time a move flashed on the board which defied their conclusion, I thought I could detect a creeping doubt that maybe, just maybe, the world was flatter than my opponent imagined. I was defeated, but invigorated, having successfully challenged a published author in a debate where we were polar opposites. I went on to use the Smith-Morra Gambit successfully twice more in the 2000 US Masters: once against the young

Hikaru Nakamura, and in the last round vs. FM Chow, who, in a perfect storybook ending, adopted the Finegold Defense himself! After an early bishop sacrifice, my knight raided the Black camp from its e6-outpost, and I won in short order. The coup prompted my objective opponent to pay the ultimate compliment – he remained unconvinced that the Finegold Defense refuted the Smith-Morra Gambit. Chow urged me to keep exploring the possibilities hidden in the gambit, and projected that in my hands the Morra may morph into a formidable weapon after all.

History has not been kind to the Smith-Morra. While the King's and Evans gambits had their time under the sun during the 19th century, the Morra has always remained in the shadows. Although the Sicilian's purest gambit did in fact debut in 1846 in Kieseritzky's practice during the height of the Romantic movement,[3] it remained eclipsed by its more accomplished brothers. Perhaps had it fallen into Morphy's hands, the world would have taken notice.[4] But alas, the gambit stayed buried in the rubble for another 100 years, only to surface again in an era where it was not welcome. Just a glance at Bronstein's famed tournament book of Zurich 1953 would tell a time traveler that the glorious games of the Romantic era had become museum artifacts.[5] The closed openings (much reviled by Morphy) ruled the day. While the masters lauded their improved defensive technique as the demise of the reckless swashbuckling play of yore, occasionally there remained a rebellion scattered across the chess kaleidoscope. The flair of the Romantic school flowed through both Bronstein and Spassky, and their reverence for the forgotten art form took center stage in their classic King's Gambit encounter. And we cannot forget Fischer's demolition of Fine in 1963, when he paid tribute to Morphy's beloved Evans Gambit. But the Romantics were fighting a losing battle, and after Spassky's King's Gambit coup over Fischer, the American genius vowed to refute the relic gambit once and for all. As the global chess level advanced through time and the game became further subjected to brutal, concrete analysis, surely the colorful, emotional play of the 19th century could not survive.

Within this hostile environment, the Smith-Morra Gambit re-emerged. While the dangerous Yugoslav attacking grandmasters, in particular Matulovic, achieved some resounding victories in the Morra, the current of history could simply sweep aside these uprisings as isolated rebellions. Despite his success, Matulovic eventually abandoned the opening, and the young gambit, without the medals of honor from the 19th century, desperately longed for a shining knight.

Sadly, no world class player would lead the charge. While Spassky still felt comfortable dabbling in the established King's Gambit, he would never dare to test the fledgling Morra Gambit. In 1960, Fischer would take up the mantle, unleashing the gambit to surprise Korchnoi. Yet despite being on the dominant end of a tense draw, Fischer would not try again. He seemed content for the gambit to remain a surprise, and nothing more.[6]

Alas, history would choose Ken Smith as the gambit's champion and name bearer.[7] The inherent risk in the gambit naturally appealed to Smith's gambling nature, who aside from being a FIDE Master and avid chess enthusiast, donned the hat of a world class poker player.[8] Smith would author a myriad of books and articles promoting the Morra, and in the San Antonio international tournament of 1972, the time came for him to showcase the virtues of the gambit to the world. However, it was not to be. Smith lost all three Morra Gambit scuffles badly vs. world class players (IM Donald Byrne, GM Larry Evans, and GM Henrique Mecking), and the harsh chess public swiftly passed its verdict on the young gambit. The popular sentiments of the day can no better be summarized than by Grandmaster and World Championship Candidate Bent Larsen. While annotating one of Smith's other games during the tournament, Larsen quipped about the opponent's choice to play the French Defense: "1...e6?, stronger is 1...c5 which wins a pawn."[9] Smith had threatened the established thinking of the day, and the grandmasters were quick to shoot his beloved gambit down. While still considered second-rate, the esteemed King's and Evans gambits were never chided in such a fashion. When Kasparov crushed both Anand and Piket in the Evans Gambit in 1994, the public praised his brilliant, if risky, play. But did Kasparov win because he played the Evans Gambit, or because he is Kasparov? Likewise, did Ken Smith lose in San Antonio 1972 because of the Morra's faulty DNA, or because he was simply outgunned by grandmasters?

The ripples of Smith's losses in San Antonio 1972 are still felt in modern times. As a teenager surveying the book store, I could not understand why such an inspiring opening faced such hostility from the chess public. Now with age and the study of history, I do. The young gambit, with virtually only 60 years of practice today, has never received its proper evaluation. Far worse, it has never even been given a chance; its life cut short, tragically pronounced dead in its second decade of testing.

This book will finally give the Morra Gambit its chance to shine. I have ventured the King's, Evans, and Smith-Morra gambits in tournament and rapid play against strong grandmasters. My results in the Morra are by far the best in these contests. In the last 8 years, I have lost only twice with the Morra Gambit in tournament play, both defeats not a result of the opening. I have faced two players over 2700 FIDE in the Morra Accepted in tournament play. In both cases, they lost in under 30 moves. Luck? Perhaps. During a phase of my career when I would lose game after game with the Evans, I would win on command in the Morra Gambit. Can this statistic simply be ignored as a result of my superior knowledge of the Morra Gambit compared to the Evans? Perhaps. But at the highest level, there is no luck in chess – all can be explained by the art of scientific analysis.

Nothing will be hidden in this book. There are no gimmicks here, no attempts to conceal novelties for later use on an unsuspecting opponent. The reader can expect the truth – nothing less. The Sicilian's only true gambit must take its rightful place in history.[10]

If gambits were viewed with skepticism in the 1950's, then in modern days, the sentiments have turned to downright scorn. The Evans Gambit has all but disappeared at the top level. Meanwhile, the King's Gambit just became the butt of a worldwide April Fool's Day joke when a 3000 core machine proclaimed it refuted at last. Naturally, many got duped![11] And 1.e4 c5 2.d4(?). Well, it just loses a pawn! The general public simply does not believe that the Romantic gambits can survive the rugged world of objective, precise, unforgiving computer analysis.

But tell that to all the grandmasters who now decline the Morra Gambit or simply don't even brave playing the Sicilian against me. Perhaps there is a crack in the armor of the materialists' mantra two plus two equals four. Perhaps there is a growing rebellion against conventional thinking. Perhaps the earth is flat after all.

As I'd do with any serious opening, I will not stop the analysis in each critical variation until I have demonstrated that White is fighting for the advantage. Yes, that is not a misprint – that **White** is fighting for an advantage in the Morra Gambit. If after studying the Morra Gambit for 15 years I did not believe I could make this claim, I would not be writing this book.

For the practical player not so much concerned about the tides of history as about maximizing chess results, I will now speak to you. In the pages ahead you will find a stockpile of heavy artillery to combat the Sicilian successfully, against players of all levels, from amateur to grandmaster. Your opponents, meanwhile, will be placed under considerable psychological strain, not only because of your imposing style of play, but because the Morra Gambit does not constitute part of their standard main line Sicilian preparations. Do not be mistaken, however – this is not simply a "how to" opening book. Rather, it expounds a philosophy of dynamic, attacking chess in general and the Morra Gambit is merely my featured guest. Thus, sprinkled across the pages you will find games which at first glance seem to have no relation to the Morra Gambit. Yet once you scale the Morra's vast, overarching theme base, the sparkling similarities will be as clear as day. Ultimately, even when you are faced with mainstream chess positions, you will be able to more successfully apply the principles of the Romantic school to your chess praxis.

Lastly, even if you have no interest in playing the Morra Gambit or doubt that it could ever be sound, your overall chess imagination and vision will improve as a result of studying this book. I dare you to push forward, and you will be exposed to possibilities you never thought existed on the chessboard. And if you finish the task, you will add a new dimension to your chess understanding, no matter what positions you choose to play. This is why Spassky's legendary coach Tolush urged him to play gambits, and why my first professional coach, IM Calvin Blocker, taught me the Smith-Morra Gambit as a youngster.

I hope this book inspires a whole younger generation to take up the forgotten art of gambit play which so enriches the possibilities in our game and chess players in general. I hope that as a result of this book, aspiring professional players have the courage to test the gambit at the highest level, pushing this fascinating opening into mainstream modern chess. And lastly, I ironically hope that after this book, the Morra Gambit Declined (which I also copiously cover) becomes the main line after 1.e4 c5 2.d4 cxd4 3.c3. After all, every player who declines the gambit tacitly admits that there is indeed much to fear! May the Smith-Morra Gambit finally have a home, a firm foothold in the 21st century, 200 years after its predecessors.

IM Marc Esserman
Cambridge, Massachusetts
June 2012

Introduction

The Much Maligned Morra

After 1.e4 c5 2.d4 cxd4 3.c3,

we reach the starting position of the much maligned Morra Gambit. I must confess that this is often the moment in my chess praxis when my heart thumps most – will my opponent accept the sacrifice in the spirit of the Romantics, or will he shun the most honorable path and meekly decline? Sometimes I wait for the critical decision for many minutes as my grandmaster foe flashes me an incredulous, bordering on insulted, look. Other times, I receive the answer almost instantaneously. Yet every time I am greeted with 3...dxc3, I could not be happier. My knight freely flows to c3, the Morra accepted appears, and we travel back in time to the 19th century. Already ahead a full tempo in development, I smile, knowing that all of my pieces will soon flood the center. My bishops will zoom to the central diagonals, and my nimble queen will influence any sector of the board she desires. Meanwhile, Black remains cramped. His queen and bishops lie sleeping, and while his queen's knight can reach c6 unharmed, the king's knight must constantly fret about the dangerous e4-e5 thrust.

The Morra Gambit vs. the King's and Evans gambits

But this only scratches at the surface of the gambit's depth. In order to fully appreciate why the Morra can endure the 21st century's rigorous analytical microscope, we must first compare the gambit to its two elder brothers which have virtually disappeared from top level chess, the King's and Evans gambits. In the King's Gambit,

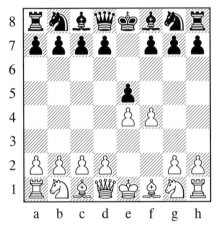

White sacrifices his king's bishop pawn for central dominance. However, his aggression comes at a hefty price – not only does he lose a pawn, but all of the squares around his king are critically weakened forever. So often it is not White's minus pawn in the King's Gambit, but a compromised king, which ultimately leads to his demise. Likewise, in the swashbuckling Evans,

the gambiteer sacrifices his queen's knight pawn to gain tempi on the black bishop via c2-c3 and d2-d4, erecting a central pawn mass in the process. But again, the price is steep, as the lunging b2-b4 undermines the solidity of White's queenside, chiefly the c3- and c4-squares. In both of these illustrious openings, if the gambiteer does not swiftly sweep Black

off the board, his game will likely become positionally bankrupt. To cast further doubt upon the ancient gambits, after 1.e4 e5, Black's king's bishop already can move, thus bringing him one step closer to castling out of danger. In contrast, in the Morra Gambit, the bishop starts buried on f8. As a result, Black's king often never escapes the pelting central crossfire.

Yet it's not all so cut and dry. To the credit of Morra bashers, Black does possess a full extra central pawn for his woes (while in the King's and Evans gambits, White sacrifices only a flank pawn.) But to take the conversation into the concrete, Black can blunt the Morra gambiteer's assault on the sensitive f7-square with ...e6, a defense not available in the classical e4/e5 gambits. The extra central d-pawn then may make an immediate impact, sliding up to d6 and plugging any holes while restraining White's e4-e5 advances. No wonder then that the solid ...e6 and ...d6 pawn duo, establishing a Scheveningen Sicilian-like fortress, is one of the most trusted ways to subdue Morra mayhem.

Yet in the final analysis, the secret to the Morra Gambit's longevity lies not solely in the tactical arena (all gambits pose immediate tactical dangers to the defender). Rather, the Morra is also firmly *positionally* grounded. For starters, a Morra gambiteer may safely castle and tuck away his king on g1 behind a healthy blanket of pawn cover. The same luxury is not available in the King's Gambit (so aptly named for throwing the white king's safety to the wind). On the other end of the board, White's rooks may rush to c1 and d1, where they will chew up central squares on the wide open c- and d-files. Take a close look at the Morra accepted starting position again – White simply has no obvious weaknesses! This fact alone can breed a doomsday psychology from the defender as he struggles to deal with reality. He knows he is up a pawn, he knows he should win easily – after all, the chess authorities said so. As all of these thoughts cloud his thinking, the freewheeling gambiteer slowly increases the pressure, his pieces ready to ravage. Even in the worst case scenario, when White's potent e4-pawn and Black's passive d6-pawn swap off and the gambiteer obtains only nebulous compensation in return, the menacing Morra rooks and imposing centralization of White's forces can still strain the defender's delicate psyche.

The d4-square – White's only true weakness

Only a keen eye can spot the one true defect in White's starting position: the d4-square. As a result of pushing 1 e4 and then shedding the c pawn, the gambiteer lacks proper pawn protection against an enemy incursion on d4. Particularly, a black knight plopping on d4, especially when supported by the e5-pawn, can virtually paralyze White. However, to access the d4 soft spot, the defender must make some serious concessions.

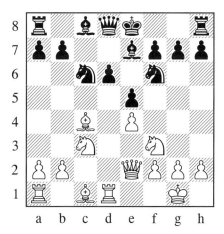

Black has just played ...e6-e5, securing a foothold on d4. In return, he surrenders the d5-square for White's pieces. But hastily probing the d5-square further with 10.♗g5(?) meets strict punishment. After 10...♗g4! Black becomes master of the center, as the highly unpleasant threat of ...♘d4 looms large. A Morra virtuoso would never allow such a beast into the heart of his camp, and instead would overprotect d4 with ♗e3! immediately. Only after the sensitive d4-square is under lock and key would White then continue his plans to conquer d5 and the rest of the board.

A good rule of thumb – Chase the black queen!

Too often the novice gambiteer believes that there is only one formulaic setup for White, namely 5.♘f3, 6.♗c4, 7.0–0, 8.♕e2, 9.♖fd1, and then hope for the best. While this sequence is normally the correct method against the d6-e6 Scheveningen defenses, thinking in these simple terms will often get you into deep trouble. In fact, the savvy defender lies awake at night wishing that you have such a misunderstanding. Achieving Morra mastery requires great mental flexibility, but if you must abide by a Morra formula, the most powerful one would be: *when in doubt, chase the black queen.*

In the Open Sicilian, White's c2-pawn obstructs his rook from participating in the fight for the c-file. As a result, Black often makes the c-file his permanent base of operations, with a rook on c8 patrolling the half-open line and the black queen comfortably perched on c7. However, in the Morra Gambit, the fully open c-file morphs into White's greatest asset. The gambiteer's lead in development ensures that his queen's rook will reach c1 first, thus serving fair warning to the black queen that c7 is no longer safe territory. The queen can be hounded on her original d8-square as well, as White's other rook can easily target her from d1. If she heads to e7, she may obstruct the harmonious development of the king's bishop and the entire kingside in turn. If she pokes her head out to b6 or a5, she comes under fire from a pawn advance b2-b4 or a sleek ♗d2 or ♗e3. If she obstinately tries to beat the queen's rook to the punch with a premature ...♕c7, White's queen's knight can harass her with ♘b5 (or even the sacrificial ♘d5) and White's queen's bishop can also get into the act with ♗f4. And if she ever plays it too cool on b8, the entombed rook on a8 will pay dearly for her cowardice. As you can see, finding a harmonious square for the queen is Black's main headache in the Morra Gambit, and if he can solve this problem, he often solves the Morra riddle. Let us now witness some queen hunting in action.

Chase #1

The following example, which made a great impression upon me as a young Morraphile, can be found in Graham Burgess's groundbreaking 1994 Smith-Morra Gambit book. Burgess featured the sequence to explain why Black cannot make simple developmental moves in the Morra Gambit and survive. We will be viewing it from a different lens, with an eye for rabidly chasing the black queen to and fro.

1.e4 c5 2.d4 cxd4 3.c3 dxc3 4.♘xc3 ♘c6 5.♘f3

In every example in this book, White's king's knight will develop to its natural f3-square.

5...d6 6.♗c4

Likewise, White's king's bishop takes aim on the aggressive "Italian" diagonal in almost all cases.[12]

6...e6

Black adopts the solid Scheveningen structure alluded to earlier, and so the gambiteer readies for the standard 0–0, ♕e2, ♖d1 plan.

7.0–0 ♘f6 8.♕e2 ♗e7 9.♖d1

The chase begins. If the queen flees to c7, White's cavalry keeps stalking her via b5.

Here the old main line of the Morra Gambit, 9...e5, prevents White's e4-e5 thrust but consequently weakens the d5-square forever.

The passive 9...♗d7 also blocks the d-file pin but interferes with the queen's guard of d6. There are just no easy answers against the Morra's flowing compensation.

9...0–0?

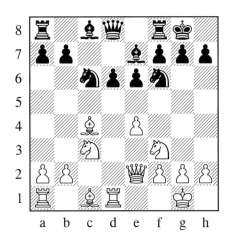

10.e5!

Black is scolded for his carelessness, and must retreat to a fallback position.

10...♘e8 11.exd6 ♗xd6

11...♘xd6 12.♗f4+– and the crushing pin decides. 12...e5 (12...a6 13.♗xd6 ♗xd6 14.♘e4+–) 13.♘xe5 only prolongs the inevitable.

12.♘b5! ♕e7

The hapless queen runs, but she cannot hide.

12...a6 13.♘xd6 ♘xd6 14.♗f4±

13.♗g5!

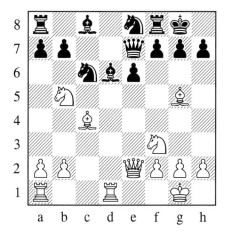

The queen has already been harried by both White's knight and rook. But now the bishop gives her the treatment, thus forcing a critical kingside weakness which will decide the outcome shortly.

13...f6 14.♗e3!

Not just any random retreat! The bishop intends further mayhem after ♘xd6 and ♗c5.

14...♗b8 15.♖ac1!

The heavy piece storm never relents. The Morra rooks reach their natural squares, and the game of hide and seek nears its conclusion. The gambiteer now menaces ♗c5 followed by ♗xe6†, winning.

15...♕f7, seeking refuge near her king, would still fail to ♗c5.

15...b6 16.♗b3!

White remains a pawn down, but the rooks are chewing up the board, creating decisive threats against Black's minor pieces. Black is bullied to the back rank, a theme you will see throughout the book.

16...♗b7

16...♗d7 17.♗c5 bxc5 18.♖xd7! ♕xd7 19.♗xe6†+– Chasing down the queen one last time.

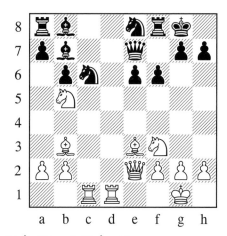

17.♗c5! bxc5 18.♗xe6†

18.♖d7?! suggests itself. But the prosaic yet stronger text gives up less material for the queen.

18...♔h8 19.♖d7!

And the hunt finally ends. White's forces doggedly swarmed the queen, never letting her out of their sights.

Chase #2

In our next example the black queen has mischief on her mind early on. She aims to end the game immediately before White's pieces swirl about.

1.e4 c5 2.d4 cxd4 3.c3 dxc3 4.♘xc3 e6 5.♘f3 ♘c6 6.♗c4 ♕c7 7.0–0 ♘f6

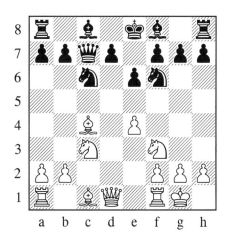

Here, so many neophytes continue with the illogical ♕e2. As the black queen just vanished from the d-file, the natural follow up ♖d1 has therefore lost its sting. While already lacking in strategy, the mindless ♕e2 makes even less sense tactically...

8.♘b5!

8.♕e2? ♘g4! and Black readies to spring the infamous Siberian trap. I banish this snare to Chapter 1 so that you will never, ever fall for it. Such a coup simply makes the Morra bashers way too happy. 9.h3?? ♘d4! And in the blink of an eye, White must either lose his queen or resign, as mate on h2 looms. What a teary tale for gambiteers worldwide. Observe once again that the fatal blow fell on the d4-square, the Morra's Achilles heel.

But if White follows the maxim of stalking the queen, he will not become the subject of public ridicule. Rather, the black queen will be reprimanded for her tricky ways, and sent back to "Siberia", or the frigid corner of the board, so to speak.

8...♕b8 9.e5!

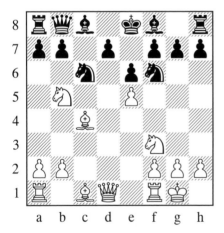

White hopes that Black continues with his greedy strategy. First he took on c3, now will he grab twice?

9...♘xe5?! 10.♘xe5! ♕xe5 11.♖e1!±

And it is open season on the queen again. Her troubles are just beginning, as we shall find out soon enough.

Chase #3

In our next display, also a main line, White has two different methods of pursuing the queen.

1.e4 c5 2.d4 cxd4 3.c3 dxc3 4.♘xc3 ♘c6 5.♘f3 d6 6.♗c4 e6 7.0–0 a6

Black takes a tempo to stop the pesky ♘b5 so that his queen can rest at c7, if only for a moment...

8.♕e2 ♘f6 9.♖d1 ♕c7

The gambiteer's bishop now sharply glares at the queen along the h2-b8 diagonal.

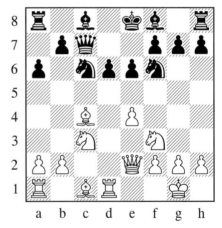

10.♗f4! ♗e7 11.♖ac1!?

The Morra rook seizes control of the c-file, reminding the queen that this is no Open Sicilian. White can give chase immediately with 11.e5!?, leading to great complications, or delay the hunt...

11...0–0 12.♗b3!

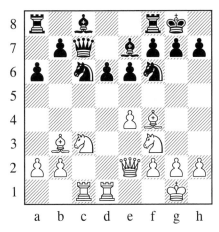

And the rook draws one step closer to its target. 13.♘d5 beckons, forcing the defender to duck and cover.

Chase #4

Our last example covers a variation favored by many strong grandmasters. Once again, the gambiteer's basic method of attack involves stalking the queen.

1.e4 c5 2.d4 cxd4 3.c3 dxc3 4.♘xc3 ♘c6 5.♘f3 e6 6.♗c4 a6 7.0-0 ♘ge7!?

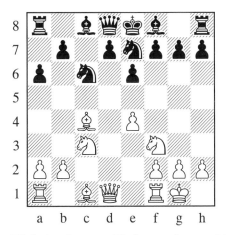

With this sly move, Black intends to establish a firm grip on the central dark squares with ...♘g6, then finish his development smoothly

after ...♗e7, castles, ...b5, ...♗b7, and ...d6. The black queen dares not venture out and wisely hides behind a solid pawn shield at d7, thus making the hackneyed ♕e2/♖d1 plan inert. White's standard e4-e5 thrust also becomes impotent, as instead of the pawn badgering the knight on f6, a knight on g6 will pester it. But the proper plan to cause chaos involves chasing the black queen, even though she may seem oh so far away.

8.♗g5!

After this powerful pin, suddenly Black cannot finish his development routinely. Note that if the black pawn stood at a7, White would already be threatening the knockout strike ♘b5!/♘d6#.

To complete the ...♘e7-g6 slog, Black must brave either 8...f6 or 8...h6, producing subtle weaknesses surrounding his kingside complex. Or the queen can nobly take matters into her own hands with 8...♕c7, although on that square her struggles have already been well documented. White can then either slowly build up the pressure with 9.♖c1, or frenetically continue the chase with 9.♘d5!.

8...♕c7

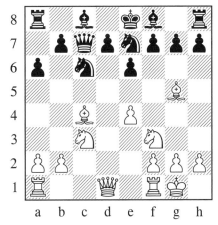

9.♘d5!

The d5-square – Ring of fire

"But didn't you just hang a piece on d5?" the skeptical reader may ask. "No, no, I merely invested the piece, and shall reap the rewards of my investment soon enough," the sage gambiteer may retort. Speaking of sacrificing knights (or bishops!) on d5, which one of these plunges on d5 would you make in your own games, and which ones, if any, are objectively sound? Some of these sacrifices on d5 you may already know, some of them you will be meeting for the first time...

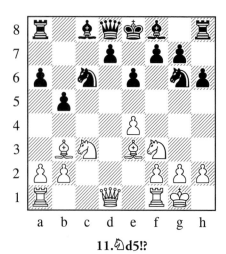

11.♘d5!?

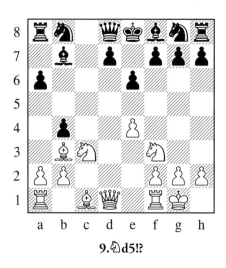

9.♘d5!?

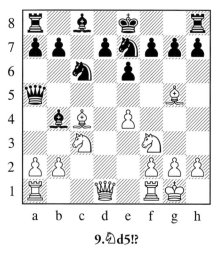

9.♘d5!?

11.♘d5!?

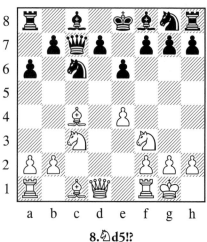

8.♘d5!?

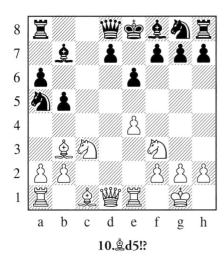

10.♗d5!?

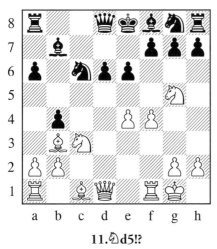

11.♘d5!?

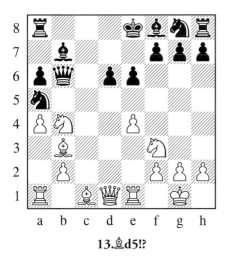

13.♗d5!?

I hope that after completing this book, you will make at least half of these "leaps of faith" on d5. And how many of these sacrifices are indeed sound? None? Half? For the few of you who guessed **all** of them, you know who you are, and you are correct! Yes, every one of these sacrifices on d5 is completely sound and offers White excellent winning chances.

The d5-square is the Morra Gambit's ring of fire, the square where all mayhem breaks loose. We have already glossed over how d5 transforms into the featured battleground in the quiet Scheveningen lines when Black blockades with ...e6-e5. However, when a White piece offers its life on d5, the position can devolve into utter chaos. Knowing when a sacrifice on d5 is good, bad, or unclear is what often separates the amateur from the virtuoso Morra gambiteer. Sometimes the sacrifice is not just optional, but forced! In such hair-raising scenarios, tossing a piece into the fire early on will likely lead to a glorious win for White. Not taking the risk, on the other hand, will yield the advantage to Black. Quite a change from conventional thinking – after all, the chess world has enough trouble accepting that White can sacrifice a pawn in the opening stages, and now it must come to terms with a maniacal gambiteer donating a whole piece, often before move 10! Now a few general considerations and rules of thumb before you contemplate taking a dive on d5.

White sacrifices a knight on d5 primarily to rip open the e-file for a direct path to the black king. Refusing the sacrifice is usually untenable, as the monstrous knight stomps on all in its wake the longer it stampedes. After Black accepts the offering, the White e-pawn typically captures back on d5, regaining not only a pawn in the process, but cutting the enemy army in two. Once on d5, the white pawn grows exponentially in strength. It may completely dominate a hapless bishop on b7 and subsequently bury the b8-knight, a8-rook, and therefore the entire Black queenside.

But that's only the half of it. From d5, the giant foot soldier may wedge further into Black's camp via d5-d6. Yes, on d6 it releases the shackled queenside pieces, but more importantly hems in Black's king's bishop, making the black king himself a fixed target for the decisive ♖e1†.

Furthermore, the gambiteer's light-squared bishop then has a free path to the bloody f7-square, the main artery of the black king. While Black did everything in his power to shield f7 from the Italian bishop, White's sacrifice on d5 stripped away the e6-pawn's last layer of defense, leaving f7 wide open for future assault. Such a fate befell the black king in Esserman – Van Wely, Orlando 2011, my most famous Morra Gambit victory.

Marc Esserman – Loek van Wely

Orlando 2011

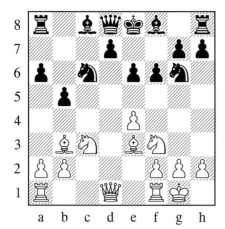

11.♘d5 exd5 12.exd5 ♘ce5 13.d6!

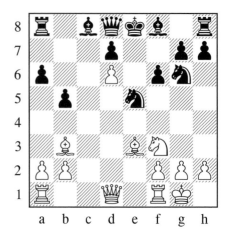

Below are a few general guidelines for when you should and should not sacrifice on d5:

1) It is rarely a good idea to sacrifice a knight on d5 when a black pawn already stands on d6, as you can no longer play the devastating d5-d6 yourself. Instead, your bishop may sit lifelessly behind the d5-pawn, and you may end up down a piece for little or no compensation.

2) If a black knight stands on c6, sacrificing on d5 sizzles with possibility. When you recapture on d5, you will gain a tempo on the c6-knight, and when it flees, you may be able to unleash the crushing d5-d6.

3) Sacrificing a knight on d5 is usually more effective when your light bishop already stands on b3. The reason is twofold – for one, your bishop is less prone to a threat from an evacuating c6 knight (via e5 or a5), which will halt your attack for a critical tempo, and secondly, the c-file will be free for your queen's rook to ravage in the moves to come.

4) You should rarely sacrifice a knight on d5 after Black has castled, unless you are immediately winning back material. The sacrifice is primarily designed to catch the king before he escapes the center. Black should be at least one, but preferably two or more moves

away from castling before you consider surging into d5. You will need these precious tempi to conduct your attack.

5) When Black wastes a vital tempo in the opening stage with ...b5-b4, hitting your knight, he is usually begging for a sacrifice on d5, and you should thank him kindly. The extra tempo spent on ...b4 is valuable time lost when he could have organized his defense.

6) If Black ventures ...♘c6-a5 to attack your bishop on b3, assuming that he is far away from castling, you must consider sacrificing even the bishop on d5 instead of retreating or letting Black happily exchange with ...♘xb3.

Of course there are no rules to follow in chess 100% of the time other than how the pieces move, but if you adhere to these guidelines you will have a much easier time making sense of the chaos surrounding the sacrifices on d5 streaming through this book. Lastly, if you are using a chess engine to assist your analysis, please take its evaluations when probing the sacrifices on d5 or other extreme situations in the Morra Gambit with serious skepticism. Like the majority of the chess public, the computer (Rybka, Houdini, Stockfish, Blowfish, or any other engine in existence) simply cannot fully fathom how White can be down a piece for seemingly little counterplay, and when it finally does start spitting out positive evaluations for the gambiteer, Black's position is often already beyond saving.

The sensitive e6/f7 complex

While an early sacrifice on d5 may give rise to the most fantastic possibilities in the Morra Gambit, there are definitely other outlandish ways to find yourself down a full piece after ten moves in the gambit and still objectively play

for the win! In particular, sacrificing a white knight or bishop on e6 or f7 is the second most common method for mayhem. As discussed earlier, when Black adopts a Scheveningen formation, he does so primarily to speed up his kingside development while shielding the vulnerable f7-pawn. When the gambiteer sacrifices on e6 or f7, however, he strips away the venerable foot soldier, leaving the black king to fend for himself in the center as chaos engulfs the board. Understand that these sacrifices work best when Black's queen's bishop fails to defend e6, either because a Black piece on d7 obstructs its guard or because the bishop felt the need to drift away from its home post towards b7. Now for a few concrete examples:

Into the Deep – 9.♘g5!

1.e4 c5 2.d4 cxd4 3.c3 dxc3 4.♘xc3 e6 5.♘f3 a6 6.♗c4 b5 7.♗b3 ♗b7 8.0–0! d6

Black chooses a Scheveningen setup, but with his e6/f7 complex severely compromised by the ill-timed ...♗b7. The gambiteer wastes no time and peppers the sensitive spot.

After 8...b4 we would descend into the chaotic world of 9.♘d5!.

9.♘g5!

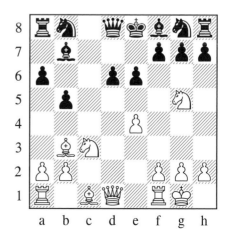

White will wreak havoc on f7 and e6 as direct sacrificial blows and the savage ♕h5 lurks. If Black stands idle, even the effortless f4-f5 will smash through.

Finegold Defense – 12.♗xe6!

1.e4 c5 2.d4 cxd4 3.c3 dxc3 4.♘xc3 d6 5.♘f3 e6 6.♗c4 ♗e7 7.0–0 ♘f6 8.♕e2 a6 9.♖d1 b5 10.♗b3 ♘bd7

We arrive at the main position of the notorious Finegold Defense. Again, Black adopts a Scheveningen formation, but obstructs the bishop's guard of e6 while his king waits in the center to receive incoming missiles. With the preconditions for a strike on the e6/f7 complex met, the gambiteer does not hesitate.

11.♘d4!?

Black lacks the time to respond with 11...♘c5 as 12.♘c6 or 12.e5! first plows through.

11...♗b7?!

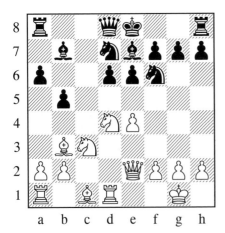

12.♗xe6! fxe6 13.♘xe6

And I went on to win in both Esserman – Chow, Chicago 2000 and Esserman – Finegold, Internet (blitz) 2006. The black king must endure a protracted central siege as White's rooks and minor pieces pillage.

Chicago Defense – 10.♘d4!

1.e4 c5 2.d4 cxd4 3.c3 dxc3 4.♘xc3 e6 5.♘f3 a6 6.♗c4 d6 7.0–0 b5 8.♗b3 ♖a7 9.♗e3 ♖d7

A main variation of the Chicago Defense. Black places his rook on the awkward square d7 to shield his queen from the menacing ♕e2, ♖fd1, and e5. However, he again blocks his queen's bishop from guarding e6 in a Scheveningen system, so the thematic response should not be hard to spot.

10.♘d4!

Target acquired.

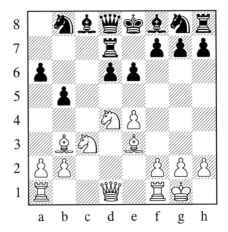

10...♘f6 11.f4!

The famous pawn advance, found principally in the Open Sicilian, is extremely effective in ripping apart the e6/f7 complex.

11...e5

Black avoids doom and gloom on e6, but in turn opens the gates to f7. It is rarely a good idea for the defender to play ...e6-e5 (or ...e7-e5) with his king more than a move away from castling, as White will have time to mount a dangerous offensive against the f7-pawn. In this case the attack features ♘g5 and ♗f7, but in other premature ...e5 positions, the gambiteer can jet his queen to b3, with themes echoing the classical e4/e5 gambits.

12.♘f3 ♗e7

Black tries to castle but it is too late.

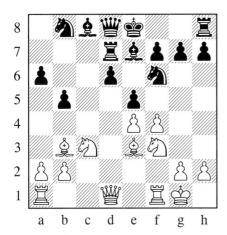

13.♗xf7†! ♔xf7 14.♘g5†+–

Showcased in Esserman – Nakamura, Chicago 2000. 14...♔e8 15.♘e6 and the knight grazes freely on e6 while the black king withers in the center once more.

In the Morra Gambit, due to White's extreme lead in development, sound sacrifices can instantly appear from just about anywhere on the board. So keep an open mind to any possibility and be alert.

Be Alert – 9.♘b5!

1.e4 c5 2.d4 cxd4 3.c3 dxc3 4.♘xc3 ♘c6 5.♘f3 d6 6.♗c4 ♘f6

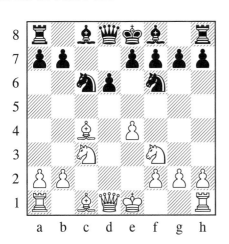

Black has developed normally and without reproach, following well established opening principles. He has obeyed the classic rule: "knights before bishops," while not wasting any time. And the necessary ...d6 inhibited White's e4-e5 thrust. Who would then think that White can seize the advantage with a forcing tactical sequence?

7.e5!

The gambiteer charges ahead regardless, ignoring Black's d6-barricade. But his advance is far from reckless, for if 7...♘xe5, then 8.♘xe5 dxe5 9.♗xf7†! nets the queen.

7...dxe5 8.♕xd8† ♘xd8

If 8...♔xd8, then 9.♘g5 hits Black from other side!

9.♘b5!

Despite making three logical opening moves, Black falls into grave danger, and if he is not inspired enough to find 9...♖b8 (which still leads to his ruin), he may get shamefully mated in only 11 moves.

9...♔d7?? 10.♘xe5†! ♔e8 11.♘c7#

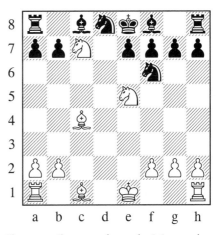

I'm sure I'm not the only Morra player to spring this embarrassing trap several times on unsuspecting opponents. Black must therefore carefully tread 6...a6! to prevent the nasty e4-e5! and ♘b5 incursion, when we would enter the theoretically touted Taylor Defense, or what some Morra skeptics like to call "Old Faithful". I shall call it "Taylor's Temple of Doom". Black aims to simply play ...♗g4 and follow up with mass exchanges after ...♗xf3, ...♘e5 and ...♘xc4. However, as we shall see, Taylor's Temple is far from the celebrated refutation the Morra bashers like to promote.

Be Alert – 11.♘xb5!

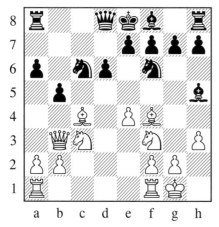

We have reached a critical position of the Taylor Defense, where Black has just threatened White's bishop with 10...b5. A lazy gambiteer may quickly retreat the bishop. The alert master, on the other hand, will notice that Black's light bishop is missing in action...

11.♘xb5!

A decisive bolt from the blue. Black's king remains many tempi away from castling, and now will be pounded on the suddenly soft a4-e8 diagonal. He cannot capture the knight due to the decisive pin ♗xb5, and if he refuses to go down quietly then...

11...♖b8 12.♘g5!

...the tag team of knight, bishop and queen lay waste to the f7-square. If now 12...e6, then

alas we have a Scheveningen structure where Black's light-squared bishop did not report for duty...

12...e6

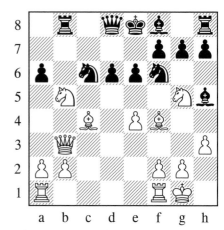

13.♗xe6! fxe6 14.♕xe6† ♗e7 15.♘xd6†+−

Pure carnage. White's pieces swarm, and his rooks lie in reserve. The rout is on!

The "Fear Factor"

Throughout the book I will be recommending sharp, yet objectively sound continuations and sacrifices. But tournament chess is not played in a science laboratory, and sometimes things go awry in the heat of battle. In these cases, even when you know you are in trouble, do not despair, for you will have the gambit *fear factor* on your side. Once you brave the Morra Gambit, you up the psychological tension, putting your opponent on the razor's edge. Now he knows that you are not afraid to sacrifice a pawn, so who knows what you will do next? You become a loose cannon, a wildcard, a jackal, a joker. This is what your opponent will likely think of you, regardless of what you think of yourself in the moment. Your opponent probably will scoff at your opening choice, but he is probably also afraid. Just remember the words of the great Mikhail Tal if ever you feel you are headed off an unsound cliff: "some sacrifices are sound, the rest are mine!"

To conclude, I will show one of my "unsound" Morra Gambit games which would have amused the Latvian genius.

Marc Esserman – Boris Kreiman

Sturbridge 2002

1.e4 c5 2.d4 cxd4 3.c3 dxc3 4.♘xc3 e6 5.♘f3 a6 6.♗c4 b5 7.♗b3 ♗b7

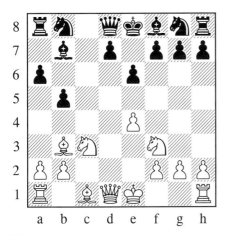

8.♕e2?!

8.0–0! Ten years ago I lacked the experience and skill to appreciate the streaming chaos after 8...b4 9.♘d5!, and instead choose to cowardly defend my e-pawn. But I promise this will be the last soft move you see from me from here on out.

8...♘c6 9.0–0 ♘ge7 10.♗g5!

Chasing the queen!

10...f6

Forcing the desired kingside concession. Now I sank into deep thought for nearly an hour. During my meditation I envisioned that after 11.♗e3, Black would respond with the unpleasant 11...♘a5!, and I would have to

beat a full retreat (normally not a good sign in gambits). So, knowing full well that my next move bordered on the unsound and even the absurd, I did it anyway. After all, you only live once, so why not enjoy giving up your pieces?

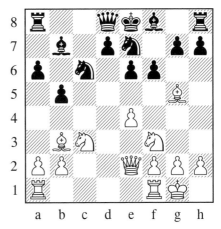

11.♖fd1!?(?!) ♕b8?

My seasoned opponent spent about 3 minutes to produce this blunder. Perhaps Kreiman feared 11.♖fd1 could have been prepared?! Or even if he suspected that it just hangs a piece, why risk coming under barbaric attack when he can just calmly subdue his weaker opponent?

11...fxg5! No fear. 12.♘xg5!? (12.♗xe6?!∓ should not net enough material for the queen.) 12...♕c7 13.♖xd7!? The insane intention behind 11.♖fd1, sound or not! 13...♕xd7 14.♗xe6

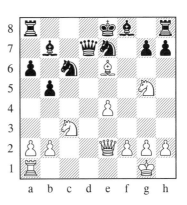

A terrifying position for a grandmaster to defend versus a master, even if he's up a rook and a bishop! The king and queen now come under heavy fire. 14...♕d6 15.♗f7† ♔d8 16.♖d1 ♘d4 17.♖xd4!+– The scintillating variation which convinced me to go for the outlandish piece sacrifice. Sure, Black can hold with the unnatural sequence 15...♔d7 16.♖d1 ♘d4 17.♕g4 ♔c6!∓, or even 12...♕b6/12...♕a5† as the queen flees from the nasty forks. However, Grandmaster Kreiman took one look at the possible danger on the field and ran for the hills. I promise you very similar experiences when unleashing Morra mayhem. Your opponents will shake in the face of such savage attacks, unless of course they are made of steel.

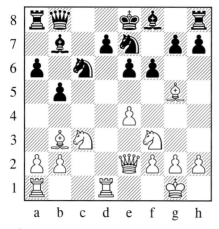

12.♗h4

Kreiman's desire to play it safe soon backfires. He had no choice but to accept the sacrifice, for as a result of his misplaced queen, I now have a raging initiative. Soon he encounters horrors far more terrifying than had he just grabbed on g5. And that's the point! There is no escaping chaos in the Morra Gambit.

12...♘g6 13.♗g3

Chase, chase, chase the queen!

13...♘ce5 14.♘xe5 fxe5

14...♘xe5 15.f4!± and after the knight vacates, the shattering f4-f5 leaves the f7/e6 complex in ruin while the bishop again stalks the queen.

15.♕g4!±

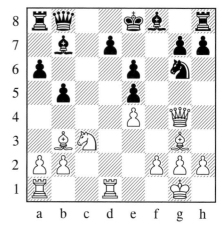

Suddenly White threatens the pulverizing ♖xd7 followed by ♕xe6† and a knockout on the c-file. The Morra "fear factor" reigns supreme.

15...♗c8

A sad necessity. The storm clouds are gathering. If 15...♕c7 16.♖ac1! further harassing the queen.

16.h4!

Pinning the bishop to its original f8-square, else h5 and ♕xg7 crunches.

16...♘f4 17.♗xf4

Happily removing Black's only active piece.

17...exf4

Kreiman intends to use the e5-square as a safe haven for his queen and the base of future operations, when he could then finally free his king's bishop and hope to castle. He must not succeed.

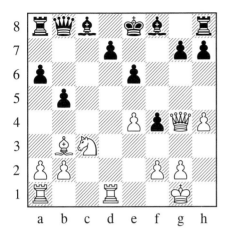

18.e5!

Emboldened, I blow up the queen's hideout and clear the path to the king. And who cares about another pawn when you have already offered to sacrifice a whole piece?

18...♕xe5 19.♖e1!

Yet another queen chase allows the rooks to harmoniously regroup along the central files, where they will pummel Black's king at last.

19...♕b8 20.♖ad1!

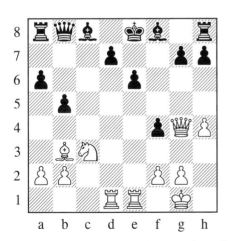

A perfect time for a photograph. All of White's pieces are ready to strike. All of Black's lie on their original squares, except for the queen of course, which is still near her home. A Morra gambiteer dreams of such moments.

The great Romantics of old smile from above, and the rest needs no comment. Or does it?

20...♖a7 21.♘d5!

The monstrous knight, often sacrificed on the d5 "ring of fire", now roams freely, immune from capture!

21...g6 22.♘f6† ♔f7 23.♘xd7! ♗xd7 24.♖xd7† ♖xd7 25.♕xe6† ♔g7 26.♕xd7† ♔h6 27.♕g4 ♗d6 28.♕g5† ♔g7 29.h5! ♖f8

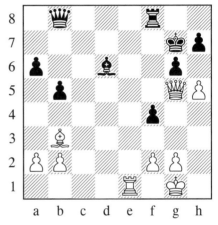

I've played flawlessly after dubiously sacrificing on move 11. But now, in massive time pressure, the fear factor suddenly betrays me, and bad nerves spoil the show. As my time ticked under 30 seconds, I uncorked 30.h6†??, and even though I'm still winning without difficulty, I found a way to flag on move 40. **...0–1**

If only the spectacle had reached its rightful conclusion...

30.♖e7†! ♗xe7 31.h6†!

Only now does the pawn advance, forcing mate.

31...♔h8 32.♕xe7!+–

Without a doubt the most painful loss of my career. Years later it still stings. But this chess tragedy motivated me to work much harder, and who knows, if it had never happened, you might not be reading this book today.

A word on the Morra Declined

Although Black can steer the struggle into positions considered far drier than the Morra Accepted by simply declining the "free" pawn on move three, I will make sure to recommend variations that are sound, but consistent with the Morra mayhem style whenever possible. This way, there will be truly nowhere for the Sicilian schemer to hide. I offer a few teasers:

Morra Declined – 3...♕a5

1.e4 c5 2.d4 cxd4 3.c3 ♕a5

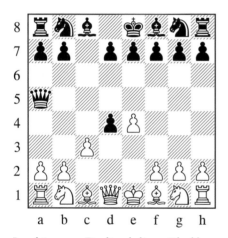

In this rare Declined line, Black's queen aspires to cramp White's style. However, after the virtually untested 4.♗d2!, the gambiteer laughs his way to a Morra accepted, but with a bishop on d2 and queen on a5, and we know who that favors!

Morra Declined – 3...♘f6

1.e4 c5 2.d4 cxd4 3.c3 ♘f6 4.e5 ♘d5

And we arrive at the Alapin variation of the Sicilian by transposition. The declining schemer will seek stodgy, sterile positions, whereas we shall strive for chaos

5.♘f3 ♘c6 6.♗c4! ♘b6 7.♗b3

And the gambiteer unveils the Alapin's version of the Morra Gambit. The schemer still desperately clings to the role of the spoiler.

7...d5 8.exd6 ♕xd6 9.0–0 ♗e6 10.♘a3!?

Run as he may, Black has no choice but to face his worst fears. He will be attacked, but will he be ready?

Of course, even if a position ever becomes "dry", you must be prepared to grind away. Most positions that amateurs may consider "boring" are actually full of life. You'd be surprised by the dangers lurking in even the simplest positions.

Morra Methodology

In the pages ahead you will find the best of my Morra Gambit analysis over thousands of hours of toil. While creating *Mayhem in the Morra*, unless otherwise mentioned, I did not consult any sources other than ChessBase Megabase 2011 and my two tireless seconds, Deep Rybka 4 and Houdini. Sometimes the computers slammed the door shut on certain variations, confirming what I already knew for years. Other times, they helped open new portals into Morra worlds never before imagined. But most exhilarating were those moments when the machines drifted aimlessly through the chaos, lost in space, desperately trying to calculate their way across chess's infinite horizon. If past or future Morra works (perhaps utilizing similar technology) happen to independently closely follow my analysis, so be it. I merely search for truth, and if analysts arrive at similar conclusions about a certain position, then we draw ever closer to the position's ultimate truth.

Now brace yourselves for a wild ride. Each narrative chapter comes equipped with an annotative theme (be it earth, wind, water, fire, cinema, or astronomy), not only to entertain, but to further enhance your memory for the vivid variations. I will begin each chapter with instructive games illustrating the key ideas in each defense against the Morra Gambit, using my own when available. In general, the chapters escalate in difficulty – near the end, you will encounter the super-advanced, theoretical sections. Geared for masters to professionals, this material will normally contain the densest analysis and sparsest commentary. The instructive games will build your understanding so that you can more thoroughly absorb the thickets of analysis. Novice players, feel free to skip the theoretical sections if you wish and focus solely on the introductory material of the chapters. The colorful games alone will provide you with more than enough bearing to play at a high level against any Morra Gambit defense. If along the way you ever feel lost, remember to read over this introduction, as it provides most of the critical themes in the gambit, and themes and ideas are more important than individual variations. I hope you are as excited as I am for the journey that lies ahead. Happy hunting!

Anonymous Candidate Master: **"He should grow up and play a REAL opening."**
Student: **"But he just beat a 2700 with it."**
Candidate Master: **"Everyone gets lucky."**

Chapter 1

Siberian Wilderness

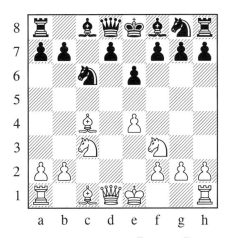

1.e4 c5 2.d4 cxd4 3.c3 dxc3 4.♘xc3 ♘c6 5.♘f3 e6 6.♗c4

We begin our adventure in the Siberian wilderness, home to the most notorious trap against the Morra Gambit. Perhaps dreamed up on a howling winter's night in Novosibirsk, the Siberian trap has left many a Morra player frozen in the cold. Like any good snare, the trapper starts out innocently enough with the simple ...e6, ...♘c6, ...♕c7, and ...♘f6, moves so common in the Taimanov Open Sicilian. The gambiteer, now playing the role of the fool, mindlessly plows forth with 8.♕e2, yet after 8...♘g4!

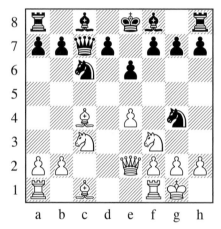

he quickly finds himself in the hunter's net. Upon 9.h3??, the trapper springs 9...♘d4!, winning the queen and collecting yet another trophy head to mount on his wall of Morra victims.

Thus, we visit the treacherous tundra first, so that your name does not appear in the Siberian trapper's collection of most memorable catches. Although the Siberian variation grows more popular each day in an Internet chess generation geared toward quick kills, the savvy Morra traveler can easily sidestep the hunter's barbs. And if you ultimately conquer the Siberian wildlands, it will be you with the trophy case – not your scheming opponent. The trapper will become the trapped, the hunter the hunted, the predator the prey. Despite its appeal, the main line of the Siberian variation will be rendered extinct by the analysis to follow. The wily trapper will then be in dire need of a new ruse, and the theoretical section covers just that. Only then will I leave you alone in the wilderness, fully armed against any trapper that may cross your path.

Marc Esserman – Gregory Braylovsky

New York (rapid) 2003

1.e4 c5 2.d4 cxd4 3.c3 dxc3 4.♘xc3 ♘c6 5.♘f3 e6 6.♗c4 ♕c7

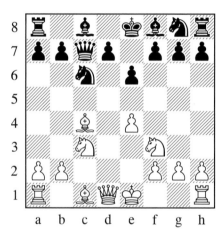

FM Braylovsky signals his intentions to spring the Siberian trap. This is always an amusing moment for me, and soon perhaps for you too. Almost all players (even titled ones!) who attempt the Siberian variation are only familiar with the one simple "Siberian" snare. They eagerly await their prey as the moment of anticipation builds.

Unfortunately for them, excitement soon turns to disappointment, and disappointment to despair. Analysis and words alone cannot serve the trapper's reversal of fortune full justice – you must experience the dramatic turnaround yourself, live in tournament play, to feel its total effect.

7.0–0! ♘f6

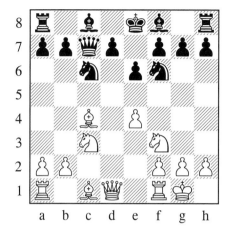

8.♘b5!

8.♕e2? No doubt the Siberian trap has reached such staggering levels of popularity because of many amateur Morra players' dogmatic approach in the opening. For them, ♕e2 and ♖fd1 comes all the time, no matter what! Such formulaic thinking must eventually lead to a gambiteer's ruin, and the Siberian is perhaps the most tragic example. Thus, this chapter appears first! The Morra Gambit encompasses much more than ♕e2 and ♖fd1, and I intend to break naive gambiteers of such dangerous habits. The plan ♕e2/♖fd1 makes little sense here as Black's queen has vacated the d-file, so White's rook would then shoot at thin air. And after 8...♘g4! 9.h3?? ♘d4!–+, you will end up on the trapper's wall. I cannot explain why 9.h3?? retains such a popularity, but from here on out, such wasteful moves like h3 and its relatives a3/a4 will only be advised under highly unusual circumstances.

Instead of 9.h3??, White may continue with the stubborn 9.♖d1, temporarily stopping the trap but allowing Black to develop freely with 9...♗c5, hitting the f2-pawn and renewing the snare. In the summer of 2011 in Spain, I witnessed such an encounter, with a young IM setting up the Siberian trap and a 2100 playing the role of foolhardy gambiteer.

As a result of ♕e2/♖d1 against the Siberian, White stood worse but somehow drew. After the game I told the Morra enthusiast that he has much better than ♕e2/♖d1 in this position, but he vehemently disagreed, insisting that ♕e2/♖d1 is theory in the Morra Gambit. What can I say? I rest my case.

After 8.♘b5, the trapper begins to feel a tad uneasy. Not only does he see his dreams of landing a fatal blow on d4 go up in smoke (the white knight guards d4), but his mischievous queen grows short of squares.

8...♕b8

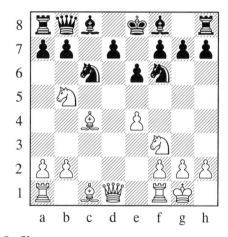

9.e5!

I recommend spending some sweet time before unleashing this sacrificial blow, preferably in a hesitant, worried manner. I always do. After all, your opponent has tried to trap you, so why not do everything in your power to spring a trap on him!

9...♘xe5

Black must refuse the bait with 9...♘g4, which we will see in Milman – Ehlvest and later in the theoretical section.

The feeble 9...a6 does not impress. White comfortably regains his pawn while retaining the initiative: 10.exf6 axb5 11.fxg7! ♗xg7 12.♗xb5± See the advanced material for the gory details.

10.♘xe5!

This powerful moves hurls the Siberian trapper into a cage with his name painted all over it!

In the past I used to play:

10.♗f4?!

An obvious pin which poses practical problems for Black.

10...d6 11.♖c1

White plots to snare the black queen on the very square she began her treachery, and in Esserman – Ehlvest, Las Vegas (blitz) 2000, the esteemed Estonian Grandmaster fell face first into the counter-trap.

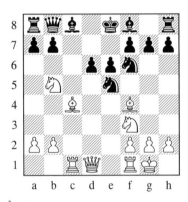

11...♗e7?

In light of the threat, Ehlvest should have responded with 11...♗d7!, reserving defensive chances far greater than after 10.♘xe5.[13]

12.♗xe5

Removing the last piece which can save the beleaguered black queen.

12...dxe5 13.♘c7†+–

And I went on to win easily after 13...♔f8 14.♘xa8, for 13...♕xc7 meets 14.♗b5† (as no e5-knight can save the queen and stop check with ...♘c6). The first of many c-file catastrophes to come!

10...♕xe5 11.♖e1!

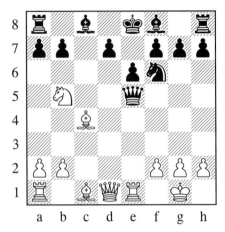

I've had this position more times than I've played 1.d4! Black is already lost, although he may not know it yet. The queen must maintain hold of c7 while staying out of the crossfire, a task which proves impossible.

11...♕c5

The alternative is only seemingly safer:

11...♕b8

Now the queen slips straight into the trap, and she will not wiggle out!

12.♕d4!

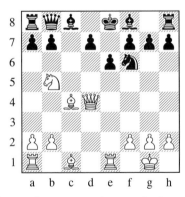

The gambiteer centralizes with this powerful queen move, courtesy of the fact that no black minor piece can push her away from her incredible outpost. A simple comparison of the state of the two queens tells you all you need to know about the position – White threatens the decisive $\mathbb{\&}$f4, capturing the black queen and placing her in his trophy case.

12...$\mathbb{\&}$h5

Black can put up creative resistance with this move. However, no amount of ingenuity will release him from the fatal trap.

The most natural 12...d6 leads to extreme pain: 13.$\mathbb{\&}$f4 e5

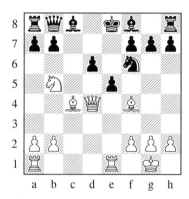

Black's pieces all lie on the back rank, waiting for the inevitable. I've caught the black queen countless times from this position, in both blitz and tournaments. 14.$\mathbb{\Xi}$xe5†! and now:

a) 14...$\mathbb{\&}$e7 15.$\mathbb{\Xi}$xe7†+–

b) 14...dxe5 15.$\mathbb{\&}$xe5+– Esserman – Ludwig, Internet (blitz) 2004.

c) 14...$\mathbb{\&}$e6 15.$\mathbb{\&}$xe6!+– Esserman – N.N, New York 2008. 15...dxe5 leads to a pretty finish, depending on one's definition of pretty. (No better is 15...$\mathbb{\&}$e7 16.$\mathbb{\&}$xf7† $\mathbb{\&}$xf7 17.$\mathbb{\Xi}$xe7†+–.) 16.$\mathbb{\&}$xe5 $\mathbb{\&}$d8 17.$\mathbb{\&}$c7†
And the queen again enters the trophy case, as 17...$\mathbb{\&}$e7 is mate in two after 18.$\mathbb{\&}$b4†.

Now you may see why I recommend pretending to think before 9.e5!. White's trap is far deeper than Black's!

13.$\mathbb{\&}$h4

The simpler 13.$\mathbb{\&}$e5!N+– wins material, as Black cannot stop both $\mathbb{\&}$c7xa8 and save his hanging knight on h5. However, the text also leads to a large advantage.

13...a6 14.$\mathbb{\&}$xh5 axb5 15.$\mathbb{\&}$xb5

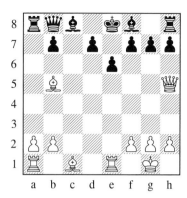

White targets e6, and Black needs to take countermeasures. The awkward 15...g6 or 15...$\mathbb{\&}$d6 would prolong the debacle.

15...$\mathbb{\&}$d6? 16.$\mathbb{\Xi}$xe6†+– $\mathbb{\&}$f8 17.$\mathbb{\Xi}$e2 b6

Here I got fancy with 18.$\mathbb{\&}$h6!? in Esserman – Shahade, Internet (blitz) 2005, which led to mate a few moves later, but 18.$\mathbb{\&}$c4+– crunches immediately.

Braylovsky decides for his queen to fight it out in the open – definitely the more challenging continuation. But of course she stands on quicksand – the open c-file! White would love to play $\mathbb{\&}$e3, but his bishop is currently hanging. How do you set the trap to snare the queen?

12.$\mathbb{\&}$f1!

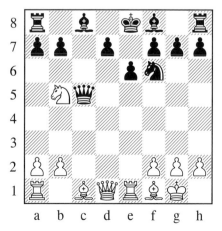

As you will see, there are no rules in chess,

only guidelines. Normally we march forward in gambit play, but sometimes we retract like a bow and arrow, only to unleash with more vigor later.

After the coiling 12.♗f1! the trap is laid clear, and White's minor pieces will banish the queen to a land where she wishes not to go. The threat of ♗e3 and ♖c1 forces Black's hand.

12...♘d5

We examine the ramifications of 12...a6 in the next illustrative game. Here I wanted to play 13.♕xd5, but after 13...♕xd5 14.♘c7† ♔d8 15.♘xd5 exd5, I merely succeed in trading pieces. Therefore I set up the threat, which as Nimzowitsch philosophizes, is stronger than the execution.

13.♗g5!

The hunter becomes the hunted. White now menaces 14.♕xd5 ♕xd5 15.♘c7#! Meanwhile, ♖c1 swirls in the frosty air. Black suffers on...

13...f6 14.♖c1 ♕e7

The queen shields her king from the fiery white rook, but in turn, entombs her entire kingside. If only the king foresaw her fate, he would have never sent her off to c7 to do his bidding so many moons ago.

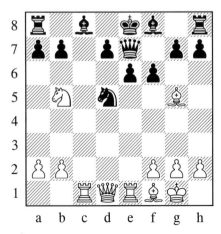

15.♗f4!

White aims to drive the queen from her hideout on e7 via ♗d6 followed by ♕xd5+–, so Black must cede the exchange. But that's not all he will lose...

15...♘xf4 16.♘c7† ♔f7 17.♘xa8

And just when the worst seems over, a final trap remains! Already paralyzed, the c8-bishop now comes under ambush. The h8-rook cannot try any heroics, as Black's other bishop also cannot move! So the exhausted queen retreats to her original square to join her comrades at their sad starting positions.

17...♕d8 18.♕d4!

The white queen's first move contains far more venom than all of Black's combined. On d4 she dominates the board.

18...♘d5 19.♗c4!

The coiled bishop lets loose, saying "Hello" to the black knight, and more importantly, to Black's king.

19...♗b4 20.♖ed1!

Only now does White's king's rook occupy d1. The "Morra rooks" now assume their natural positions, rounding up any enemy pieces in their wake.

20...♘b6

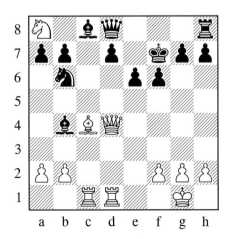

21.♗xe6† ♔xe6 22.♘c7†

The white knight gallops back into the fray, as Black's pieces lie helpless.

22...♔f7 23.♕xb4 d5 24.a4

And Black had seen enough. After the unstoppable a4-a5, Braylovsky's position completely collapses.

1–0

Marc Esserman – Kapil Chandran

Sturbridge 2010

1.e4 c5 2.d4 cxd4 3.c3 dxc3 4.♘xc3

My young opponent, a top-ranked 12 year-old, fearlessly intends to spring the Siberian trap. But he gets a lesson in the style of the old masters.

4...e6 5.♘f3 ♘c6 6.♗c4 ♕c7 7.0-0 ♘f6 8.♘b5 ♕b8 9.e5

Here again, although all the moves were now known to me for years after the Braylovsky game, I pretended to think deeply for ten minutes, and the ploy worked, for my naive opponent grabbed on e5 instantly after my move! I must say, I tried the same psychological trick on the precocious IM Daniel Naroditsky in an entirely different position, and after the game, he politely asked: "Were you trying to trick me by pretending to think?!" Naturally I responded yes with a smile.

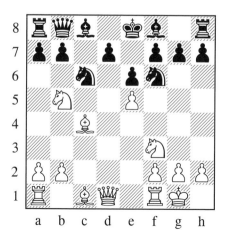

9...♘xe5?! 10.♘xe5 ♕xe5 11.♖e1 ♕c5 12.♗f1 ♘d5

So far all is familiar to us, but Black can now venture:

12...a6

This has the idea of sacrificing his queen.

13.♗e3 ♕c6

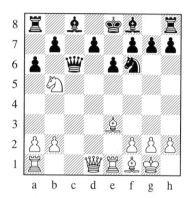

White should now continue with the exotic: 14.♘a7!+–

The gambiteer must not "win" the queen with 14.♖c1?, for after 14...axb5! 15.♖xc6 bxc6∓ Black nets two pawns, a knight, rook, and a very compact position for the queen. The tables have dramatically turned, and White, once again the hunted, must hope for a draw. 14...♕c7

Black must sacrifice the exchange with 14...♖xa7 to avoid further hardship, but his position remains untenable: 15.♗xa7 b5 16.a4 White, with his developmental and material advantage (and fearsome Morra rooks), should crush.

15.♖c1 ♕d8

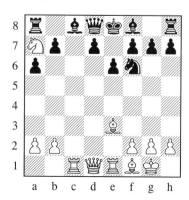

16.♕c2!

And suddenly the bishop lies trapped on its original square, just as in the Braylovsky game. The sojourns of Black's "Siberian" queen are again the culprit.

16...♗b4

This desperate lung offers only a glimmer of hope.

17.♘xc8 ♗xe1 18.♗b6!

And the queen is trapped yet again – this time not in the open wilderness, but on her home square! 18.♘d6† intending ♖xe1 also wins routinely.

13.♗g5! a6

A new move for me! I was again on my own in the Siberian wildlands, but fortunately I brought my hunting gear.

14.♖c1 ♕b6 15.♕xd5 axb5 16.♗xb5

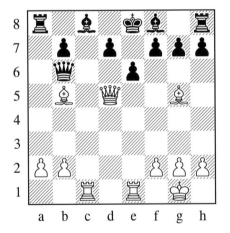

The smoke clears, and the gambiteer regains just one of the two sacrificed pawns. The materialists rejoice in their pawn advantage, but they celebrate prematurely, for Black can resign at once! The blow ♖xc8† will annihilate; any attempt to escape the danger leads to equally crushing consequences. Can you find Black's only two defensive gasps, and White's two finishing strikes?

16...♕d6

16...♕d6 holds d7, but now White channels the great Morphy after 17.♕c4!, threatening a romp after ♕xc8†. If Black either guards the trapped and targeted bishop with 17...♕b8, or gives his king air with 17...f6, the blazing 18.♖xe6† decides.

The game move shields d7, but interferes with the queen's guard to the vital e6-pawn. The gateway to the black king flies open:

17.♖xe6†!
1–0

Black resigned, not wishing to experience the end...

17...fxe6 18.♕xe6† ♔f8 19.♕f5†!

19.♗e7† may win the queen, but the text move leads to forced mate.

19...♔e8

19...♔g8 20.♗c4#

20.♖e1†

20.♖xc8†! is an even faster, more elegant and economical mate: 20...♖xc8 21.♗xd7#

20...♗e7 21.♖xe7† ♔d8 22.♖xd7† ♔e8 23.♖d8#

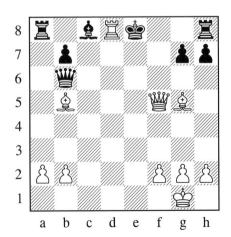

Mating in the style of the famous Morphy opera box game, toward which we now take a slight detour for those who are not familiar, or more likely... have forgotten.

Afterwards, Chandran asked where he went wrong, and I, not wanting to give any secrets away, responded: "By taking on c3, of course." But now, as the truth comes out, the real answer clearly was: "In choosing the Siberian trap."

Paul Morphy – Duke Karl & Count Isouard

Paris 1858

This is my favorite chess game, not only for its beauty, but for the powerful principles it preaches. Morphy vs. the Duke of Brunswick and Count Soured, conducted in a Paris opera box during intermission, is the first game my coach showed me, and the first game I show any student, regardless of strength. Its lessons will appear again and again throughout this book, so now is as good a time as any to pay it careful study.

Treating the game like a great piece of music, I will not interrupt its flow with comments – make your own notes and take from it whatever treasures you like. In brief, observe how Morphy's opponents fall behind in development after 3...♗g4?! and never recover. Morphy not only develops with ease, but forcefully impedes the Count and Duke's development every step of the way (note 7...♕e7 in particular!). With 9...b5?! Black, already woefully lagging behind, stubbornly lashes out (rarely wise), and the rest is history.

1.e4 e5 2.♘f3 d6 3.d4 ♗g4?! 4.dxe5 ♗xf3 5.♕xf3 dxe5 6.♗c4 ♘f6 7.♕b3 ♕e7 8.♘c3 c6 9.♗g5 b5?!

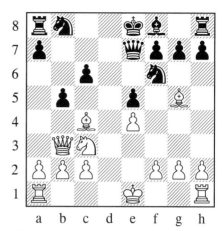

10.♘xb5! cxb5 11.♗xb5† ♘bd7 12.0–0–0! ♖d8

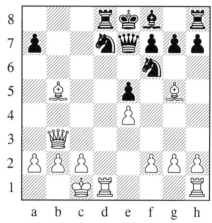

13.♖xd7! ♖xd7 14.♖d1 ♕e6 15.♗xd7† ♘xd7 16.♕b8†! ♘xb8 17.♖d8#

Lev Milman – Jaan Ehlvest

New York (rapid) 2003

The young IM Lev Milman was once a swashbuckling Morra gambiteer in his teenage years. However, with maturity comes wisdom, and he now prefers more mainstream openings. Hopefully after reading this book Lev may be convinced yet again that playing the Morra Gambit can often be the wise choice!

1.e4 c5 2.d4 cxd4 3.c3 dxc3 4.♘xc3 ♘c6 5.♘f3 e6 6.♗c4 ♕c7 7.0–0 ♘f6 8.♘b5 ♕b8 9.e5

In 2003 Lev and I spent considerable time analyzing the Morra together and developing new ideas. Lev always had a very creative approach, as you will witness in the following miniature. One afternoon, we were studying the Siberian variation, and I mentioned that if he ever faced Ehlvest, he may very well get the position you see on the board. Ehlvest, as I suspected, might simply dismiss my Las Vegas victory as a lucky blitz coup and make a small improvement, rather than recognize the Siberian's overarching flaws and abandon the primitive trap entirely. Ironically, that very evening, Lev got a chance to use our preparation against Ehlvest in the New York Masters weekly rapid tournament, and the result went down as one of the Morra Gambit's most famous scalps!

9...♘g4!

Ehlvest indeed learns his lesson from Las Vegas and deviates. But he still fails to appreciate the difficulties that lie ahead; Lev soon makes him hyper-aware.

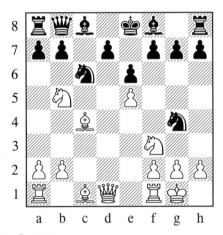

10.♘d6†!?

Lev immediately hops into d6, establishing a long-term bind on the dark squares. However,

I disagreed with him then and now – the developing 10.♗f4 first is best, as we shall see in the theoretical section. Only after Black wastes more time with ...a6 should White's knight settle on d6. In a practical (especially rapid) game, this quibble can become irrelevant, as Lev emphatically demonstrates.

10...♗xd6 11.exd6

The d6-pawn now splits the board in two, and White will gear up for a decisive kingside assault while Black's queenside sleeps.

11...b5

Black longs to free his cramped queenside. If he succeeds while simultaneously parrying White's threats, then he will seize the advantage. But such a daunting task remains a far way off.

12.♗b3

12.♗d3? ♕xd6 and the cornered queen escapes.

12...0–0 13.h3

13.♖e1?! is an imprecision, as Ehlvest would then win a valuable tempo towards liberating his queenside after 13...♕b6!.

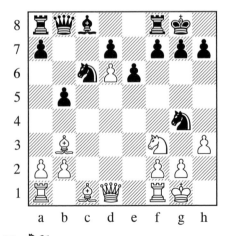

13...♘f6

Ehlvest could also have tried to swap the dangerous white kingside knight with

13...♘ge5!?. After White exchanges, Black's remaining knight can aid the king's defense by going to g6, while Black's bishop would hurry to b7. Note that such a defensive scheme would not be available if White's bishop already stood on f4.

14.♖e1

14.♗g5?! seems logical, as the capture on f6 would destroy Black's kingside. However, Black coolly responds 14...♘e4!, gaining more time for his precarious defense. If White then tries a quick kingside attack, Black has the resources to counter: 15.♕c2 ♘xg5 16.♘xg5 g6

Lev's move stops ...♘e4 and prepares the way for ♗g5. Ehlvest does not sense the cage forming around his king, and subsequently reacts with insufficient energy.

14...a5?

14...♘a5! 15.♗c2 ♘d5! 16.♘g5 and now not 16...h6? 17.♘h7±, but instead 16...f5!∓ would allow Ehlvest to miraculously escape the lion's den, as the f5-pawn shields the vulnerable diagonal road to his king, while the d5-knight can return to f6 if necessary. Such defensive motifs involving a timely ...f5! are common in the 9...♘g4! sub-variation of the Siberian, and Ehlvest very likely would have avoided the history books if he had found this plan.

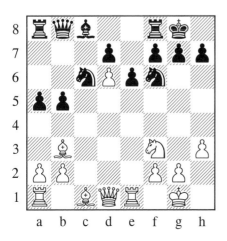

15.♗g5!+−

Black's position is beyond hope. His major pieces are in a slumber and even if they arise cannot reach the beleaguered king.

15...a4 16.♗xf6 gxf6

The computer's attempt is:
16...axb3!
  Leaving the bishop on f6 is an amazing try which ultimately fails.
17.♘g5! gxf6 18.♕h5 fxg5 19.♕xg5† ♔h8 20.♕f6† ♔g8

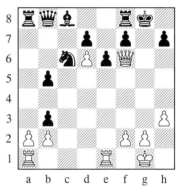

Great precision is still required. How would you seal the deal? White may be down two pieces, but the trap will soon slam shut. However, if 21.♖e4? then Black responds with the incredible 21...♖a4!!. The rook busts out of his cage just in time to reach the king's aid, albeit from the opposite side of the board! White would then be forced to settle for perpetual check. If 21.♖e3?, then Black's queen joins the circus via 21...♕xd6!, meeting 22.♖g3† with 22...♕xg3, saving the day just in time.
21.♖ad1!!
  White finds a way to freeze the black queen, permanently. So the frigid Siberian queen nobly accepts the inevitable, giving her life to create a new queen on a1 who will join the defense from the opposite corner of the board!
21...bxa2 22.♖e3 ♕xd6□ 23.♖xd6 a1=♕† 24.♔h2 ♕b1!

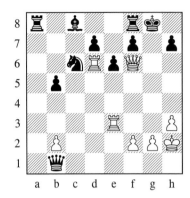

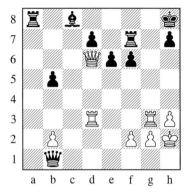

Black's Herculean defensive labors border on the absurd – the new queen now plans to sacrifice herself on g6 after ☖g3†, when Black would then be winning! But the ruthless gambiteer soon snuffs out all hope of a miracle. No queen, (either on b8 or b1!) can escape White's version of the Siberian trap!

25.☖dd3!

Preventing Black's desperado. Further spirited efforts to get away prove futile.

25...♘e5 26.♕xe5 f6 27.☖g3† ♔h8

27...♔f7 28.♕h5† ♔e7 29.♕xh7† ☖f7 30.☖xd7†! ♗xd7 31.♕xb1 and White snares Black's queen at last!

28.♕d6!

White's queen triumphantly appears at the scene of the trap (where the d6 wedging-pawn got the attack rolling). Now she aims for e7 and mate...

28.☖df3?! fails spectacularly to 28...☖a1! as the a1-rook salutes the black king from the opposite corner! 29.☖g5 (29.☖g4 ♕h1† and the queen waves from the other corner! 30.♔g3 ☖g1!–+) 29...♕g1† (29...♕h1† 30.♔g3 ☖g1?? 31.♔h4! ☖xg2 32.☖xf6+–) 30.♔g3 ♕c1! 31.☖xf6 ♕xg5†! 32.♕xg5 ☖g8–+ Simply incredible defense!

28...☖f7

28...☖e8 29.♕f4 ☖f8 (29...♕xb2 30.☖d4!+– and the black queen is shut out for the last time!) 30.♕g4+–

29.♕xe6!+– dxe6 **30.☖d8† ☖f8 31.☖xf8#**

A beautiful finish to one of the deepest combinations I have ever encountered!

17.♗c2+– ♘b4

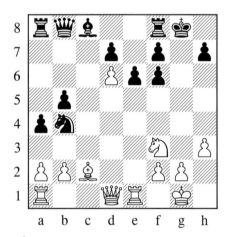

18.♗b1!?

Although simple and strong, this does not show just how confined Black's position truly has become. There are a couple of more startling wins:

18.♘g5!? also wins after 18...fxg5 19.♗xh7†.

18.♗xh7†! ♔xh7

If Black feebly declines the sacrifice, his king meets the same fate: 18...♔g7 19.♘e5!+– fxe5 (19...☖h8 20.♕h5 fxe5 21.♕g5† ♔f8 [21...♔xh7 22.☖e4] 22.♕e7† The d6-wedge now directly assists the white queen in the

final mating blows. 22...♔g7 23.♖e4+-)
20.♕g4† ♔f6 21.h4! (Or the simple
21.♕h4† and 22.♖e3 silences.) Observe
how the d6-pawn again helps to weave the
mating net.

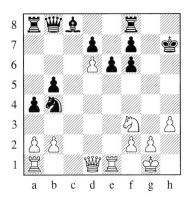

19.♘e5!+-

Black's rook stays frozen on f8 due to ♕h5†/
xf7 and mate.

Sacrificing the knight on the other square
also wins: 19.♘g5† ♔g6 (19...♔h6 20.♘h7
♖g8 21.♘xf6 ♖g6 22.♕h5† ♔g7 23.♘e8†
♔f8 24.♖e5 ♖a6 25.♕h8† ♖g8 26.♕f6) But
only after 20.♘h7!! ♔xh7 21.♕h5† ♔g7
22.♖e4 ♖g8 23.♖g4†.

19...fxe5

White's queen and rook now mop up.
20.♕h5† ♔g7 21.♕g5† ♔h7

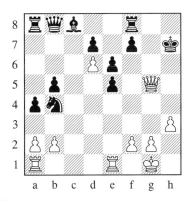

22.♖e4 with mate.

18...♘d5 19.♘h4! ♕xd6

The black queen finally escapes, but her king
remains in the noose.

20.♕g4† ♔h8

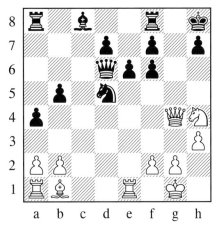

21.♘f5!

A pretty finish for Lev (Russian for "Lion")
Milman. After two short losses I doubt whether
Grandmaster Ehlvest will dare venture the
Siberian trap again.

1–0

We now begin our first theoretical section of
the book. For my less experienced (or busier!)
readers, you can simply go on to the next
chapter if you wish – rest assured, you have
more than enough information on how to
combat the Siberian trap up to the master level
and beyond. As I expect the audience in these
sections to generally be more advanced, I may
not always have as many descriptive comments
here as in the earlier chapter sections, and
instead often launch into *Informator*-style
analysis.

Theory I

1.e4 c5 2.d4 cxd4 3.c3 dxc3 4.♘xc3 e6
5.♘f3 ♘c6 6.♗c4 ♕c7 7.0–0 ♘f6 8.♘b5
♕b8 9.e5

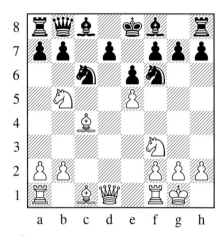

9...♘g4

Before exhausting 9...♘g4, we must first take a deeper look at the other reasonable alternatives for Black:

9...♘xe5?! 10.♘xe5 a6!?

Black can try and escape his fate with this zwischenzug, but White keeps throwing barbs.

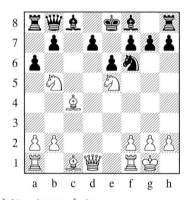

11.♗f4! axb5 12.♗xb5

The threat of ♘xd7 decides, so the queen flees to the edge.

12...♕a7 13.♖c1!?

The sharpest option, eyeing ♖xc8 and ♗xd7†+−, so Black must protect the sensitive d7-square somehow.

13.♘c4!?± is simple and strong, heading for the weak d6-square and a permanent dark-squared bind.

13...♗c5

If 13...b6, White can simply strengthen his position with 14.a4 among other alternatives, and if 14...♗c5, then 15.♗g5 would unleash a raging kingside attack if Black dares to castle. Black can try and improve with 14...♗e7!?, although after 15.♘xd7! ♗xd7 (15...♘xd7 16.♖c7 ♕b8 17.♖xd7 ♕xf4 18.♖d8#!) 16.♖c7 ♕xc7 17.♗xc7 ♗xb5 18.axb5 0–0 White finally wins the Siberian queen, but Black can try to hold this difficult ending.

14.b4!

This decoying Evans Gambit-like motif pries open the c-file.

14...♗xb4

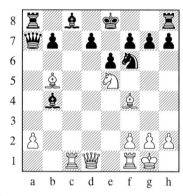

15.♗g5!N

And now the threat of ♖xc8† heats up the frosty air, as White will then snap off with ♗xd7†, ♗xc8 and ♕d7† and mate on f7. Black cannot parry all the threats.

The immediate 15.♖xc8† ♖xc8 16.♗xd7† ♔e7 17.♗xc8 ♖xc8 only led to a draw in Deak – Percze, Hungary 1997.

15...0–0?

15...♗e7 16.♖xc8† ♖xc8 17.♗xd7†+− The king will be lonely indeed with his queen on the opposite end of the board.

15...b6 16.♕d4!+− Again we see this thematic powerful centralizing move. If Black now gives chase with 16...♗c5, then 17.♕f4, and threats on c8 will renew if the bishop moves from c5, combined with unrelenting pressure on the f7-square.

16.♗xf6 gxf6 17.♕g4† ♔h8

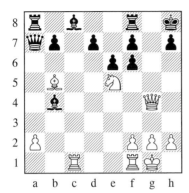

18.♕h4! fxe5 19.♕f6† ♔g8 20.♖c4!

The c-file now becomes a highway to the black king.

20...♖e8 21.♖g4† ♔f8 22.♖g7 ♖e7 23.♖xh7

The miserable black queen can only save the king for one move with 23...♕xf2†!.

Although 10...a6 seems the best choice in a rotten position, I have never seen it in my practice and only once in all the games of my students. By and large you will face the natural 10...♕xe5, which as you have already witnessed, leads Black to ruin.

9...a6?! 10.exf6 axb5 11.fxg7! ♗xg7 12.♗xb5 0–0

GM Jobava faced this position ten years ago and won on the Black side, but White did not play correctly.

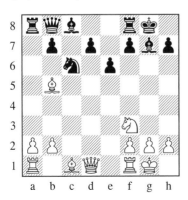

13.♗e3!

The gambiteer should speed ahead, unconcerned about the b2-pawn.

13...♗xb2 14.♖b1± ♗g7

14...♗f6 aims to meet the binding 15.♗c5 with 15...♗e7, but it offers little salvation, as White lifts his rook with 15.♖b3! and danger looms on the horizon for the black king.

15.♗c5! ♖e8 16.♗d6 ♕a7 17.♘g5+– h6 18.♘xf7! ♔xf7 19.♕h5† ♔g8 20.♕xe8† ♔h7 21.♗d3#

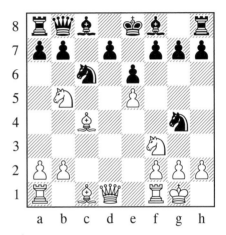

10.♗f4!

The improvement over Milman's 10.♘d6†?! vs. Ehlvest. I never understood why White should rush the check, as after 10.♗f4 Black cannot grab on e5...

10...a6□

10...♘gxe5? 11.♘xe5 ♘xe5

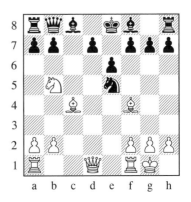

12.♗xe6! A shocking bolt. (12.♖c1+– is also good enough.) 12...dxe6 (12...fxe6 13.♕h5†) 13.♖c1! f6 14.♘c7† ♔f7 15.♗xe5 fxe5 16.♕h5† g6 17.♕f3† ♔g8 18.♘xa8 Black's position is in tatters. 18...♗d6 (18...♕xa8 19.♖c7+– offers a picture of complete domination.) 19.♕f6+–

11.♘d6† ♗xd6 12.exd6

As the e5-pawn remained taboo, Black had no choice but to waste a tempo on ...a6 – this slight loss of time makes all the difference! We will analyze both 12...b5 and 12...0–0 for Black, the only two reasonable moves, which, as it turns out, aren't so reasonable after all. White's dark-squared bind is simply too strong. Note that Black cannot play 12...f5? immediately due to 13.♗xe6! and 14.d7†.

12...b5 13.♗d5!!

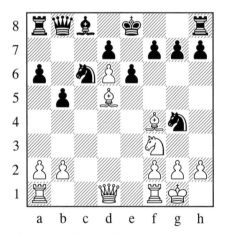

This beautiful shot defies superlatives. It is the first of many sacrifices you will see on the d5-square in the book, and one of the least obvious. Black must eliminate the menacing bishop, as it exerts an overwhelming central pull.[14]

13...exd5

13...♕b6?! 14.♖c1± exd5 (14...♗b7 15.♗xc6 dxc6 16.d7† ♔f8 17.♕d6† ♔g8 18.♕c7 and White queens easily!) 15.♕e2† ♔f8 16.♖xc6+–

13...♗b7? 14.♗xc6! ♗xc6 (14...dxc6 15.d7†) 15.♘d4! The main tactical justification for the ♗d5 raid – Black now loses a piece, as 15...♘f6 16.♘xc6 dxc6 17.d7† snares the queen.

14.♖e1† ♔f8

The lack of coordination in Black's position rings alarm bells, and now his king has gone running. White is down a full piece and a pawn, but no matter – Black is lost. A decisive strike must soon follow...

15.♘g5!

The deeper tactical justification behind 13.♗d5!! reveals itself. White intends an invasion on e7, with the d6-pawn as the lever.

15...♘h6

15...♘f6 16.♖e7! ♕b6 17.♖xf7† ♔g8 18.♖xf6+– Smothering.

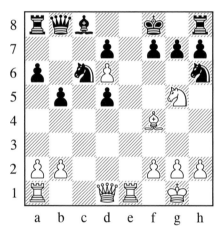

16.♖e7 ♕b6

16...♗b7 17.♕h5+–

17.♕xd5 ♘xe7 18.dxe7† ♔xe7

White is now down a whole rook, but Black will be down a king.

18...♔e8 The Siberian trapper intends to use the e7-pawn as a shield, often useful in cool castled positions – however, not in the fiery center!

White now drags the king out of his cave. 19.♘e4 ♗b7 20.♘d6† ♔xe7

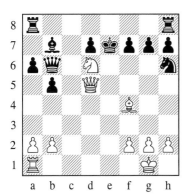

21.♕e5† ♔d8 (21...♔f8 22.♗xh6 gxh6 23.♕xh8† ♔e7 24.♖e1† ♔xd6 25.♕e5† ♔c6 26.♖c1†) 22.♕xg7 and simple butchery succeeds.

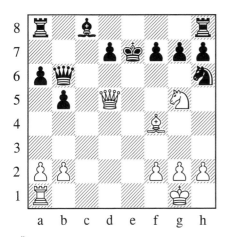

19.♘e4!+–

19.♖e1†?! ♔d8 20.♕xf7! A gorgeous sacrifice which nearly wins instantly. 20...♕f6! A saving grace... sort of. 21.♕d5 ♖e8 22.♖xe8† ♔xe8 23.♕xa8±

19.♕xa8? ♕b7! forces the queens off.

19...f6

Black has no defense:

19...♕e6 20.♗d6† ♔d8 21.♕xa8+–

19...♗b7 20.♕g5† f6 (20...♔f8 21.♗d6† ♔g8 22.♘f6#) 21.♕xg7† ♘f7 22.♘d6 ♖hf8 23.♖e1†+–

19...♔f8 20.♗d6† ♔g8 21.♕e5

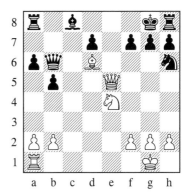

White's pieces swarm. The threat of ♘f6† is irresistible: 21...♕d8 22.♘f6†! gxf6 23.♕g3†+–

20.♘d6 ♕c6 21.♖e1† ♔d8

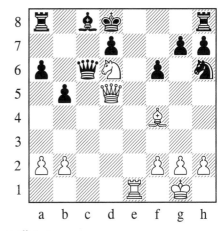

22.♕d2!!

After this subtle, devastating move, White's dark-squared domination is complete.

22...a5 23.♕e3+–

Catastrophe for the defenseless black king looms.

23...♗b7 24.♕e7† ♔c7 25.♘c8†

A humorous finish.

25...♔xc8 26.♕e8† ♖xe8 27.♖xe8#

So 12...b5 loses brilliantly to an avalanche of chaos. If Black cannot keep the balance with 12...0-0, then we can all but dismiss the Siberian trap as simply that, a superficial trap!

Theory II – 12...0-0

1.e4 c5 2.d4 cxd4 3.c3 dxc3 4.♘xc3 e6 5.♘f3 ♘c6 6.♗c4 ♕c7 7.0-0 ♘f6 8.♘b5 ♕b8 9.e5 ♘g4 10.♗f4! a6□ 11.♘d6† ♗xd6 12.exd6 0-0

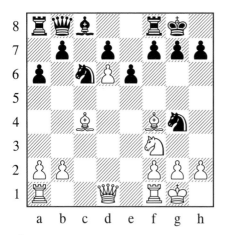

13.h3!N
A calm, effective novelty. But fear not, chaos comes soon.

13...♘f6
Instead of this retreat, Black can try the more ambitious:
13...b5 14.♗d5!
Again the bishop is sacrificed on this square, even against the castled king, as White has the luxury of chopping the knight on g4. The softer 14.♗d3 is playable but not as precise, as Black can summon defensive resources with 14...♘f6 (similar to

Ehlvest's early missed chance vs. Milman). Here 14.♗d5! drives a stake into the heart of Black's position, sowing the necessary confusion to ensure that he cannot coordinate his defense properly. In addition, the bishop sacrifice rips the e6-pawn away from its defense of f5, a square where the white knight will soon wreak havoc.

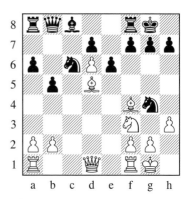

14...exd5
The most obvious and strongest retort, but Black's defensive labors remain Herculean.
14...♘xf2 15.♖xf2 exd5 16.♘h4± and Black's naked king may soon be mated. A possible continuation is: 16...♗b7 17.♕g4 ♔h8 18.♖e1 ♕a7 (18...♘d4 19.♗h6+−) 19.♘f5 ♖g8 20.♘e7+−
14...♘f6? 15.♗xc6 dxc6 16.d7 ♕xf4 17.d8=♕+− Two queens are better than one!
15.hxg4 ♘d8!
The knight desperately tries to reach his king.
16.♘h4!
But White's knight has the same idea...
16...♘e6 17.♕d2
I doubt Black can hold this position, either in theory or in practice. You take Black, I'll take White!
17...♗b7 18.♘f5 ♔h8
18...g6 19.♘e7† It's rarely a good sign when a knight gets to e7 supported by a pawn on d6! 19...♔h8 20.g5 A second dark-squared wedge ends all debate. 20...♘xf4 21.♕xf4

f6 22.gxf6 ♖f7 23.♖ac1 ♕f8 24.♖c7 ♖xf6 25.♕e5 ♗c6 26.g4 White cavalierly brings a pawn to g5, winning easily. 26...g5 (26...♕g7 27.♘xc6) 27.f4+–

19.♖ac1

White may threaten ♖c7, when the d-pawn eagerly waits to capture on c7 and become a queen.

19...♕d8 20.♖fe1 ♖c8

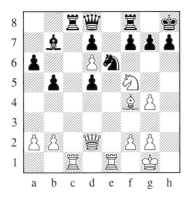

21.♖c7!

The shots now flow freely.

21...♘xc7

Declining the sacrifice with 21...♗c6 only leads to more mayhem: 22.♗h6!+– ♖g8 (22...♕f6 23.♖xe6+–) 23.♖xe6! The c-rook, initially only victimizing Black on vertical lines, will now operate laterally to help deliver the decisive blow. 23...dxe6 (23...fxe6 24.♘xg7! ♖xg7 25.♕d4 ♕g8 26.♗xg7† ♕xg7 27.♖xc8#) 24.♖xf7! And extreme chaos erupts around the black king. 24...exf5 25.♕c3+– Black suffers from catastrophic material loss.

22.dxc7 ♖xc7 23.♗xc7 ♕xc7 24.♕g5 ♖g8 25.♖e8

Black can only avert mate by giving up his queen.

14.♘e5!

This simple and strong move ensures that Black will not be able to complete his development routinely.

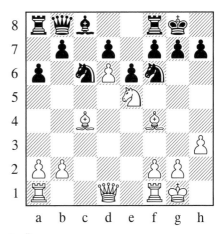

14...♘a5

This awkward move only encourages White's attack, which now becomes unstoppable.

14...♘xe5?! 15.♗xe5± must lead to disaster for Black, following the themes we already studied in Milman – Ehlvest.

14...b5? 15.♘xc6!+– demonstrates the point behind White's play – that ...b5 remains impossible and Black therefore struggles to untangle. I reached this position against an unlucky Boston teammate of mine last fall, and soon got the privilege of frolicking about with two queens in the early middlegame. But since the same teammate is featured later on in another chapter where I promote to a queen on d8 before move 30, I figure it's best to only identify one of his losses by name... 15...dxc6 16.d7! ♕xf4 17.d8=♕ Esserman – Unnamed teammate, Rhode Island (blitz) 2011.

14...♘b4!?

Possibly Black's only defense. Watch in disbelief at the land mines he must dodge for merely the hope of salvaging a draw by repetition.

15.♗b3 ♘bd5 16.♗g3 b5 17.♖e1 ♗b7 18.♗xd5! ♗xd5 19.♗h4 ♕xd6 20.♗xf6 gxf6 21.♕g4† ♔h8

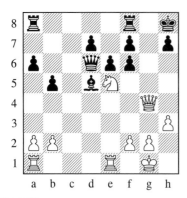

22.♕h4! ♕e7

  22...fxe5?! 23.♕f6† ♔g8 24.♖xe5 h6 25.♖d1!
À la Milman – Ehlvest again! 25...♖fc8
26.♖dxd5! (26.♖d3 ♕f8!)   26...♖xd5
27.♖xd5 exd5 28.♕xh6±

23.♖ad1 ♗c6

  23...♕d8?! 24.♘xd7! ♕xd7 25.♕xf6† ♔g8
26.♖e3+−

24.♘g4!?

  24.♘xd7 ♗xd7 25.♖xd7 ♕xd7 26.♕xf6†=

24...♖g8

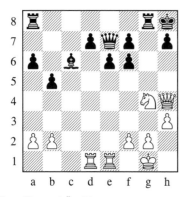

25.♖e5! ♖g7 26.♘xf6!

  The position nears explosion!

26...♗xg2

  26...♖xg2†? 27.♔f1 ♖g7 28.♖h5+−

27.♔h2 ♗c6 28.♖g1 ♕d6! 29.♖xg7 ♔xg7!

  29...♕xe5†? 30.♖g3 ♕f5 31.f3 ♖c8
32.♕h6+− provides a cold shower for the
Siberian trapper.

30.♕g5† ♔f8

  30...♔h8? 31.♘h5+−

31.♘xh7† ♔e8 32.♘f6† ♔f8=
Survival of the fittest!

15.♗d3 ♘d5 16.♗h2 f5

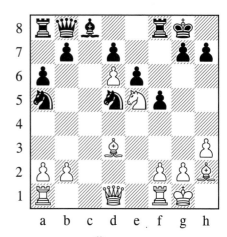

17.g4!± fxg4 18.♕xg4

And the highway to the black king is all clear.

18...♘f6 19.♕h4 ♕xd6

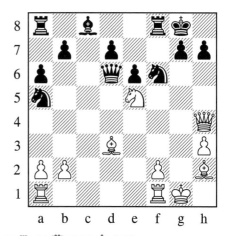

20.♖ad1 ♕e7 21.♗xh7†+−

I am confident that with the white pawn
on d6 acting as a destabilizing wedge in the
Black camp, the gambiteer will always retain
excellent theoretical chances for a sizeable
advantage in the mainline Siberian, even if
improvements are found. And in practice, as

all of these variations clearly show, the Siberian trap is extremely difficult for Black to handle if White comes fully armed. I cannot imagine a professional player choosing the Siberian after reading this chapter, unless of course he is a glutton for punishment. Therefore, in an attempt to revitalize the variation, I propose an "improved" version of the Siberian trap in the theoretical conclusion.

Theory III

1.e4 c5 2.d4 cxd4 3.c3 dxc3 4.♘xc3 e6 5.♘f3 ♘c6 6.♗c4 ♘f6!

I first faced the "Improved Siberian" in 2001, and immediately could sense the danger ahead. I sank into deep thought, and the longer I pondered, the funnier the looks my master opponent threw my way. He seemed to be asking: "What on earth are you thinking about here for over an hour...?" I then suspected he probably did not appreciate the significance of his move-order improvement. I could just castle here, when 99% of players would transpose to the Siberian main line after 7...♕c7. But I couldn't gamble, and continued with 7.♕e2!.

7.♕e2!
  7.0–0?! ♘xe4! is the point!

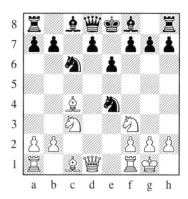

This simple fork trick is almost never played, but it solves Black's problems after 8.♘xe4 d5. During the game I did not trust White's resulting position – even now I'm sure Black should be the only one fighting for an advantage here. Siberian players take note – you now have a second trick to hide up your sleeves. I fully expect 6...♘f6 to become the Siberian's main line after this book's release.

7...♕c7
  White averted the fork trick with 7.♕e2 but has clearly made a concession – the queen is misplaced and after 8.0–0 ♘g4! the Siberian trapper is back in business. Therefore, Morra gambiteers must adopt a different method of attack.

8.e5

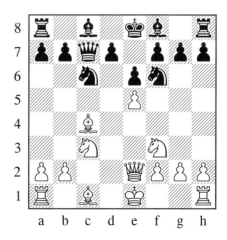

This brings us to the other main path in the Siberian, but White should only aim for this variation if Black forces his hand with the accurate 6...♘f6!.

8...♘g4

Black may eagerly attempt to free his restricted d-pawn, but it proves premature: 8...d5?! 9.exf6 dxc4 10.♗g5!

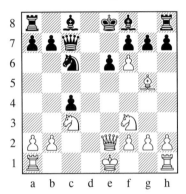

This active move is clearly superior to simpler captures.

10...♘b4

Black must try to hold on tight to his extra c-pawn, though it proves futile. Alternative defenses get even uglier:

10...e5? 11.0–0–0! with shades of the Morphy opera box game! 11...♗g4 12.♖he1+–

10...h6 11.♗h4 g5 12.♗g3 A position akin to the Moscow Gambit of the Semi-Slav appears; we could call it the "Morra Moscow." 12...♗d6 13.♖d1 ♗xg3 14.hxg3±

11.0–0 ♘d3 12.♖fd1! ♗d7 13.b3!

Black's attempt to hold his second extra pawn proves costly, and his position begins to creak.

13...h6

13...♗c6 14.bxc4±

14.♗e3 ♗c6

14...gxf6 15.♘d5 ♕d8 16.bxc4±

14...♕a5 15.bxc4 ♕xc3 16.♗d4±

15.bxc4 ♘e5 16.♘d5! exd5 17.cxd5+–

Black's lack of development does him in yet again.

9.♗f4

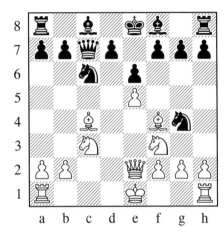

The Siberian trapper now has two choices, leading to drastically different landscapes. He can either open the game with 9...f6, or attempt a lockdown with 9...d5. One devolves into mayhem, the other becomes a "refined" positional struggle.

9...f6!?

9...d5!? 10.♗b3!

White does not release the central tension with 10.exd6?!, which simplifies Black's defensive task. Sometimes in the Morra Gambit you can trade the white e-pawn for Black's d-pawn if you can generate sufficient piece play, but this is not one of those cases. The resulting positions after 10.♗b3! bear a direct resemblance to some gambit variations of the French Defense.[15] First, Black must alleviate the g4-knight's suffering. But even if he does, White can generate heavy pressure on the c-file. If Black breaks prematurely with ...f6 to get air, he often pays severely. White has more than full compensation here. Now get ready for some thickets.

10...♗c5!?

a) 10...♘a5?! 11.0–0 ♘xb3 12.axb3 ♗c5 13.b4!± ♗e7 (13...♗xb4 14.♕b5†) 14.♖fc1 ♕b6 15.h3 White exploits his trumps – the open c-file and Black's wayward knight – on back-to-back moves. 15...♘h6 16.♘b5 0–0 17.♗e3 ♕d8 18.♘c7+–

b) 10...f6?? 11.♘xd5! exd5 12.exf6†+–

c) 10...♗e7 11.0–0 and now:

c1) 11...f6? 12.♘b5 (12.exf6?? ♕xf4 13.fxe7 ♘d4! and the old Siberian trap snares White yet again!) 12...♕b8 13.exf6! Now Black no longer has the infamous trick. 13...♕xf4 14.fxe7 ♘ce5 15.♘bd4 ♔xe7 16.♖fe1±

c2) 11...0–0 12.♖ac1± White's overall pressure and looming threat of h2-h3 causes great mischief, as Black is offered no salvation by: 12...f6? 13.exf6 ♕xf4 14.♘xd5 exd5 (With Black's queen hanging, the trap no longer works: 14...♘d4 15.♘xf4±) 15.♗xd5† ♔h8 16.fxe7 ♖e8 17.♖xc6+–

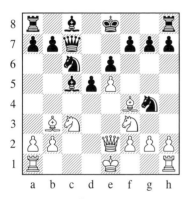

11.0–0 0–0 12.h3 ♘f6!

a) 12...♘h6?! The wayward knight now contributes to the wreckage of Black's kingside. 13.♗xh6 gxh6

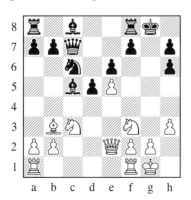

14.♗xd5! exd5 15.♘xd5 ♕d8 16.♘f6† ♔g7 17.♕e4 ♖h8 18.♘h5† ♔f8 19.♕f4+–

b) 12...♘xf2!? Logical but overambitious. 13.♖xf2 f6 14.♘xd5! and:

b1) 14...♘xf2†?! 15.♕xf2 exd5 16.♗xd5† ♔h8 The fun is just beginning... 17.♘h4!

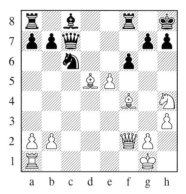

The threat of ♘g6† renders Black defenseless. 17...♗f5□ (17...g5 18.♗xg5 ♕xe5 19.♘g6† hxg6 20.♕h4† ♔g7 21.♕h6#) 18.exf6 ♕a5 (18...♕d7 19.fxg7† ♕xg7 20.♗xc6 bxc6 21.♕c5!+–) 19.fxg7† ♔xg7 20.♗xc6 bxc6 21.♗d2+– The calm before the winter storm.

b2) 14...exd5 15.♗xd5† ♔h8 16.♗e3±

13.♖ac1 ♘d7 14.♖fd1

White quietly increases the positional pressure. If Black tries to liberate himself...

14...f6?

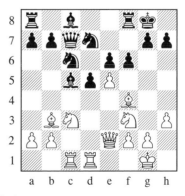

15.♖xd5!

You guessed it!

15...exd5

15...fxe5 16.♘g5! ♖xf4 (16...exd5 17.♘xd5
♕d8 18.♕h5+–) 17.♘xe6+–
16.♘xd5 ♕d8 17.exf6! ♔h8 18.fxg7† ♔xg7
19.♘g5+– (19.♗d2+–)

Therefore, after 14.♖fd1 Black must suffer
on in passivity.

With 9...f6, Black forces matters, and he
certainly gets what he wishes!

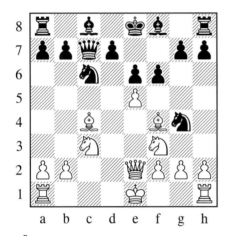

10.♘d5!?

The gambiteer may also fling the knight to
b5, intending with ♘d6† to obtain a dark-
squared bind similar to positions we have
studied earlier. However, I prefer the violent
text – it's hard to pass up another opportunity
to sacrifice on d5!

10.♘b5!?∞
In fact, I played this simpler move back
in 2001 when I first faced the "Improved
Siberian", and went on to win with the
standard dark-squared clamp (Esserman
– Storch, USA 2001). It remains just as
viable as the more violent knight thrust. If
you feel confused or unconvinced by the
main analysis following 10.♘d5, then I
can confidently recommend this simpler
alternative.

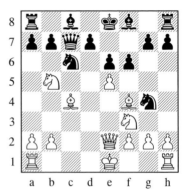

10...♕a5†
10...♗b4†? 11.♘d2!± and Black cannot save
all his hanging pieces.
10...♕b8?! 11.♘d6† ♗xd6 12.exd6± and
White obtains an excellent version of the
dark-squared binds we have previously
analyzed. Use your knowledge gleaned from
the earlier parts of the chapter to navigate
this terrain.
11.♗d2 ♕d8
11...♕b6?! 12.exf6 ♘xf6 13.♗f4 ♗b4†
14.♔f1 0–0 15.♗c7→
12.♘d6† ♗xd6 13.exd6∞
10...♕a5† followed by 11...♕d8 is Black's
best hope to survive, as the Siberian queen has
more spacious living quarters on the d8-a5
diagonal than in the b8 sinkhole. Both sides
have chances in this lush and wild Siberian
position.

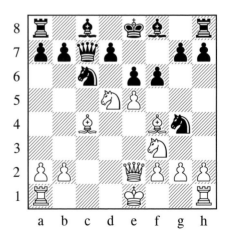

10...♕a5†□

Black cannot grab the invading knight – usually a ominous sign.

10...exd5 11.exf6†!± ♘ce5

11...♘ge5? 12.♗xe5! ♘xe5 13.♘xe5+–

12.♘xe5 ♘xe5 13.♕h5† g6

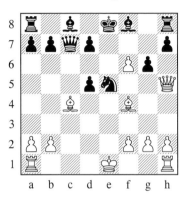

14.f7†!

This bone-chiller finishes Black.[16]

14...♚e7?

14...♚xf7 15.♗xd5† and Black's king lands in the crossfire: 15...♚e8 16.♕xe5† ♕xe5† 17.♗xe5 ♗b4† 18.♚e2 ♖f8±

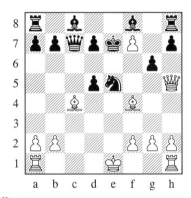

15.♕g5†!

Another great in-between move ends all resistance.

15.♕xe5† ♕xe5† 16.♗xe5 dxc4 17.♗xh8 d5±

15...♚e6

The black king is very brave indeed. But bravery and foolhardiness sometimes go hand in hand.

16.0–0+–

White dominates. You can work out all the variations yourself – I will only give one incredible line.

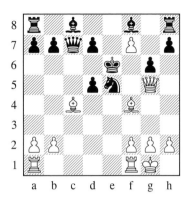

16...d6 17.♗xd5†! ♚xd5 18.♗xe5 dxe5 19.♕f6 ♗c5 20.♖ad1† ♗d4 21.♖xd4†! exd4

Black is a whole rook and piece up; I've heard that excuse before!

22.♕f3†! ♚d6

22...♚e6 23.♖e1† ♚d7 24.♕f6+–

23.♕f4†! ♚d7 24.♕xd4† ♚e7 25.♕xh8

Having collected one rook, White will either promote the pawn or pick up the other rook, since 25...♚xf7 would lose Black his Siberian queen.

11.♗d2 ♕d8

After the excitement of 10.♘d5 exd5, our final analysis in Siberia is a bit tamer!

12.exf6 ♘xf6

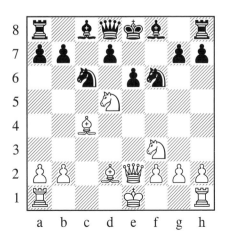

Now you must make a critical decision – what result are you playing for? After 13.♗g5 ♕a5† 14.♗d2 ♕d8 15.♗g5, you may earn a draw by repetition in the style of the ...♕a5/♗d2 Sveshnikov Sicilian. Morra bashers will urge you to do just this, but if you wish to win, you've come to the right place. You certainly won't find any lame draws by repetition recommended after 15 moves in this book.

13.♘xf6†!? ♕xf6 14.0–0! ♕xb2!?

If Black doesn't grab the pawn and instead develops, White's active piece play ensures full compensation: 14...♗e7 15.♗c3⩲

15.♖ab1 ♕f6

Now White is two pawns down – if you're afraid, take the draw!

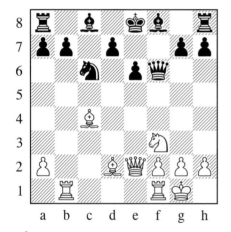

16.♗d5!

Applying more central pressure in what I like to call a "freestyle" position.

16...♗e7 17.♗xc6 bxc6

The gambiteer seeks a long-term positional grip.

18.♗g5 ♕f8

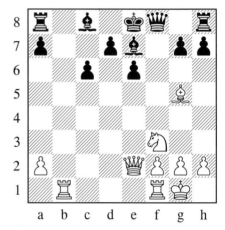

19.♘e5!?∞

The sad state of Black's queenside makes playing White's position preferable to forcing a draw. White intends to meet ...♗xg5 with ♕h5†, thus plundering the dark squares. Black should be able to hold the balance, but a hard struggle lies ahead.

19.♖fd1!? ♗xg5 20.♘xg5 ♕e7 21.♕h5† g6 22.♕h6 is an alternative binding continuation. At last we can finally escape the Siberian wilderness with a full awareness of the pitfalls that await us in its treacherous tundra. While White's chances are heavily favored in the Siberian main line, in the "Improved Siberian" the battle rages fierce. May the best player win!

Chapter 2

The Scheveningens

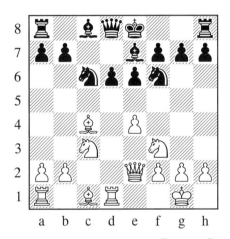

**1.e4 c5 2.d4 cxd4 3.c3 dxc3 4.♘xc3 ♘c6 5.♘f3 d6
6.♗c4 e6 7.0–0 ♗e7 8.♕e2 ♘f6 9.♖d1**

After braving the Siberian tundra, we now fly to far different terrain – the beaches of Scheveningen. Named after the Dutch town where the famous Sicilian structure debuted in the 1920's, the Scheveningen is one of Black's most sturdy and flexible defensive systems against White's wave of initiative in the Open Sicilians. So too in the Morra Gambit, Black can erect the small but stable e6/d6 central pawn duo to stem the tide of White's rapid development.

The defender's plan is simple – build the e6/d6 pawn dam, then quickly develop and castle, solving all problems. Yet as the Dutch well know, water's unrelenting flow has a way of breaching even the finest of walls. Against the Scheveningens, the gambiteer should swim alongside the traditional current of Morra theory with a quick 0–0, ♕e2, and ♖d1, and soon the cracks will begin to show in the enemy camp.

In Part I of the Scheveningens, Black hopes to stop White's swelling pressure with 9...e5.

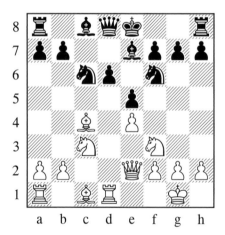

This is considered the classical main line of the Morra Gambit. Yet after this necessary compromise to the Scheveningen structure, the floodgates open, and White's pieces bathe freely on the weak d5-square.

The "Morra rooks", stationed on c1 and d1, support the surfing minor pieces, and if the defender is not careful, his position may quickly collapse amidst the torrential downpour.

In Part II (covered in the next chapter), the dam builder constructs a slightly different fortress – the black queen seeks dry ground from the waves on the d-file at c7, and the a6-pawn plugs the hole on the b5-square.

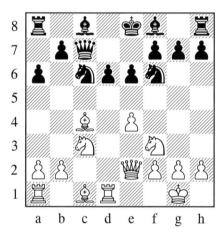

But water can adapt to any shape and crash its way through. Here the gambiteer must adapt in turn and fling his dark bishop to f4, where it threatens to drench Black after e4-e5!. Black may stop this leak, but water swirls from all angles after the queen's rook glides to c1, dousing the black queen.

Thus, when facing the Scheveningens, it's wise to remember a quote from the famous martial artist Bruce Lee:

Be formless, shapeless, like water. Now you put water into a cup, it becomes the cup. You put water into a bottle, it becomes the bottle. You put it in a teapot, it becomes the teapot. Water can flow, or it can crash. Be water, my friend.[17]

Lev Milman – Carlos Obregon

Villa Giardino 2002

1.e4 c5 2.d4 cxd4 3.c3 dxc3 4.♘xc3 ♘c6 5.♘f3 d6 6.♗c4 e6 7.0–0 ♗e7 8.♕e2 ♘f6 9.♖d1

Black has erected the fortress, although in this game he mixes systems, thus creating the flimsiest of dams.

9...♕c7?

The floodgates now burst open. If Black wishes to dodge the d1-rook via ...♕c7, he must first spend time earlier with ...a6 to plug the hole on b5 (the subject of the Scheveningens Part II). Of course, 9...a6 is out of the question here, as White crashes through with 10.e5!.

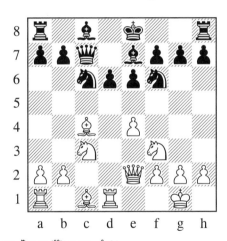

10.♘b5! ♕b8 11.♗f4±

Naturally, the bishop chases the queen, and the once sturdy Scheveningen loudly creaks.

11...♘e5

Black can try and patch the broken dam with the desperate 11...e5, but then White obtains a superior version of this chapter's main line. In addition to White being given the luscious d5-square, Black's queen remains stranded in "Siberia" – we already know what a frigid place b8 can be!

Continuing with 12.♗g5, the gambiteer threatens to further breach the dam's already shattered structure by ♗xf6. For a more penetrating analysis, please refer to the advanced material later.

12.♘xd6†!

Let the mayhem begin!

12...♗xd6 13.♖xd6 ♕xd6 14.♘xe5

For the small price of sacrificing the exchange, Milman shreds the Scheveningen structure. Meanwhile, Black's queen remains battered by the waves. Black, a young master, now completely collapses amidst the swelling pressure – a very common occurrence in the Morra Gambit.

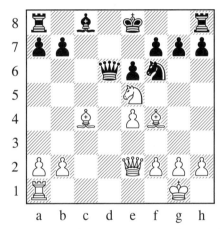

14...0–0 15.♘g6! ♕c6?? 16.♘e7† ♔h8 17.♘xc6+–

Lev went on to win easily, with Black drifting a queen for a rook down, his position awash.
...1–0

RawFishStomach (Esserman) – Mincho

Internet (blitz) 2011

1.e4 c5 2.d4 cxd4 3.c3 dxc3 4.♘xc3 ♘c6 5.♘f3 e6 6.♗c4 d6 7.0–0 ♗e7 8.♕e2 ♘f6 9.♖d1 e5

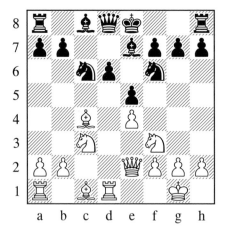

We reach the classical main line of the gambit, the most strategic variation of the opening, or what I like to call the "Ruy Lopez" of the Morra Gambit. As a result of this Scheveningen's more positional nature, expect to see more concepts discussed in the analysis and maneuvers featured in the games. But don't be alarmed if the position quickly takes a sharp turn, for even in the most protracted positional struggles, chaos still lurks. Many Morra manuals give here 10.h3?, revealing their great fear of the pinning ...♗g4. I can sympathize with their concern, as we cannot allow Black to gain supremacy of the d4-square for his knight after ...♗g4xf3 and ...♘d4. But remember, this is gambit play, and passive pawn moves in the early phases of the struggle like h3 or a3/a4 cannot be advised unless under the most dire of circumstances. Such limp moves may come later to incrementally improve the position, but only after you have established a dominant lead in development to justify the pawn sacrifice. Therefore, we waste no time and stream forward while overprotecting the weak d4-square.

10.♗e3!

Not 10.♗g5?, as after 10...♗g4! White has no choice but to drift backwards to e3.

10...♗g4

As this game will show, the only thing we have to fear about ...♗g4 is the fear of ...♗g4 itself.

11.♖ac1 0–0 12.h3

Only now, with all of our pieces developed and in optimal central positions, do we start with the flank pawn moves.

12...♗xf3

We investigate the ramifications of 12...♗h5!? 13.g4 ♗g6 14.♘h4! later on.

13.♕xf3±

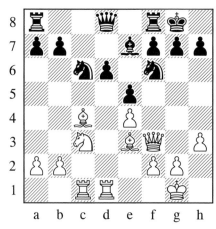

Despite being a pawn down in a "calm" position, the gambiteer retains a clear long-term pull. In addition to possessing the two bishops, his rooks own the prime "beachfront property", and his minor pieces are eager to surf on the d5-square. As for Black, he floats in a true defensive position. He lacks any meaningful targets for counterplay, while his extra d6-pawn lies backwards and under siege – his e7-bishop, meanwhile, drowns in defense of d6.

13...♖c8 14.♕e2

This smooth regrouping maneuver stifles any tricks on the c-file and secures the advantage.

14...a6 15.a3

As you will see over and over in the main line, gaining space and inundating Black's queenside with a3 and b4 is the next logical step towards victory after the opening phase.

15...♔h8 16.b4 ♘e8

This backwards move allows the white knight to dock into d5, but in return Black gives his suffocating bishop a little air. He eventually hopes to swap it off for its dominant counterpart on e3.

17.♘d5 ♗g5 18.♗b6

But this wish turns out to be a dream. Note that ...a6, while plugging the b5-point, has caused more harm than good, as the b6-square now drips with white pieces. Water, after all, cannot be stopped.

18...♕d7 19.♖c3!?

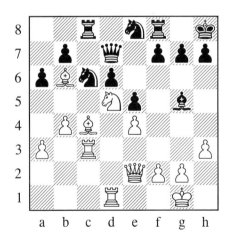

19...g6

Black should have continued with his retreating strategy and eliminated the towering knight on d5 with 19...♘e7, but in a blitz game such a sublime maneuver requires extreme deftness.

20.h4!

This move, inspired by my study of a very similar sacrifice in the Sveshnikov Sicilian (which you will see in a related game at the chapter's end) is a natural reaction to ...g6. If Black does not accept the offering, then h4-h5 next sends ripples throughout the kingside.

20...♗xh4 21.♖h3

The point – the h-file rips open as White's heavy pieces surge towards the black king.

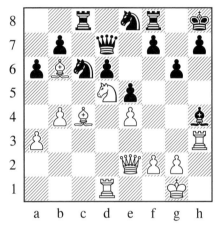

21...♗g5 22.♗e3 ♗xe3?

Black can ill afford this critical weakening of the dark squares. Not only will the kingside be drenched, but the b6-square floods as well. Again, the constricted 22...♗d8 was best, but exchanging is the most natural reaction to such torrential pressure.

23.♕xe3+–

Black must now choose between getting mated and giving the exchange. White decides for him.

23...f5 24.♘b6 ♕c7 25.♘xc8 ♕xc8 26.♕h6 ♘f6 27.♖xd6

The final heavy piece crashes through.

27...♘h5 28.♖xg6!

A flashflood!

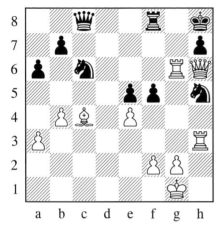

28...♘e7 29.♖xh5
1–0

Marc Esserman – Mark Ginsburg

Miami 2007

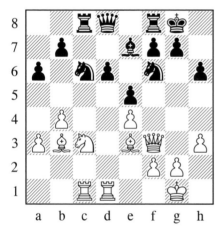

The position above corresponds nearly exactly to a moment from our last game adventure (right before Black retreated with 16...♘e8). Here IM Ginsburg hits upon a similar plan to trade off his suffering dark-squared bishop, but chooses h7 for his knight instead. This option was impossible in the previous game, as Black had tried ...♔h8 rather than ...h6. But the subtle pawn slide also has its flaws – in particular g6 may "leak" and h6 itself may become the target for a sacrificial blow.

16...♘h7 17.♖c2

I could have continued as before with ♘d5 and ♗b6, but alas, I was weaker then. At least I knew better than to let the bishops swap. After 17.♘d5! ♗g5 18.♗b6 ♕d7 19.♖c3! ♘f6 20.♖cd3± White's fully coordinated army effortlessly flows across the board. The d6-pawn is now ripe for the plucking, as the impetuous bishop has skirted his defensive duties. If now 20...♘xd5, then 21.♖xd5, and White bathes on d5 forever.

17...♔h8?!

Of course I still had the sense to plan for 17...♗g5. Namely, I eyed the ever-swirling tactic in the Scheveningens, 18.♗c5!?. But in this case, both combatants overlooked that Black could then sacrifice his queen with the thematic 18...dxc5! 19.♖xd8 ♖cxd8, securing a dominating bind on the dark squares, thus ensuring that White's swelling initiative would quickly subside. Observe that at the end of this instructive variation, Black's knight dines on the d4-square, always the Achilles heel of the Morra Gambit! Rather than basking on d5 itself, White's knight would then have to beat a sad retreat with 20.♘e2∓.

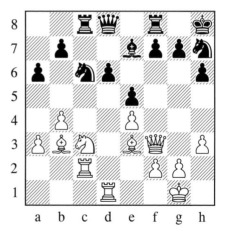

After the move played in the game, 18.♘d5!± suggests itself, but I have more ambitious plans for the beast – to swim to f5 via g3, a tour very familiar to us from the famous lines of the Ruy Lopez.

18.♘e2!? ♕d7 19.♘g3

Black now takes drastic measures to prevent the knight from reaching the sacred waters on f5.

19...♘d4 20.♗xd4 ♖xc2

21.♗xc2?!

Completely against the Romantic spirit! Who cares about restoring material equality when you can be down an exchange instead:

21.♗xe5!±

White smashes the Scheveningen structure with a few crackling lightning bolts.

21...♖c6 22.♘f5

The wayward knight finally reaches its destination. There is simply no comparison between White's foaming and Black's flailing pieces.

22...f6

After 22...♗f6 23.♗xf6 ♘xf6 24.e5! White's fluid e-pawn bursts forward, washing away any memory of Black's e5-pawn dam which once firmly stood in its place.

23.♕g3 ♘g5 24.♗d4

Threatening the pulverizing h3-h4.

24...♗d8 25.♗d5!

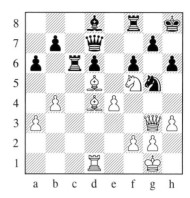

The contrast between activity and passivity shines brighter with every move!

25...♖c7 26.h4 ♘e6 27.♗b6+–

With ♗xe6 coming next, Black's kingdom finally crumbles.

21...exd4 22.♖xd4 ♗f6 23.♖d3 ♗e5

White still stands better, but Black has stemmed the rising tide, for now.

24.♕e3 ♕c7 25.♗b3 ♖c8

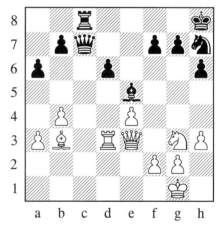

Once more, I miss a great chance to shatter Ginsburg's e5-blockade.

26.♘e2?

26.f4! simply wins, as 26...♕c1†, the move I feared, fails to a nasty fork: 27.♕xc1 ♖xc1† 28.♔f2! ♗xf4 29.♘e2!+– A petite, but non-trivial combination.

Black must therefore give ground on e5 with 26...♣f6, but then the d6-pawn collapses: 27.♘f5 ♜d8 28.♕d2+–

After so many mistakes by both sides, it is only fitting that the game eventually ended in a draw. A slippery, sloppy, yet instructive encounter.

...½–½

Marc Esserman – Emmanouil Kazakos

Paleochora 2011

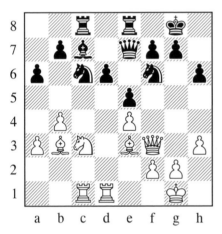

After some lengthy maneuvering flowing from yet another ...♣g4xf3 position, it is now high time for me to crash through. Black's dark-squared bishop again ranks as his dampest piece, having somehow drifted to c7 (a square normally fit for a queen in most Sicilians, but maybe not a Morra). His queen, meanwhile, awkwardly assumes the bishop's normal defensive post at e7. As a result of this strange bishop/queen reversal, I decided to lash out with my g-pawn, intending a quick g4-g5, and if ...hxg5, then ♣xg5 (pinning the knight against the misplaced queen) and ♘d5, winning...

23.g4?

But simply diving in with the knight (avoiding preliminary pawn forays) would have

busted Black's already battered Scheveningen: 23.♘d5!N ♘xd5 24.♣xd5

The pristine 23.♘d5 has effectively exposed Black's structural defects – as a result of eliminating the f6-knight, White's queen can now work her magic on the kingside, supported by her dark-squared archer on e3 and hungry rooks. And as for White's golden d5-bishop, it simply walks on water, surfing throughout the board. White's numerous threats (♣xc6, ♕g4 or ♕h5 followed by ♣xh6) cannot be stopped. The following sample variations illustrate varying positional and tactical methods for seizing victory.

24...♣b8

24...♕d7 25.♕g4 ♕xg4 26.hxg4± and although the most dangerous pieces evaporate, Black remains crippled: 26...♘d8 27.♜d2 ♘e6 28.♜dc2+–

24...♣d8 25.♕g4+–

25.♕h5 ♘d4

After 25...♕f6 26.♜c3 White threatens to double on the c-file or swing to the kingside. 26...♘e7 27.♜xc8 ♜xc8 28.♣xb7+–

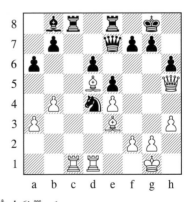

26.♣xh6! ♜xc1

26...gxh6 27.♜xc8 ♜xc8 28.♕g4† and Black's stray pieces lie in the wreckage.

27.♜xc1 gxh6 28.♕g6† ♚h8 29.♕xh6† ♚g8 30.♚f1!

Silencing Black's gasp on e2, and after the second rook wave to c3-g3, the story would end.

30...♕f8 31.♕g6† ♔h8
  31...♕g7 32.♗xf7†
32.♗xf7 ♖e7

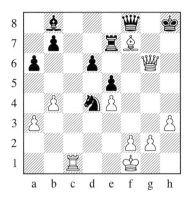

33.♖c8! ♖xf7 34.♕h5† ♔g7 35.♕g5† ♔h8
36.♖xf8† ♖xf8 37.♕e7 ♖g8 38.♕xb7+–
A fitting conclusion – after ♕xa6, White
easily springs new queens, and Black's bishop
remains miserable right to the final move.

23...♗b8!
Now, like falling into cold water, I suddenly
knew I had pitched my advantage, as the g4-
advance proves to be nothing more than a
gaping kingside weakness. Black's position is
supposed to leak, not White's.

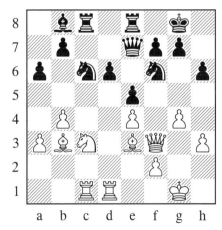

24.♔g2
The point of Black's 23rd move is: 24.g5?
hxg5 25.♗xg5 ♘d4!–+ This knight thrust, the

Morra's "kryptonite", strikes again! White's
superficial pinning tricks fail against Black's
central and c-file counterplay. 26.♖xd4 exd4
27.♘d5 ♖xc1†! 28.♗xc1 ♘xd5

**24...♘d4 25.♗xd4 exd4 26.♖xd4 ♕e5
27.♖dd1 d5!?**

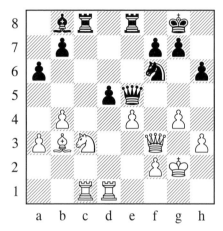

And now, in mutual time pressure, Black is
having all the fun, while I must assume the
tragic role of "dam builder". Thus, I lost only
my second tournament game in the Morra
since 2003. But my personal failings are of
little theoretical interest – clearly my defeat is
in no way the fault of the Morra Gambit, and
that's what ultimately matters.
...0–1

Marc Esserman – William Collins

Harvard (blitz) 2010

So far we have only swum in the channels of
Black's ...♗g4xf3. Now we consider other c8-
bishop developments, and what better way
than by introducing another character to the
lexicon of chess mythology, "Sir William"
Collins. Billy – the chess magician – Collins,
near chess master and super-grandmaster
trash-talker, is a man of many nicknames and
talents. My sparring partner Billy is always

searching for that elusive victory notch on his belt against the Morra Gambit – or against any titled player who dares cross his path, in any opening! So if you are brave enough, then fly to Cambridge, MA, and face this Boston chess legend in the flesh. The battle will be fierce, but be sure to bring along some thick skin with all that chess knowledge, because when you do blunder, and eventually you will, then you will surely get an earful!

1.e4 c5 2.d4 cxd4 3.c3 dxc3 4.♘xc3 ♘c6 5.♘f3 d6 6.♗c4 e6 7.0-0 ♘f6 8.♕e2 ♗e7 9.♖d1 e5

Billy has tried everything under the sun in our Morra matches, but when he desperately wants that notch, he always goes for the classical main line, or "Old Betsy" as he calls her.

10.♗e3 0-0 11.♖ac1 ♗e6!?

On e6, the bishop's other main path, it now actively fights for control of the critical d5-square. We will examine this move in greater detail in the theoretical section.

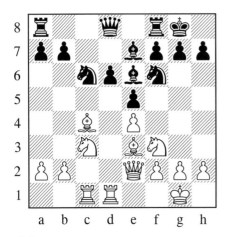

12.b4!

The most energetic way to fight for the advantage.

Note that the obvious 12.♗xe6 fxe6 13.♕c4

fails to 13...♕d7, and after 14.♘g5 ♘d8! White will soon beat a sad retreat.

12...a6

If 12...♘xb4, then 13.♘xe5 and the storm surges.

If 12...♖c8, then only now does the gambiteer strike with 13.♗xe6 fxe6 14.b5! ♘a5, and after 15.♘xe5, White obtains a large edge. 12.b4 is a slippery move indeed!

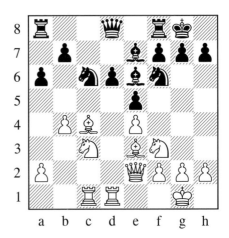

13.a3!?

A mysterious pawn move, seeming to merely guard b4. Many of my opponents, including Billy, have been hypnotized by its charms.

13...♖c8?

When Billy first heard from me about this book's upcoming release, he hungered to read about the secrets of the thematic b2-b4 so that he could once and for all put an end to the Mayhem in the Morra. Well Billy, are you reading, "catdog"? Black may play 13...♗xc4!? 14.♕xc4 ♖c8, but after 15.♕b3 White retains lasting light-squared pressure. Although the computer here shouts "equal", water may slowly submerge the Scheveningen fortress and silence its claims.

14.♗xe6!

Now White snaps off the bishop. Clearly the tide has turned.

14...fxe6 15.♕a2!

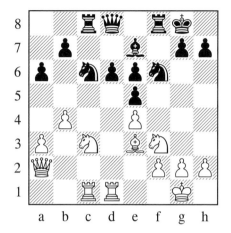

The mystery behind 13.a3 reveals itself – a secret hideout for the queen on a2 appears.

15...♕d7 16.♘a4!±

The other idea behind the timely ♗xe6! The knight cruises to c5 or to the fresh hole on b6 that ...a6 left in its wake. Water breaches the dam from all sides, and Black cannot plug all the gaps. Although I've executed the sequence with ♗xe6, ♕a2, and ♘a4 at least 20 times online and during live blitz and simuls, the position after 13.a3 does not seem to appear in any database, showcasing just how ripe the field for innovation remains in the Morra.
...1–0

We leave our featured blitz game now, as it is interesting to analyze Black's desperado, the old familiar trick ...♘d4 (which I've faced a few times, and of course once against Billy).

16...♘d4 17.♘xd4 ♖xc1

17...exd4 18.♘b6 ♖xc1 19.♖xc1 transposes to our main line.

18.♖xc1 exd4

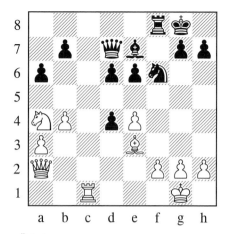

19.♘b6!

Try as he might, Black cannot hold off the onslaught.

19...♕e8 20.♕xe6† ♕f7

20...♖f7 21.♖c8+–

21.♕xf7† ♖xf7 22.♗xd4 ♘xe4

The dam builder finally stands on level ground, material-wise at least, but White's dominance of the c-file sweeps him away.

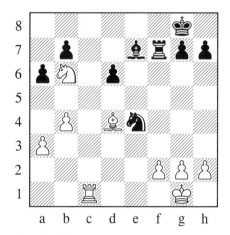

23.♖c8† ♖f8

23...♗f8 24.♘d5±

24.♖c7 ♗f6 25.♗xf6 ♖xf6 26.f3+–

Black's queenside foundation collapses at last.

Marc Esserman – Thomas Bartell

US Chess League, Internet 2009

1.e4 c5 2.d4 cxd4 3.c3 dxc3 4.♘xc3 ♘c6 5.♘f3 d6 6.♗c4 e6 7.0–0 ♗e7 8.♕e2 ♘f6 9.♖d1 e5 10.♗e3 0–0 11.♖ac1 ♗d7!?

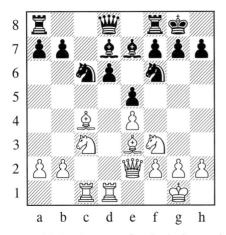

An odd development for the bishop, which I had never seen before at this juncture, nor since. But the move, played instantly by Bartell and therefore likely prepared, has its theoretical interest – not only does the bishop block the d-file, stopping tactical thrusts like b2-b4, but it also avoids the other forcing skirmishes we have already seen in the 11...♗g4 and 11...♗e6 lines. Therefore, as the bishop will eventually find its way to e6 or g4 when Black feels the time is right, we can brand 11...♗d7 as a useful, albeit passive waiting move. In the absence of anything else to do, I continued with the standard queenside expansion.

12.a3 a6 13.b4 b5 14.♗b3 ♗e6

Only now, like a good soldier, does the bishop glide to e6 with "sandbags" in tow, to stop any potential flooding on the light squares. Much to my concern, I realized that unlike in Esserman – Collins, I cannot grab on e6 and play ♕a2, as after ...♕d7 the reply ♘a4 is impossible due to Bartell's inclusion

of ...b5. The light-squared holes would then be sealed shut forever, and my hopes of obtaining an advantage quashed. Hungry to prove the power of the Morra Gambit to the rabid Internet crowd following this US Chess League match, I recklessly pushed forward...

15.♘d5 ♗xd5

15...♘xe4? of course loses to 16.♗b6!.

16.exd5!

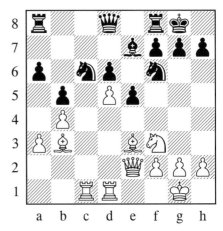

Before we continue, I must explain why we are studying this encounter last in the chapter. This game caused quite a stir in the US upon its dramatic finish, perhaps because behind all the loud fireworks, it quietly challenged the popular myth that Black should seize the advantage in the Morra without dripping too much sweat. But the game also created a sensation amongst my students, much to my dismay. These aspiring gambiteers would properly sink a piece into d5 in the Scheveningens, but upon its capture would take back on d5 with a pawn, without hesitation! Oh the horror! Of course, exd5 is normally doubly bad for White. This "blunder" firstly plugs the critical d5-hole, and secondly shields the d6-pawn from the d1-rook's unrelenting pressure. In a few more moves, my wayward students would be inexorably lost at sea, thus proving

Larsen right that the Morra Gambit indeed drops a pawn. Fortunately though, you will not suffer their fate, as I have already provided countless examples where White successfully captures back on d5 with a piece! But rules, in chess and life, are sometimes made to be broken...

16...♞b8?!

In hindsight, Black had to play the unnatural 16...♞a7, after which the chances would be about equal. Both sides have their plusses. In White's favor are the two bishops, extra development, space, and the domination of the c-file (in particular the weak c6-square). In Black's favor are the dreaded extra center pawn, and his greatest positional leak solved – the d5-square. But the battle is contested in the arena, not the analytical science laboratory, and thus Black did not hear the rushing current approaching.

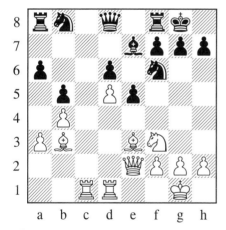

17.♞xe5!

Gushing through Black's stone-like blockade. The violent turn of events no doubt inflicted as great a psychological blow as the objective damage of the move itself.

17...dxe5 18.d6 ♝xd6

I expected the clinging defense:
18...♞bd7

At the time I remained undecided how to proceed. By happenstance, White has a devastating shot which foreshadows the game's end.

19.g4!+–

Freezing Black's minor pieces as the marauding Morra rooks flood the board. Black is defenseless to the incoming g4-g5 and a multitude of pins.

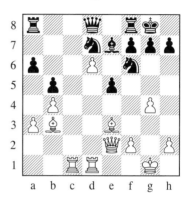

19...♝xd6

19...♞e4 20.dxe7 ♛xe7 21.♖c7 (or 21.♗d5+–) 21...♖ad8 22.♛f3 ♞d6 23.♗c5!+–

20.♖xd6 ♛e7

20...♞e4 21.♖d3 ♖c8 22.♖cd1 ♞c3 23.♛c2 ♞xd1 24.♛xd1 ♖c7 25.♗b6!+–

21.♛d1 h6

21...♖fd8 22.♖c7+–

22.♖c7 ♖ad8 23.g5! hxg5 24.♗xg5

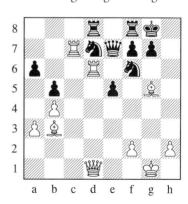

Supreme swelling abounds!

19.♗c5 ♗xc5

19...♘e8 20.♗d5!+– and the bishops stream through.

20.♖xd8 ♗xf2†?!

Bartell did not intend to float away with 20...♖xd8 21.♖xc5 ♘bd7 22.♖c7, and instead picks up a pawn for his suffering.

21.♕xf2 ♖xd8

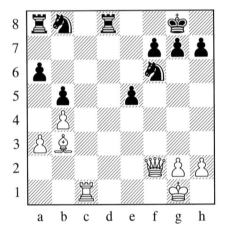

Black might have weathered the storm, if not for one little pawn move. But such "if only" thinking holds no weight in chess.

22.g4!+–

This bludgeoning blow blasts Black's king to smithereens.

22...a5

22...h6 seeks but does not find solace: 23.h4! ♖d4 24.♖c8† ♔h7 25.♕f5† g6 26.♕xf6+–

22...♖f8 23.g5 ♘e4? (23...♘fd7 24.♗d5+– Flowing...) 24.♕xf7†! and crashing... 24...♖xf7 25.♖c8#

23.g5 ♘fd7 24.♕xf7† ♔h8 25.♕e7 ♖f8

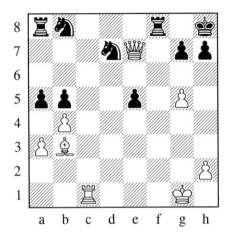

26.♕xf8†! ♘xf8 27.♖c8

Black resigned, leaving some elegant conclusions to the imagination: 27...g6 28.♖xf8† ♔g7 29.♖g8# or 27...♘bd7 28.♖xa8 h6 29.g6 e4 30.♗e6 e3 31.♗xd7 and only water remains on the earth.

1–0

A month later, the New York Times featured this game in its weekly column, titling the article "An Often Shunned Opening, for Good Reason", and continuing: "Some openings are perennially popular. Others are rarely used, particularly among elite players, and often for good reason."[18] Thus, the myth of the big, bad, unsound Morra, passed on from generation to generation, endures today, despite the dent this game wedged in its armor. After all, the author later concedes that among the risky gambits, the Morra is "among the most respectable. By investing a pawn, White obtains a significant initiative. Black can defuse this advantage, but it takes patience." Ah, patience, a significant victory indeed! Read through the article if you will, and answer my question. Do you get the nagging feeling, as I do, that the reason many top players shun the Morra Gambit is because it's too chaotic, or simply, just too much fun!?

Theory I – 9...♕c7? 10.♘b5!

1.e4 c5 2.d4 cxd4 3.c3 dxc3 4.♘xc3 ♘c6 5.♘f3 d6 6.♗c4 e6 7.0–0 ♘f6 8.♕e2 ♗e7 9.♖d1 ♕c7?

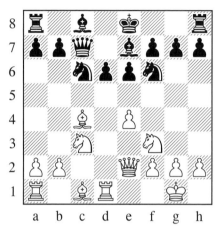

10.♘b5! ♕b8 11.♗f4± ♘e5

11...e5 12.♗g5 a6 13.♗xf6 gxf6 14.♘c3 ♗g4

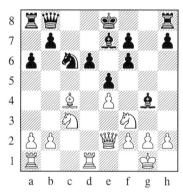

Black tries the usual trickery on the d4-square, but with his queen on b8, White sacrifices the exchange and easily seizes the initiative: 15.h3 ♘d4 16.♖xd4! exd4 17.♘d5 ♗xf3 (17...♗e6 18.♘xd4+– or 17...♗h5 18.♘b6 ♖a7?! 19.♗b5†!+–) 18.♕xf3 ♕d8 19.♖d1 ♖c8 20.♖xd4 Black cannot castle as ♗d3, e5 and ♖g4 would follow, when he can resign.

12.♖xd6!

12.♘xd6†! ♗xd6 13.♖xd6 ♕xd6 comes to the same thing.

12...♗xd6 13.♘xd6† ♕xd6 14.♘xe5

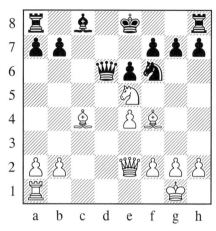

As the following variations show, Black cannot consolidate in time to capitalize on his material advantage.

14...♕e7

14...0–0 15.♘g6±

14...♕b6 15.♗b5† ♔f8 (15...♗d7 16.♘xd7 ♘xd7 17.♖d1 ♖d8 18.♕d3 0–0 19.♗xd7+– or 15...♔e7 16.♕c4+–) 16.♖d1 ♔g8 17.♗e3 ♕c7

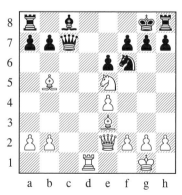

18.♕c2! ♕e7 19.♗c5 ♕c7 20.♗xa7+–

15.♗b5† ♔f8 16.♖d1!±

Suppressing Black's queenside, permanently.

16...a6 17.♗a4 ♚g8

17...b5? 18.♘c6+–

18.♕c2!

Sending ripples towards the h7-square.

18...h6 19.♗b3 ♚h7

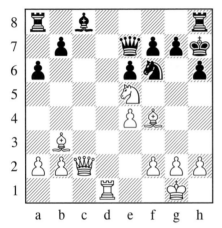

20.♘xf7! ♕xf7 21.e5† ♕g6 22.exf6 ♕xc2

22...gxf6　23.♕c7†　♕g7　24.♗c2†　f5
25.♕xg7†+–

**23.♗xc2† g6 24.♗e5 ♖f8 25.♖d3 b5
26.♖g3+–**

Thus we can toss 9...♕c7? into the ocean.

Theory II – 11...♗g4 12.h3 ♗h5 13.g4

**1.e4 c5 2.d4 cxd4 3.c3 dxc3 4.♘xc3 d6
5.♘f3 e6 6.♗c4 ♘c6 7.0–0 ♘f6 8.♕e2 ♗e7
9.♖d1 e5**

9...♗d7 10.♘b5 ♕b8 11.♗f4 ♘e5 Karaklaic –
Gravseth, corr. 1957. (11...e5 12.♗g5 a6 13.♗xf6
gxf6 14.♘c3⩱) 12.♘xd6†!?N Compared to page
59, Black has the extra move ...♗d7, but still
the sacrifice is decent. 12...♗xd6 13.♖xd6 ♕xd6
14.♘xe5 ♕e7 (14...♕b6 15.♖d1 a6 16.♘xd7
♘xd7 17.♗d6 intending e4-e5 with full
compensation) 15.♖d1 0–0 Black may as well
return the material. (15...♖d8 16.♘xd7 ♘xd7
17.♗d6 with a dangerous initiative) 16.♘xd7

♘xd7　17.♗d6± White regains the exchange
while keeping the slightly more active position.

10.♗e3 0–0 11.♖ac1 ♗g4

11...♗g4?! 12.♗c5!± and the knight has
nothing better than returning with 12...♘f6.
White's bishop can now reroute to a3, but only
after 13.h3, preventing ...♗g4 (thus securing
the d4-square).

12.h3

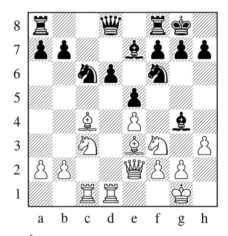

12...♗h5

12...♗xf3 13.♕xf3±

13.g4 ♗g6

The bold 13...♘xg4 fails to impress: 14.hxg4
♗xg4 15.♔g2 ♚h8 16.♖h1±

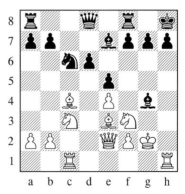

White dominates the d5-square, and plans
to either double rooks on the h-file, or reroute

for defense via ♕d1 and ♗e2. 16...f5?! 17.♗e6! ♕e8 18.♖xh7†! Crashing through. 18...♔xh7 19.♖h1† ♔h5 (19...♔g6 20.exf5† ♗xf5 21.♘xe5† ♘xe5 22.♕h5† ♔f6 23.♕xf5#) 20.♘xe5! ♘xe5 21.♖xh5† ♔g6 22.exf5† ♔f6 23.♘d5#

14.♘h4!

I found this powerful idea in 2004 and have used it countless times in blitz/rapid, always obtaining strong results. At a glance it seems that White drops material, but Black cannot tactically exploit this strategically significant move. Nowadays, the top engines agree that this is White's best course after 11...♗g4.

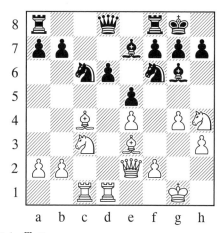

14...♖c8

14...♗xe4?? 15.g5!+– must be a blind spot for my opponents, as I've won like this in blitz probably a dozen times, even against titled players. So is 14...♘xe4?? 15.♘xg6 ♘xc3 16.♘xe7†+–.

14...♘d7!? Here, and in this whole variation, you must decide whether to play for long-term positional pressure after taking the g6-bishop, or for a kingside pawn assault after bringing the knight to f5. In this exact position, both moves promise an advantage, but at other moments, perhaps only the stable exchange on g6 suffices. 15.♘xg6 (15.♘f5!? ♗xf5 16.exf5 ♖c8 17.♕d2 ♘b6 18.♗f1± For all you positional grinders out there, this may be your

Morra variation!) 15...hxg6 16.a3 a6 17.♗a2± With a lasting light-squared bind.

15.a3!?

I have habitually played the aggressive 15.♘f5 in these positions, but against precise defense here, it may not be best: 15...♗xf5 16.exf5 If Black is not alert, he will get run over by g5-g6. 16...h6 17.a3 a6 Now the violent pawn storm 18.h4?! b5 19.♗b3 ♘d7∓ is easily weathered, so White should play any calm move like 18.♗a2±.

15...♘e8

15...♘d7 16.♘xg6 hxg6 17.♘b5! Eyeing the d6-pawn promises White an advantage.

16.♘xg6!

16.♘f5?! allows Black to solve the problem of his bishop with 16...♗g5.

16...hxg6

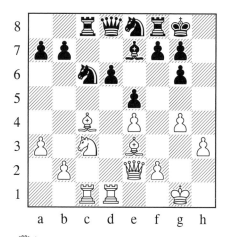

17.♕d2!

The key subtlety, justifying the plan with 15.a3 and 16.♘xg6. White must keep the e7-bishop submerged.

17...♘c7 18.♘d5 ♘xd5 19.♗xd5 ♕d7 20.♔g2±

White's positional pressure endures deep into the middlegame.

Theory III – 11...♗e6 12.b4!?

1.e4 c5 2.d4 cxd4 3.c3 dxc3 4.♘xc3 d6 5.♘f3 e6 6.♗c4 ♘c6 7.0-0 ♘f6 8.♕e2 ♗e7 9.♖d1 e5 10.♗e3 0-0 11.♖ac1 ♗e6

This leads to some of the sharpest, unexplored waters in the main line. Let's take a brief look.

12.b4

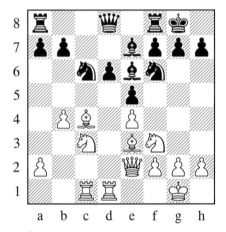

12...♘xb4!?

12...♗xc4 13.♕xc4 ♖c8 14.♕b3⩲ with a gripping bind, as in the ...♗g4 variations.

12...♘g4!? 13.♗d2! ♘f6

13...♘xb4 Playing the knights to g4 and b4 is certainly not very "human" chess. 14.♗xe6 fxe6 15.♕c4 ♘xf2 (15...d5!? 16.exd5 ♘xf2 17.♔xf2 ♖c8 18.♕g4 ♘d3† 19.♔f1 ♘xc1 20.♕xe6† ♔h8 21.♖xc1∞) 16.♕xe6† ♔h8 17.♔xf2 ♘d3† 18.♔e2 ♘xc1† 19.♖xc1 ♖c8 20.♘d5 ♖xc1 21.♗xc1± The chaos has subsided, and White retains his bind.

14.♘d5!

14.♗e3=

14...♗xd5

14...♗g4 15.♗c3∞

15.exd5 ♘b8∞

Another structure familiar to us from the

Esserman – Bartell analysis. The following gives a flavor of how Black may be outplayed.

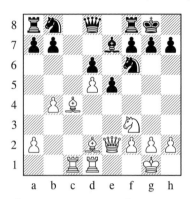

16.a4 ♘bd7 17.a5 ♖c8 18.♗b3 ♖xc1 19.♖xc1 ♘e8?!

Rushing to prepare the standard ...f5 proves fatal.

20.♕b5! b6 21.♗a4 ♘ef6 22.a6 ♖e8 23.♕c6 ♕b8 24.♕b7 ♕xb7 25.axb7 ♖b8 26.♖c8† ♗f8 27.♗c6+–

13.♘xe5!

After his gutsy 12th move, Black gets the violent struggle he seeks.

13.♗xe6 fxe6 14.♘xe5 will just lead to a transposition after 14...♖c8 or 14...♕a5, but playing the knight forward first gives Black an extra chance to go wrong.

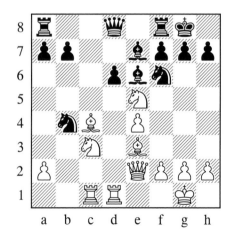

13...♖c8

13...♗xc4? 14.♘xc4! is great for White as e4-e5! busts through.

13...♕a5 14.♗xe6 fxe6 15.♘f3!⩲ White will sink the knight into e6. Black can prevent the incursion via 15...♘g4, but then after 16.♗d2, he faces a whole new cast of problems.

14.♗xe6 fxe6 15.♘f3

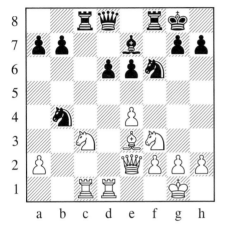

White aims for the creaking e6-square with another attacking wave. Possible continuations are:

a) 15...♘g4?! 16.♘d4! ♘xe3 17.♘xe6± ♕b6 18.fxe3 ♖fe8 (18...♖f6 19.♘d5+–) 19.♘a4 ♕a5 20.♖xc8 ♖xc8 21.♕g4 ♕e5 (21...g6 22.♘f4 crashing on g6) 22.♘xg7!+–

b) 15...♕d7 is not met by 16.e5? ♘fd5∓, but with the simple 16.♗xa7±.

c) 15...d5 16.♘g5!⩲

Perhaps more than any other Morra variation, the main line contains themes that will directly enrich your Open Sicilian play. When my coach, IM Blocker, first taught me the Morra, he placed particular emphasis on the main line and the fight for the d5-square, using it (and the entire opening) as a stepping stone to more fully appreciate the vast Open Sicilian. He

never anticipated that I would become such a Morra "maniac". Sorry, Calvin, I apologize, but in the following game I hope to vindicate your teaching philosophy. Observe the striking similarities between this game, which I leave largely unannotated for your quiet study, and the ideas we have just absorbed.

Marc Esserman – John Fedorowicz

US Chess League, Internet 2011

1.e4 c5 2.♘f3 ♘c6 3.d4 cxd4 4.♘xd4 ♘f6 5.♘c3 e5 6.♘db5 d6 7.♗g5 a6 8.♘a3 b5 9.♘d5

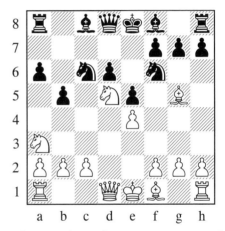

9...♗e7 10.♗xf6 ♗xf6 11.c3 0–0 12.♘c2 ♗g5 13.a4 bxa4 14.♖xa4 a5 15.♗c4 ♖b8 16.♖a2 ♔h8 17.♘ce3 g6 18.h4!

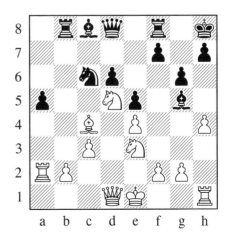

18...&xh4 19.g3 &g5 20.f4 exf4 21.gxf4
&h4† 22.&f1 f5 23.b4! fxe4 24.&ah2 g5

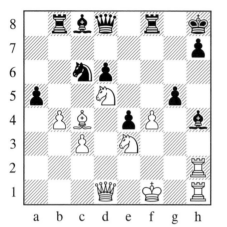

25.&e2!! &b7 26.b5 &e5 27.fxe5 dxe5
28.&b1

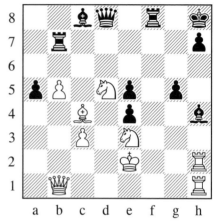

28...&d6

28...&f4!? 29.&xf4 exf4 30.&xe4 &e7
31.&xh4! gxh4 (31...&xe4 32.&xh7#)
32.&xf4+−

**29.&xe4 &bf7 30.&xh4 gxh4 31.&xh4 &g7
32.&d3
1–0**

Chapter 3

The Scheveningens II

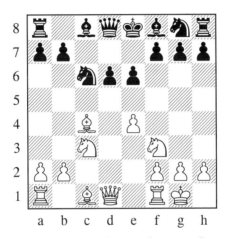

1.e4 c5 2.d4 cxd4 3.c3 dxc3 4.♘xc3 ♘c6 5.♘f3 d6 6.♗c4 e6 7.0–0

When the "Magician from Riga" waves his wand in the Morra, even the sea itself will part.

Mikhail Tal – Neibult

USSR 1991

1.e4 c5 2.d4 cxd4 3.c3 dxc3 4.♘xc3 ♘c6 5.♘f3 d6 6.♗c4 e6 7.0-0 ♘f6 8.♕e2 a6 9.♖d1 ♕c7 10.♗f4!

The bishop assumes its natural post in the ...a6/...♕c7 Scheveningen, riding the crest of the h2-b8 diagonal. Fearing for his queen's safety, Neibult cements the e5-hole, but leaves the c-file channel wide open.

10...♘e5?!

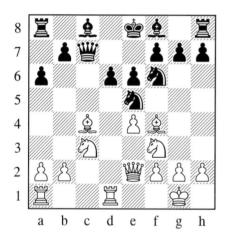

11.♗b3?!

While surfing the thunderous waves of the Morra, even history's most legendary tactician may miss a sparkling combination.

After the shocking 11.♗b5†!N, Tal would have immediately crashed through: 11...axb5 12.♘xe5! dxe5 13.♘xb5!± White storms forward and Black's entire queenside will soon fall. For example: 13...♕b8 14.♕c4! ♗e7

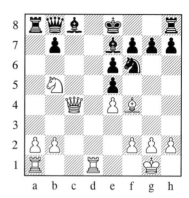

15.♗xe5!+– (15.♘c7†±) 15...♕xe5 16.♘c7† ♔f8 17.♘xa8 ♗d7 18.♖xd7! Smashing the last reserves. 18...♘xd7 19.♕c8† ♗d8 20.♕xd8# We shall analyze this novelty more deeply in the theoretical section on page 85.

Tal allows the e5-blockade to endure, but will use his genius to break through nevertheless.

11...♗e7 12.♖ac1

The Morra rooks are ready to rock and roll.

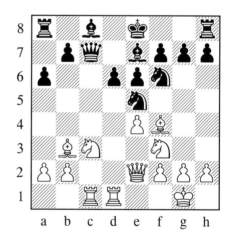

12...♕b8 13.♘d4!

The cavalry charges into the center, making way for the barricade-busting f2-f4 pawn storm. By simultaneously avoiding exchanges, Tal maintains full-scale attacking possibilities.

13...0-0 14.♗g3 ♘ed7?

Black must continue his development – a very tense fight would lie ahead after: 14...♗d7 15.f4 ♘c6∞

15.f4!

As his pieces drown amongst themselves, Neibult desperately lashes out and quickly sinks.

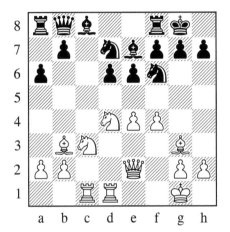

15...e5?

Opening up the floodgates for Tal's suddenly swarming forces (b3-bishop, f5- and d5-knights, and c4-queen).

16.♘f5+– ♖e8 17.♕c4! d5 18.♘xd5 ♗c5† 19.♔h1 ♖e6

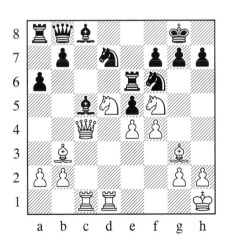

20.♕xc5!

The great wizard strikes!

20...♘xd5

20...♘xc5 21.♘xf6† gxf6 22.♖d8† ♖e8 23.♖xe8#

21.♖xd5

Always leave a queen hanging when you can – the crowd will love you for it.

21...exf4

21...♘xc5 22.♖d8† ♖e8 23.♖xe8#

22.♘e7† ♔f8

22...♔h8 23.♖xf4! ♕xf4 24.♕xc8† ♖xc8 25.♖xc8† ♘f8 26.♖xf8#

23.♖xd7 ♗xd7 24.♗xe6

And ♘c6† will win the stranded black queen finally.
1–0

Milan Matulovic – Aleksandar Bradvarevic

Yugoslavia (ch), Sombor 1957

1.e4 c5 2.d4 cxd4 3.c3 dxc3 4.♘xc3 ♘c6 5.♘f3 d6 6.♗c4 e6 7.♗f4 a6 8.0–0 ♗e7 9.♕e2 ♘f6 10.♖fd1 ♕c7

Over 50 years ago, Grandmaster Matulovic, the first master of the Morra, correctly spotted the clearest way to navigate the ...a6/...♕c7 Scheveningen waters. White's rook springs to c1, his bishop drops back to b3, and ♘c3-d5 threatens to shatter the fortress.

11.♖ac1 0–0 12.♗b3 ♖d8

Black must not allow the ♘d5 blow, and instead should send his queen drifting with the awkward 12...♕b8!?∞, which we exhaustively analyze in the theoretical section.

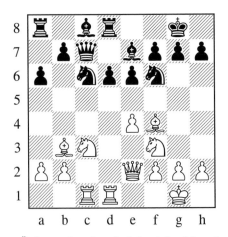

13.♘d5! exd5 14.exd5 h6 15.dxc6 bxc6

Note how all of White's pieces, especially his rooks and bishops, now flow freely towards their targets. Black may have extra pawns in the center, but they will be subjected to a ferocious assault.

16.♘d4± ♗b7

16...c5!? 17.♘c6! ♕xc6 18.♕xe7 and the queen and bishops plunder on f7 or d6.

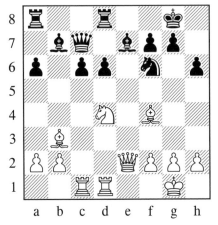

17.♘xc6!

Washing away the last obstacle of c-file resistance. White's powerful bishops and heavy artillery now loot the wreckage of Black's position. A flawless performance by Matulovic in the infancy of Morra theory.

17...♗xc6 18.♗a4 ♗f8 19.♗xc6 ♖ab8 20.b3 a5 21.♕a6 ♘d7 22.h3 ♖b4 23.♗xd7 ♕xd7 24.♗d2 ♕b5 25.♕a7 ♖e4 26.♕xa5 ♕xa5 27.♗xa5 ♖a8 28.b4 d5 29.a3 ♖c4 30.♔f1 f6 31.♔e2 ♖e8† 32.♔f3 ♖ec8 33.♖xc4 dxc4 34.♖d8 ♖xd8 35.♗xd8 ♗d6 36.♔e4 ♗e5 37.a4 ♔f7 38.a5 c3 39.♔d3
1–0

Marc Esserman – Anya Corke

Harvard (blitz) 2011

50 years later, on the streets of Harvard Square, Matulovic's plan endures the sands of time.

1.e4 c5 2.d4 cxd4 3.c3 dxc3 4.♘xc3 ♘c6 5.♘f3 d6 6.♗c4 e6 7.♗f4 a6 8.0–0 ♗e7 9.♕e2 ♘f6 10.♖fd1 ♕c7 11.♖ac1 0–0 12.♗b3 ♖e8

12...♘h5!? forces White to redirect the bishop, which alleviates but does not prevent the onslaught: 13.♗d2 ♘f6 14.♘d5±

13.♘d5 exd5 14.exd5

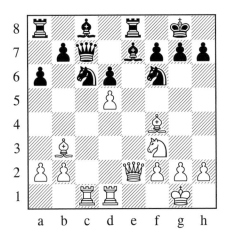

14...♗d7?

Under pressure from Matulovic's powerful knight sacrifice and my lightning-speed moves, Corke's defenses crack. But Black's position is already waterlogged.

14...♗f8 15.♕c2! Increasing the stream of c-file force. 15...♗g4 16.dxc6 ♖ac8 (16...bxc6?! 17.♕xc6 ♕xc6 18.♖xc6±) 17.cxb7 ♕xb7 18.♘d3 ♖xc1 19.♖xc1± With nagging positional pressure.

14...♘xd5!? 15.♗xd5 ♗g4 16.♕c4 ♗h5

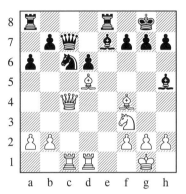

17.♘d4!?± (or even the rousing 17.g4!? ♗g6 18.♘d4±) and White's forces swell violently.

15.dxc6 ♗xc6

15...bxc6 16.♘g5! and f7 bursts: 16...♘d5 17.♗xd5 ♗xg5 18.♗xf7† ♔xf7 19.♕h5† ♔g8 20.♕xg5±

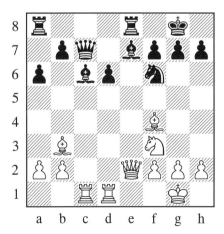

16.♗xf7†!

Now the rip tide drags the black king permanently under.

16...♔xf7 17.♘g5†
1–0

Black resigned, faced with 17...♔f8 18.♕e6! (18.♘e6†+−) 18...♗d8 19.♗xd6† ♕e7 20.♕f7# or 17...♔g6 18.♕d3† ♔h5 19.♘e6 ♕d7 20.♘xg7† ♔g4 21.♕g3#.

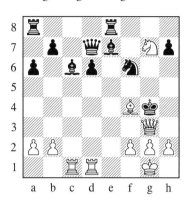

11.e5!?

Lastly, before embarking on the theoretical section of the chapter, we shine light on a move which you must carry in your Morra beach bag, regardless of whether you decide to unleash its torrential energy on an unsuspecting opponent.

1.e4 c5 2.d4 cxd4 3.c3 dxc3 4.♘xc3 d6 5.♘f3 e6 6.♗c4 ♘c6 7.0–0 a6 8.♕e2 ♘f6 9.♖d1 ♕c7 10.♗f4 ♗e7 11.e5!?

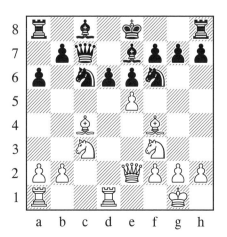

The most violent, direct approach, ripping apart the Scheveningen structure at its seams. Black must now find an unnatural only move, or else his position combusts immediately.

11...dxe5?!

11...♘h5! stalls White's streaming piece flow, as 12.exd6?! ♘xf4 13.dxc7 ♘xe2†∓ neutralizes the swells, and after ...♗d7 and ...♖c8, Black will regain his extra pawn with ease. Instead, White must muddy the waters and sacrifice two pawns with 12.♗g5!, reaching a choppy position which we painstakingly wade through later in Hague – Plaskett (see page 87).

Oh the seductive siren 11.e5!?, for just one slip, and the sturdy Scheveningen shatters.

12.♘xe5± ♘xe5 13.♗xe5 ♕a5 14.a3! 0–0 15.b4 ♕b6

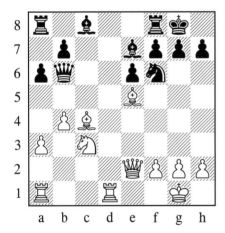

In such fluid Morra positions (when White's central e-pawn exchanges for Black's d-pawn), the gambiteer must possess heavy piece pressure to obtain sufficient compensation for the pawn. During my frequent blitz exploits in this position, I have routinely flaunted my superior freedom of movement to swing the rook from d1-d3-g3/h3 for decisive action.

16.♖ac1!±

16.♖d3!? ♗d7 17.♖g3 ♗c6 (17...g6∞) 18.♕d2! ♔h8? (18...g6)19.♕g5!+− ♖g8

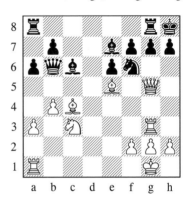

Now I won sloppily with 20.♖h3 ♖ad8 21.♗d3 ♖xd3 22.♖xd3+− in one such encounter.

But the smooth 20.♗d3! brushes Black aside: 20...♖ad8 (20...h6 21.♖h3 ♘h7 22.♕xh6+−) 21.♗xh7! Crashing through. 21...♘xh7 22.♗xg7† ♖xg7 23.♕xg7#

But instead of 16.♖d3, whose success is not guaranteed without Black's mistake on the 18th move, that slippery fish Rybka swims its way to a decisive advantage with 16.♖ac1.

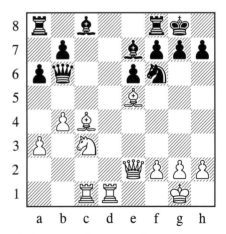

The Morra rooks assume their posts, spraying into the open board. Black's queenside starts to sink (16...♗d7? 17.♗xf6+−), and the queen herself falls next.

16...♖d8 17.♘a4!

Chase, chase, chase the queen until she drops.

17...♕c6

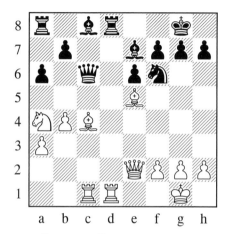

18.b5! ♖xd1† 19.♖xd1 axb5

With 19...♕e8 she may save herself, only to leave her rook stranded: 20.♘b6 ♖a7 21.♗b8+−

20.♗xb5 ♕e4 21.♕xe4 ♘xe4 22.♘b6 ♖a5 23.a4!+−

And the black bishop lies at the mercy of the storm.

Come now, and bring your boards as we ride the waves of theoretical analysis through the ...a6/...♕c7 Scheveningen, and you can ultimately decide which move (11.e5!? or 11.♖ac1) you wish to surf.

Theory I – 10...♘e5 (with ...♗e7)

Before we get to the main lines, first we must dismiss any notion that Black can plug the gaps with an early ...♘e5.

1.e4 c5 2.d4 cxd4 3.c3 dxc3 4.♘xc3 d6 5.♘f3 e6 6.♗c4 ♘c6 7.0–0 a6 8.♕e2 ♗e7

9.♖d1 ♕c7 10.♗f4 ♘e5?!

This position, which featured in German IM Langrock's 2006 book "The Modern Morra Gambit", may look the same as the Tal – Neibult game, but it is not! Here the black bishop stands on e7 and the knight on g8, whereas in Tal's Morra miniature the knight stood on f6 and the bishop on f8. A slight detail, and while the themes may be the same (crashing through on the c-file), the precise tactical execution in each position distinctly differs.

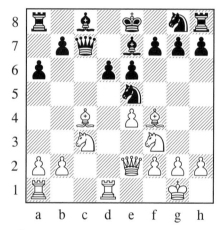

11.♗xe5!

Quickly giving up the bishop followed by a c-file invasion leads to success, whereas in the position from Tal's game, it does not yield a clear advantage.

11...dxe5 12.♖ac1!±

White can also sacrifice immediately:
12.♗b5†±

Langrock highlights games stemming from this, although correctly noting that 12.♖ac1 works as well. I will quickly summarize his sources.
12...♔f8

Langrock gives the variation: 12...axb5 13.♘xb5 ♕a5 14.♖ac1 ♘f6 15.♘c7† ♔f8 16.♘xa8 ♕xa8 17.♕c4! ♗d7 18.♖xd7! Note that this same tactic will appear in the

Tal – Neibult analysis as well. 18...♘xd7
19.♕c8†+–

13.♖ac1

White achieves a decisive attack.

13...axb5 14.♘xb5 ♕a5 15.♖c7! b6 16.♘xe5

16.♖xe7 also wins.

16...♗a6

16...f6 17.♖d8†! ♗xd8 18.♖f7† ♔e8

19.♘d6# Roselli – Tereschenko, corr. 1972.

17.♕h5! g6

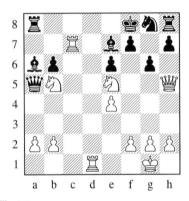

18.♖xe7!

A gorgeous finish.

18...♘xe7

If 18...♔xe7 then 19.♖d7† silences.

19.♕h6† ♔g8

19...♔e8 20.♘c7#

20.♘d7 f6 21.♘xf6† ♔f7

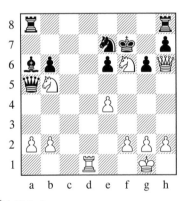

22.♘h5! 1–0

Jansen – Hadley, corr. 1998. After
22...gxh5 Black is quickly mated: 23.♘d6†

♔g8 24.♕xe6† ♔g7 25.♕f7† ♔h6 26.♕f6†
♘g6 27.♘f7#

The natural 12.♖ac1, delaying the sac for later,
seems cleaner to me, but it's a matter of taste.

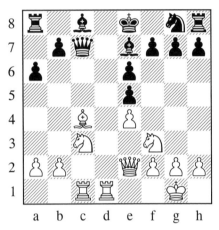

12...♘f6

12...♕a5 13.♗b5† transposes to the above
lines.

After 12...♕b8 White again wins with
13.♗b5†!+–, or with the more spectacular:
13.♘a4! b5 14.♗xb5† axb5 15.♖xc8†! ♕xc8
16.♕xb5† ♔f8 17.♘b6 ♕a6 18.♘d7† ♔e8
19.♘f6† ♔f8

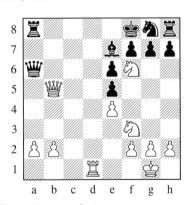

20.♕e8† ♖xe8 21.♘d7#

12...♗d7 13.♘b5! A standard Morra c-file
clearance theme, already seen in Esserman

– Ehlvest on page 34, re-emerges. 13...♕b8
(13...axb5 14.♖xd7!) 14.♖xd7 ♔xd7 15.♕d2†
♗d6 (15...♔e8 16.♘c7†! ♔f8 17.♘xa8 ♕xa8
18.♗xe6 fxe6 19.♕d7+–)

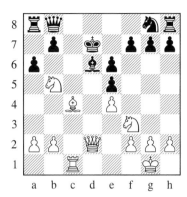

16.♘xd6 ♕xd6 17.♘xe5† ♔e7 18.♕xd6†
♔xd6 19.♘xf7†+–

13.♘b5! ♕b8

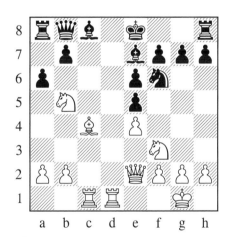

14.♘c7†+–

Now, fully armed with these motifs, we can
more easily appreciate Tal's missed opportunity,
and more importantly, not confuse the two
positions!

Theory II – 10...♘e5 (with ...♘f6)

**1.e4 c5 2.d4 cxd4 3.c3 dxc3 4.♘xc3 ♘c6
5.♘f3 d6 6.♗c4 e6 7.0–0 ♘f6 8.♕e2 a6
9.♖d1 ♕c7 10.♗f4 ♘e5?!**

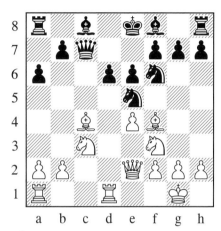

11.♗b5†!N
We saw 11.♗b3?! in Tal – Neibult above.

11.♗xe5?!
  This does not work here, as Black can
  simultaneously develop his bishop and blunt
  the c-file pressure.
11...dxe5 12.♗b5†?
  12.♖ac1 ♕a5 13.♗b5† ♗d7 and Black just
  holds, as he can now block the check, a
  resource unavailable to him in the previous
  analysis (without ...♘f6). 14.♖xd7† ♔xd7=
12...axb5! 13.♘xb5 ♕b6! 14.♖ac1 ♗c5!
  Black readies to castle as the tactics now
  work in his favor.
15.b4

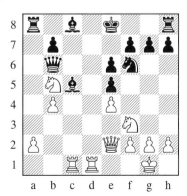

15...♗xf2†!

The subtle difference in move order.

16.♔f1 0–0

And Black was winning in Szava – L. Kovacs, Hajduboszormeny 1996. Such nuances reveal the importance of understanding each ripple of the position in our rich game.

11...axb5

Now White busts through. Declining the sacrifice does not lessen the never-ending piece current flowing Black's way. I give some highlights.

11...♘c6 12.e5!±

11...♗d7 12.♗xd7†! ♘fxd7
　12...♘exd7 13.e5±
13.♖ac1

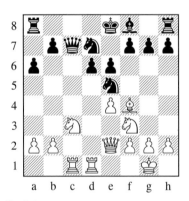

13...♘xf3†

　a) 13...♕c4 14.♗xe5 ♕xe2 15.♘xe2 ♘xe5 16.♘xe5 dxe5 17.♖c7 b5 18.♖dd7± and White's pigs splash on the 7th.

　b) 13...♕a5 14.♘xe5 ♘xe5 15.b4! ♕xb4 16.♗xe5 dxe5 17.♕d3 Heavy piece high tide. 17...♕d4 18.♕g3±

　c) 13...♘c6 gives White a pleasant choice between 14.b4± and 14.♘d5±.

14.♕xf3 ♕b6 15.e5!

Get a front row seat as the Scheveningen structure tumbles.

15...♘xe5

15...d5 is no better:

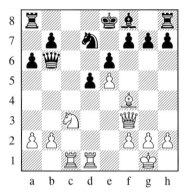

16.♖xd5! exd5 17.♘xd5+– ♕xb2 18.♘c7† ♔d8 19.e6 fxe6 20.♘xe6† ♔e8 21.♘c7† ♔d8 22.♖d1 ♖c8 23.♖xd7†! Bulldozing. 23...♔xd7 24.♕d5† ♔e7 25.♕d6† ♔f7 26.♕e6#

16.♗xe5 dxe5 17.♖d7!

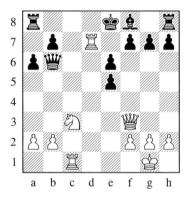

Tossing the king into the water!

17...♔xd7

　17...♗e7 18.♖xb7+–

18.♕xf7† ♗e7 19.♘a4! ♕b5 20.♘c5† ♔d8
　20...♔d6 21.♕xe6†+–

21.♘xe6† ♔d7 22.♖c7†+–

What a rush.

12.♘xe5!± dxe5 13.♘xb5

Now, after the proper tactical execution, the themes from the previous analysis will sharply resonate.

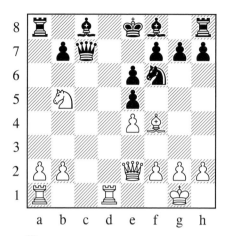

13...♕a5

13...♕b8 14.♕c4! ♗e7 (14...exf4 15.♘c7†
♔e7 [15...♕xc7 16.♕xc7±] 16.♕b4#)
15.♗xe5! ♕xe5 16.♘c7† ♔f8 17.♘xa8 ♗d7
18.♖xd7! Remember? 18...♘xd7 19.♕c8†
♗d8 20.♕xd8#

14.♗d2!

The weary queen never rests.

14...♕b6

14...♗b4 15.♗xb4 ♕xb4 16.♘c7†±

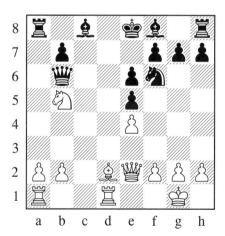

15.♗e3!

No ...♗c5 blunting this time.

15...♕a5 16.♖ac1 ♗d7 17.♘c7† ♔d8

18.♘xa8 ♕xa8 19.♗g5+–
Razing the last barricade.

19...♔e8 20.♗xf6 gxf6

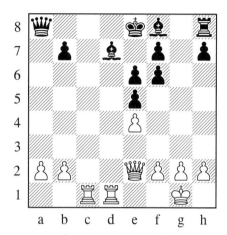

**21.♖xd7! ♔xd7 22.♕b5† ♔d8 23.♕d3†
♔e8 24.♖c7+–**
The pig bathes on the 7th yet again.

24...♕a4 25.♖c8† ♔e7 26.♕d8#

Now we are ready to surf mainstream
...a6/...♕c7 theory.

Theory III – 11.e5!?

Ben Hague – Jim Plaskett

West Bromwich 2005

The fact that Black, an experienced
grandmaster, goes down violently against an
FM even after playing the best defense, shows
just how dangerous the swashbuckling 11.e5!?
can be in practice.

**1.e4 c5 2.d4 cxd4 3.c3 dxc3 4.♘xc3 ♘c6
5.♘f3 e6 6.♗c4 d6 7.0–0 ♘f6 8.♕e2 ♕c7
9.♖d1 ♗e7 10.♗f4 a6**

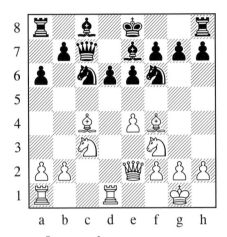

11.e5!? ♞h5! 12.♗g5! dxe5?!

Black should exchange the bishops first as we shall see below, but even then the defense remains murky.

13.♗xe7 ♞f4 14.♕e4

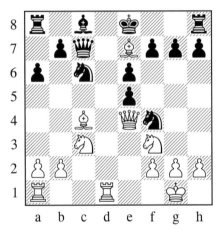

14...♚xe7

14...♕xe7 maintains castling privileges, but gives back one of his two extra pawns and leads to shipwreck: 15.♞xe5 ♞xe5 16.♕xe5 ♞g6 (16...♕f6 17.♗b5†! axb5 18.♕xb5† ♚f8 19.♕b4† ♚g8 20.♞e4! ♕h4 21.g3+– forces catastrophe after, for example, 21...♞h3† 22.♚f1.) 17.♕xg7±

14...♞xe7 15.♞xe5 ♞eg6
    15...♞fg6 16.♞b5! Black must be punished

before he castles. 16...axb5 17.♗xb5† ♚f8 18.♖ac1 ♕a5 (18...♕b6 19.♖xc8†+–)

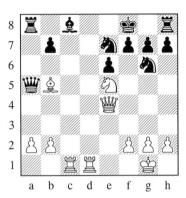

19.♕b4!+– White weaves a sparkling net, catching a king. 19...♚g8 20.♞xg6 hxg6 21.♕xe7 ♕xb5 22.g4!! Threatening mates using the back rank and the h-file! 22...♗d7 23.♖xd7 ♖f8 24.♕xf8†! ♚xf8 25.♖c8#
16.♞xg6 hxg6 17.♖d4→

15.g3

Both sides are swimming through the chaos now. Black stays two pawns up, but his king remains lost at sea.

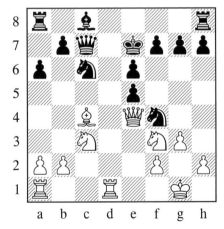

15...♞g6 16.h4 f5 17.♕e3 e4 18.♕c5†

Launching with ♞g5!? would have ushered in a tsunami-like attack. I'll show some pearls:

18.♘g5!?

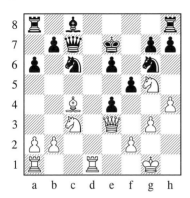

18...♕a5

18...h6? 19.♕c5† ♔f6 20.♘xe6! (or 20.♘d5†! exd5 21.♖xd5+–) 20...♗xe6 21.♘d5†! ♗xd5 22.♖xd5+– The black king suffers from heavy exposure.

18...♘ce5 19.♗b3 (19.♗xe6!± also leads to mayhem – swim at your own risk!) h6 20.♖ac1!± With ravaging sacrifices on e4 or e6 to follow.

19.b4!→ ♕xb4

19...♘xb4 20.♘xe6! ♗xe6 21.♕g5† ♔f7 22.♖d7†!±

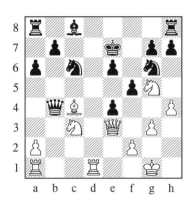

20.♗xe6! ♗xe6 21.♖ab1!

The tanks rage forward.

21...♕c4 22.♖xb7† ♔f6

22...♔f8 23.♕c5†! ♕xc5 24.♘xe6†+–
22...♔e8 23.♖d6! ♗c8 24.♖xg7+– and the Morra rooks have an exotic feast.

23.♘gxe4† fxe4 24.♕g5#

18...♔e8 19.♘d4

No matter what the computer may say, such positions are extremely disturbing in the heat of battle (and for machines too, not just mortals). Although he defends admirably, eventually Plaskett succumbs to the Morra's insatiable lust.

19...♕e5 20.♕b6 ♘ge7 21.♘ce2 ♔f7 22.f4 ♕a5 23.♕b3 ♘d8 24.♖ac1

∓ is the assessment from the "Fish" (Rybka), but I doubt Plaskett felt that way in the game.

24...♖e8

24...b5 25.♗xe6†!→

25.♔h2 ♘ec6?

The correct defense is 25...b5!–+ only now, as Plaskett's previous move has bolstered the e6-breach: 26.♗xe6† ♗xe6 27.♘xe6 ♘xe6 28.♖d6 ♘g6 29.♖cc6 ♘gf8! Please forgive the grandmaster for missing these maneuvers under pressure.

26.g4 ♘xd4 27.♘xd4 ♔f8 28.gxf5 exf5

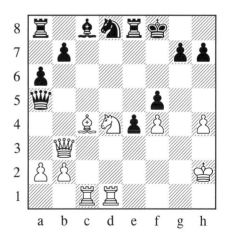

The end is near.

29.♗g8! h6 30.♗h7!

Penetrating the kingside by highly original means.

30...♔e7 31.♖xc8!+– ♖xc8 32.♘xf5† ♔f6
32...♔f8 33.♕g8#!

33.♕g3!
White's queen swims the freestyle in the open water.

33...♕xf5 34.♗xf5 ♔xf5 35.♕h3† ♔f6 36.♕xc8 e3 37.♖xd8
A wildly entertaining game, showcasing the practical power of 11.e5!?.
1–0

Theory IV – 11.e5!? ♘h5! 12.♗g5! ♗xg5!

1.e4 c5 2.d4 cxd4 3.c3 dxc3 4.♘xc3 ♘c6 5.♘f3 e6 6.♗c4 d6 7.0–0 ♘f6 8.♕e2 ♕c7 9.♖d1 ♗e7 10.♗f4 a6 11.e5!? ♘h5! 12.♗g5! ♗xg5! 13.♘d5!
13.♘xg5?! ♘f4 14.♕e3 dxe5∓

Black must pass through these rough waters if he wishes to set foot ashore after 11.e5.

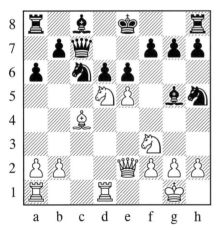

13...♕d8 14.♘xg5 ♘f4!
The immediate recapture is less convincing: 14...♕xg5?! 15.♘c7† ♔f8 16.♘xa8 ♘xe5
16...♘f4!? and my intuition says Black should get the better ending an exchange down for two pawns, but the situation remains muddled: 17.♕f3 ♘xe5 18.♕g3

♕xg3 19.hxg3 ♘xc4 20.gxf4 ♔e7 21.♖ac1 ♗d7 22.♖xc4 ♖xa8 23.♖c7 ♖b8 24.♖d3 ♔d8 25.♖dc3 and Black cannot dislodge the rook.
17.♘b6 ♘f4 18.♕f1∞
A hilarious position, depending on your sense of humor.
18...♘g4?! 19.♖d4!

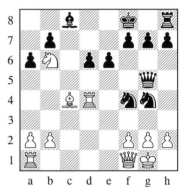

White dramatically stops Black's looming ...♘h3† then ...♘e3† trick by setting up the remarkable ♖g4! interference. Not exactly what the old masters had in mind when they spoke of "piece coordination"...
19...e5 20.♖xf4! ♕xf4 21.g3 ♕f5

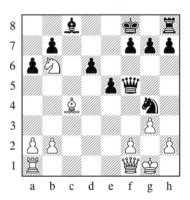

22.♖c1±
The bishop sinks again.
22...♗d7 23.♗d3 ♕e6 24.♖c7
White penetrates in force.

15.♕f3 ♕xg5 16.♘c7† ♔d7

Black reaches a superior version of the variation we saw above, with the black king fully engaged in the fight. The similar 16...♔d8!? is also possible.

17.♘xa8 ♘xe5 18.♕g3 ♕xg3 19.hxg3 ♘xc4 20.gxf4

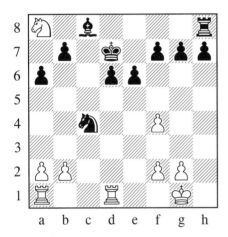

20...b5!?∓

20...d5∓

21.b3 ♗b7!

21...♘a5?! 22.♖ac1 ♘c6 23.♘b6† ♔c7 24.♘a8†! ♔d7=

22.bxc4 ♖xa8∓

White even went on to win this endgame in Hlavac – Necesany, e-mail 2003. However, in a theoretical laboratory, these positions are clearly unacceptable for White, and while the computer thinks Black only has ∓, I feel the advantage lies much closer to −+. But I presented all of this analysis for you to appreciate just how difficult Black's task remains in the arena. At the highest level 11.e5 should receive a ?!, but I still give it a !? for the move's practical value. Whether or not you dare play 11.e5!?, I leave up to you.

Finally, we move on to the more reputable main line.

Theory V – 11.♖ac1 0–0 12.♗b3 ♕b8!?

1.e4 c5 2.d4 cxd4 3.c3 dxc3 4.♘xc3 ♘c6 5.♘f3 d6 6.♗c4 e6 7.0-0 ♘f6 8.♕e2 a6 9.♖d1 ♕c7 10.♗f4 ♗e7 11.♖ac1 0–0 12.♗b3 ♕b8!?

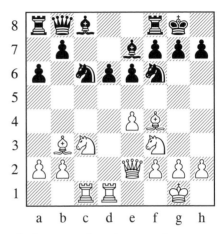

Black must play this crouching move to avoid ♘c3-d5 and stay on level terms.

13.e5!?

We search for more than the equal position that White can force with: 13.♘a4 b5 (13...♕c7 14.♘c3= just repeats. 13...♘d7?! 14.♕d2 e5 15.♗e3± à la Scheveningens Part I.) 14.♖xc6 bxa4 15.♗xa4 ♗d7 16.♖c4 ♗xa4 17.♖xa4 ♕b5 Drying out the position. 18.♕xb5 axb5 19.♖xa8 ♖xa8 20.♗xd6 ♗xd6 21.♖xd6 ♘xe4 22.♖b6 ♔f8 23.a3 ♖d8 24.♔f1 ♖d5=

An improved version of 11.e5 awaits! Again, White leverages on his fluid piece play in light of his missing center pawn to offer full compensation for the material and hopefully more. Rook lifts and kingside attacks abound.

13...♘h5

13...dxe5?! 14.♘xe5→

14.♗g5!?

We see the same dance as after 11.e5, but to a different tune. Now Black only gets one pawn for his troubles!

14...dxe5

14...♗xg5? 15.♘xg5 ♘f4 16.♕c2 g6 17.exd6+−

15.♗xe7 ♘xe7 16.♘xe5 ♘f6∞

16...♘f4 17.♕e3 ♘fg6 (17...♘fd5!? may offer the best hope for Black to equalize after 18.♘xd5 ♘xd5.) 18.♘xg6 hxg6 (18...♘xg6 19.♘a4!± plopping on b6 with an everlasting bind.) 19.♕g5!±

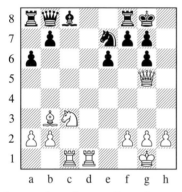

19...♘c6 20.♘e4 ♕e5 21.♕xe5 ♘xe5 22.♖c7± Black's shallow knight maneuvers have left him awash.

We reach a critical impasse. White must act decisively before Black squirms out. This may involve playing for a calm, gripping queenside bind with full compensation, or a bridge-burning, wild attack. In the second, more spirited plan, White should redirect his now blunted Italian bishop towards the black king, lifting at least one rook, and dousing the black king with the bayonet charge g4-g5. In theory Black can defend but the variations are worth including for their spectacular and instructional value.

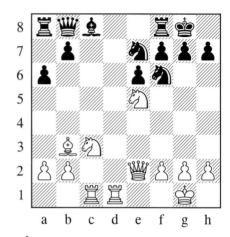

17.♗c2!?N

17.♘a4!?∞ is the reliable positional approach. On 17...b5, White's knight jumps into c5, thus obtaining excellent long-term positional pressure, thanks to his active knights and rooks.

17...♘ed5

17...♘g6 blunts the attack, but allows White to switch gears for a queenside bind: 18.♗xg6! hxg6 19.♕e3±

17...b5! 18.g4!?
18.♘g4?! ♘fd5?! (18...♘xg4! 19.♕xg4 ♘g6∓) 19.♘xd5 ♘xd5

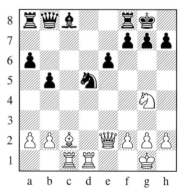

20.♖xd5! exd5 21.♕d3 Suddenly White stirs up a massive attack. 21...f5 22.♕xd5† ♔h8 23.♘e5→
18...♗b7?!

After this, Black may feel cold water.
He must instead find the precise 18...♘fd5∓,
bolstering the defenses (Δ...♘f4-g6 in
many variations) while exploiting White's
bankrupt positional play.

18...b4? 19.g5 bxc3 20.gxf6 gxf6

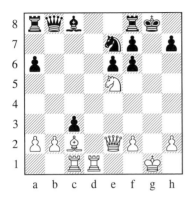

21.♘c6! ♘xc6 22.♗xh7†!+− With decisive
rook lifts.
19.g5 ♘fd5 20.♖d4!
Preventing the knights from coordinating
and readying for mayhem.
20...♘g6 21.♗xg6 hxg6 22.♘xg6!→

18.♖d4! b5?!
18...♕d6 19.g4!→
Black is about to wish he had played ...b5 a
move earlier.

19.♘xd5 exd5

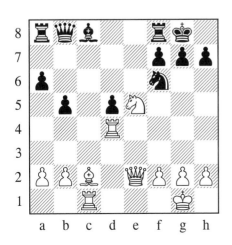

20.♗xh7†!
Flash lightning.

**20...♘xh7 21.♘c6 ♕b6 22.♖h4! g6 23.♘e7†
♔g7 24.♖c6!**
The Morra rooks run wild.

**24...♕b7 25.♕d2 g5 26.♖xh7† ♔xh7
27.♕d3†!**
27.♕xg5 is also good enough.

27...♔g7

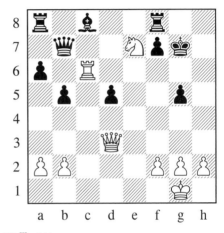

28.♖g6†!
Streaming chaos!

28...fxg6 29.♕xg6† ♔h8 30.♕h6#

Theory VI – 14.♗e3 and 15.♗b6!

To conclude the Scheveningens, I offer up
one more original treatment for the main line
which will attract the bravest of gambiteers.

**1.e4 c5 2.d4 cxd4 3.c3 dxc3 4.♘xc3 ♘c6
5.♘f3 d6 6.♗c4 e6 7.0–0 ♘f6 8.♕e2 a6
9.♖d1 ♕c7 10.♗f4 ♗e7 11.♖ac1 0–0 12.♗b3**

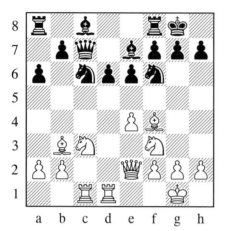

12...♕b8 13.e5 ♘h5 14.♗e3!?N dxe5 15.♗b6!

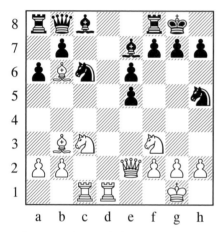

White sacrifices a full two pawns, but sinks Black's queenside into total oblivion. Feel the nebulousness of the position!

As a postscript to the chapter, here are two related games. First watch as a young Kasparov handles a Vaganian Gambit in a very Morra-like fashion.

Semon Palatnik – Garry Kasparov

Kislovodsk 1982

1.d4 ♘f6 2.c4 c5 3.♘f3 cxd4 4.♘xd4 e5 5.♘b5 d5 6.cxd5 ♗c5 7.♘5c3 0–0 8.a3 a5

9.e3 e4 10.♘d2 ♕e7 11.d6 ♗xd6 12.♘dxe4 ♘xe4 13.♘xe4 ♖d8!

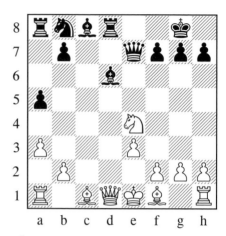

14.♘xd6

14.♗d3 ♗f5 15.♕c2 ♖a6!→

14...♖xd6 15.♕c2 ♘c6 16.♗d3 ♘d4! 17.♗xh7†

17.♕c3 ♗g4!–+ 18.0–0 ♘f3† 19.♔h1 ♖h6 20.h3 ♕d6 21.g3 ♖xh3† 22.♔g2 ♖h2#

17...♔f8 18.♕e4 ♘b3! 19.♕xe7† ♔xe7 20.♖b1 g6 21.e4 ♘xc1 22.♖xc1 ♗d7 23.0–0 ♗c6 24.♖fd1 ♖ad8 25.♖xd6 ♖xd6 26.h4 ♔f8 27.h5 ♔g7 28.hxg6 fxg6 29.♗xg6 ♔xg6 30.f3 ♖d2 31.b4 a4 32.♖c3 ♖b2 33.♖e3 ♔g5 34.g3 ♗b5 35.e5 ♔f5 36.e6 ♖b3 37.♔f2 ♖xe3 38.♔xe3 ♔xe6 39.♔d4 ♔d6 40.g4 ♗d7 41.g5 b5 42.g6 ♔e6 0–1

Marc Esserman – Phillip Nutzman

Somerville 2009

My best ♗h7 maneuver (to compare with Hague – Plaskett), inspired by a lifetime of Morra play.

1.e4 c5 2.♘f3 e6 3.d4 cxd4 4.♘xd4 a6 5.♗d3 ♕c7 6.0–0 ♘f6 7.♗e3 d5?! 8.exd5 ♘xd5 9.♘c3 ♘xe3

9...♘xc3 10.bxc3 ♕xc3⩲

10.fxe3 ♝d6 11.♕h5 ♘c6 12.♘cb5! axb5 13.♘xb5 ♝xh2†

13...♕e7? 14.♖xf7+−

14.♔h1 ♕e7 15.♔xh2 ♘d8□ 16.♖ad1 h6

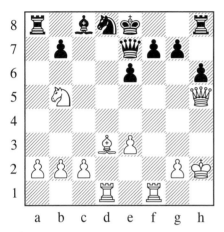

17.♝h7!!+−

17.♕g6? ♕h4†!−+

17...♖xh7

17...♖a5 18.♕e5! ♖xb5 19.♕xb5† ♝d7 20.♕d3+−

18.♘d6†! ♔f8

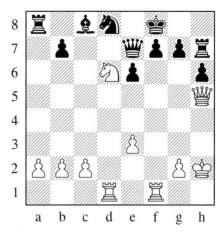

19.♘xf7! ♘c6

19...♘xf7 20.♖d8† ♕xd8 21.♕xf7#

20.♘e5† ♔g8 21.♘xc6
1–0

Black resigned, in view of: 21...bxc6 22.♖d8†! (or 22.♕f7†!) 22...♕xd8 23.♕f7† ♔h8 24.♕f8† ♕xf8 25.♖xf8#

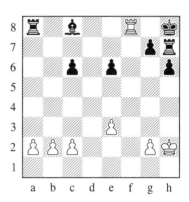

"A belief in the existence of Santa Claus is more rational than imagining White has adequate compensation after the unwarranted 3.c3?"
– Former World Championship Challenger, Grandmaster Nigel Short

Chapter 4

Into the Deep

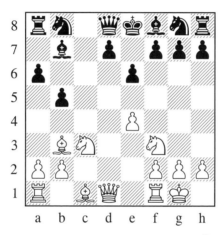

**1.e4 c5 2.d4 cxd4 3.c3 dxc3 4.♘xc3 a6
5.♘f3 e6 6.♗c4 b5 7.♗b3 ♗b7 8.0–0!**

Prepare yourself as we take the plunge into some of the deepest waters found in the Morra Gambit and, perhaps, all of chess. After Black plays a quick ...e6, ...a6, ...b5 followed by ...♗b7, he threatens to win White's proud e4-pawn immediately with ...b4.

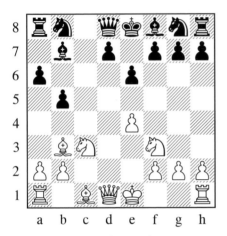

But the daring gambiteer, always true to style, does not flinch and simply castles, preferably with a grin! For he knows that, regardless of whether or not his hapless opponent is aware, both parties are about to descend 20,000 leagues under the chess sea.

Yet before we plummet into the abyss of complications after ...b4, we first skim the ocean's surface when Black refuses to make a dive for White's e4-pawn and calmly continues with 8...d6. However, our cursory tour of shallow sea lasts not even a move, for after the seismic 9.♘g5!

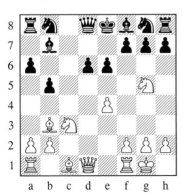

any illusions Black has of keeping his head above water are resolutely blasted. Instead we drag the deluged defender further and further into the depths of the gambit, to a point from which there is no return.

As we descend deeper and deeper, we delve into the position after 8...b4, and only here can we finally hope to venture into the darkest, most mysterious trenches of the Morra Gambit. On 8...b4, the intrepid gambiteer does not merely sacrifice a pawn with 9.♘a4?!. Rather, he drops a whole piece into the deep after 9.♘d5!, as early as the 9th move! If you do not plow deeper with 9.♘d5, you have no hope of survival against Black's ambitious setup. If you do, and you keep your wits and nerve under great pressure, I promise it will be your opponent who becomes lost amidst the drowning sea of chaos. If you ever feel hopeless or even scared in the Morra's trenches, feel free to bring your computer programs along for the ride to perhaps shine a bit of light on the surrounding positions, but be forewarned – after 9.♘d5, we have entered the abyss, and your engines will inevitably malfunction, spitting out nonsensical evaluations which prove that even they are out of their league down in the dark hallows of the deep. If you don't believe me, then bring them, but they will only cloud your mind as you try and make sense of the chaos that you can barely see before you.

On 9.♘d5, as Tal so aptly put it, you have taken "your opponent into a deep, dark forest where 2+2=5, and the path leading out is only wide enough for one."[19] Come now, and follow along closely with your mind's eye wide open as you witness sparkling combinations never before seen on the chessboard, and it will be you, and not your opponent, who re-emerges from the trenches alive to tell the tale.

wHySoSeRiOoOus (Esserman) – Reti

Internet (blitz) 2010

1.e4 c5 2.d4 cxd4 3.c3 dxc3 4.♘xc3 a6 5.♘f3 e6 6.♗c4 b5 7.♗b3 ♗b7 8.0–0!

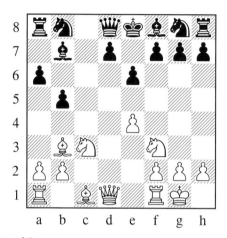

8...d6

As promised, we start out at the surface rather than immediately entering the sea of chaos after the more extreme 8...b4. With 8...d6 Black intends to complete his development via the flexible and dynamic ...♘bd7, ...♘gf6, ...♗e7, ...0–0. The possibility of ...♘c5 then looms large, thus undermining the anchor of White's position (the b3-bishop) while engulfing the e4-pawn even further. If Black's pieces are allowed to effortlessly flow towards such a structure resembling the powerful Najdorf so common in the Open Sicilian, then the only chaos on the board will be that of White's uncoordinated forces strewn across the battlefield. Black's aggressive queenside expansion must therefore be swiftly punished before his plans are set in motion. Too many times over the years I missed the mark – the hackneyed 9.♕e2, for example, fails to inspire, as Black simply responds with ...♘f6 and ...♘bd7, blunting any d-file subterfuge. 9.♘d4 also lacks sufficient thrust, as Black again smoothly plays 9...♘f6, which

prepares to castle, eyes the e4-pawn once more, and calls White's bluff to prematurely sacrifice on e6.

9.♘g5!N

Necessity, as they say, is the mother of invention, and it is out of great respect for Black's potential defensive possibilities here that I subjected this position to deeper study. The radical 9.♘g5! now adds to the flavor of standard ♘d4 Sicilian motifs. Remember, with black pawns on d6/e6 and the light-squared bishop missing from defensive duty on c8, you should often target the e6/f7 pawn core and prepare for a sacrifice and/or a quick f4-f5 pawn blast. However, unlike ♘d4, playing the knight to g5 does not allow the opponent to plod along the surface of the position with simple moves. If he insists...

9...♘f6? 10.e5!+−

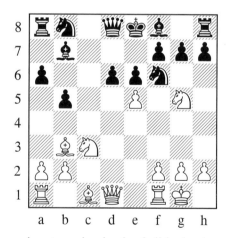

...then into the depths shall he be dragged, where there is no escape. Thus the first tactical point of 9.♘g5 emerges – if 10...dxe5, then 11.♕xd8 ♔xd8 12.♘xf7† decides immediately. Black is now utterly buried. If he wishes to unlock the deeper points behind 9.♘g5, he needs to play a deeper defense, which we will examine later. But for now, it is too late. Yes, in the Morra, time often accelerates and compresses – nine whole moves can decide a man's fate.

10...♘d5 11.♘xd5 exd5 12.♗xd5 ♗xd5 13.♕xd5 ♖a7 14.♖e1

It's always a pleasure to surround a stationary target such as a black king on e8.

14...♖e7 15.e6 fxe6 16.♘xe6

White's knight alone trumps all of Black's immobile forces. We need not mention the other white pieces ready to rampage.

16...♕d7 17.♗g5 ♘c6 18.♗xe7 ♘xe7 19.♕a8† ♔f7 20.♘d8† ♔g8

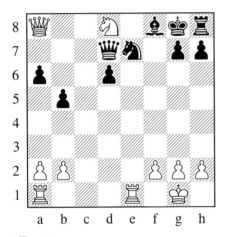

21.♖xe7!

Black resigns. An amusing ending, with the knight on d8 and queen on a8 poised to deliver mate. As Maximus once shouted to the roaring crowd after a brutal, swift victory in the epic movie *Gladiator*: "Are you not entertained? Are you not entertained? Is this not why you are here?"

1–0

Marc Esserman – Matthew Herman

Internet (blitz) 2011

1.e4 c5 2.d4 cxd4 3.c3 dxc3 4.♘xc3 e6 5.♘f3 a6 6.♗c4 b5 7.♗b3 ♗b7 8.0–0! d6 9.♘g5! ♘f6?

American Senior Master Matthew Herman is an extremely talented player with all the gifts to become a strong grandmaster. Throughout the last decade he tortured me with his pet system against the gambit in our training games, and whenever I did win, I routinely had to pass through lost positions before pulling off a swindle. Fortunately, this book is not about tricks, but rather good, sound moves, and I am glad that you will be able to skip all of my painful failed experiences and play the best continuations. Sorry for including 9...♘f6? for a second time, but it shows that even pros well familiar with this defensive system will fall prey to the power of 9.♘g5!. In fact, in the handful of games I have had the pleasure of unleashing 9.♘g5, every single one of my opponents has fallen into the pit after 9...♘f6?.

10.e5 ♘g8

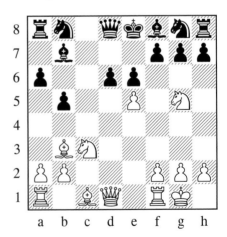

Of course, many moves now win, as Black cannot hope to survive after ...♘g8. But as you may have noticed, I have a problem with sacrificing pieces.

11.♘xe6+– fxe6 12.♗xe6

This position should serve as a good primer for our more in-depth analysis of 9.♘g5. Note in particular how White's "Italian" bishop dominates the center of the board – Black's king will never leave the center, and as we know, the center is not a regal spot for a king in gambit play.

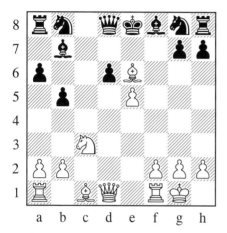

12...d5

12...dxe5 13.♗f7†! ♚e7 14.♛b3+– and the king drowns on e7 as mate on e6 looms. If Black struggles on, then at the very least the g8-knight hangs.

13.♘xd5 ♘c6 14.♗e3

You know the end draws near when a hostile bishop and knight wreak such havoc so close to a helpless king.

14...♗c8 15.♗xg8

Another way is: 15.♗b6 ♛g5 16.♘c7† ♚e7

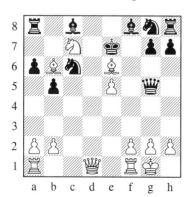

17.♛d6# (or 17.♗c5#) A fine example of why the king needs a home away from the volcanic center.

15...♖xg8 16.♗b6 ♛g5 17.♘c7† ♚f7 18.♛d5† ♚g6 19.♛xc6†
1–0

9.♘g5! – Basic analysis

1.e4 c5 2.d4 cxd4 3.c3 dxc3 4.♘xc3 e6 5.♘f3 a6 6.♗c4 b5 7.♗b3 ♗b7 8.0–0! d6 9.♘g5!

Of course Black must sense the danger and rise to the defensive challenge. But I believe that even while exhibiting the greatest defensive skill, he still cannot fight the gravity of the position, which pulls him deeper and deeper into the abyss on every move. I will merely whet the appetite with a few basic plans and some spectacular treasures after 9.♘g5. If you wish to go further, you can explore on your own, but the main ideas are laid out before you below.

9...♘c6

Black may be tempted by the following obvious retort, telling the invading knight to evacuate enemy waters:

9...h6?!

The gambiteer has two promising rejoinders – to sacrifice immediately on e6, or to increase the pressure.

10.♕h5!?

10.♘xe6 fxe6 11.♕h5† Although White is a piece down, he has a clear advantage, for the marooned black king floats in the center as White's shark-like rooks and minor pieces circle about.

Bringing the queen out is the saner alternative, but chaos flows here as well. Many may criticize moves such as ♘g5 and ♕h5 as "primitive" or "barbaric", while favoring more refined positional opening sequences like 1.♘f3, 2.g3, 3.♗g2 and 4.0–0. And to these pundits I say, yes, ♘g5 is indeed savage and raw. But the last time I checked, the goal of chess was to deliver checkmate, so in fact these moves are as refined as any.

10...g6 11.♕h3!

The gambiteer gears up for the decisive blow on e6 (similar to the Herman game, except that the white queen now assists from her island on h3).

11...♕e7

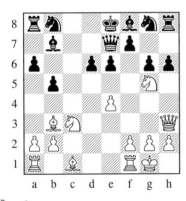

12.♘xe6!

Certainly 12.f4 first or 12.♘xf7!? also offer rich attacking chances, but the violent text seems most effective.

12...fxe6 13.♗xe6

White's bishop on e6, like a Samurai sword, slices Black's position in half – remember this attacking motif!

13...♘f6 14.♘d5 ♘xd5 15.exd5 ♗g7 16.♖e1±

If 9...♗e7, White bombards with 10.f4!, and if Black dares to grab the knight, then after fxg5! White's rook propels piercing cannon-fire towards the enemy king.

10.f4!

A whirlpool is forming down below, and Black edges closer and closer to the brink.

10...b4?

And with this final time sink, he is swept in.

11.♘d5!?

11.f5! wins immediately and without much drama (well, there is some action – White sacrifices a piece...), but why sacrifice just one piece, when you can sacrifice two?

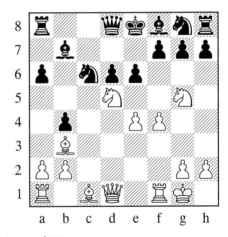

11...exd5?!

Black must decline this gift with 11...♘f6, but is in a greedy mood. First, he took the pawn on c3. Now he cannot control himself and eats the knight on d5. Fortunately for him, he is about to receive another present. Greed is good, sometimes... (To mock Gordon Gekko's famous words from the movie *Wall Street*: "Greed, for lack of a better word, is good.

Greed is right. Greed works. Greed clarifies and cuts through and captures the essence of the evolutionary spirit.")

12.♘xf7!±

An outlandish conclusion. Black cannot gorge on the second Trojan horse, as he is quickly swarmed after ♕xd5†. He therefore must insert ...♕b6† first, then shuttle his king to the d8-escape cavern, but no about of cunning can save him now – he is in too deep! At variation's end, White remains a piece down, but the pressure still swirls. Soon, more Black forces will fall. What a rare chess treasure – a sound, fantastic double knight sacrifice as early as moves 11 and 12!

12...♕b6† 13.♔h1 ♔xf7 14.♕xd5† ♔e8 15.♕f7† ♔d8 16.♕xf8† ♔c7 17.♕xg7† ♘ge7 18.f5!±

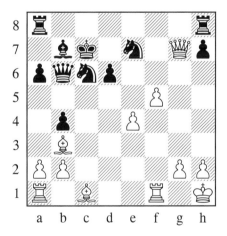

But now, gather all your energy as we dive even deeper to unlock the mysteries of a revolutionary knight sacrifice which may forever alter your understanding of chess. I, for one, morphed into a different chess player when I first discovered that the "insane" 9.♘d5! was in fact objectively sound.

Marc Esserman – Justin Sarkar

Miami 2008

1.e4 c5 2.d4 cxd4 3.c3 dxc3 4.♘xc3 e6 5.♘f3 a6 6.♗c4 b5 7.♗b3 ♗b7 8.0–0! b4

"And here... we... go."[20] – The Joker.

9.♘d5!

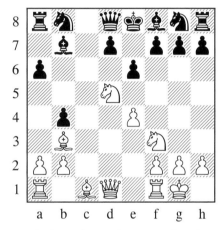

IM Sarkar admitted to me after the game that he always considered this sacrifice to be a joke, and this opinion is echoed in Palliser's 2007 book *Fighting the Anti-Sicilians*, which dismisses the speculative sacrifice as unsound.[21] Justin, perhaps too trusting of authority here, decided to follow Palliser's recommendation and confidently grabbed the beast, but as he soon learned, nothing is as it seems in the Morra's darkest trenches. Such an "absurd" move, which seemingly sacrifices a whole piece for "nothing", just like the Morra Gambit as a whole, simply offends what many consider to be "proper" chess!

After I uncorked 9.♘d5, a few grandmasters flashed some very colorful faces when glancing at my board while strolling away from their own matches. Even one of my own coaches, Grandmaster Anatoly Lein, harshly rebuked me when I first showed him 9.♘d5 over a year before this game, but for a more humorous reason: "So what; why do I have to take it?!" he barked. So the radical, provocative knight sacrifice has its detractors – both those who claim it virtually hangs a piece, and those who deride the idea as all nice and bubbly but ultimately nothing but a bunch of hot air.

However, what if I were to argue that 9.♘d5 is not only sound, but nearly impossible to defend against perfect attack? Surely that would ruffle some feathers. Yes, my great coach concluded from our analysis that "you underestimate defense, my friend", voicing the opinion of many in modern chess that defensive technique has risen over the years to overtake the more primitive Romantic attacking arts. But perhaps the defensive school also underestimates the attack. Such is the great beauty and depth of chess, when a single move can ignite such intense passions.

During the Miami Open 2008 post-tournament festivities, only one grandmaster took my side that Black has already fallen into the abyss after 9.♘d5, but he was well beyond inebriated during this revelation. This may not come as a surprise, as 9.♘d5 may also be mocked as part of the "drunken" style.

9...exd5

Firstly, the knight must be taken! Sometimes after ♘d5 in the Morra, Black can play matador and dance with the angry bull on d5, but not here. I offer one fantastic variation: 9...♗c5 10.♗g5! f6 (10...♘e7 11.♖c1+–) 11.♘e5!

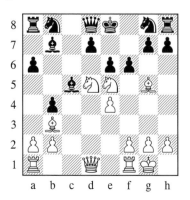

And the threat of ♕h5† decides. Whereas two moves earlier Black had the simple choice of whether or not to grab a knight, now he can capture three different white pieces on the 5th rank. But of course, Tal would utter his famous words: "He can only take one of them at a time!"

10.exd5!

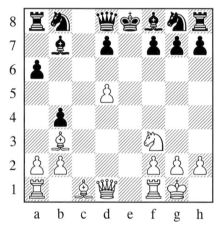

While the rest of the game may appear like magic, it is firmly rooted in ruthless positional logic. When I lecture on this position, I always ask students: "What is White's most effective piece?" Please don't pick the queen, or else this would be quite a lame question. Take a moment to answer...

Yes, the d5-pawn! White may be down a piece, but the d5-pawn buries Black's entire queenside. The bishop and knight gasp for air, and the a8-rook lies entombed. You can even brush these pieces off your board for dramatic effect – they are caught in the vortex, and will not exist for the next few moves. Add to the equation that the gambiteer threatens the decisive ♖e1† (Black cannot block the check as the d5-pawn swallows pieces via d5-d6), plus all of White's other pieces burst with energy as Black's king awaits punishment in the center, and as you can clearly compute, White has more than enough compensation for a measly piece.

10...d6

While it is the attacker's obligation to ensure that Black's queenside remains buried at the bottom of the ocean, so too the defender must fight to escape his fate. Sarkar's last move simultaneously prevents White's crippling d5-d6 advance while allowing his queenside a breath with ...♞bd7. We cover the only other logical try, 10...♝d6, next.

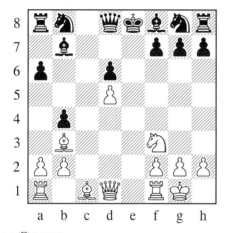

11.♕d4!?N

The gambiteer uses his superior freedom of action to the fullest, centralizing the powerful queen where she radiates waves of energy across the board. Specifically, Black can no longer play the natural 11...♝e7 as 12.♕xg7 looms, and if 12...♝f6 to save the stray rook, then 13.♖e1† and the black king sinks.

11...♞f6 12.♕xb4!

Normally I would not waste time floating around with my queen when trying to capitalize on a lead in development. However, the rippling 12.♕xb4 is no mere queen move. Rather, it sends serious shock waves towards the bishop! Every Black defense leads further down the trench.

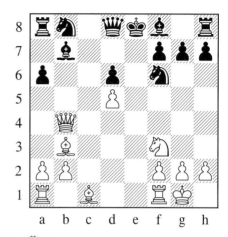

12...♕c7

Justin resists valiantly, but his queen now falls onto one of the Morra Gambit's main fault lines – the shaky c-file.

On 12...♕d7, White wins easily with 13.♝a4.

At the tournament party (we like to dance in Miami), one of the "materialistic" grandmasters argued that Black's sinking ship might be salvaged by the backwards:
12...♝c8
But the following variation left no doubt that defensive hope does not spring eternal.
13.♖e1† ♝e7 14.♝f4!
Loading up for decisive action on d6, so Black finally drifts to "safety".
14...0–0

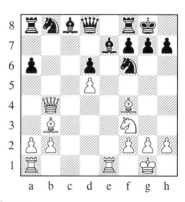

15.♖xe7!

White now tosses his rook into the pit, if only to win the black queen.

15...♕xe7 16.♗xd6 ♕d8 17.♗e7! ♕e8 18.♖e1

Threatening a discovery on f6.

18...a5

18...♘fd7 19.♗h4 nets the queen in open water.

18...♘g4 gives the queen a flight on d7, but 19.♗a4 ends this dream, for if 20...♗d7 then 21.♗xd7 and White collects either Black's stray rook or knight.

You may peruse the following sample of Black's most accurate, but still futile defense during your leisure diving hours.

19.♕a3 ♘g4 20.♗c2

20.♗a4 no longer works as the white queen's tentacles do not reach the g4-knight anymore.

20...f5

Black, under severe pressure, must prevent 21.♗xf8 ♕xf8 22.♗xh7†!, which would nab the queen once more.

21.h3 ♘h6 22.♗xf8 ♕xf8 23.♖e7! ♘d7 24.d6

The crushing d-pawn pins Black further and further down.

24...♘f6 25.♗a4 ♔h8 26.♘g5 ♖b8

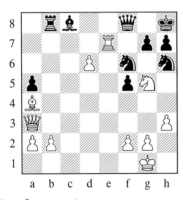

27.♖e8! ♘xe8 28.d7!

I told you the d-pawn was the positional secret to the mysterious 9.♘d5 sacrifice... now the great pawn will actually become a queen itself!

28...♘d6 29.♘e6!+−

13.♗f4!?

I could have played 13.♗g5! as well, which ends all resistance. I will leave you alone to explore this minor detail in the crevasses of the position if you so desire.

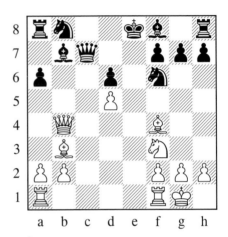

13...♘bd7

The deflectionary shot 13...a5 is Black's best last ditch effort, but after 14.♖fe1† he still should spiral downward. The black king suffers, as 14...♗e7 fails instructively: 15.♖ac1! ♕xc1 Desperation! (15...♕d7 16.♕xd6+− or 15...axb4 16.♖xc7+−) 16.♕xb7! And the entire Black queenside falls to the raiding white queen – a recurring theme.

14.♖fe1†

Justin has played the most natural defensive moves, and yet is already completely lost. Ultimately this stands not only as a testament to the power of 9.♘d5, but to the stunning power of precision sacrificial attacking in general.

14...♔d8

Of course 14...♗e7 collapses to 15.♗xd6. Thus Black's king enters the darkest corner of the abyss.

15.♖ac1! ♕b6

Justin surely wished to block the attacking forces via 15...♘c5, but after the crusher 16.♖xc5, White crashes through: 16...♕xc5 (16...dxc5 17.♗xc7†+–) 17.♕xb7+– Amidst a variety of menacing threats, the f7-pawn at the very least goes.

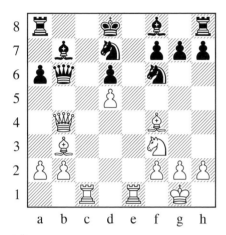

16.♘g5!!

I envisioned this outstanding knockout blow during a long think before my 12th move, and much to my excitement it actually found its way onto the canvas.

Justin resigned immediately, as ♘xf7† will send the king into oblivion. Take special notice of the "Morra rooks", which elegantly lay the foundation for the final strike. Black may cheat his fate for a move with 16...♗e7, but then the obvious 17.♘xf7† wins anyway, or White can sacrifice his queen yet again for further approval from the masters of old: 17.♕xd6!! ♕xd6 (17...♗xd6 18.♘xf7#) 18.♗xd6 And the violent whirlpool finally drags the black king to the bottom. 18...♖e8 19.♘xf7#

1–0

10...♗d6 introduction

1.e4 c5 2.d4 cxd4 3.c3 dxc3 4.♘xc3 e6 5.♘f3 a6 6.♗c4 b5 7.♗b3 ♗b7 8.0–0 b4 9.♘d5 exd5 10.exd5!

We now probe Black's only other reasonable defensive chance in the Sarkar game:

10...♗d6

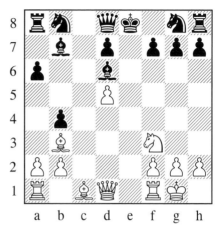

This move intuitively appeals to me more, as Black quickly develops part of his kingside and prepares to castle.

However, unlike 10...d6, it does nothing to save Black's drowning queenside pieces. If you brought your computer engines along for the ride, now would be a good time to fire them up and watch as they sputter and spit out nonsense as we delve deeper and deeper.

11.♖e1† ♘e7?!

As you may have noticed, your computer will probably assess this position as clearly favorable to Black. After all, it's hard to blame your cold, emotionless friend, as Black will calmly castle out of the danger...

We will examine the forced 11...♔f8 soon before moving onto the most advanced material.

12.♘g5!

But now the silicon "oracle" may switch its assessment to =. Could castling perhaps not be the great escape out of the trenches?

12...0–0 13.♕h5! h6 14.♘e4

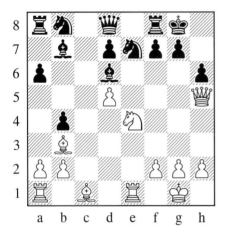

By now your machine should "see" the great vortex on the horizon. The normally waterproof engines switch from "equal" to "White is clearly better" to "White is winning." This is just one of the many "computer confusion" moments found throughout this chapter and the book. Well, if the Morra Gambit can do this to the world's greatest computers, the beasts that reign supreme throughout our chess world, then imagine what it can do to your hapless opponents.

In addition to the transparent ♘xd6, White also threatens the devastating ♗xh6 and a renewed assault on the king. Black cannot simultaneously parry both threats and enters a state of freefall. Note that White's superiority in attacking force emanates primarily from the wedging d5-pawn, which prevents Black's sleeping queenside from rescuing the king.

14...♕c7 15.♗xh6+– ♗xh2†

This desperado puts up maximum resistance against the current, but a black hole is a black hole – there is no escape.

After 15...gxh6 16.♕xh6 f6 White has multiple wins – I'll just offer two which give the d-pawn a starring role: 17.♘xd6 ♕xd6

18.♖xe7 ♕xe7 19.d6†+– or 17.♘g5! fxg5 18.♖xe7 ♗xe7 19.d6† ♖f7 20.♕g6† ♔h8 21.♗xf7 The d-pawn doesn't even bother to capture the queen, but just watches from the side as White's heavy pieces deliver checkmate.

16.♔h1 ♕e5 17.♗g5!+–

Menacing mayhem everywhere! 18.♘f6†, winning the queen, is just the largest of many threats.

17...♘xd5

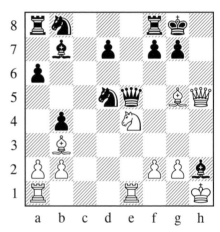

Amazingly, all these moves were played long ago in Zelic – Sermek, Makarska 1995, in which Black somehow managed not only to survive, but win! Perhaps this explains why White's decisive attack stayed buried under the rubble for so long. (I for one had no idea this encounter existed until writing up this chapter, but I had reached this position independently in my analysis in 2005.) Here Zelic played the illogical 18.♗xd5?, parting with his golden Italian bishop and allowing Black a great reprieve.

But to complete the picture of total domination, White needed only to bring his last inactive piece into the fray.

18.♖ad1!N+–

The threat of winning the queen reappears, as White intends 19.♗xd5 ♗xd5 20.♘f6†. Black's only reprieve now would be to resign.

18...g6

White can keep the queens on and play for a dramatic mate, or play the role of the butcher.

19.♕xh2 ♕xh2† 20.♔xh2 ♘b6 21.♘d6

Collecting the rook after ♗e7, or a sadist may weave a queenless mating net instead with ♔g3!, intending final destruction via ♖h1 and ♘/♗ to f6.

10...♗d6 11.♖e1† ♔f8

1.e4 c5 2.d4 cxd4 3.c3 dxc3 4.♘xc3 e6 5.♘f3 a6 6.♗c4 b5 7.♗b3 ♗b7 8.0–0 b4 9.♘d5! exd5 10.exd5! ♗d6 11.♖e1† ♔f8

We now curtly discuss the critical line before losing ourselves in the theoretical maze of complications to come. With 11...♔f8, Black sidesteps immediate danger, but forfeits castling privileges forever. This concession, coupled with Black's hopeless queenside, offers the gambiteer all the chances for an advantage, provided that he pursues the attack with the vigor worthy of his name. If not, he will simply be down a piece for "nothing", much to the thrill of the materialists.

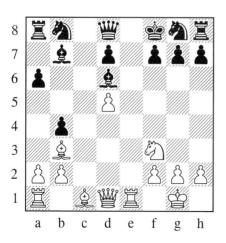

12.♕d4!

To summarize one of Nimzowitsch's tenets in his timeless positional treatises, "When in doubt, centralize."[22] Now, over 80 years on, we use his very teachings to help shed light on one of the wildest attacking positions in chess. Black must proceed with the utmost caution to avoid falling over the edge. Unfortunately for him, all of his obvious developing moves fail to prevent the downward surge. For now, we will only examine the most logical one.

12...♘f6?! 13.♘h4!+−

White plunders on the fertile f5-square. Observe how the black bishop remains chained to d6 – it must keep the lusting d5-pawn at bay while guarding against many other lurking hazards.

13...♕c7

Black stubbornly clings to the blockade on d6, but he is in for the cruelest of surprises. We can see some of the other hazards after: 13...♔g8 14.♘f5 ♗f8

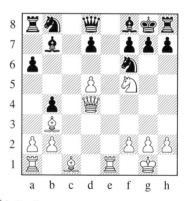

15.♗h6! g6
  Upon 15...gxh6, the incoming rook lift will decide.
16.d6!
  The d-pawn's lust to expand knows no bounds.[23]
  16.♗xf8 ♔xf8 17.♖e7 also wins.
16...gxf5 17.♖e7!! ♗xe7 18.dxe7 ♕xe7 19.♕h4!

With an unstoppable mate on Black's shattered dark squares.

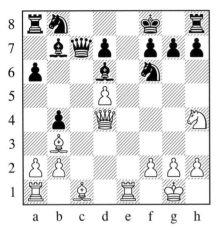

14.♕xf6!

Another flashy queen sacrifice. Some say the greatest depths house the greatest pearls.

**14...gxf6　15.♗h6†　♔g8　16.♖e8†　♗f8
17.♖xf8#**

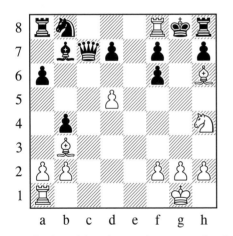

Well, if you like what you've seen so far, then grab a seat for the rest of the trip, for it's about to get a whole lot crazier. So be brave, come and enter the darkest abyss. Do not worry if you cannot make sense of all the chaos surrounding you – I promise you won't be the only one suffering from vertigo way down below.

Theory I – 10...♗d6

**1.e4 c5 2.d4 cxd4 3.c3 dxc3 4.♘xc3 e6 5.♘f3
a6 6.♗c4 b5 7.♗b3 ♗b7 8.0–0! b4 9.♘d5!**

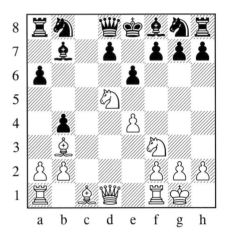

9...exd5□

The following variations prove beyond a doubt that Black has no choice but to accept the sacrifice:

9...d6? is simply met by 10.♘xb4± or 10.♗a4† first, followed by ♘xb4.

9...♘f6?! 10.♖e1!?
Now Black definitely cannot take on d5!
White has several other options:
a) 10.♘xf6† gxf6 11.♕d3 a5 12.♖d1⩱
b) 10.♗f4 exd5 11.exd5 ♗c5∞
c) The logical 10.♗g5 also leads to a advantage: 10...h6 11.♗xf6 gxf6

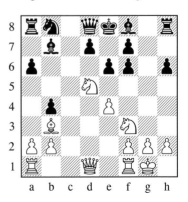

12.♕d4 ♗e7 (12...exd5 13.♖fe1 dxe4
14.♖xe4† ♗e7 15.♖xe7† ♚xe7 16.♕xb4† d6
17.♕xb7† ♘d7 18.♕d5+–) 13.♘xe7 ♕xe7
14.♖ac1 ♘c6 15.♕e3± It is not clear what
Black should do with his king.

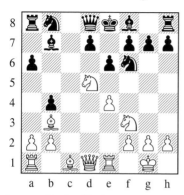

10...♗c5 11.♘xf6† ♕xf6?

11...gxf6 is the only way to continue, but
Black becomes hopeless on the dark squares
and his kingside is shattered: 12.♗e3!±
12.♗g5 ♕g6

With 12...♕xb2, Black's queen would drift
too far from the action.

13.♖c1

13...d6 14.♖xc5! swiftly decides.

13...♗e7 14.♗xe7 ♚xe7 15.♖c7 ♗c6 16.♘e5+–

9...♗c5?! 10.♗g5 f6

10...♘e7?! 11.♖c1 overloads on the minor
pieces.

11.♘e5!±

Centralizing!

11...fxg5 12.♕h5† g6 13.♘xg6 hxg6 14.♕xh8

This spells disaster for the black king.

14...♚f8 15.♖ac1 d6

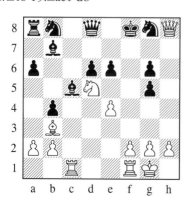

16.♖xc5!

Removing Black's only active piece and
clearing the path towards the king on the f-file.

16...dxc5 17.f4! g4

Opening up the f-line would be catastrophic
for the f8-king, but White will still have his
way.

18.f5! gxf5 19.exf5 ♗xd5

19...e5 20.f6+–

20.fxe6† ♚e7 21.♕h4† ♚e8 22.♕h5†

White can do as he pleases, but this leads to
mate in 4.

10.exd5 ♗d6

We shall get to the truth about 10...d6 after
first exhausting 10...♗d6.

11.♖e1† ♚f8□

11...♘e7 12.♘g5+– was covered earlier.

12.♕d4!

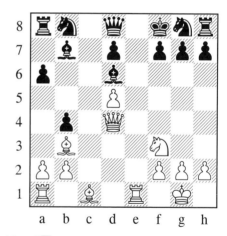

12...a5□

Ironically, this non-developing flank pawn
move is Black's only hope of combating White's
overwhelming central pressure. Although it
fails to develop a piece, it frees the a6-square
for Black's rook to bolster the d6-blockade
laterally along the 6th rank, thus boosting
defensive morale. All other logical tries fail –
we now bury them one by one.

12...♘f6?! 13.♘h4+– as noted earlier.

12...♘e7? fails rather routinely. 13.♗g5! White now threatens ♗xe7 and d5-d6 followed by doom on f7. Black is powerless to prevent the pain. 13...♔g8 (13...f6 14.♗xf6+–) 14.♗xe7 ♗xe7 15.d6

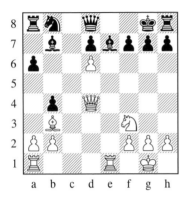

15...♗f6 16.♕c4 ♕f8 17.♕xf7†!♕xf7 18.♖e8#

12...h6?!

This takes away key squares from the attacker's forces but does little to secure the d6-blockade, so White strikes at the most sensitive point. Your computers, if they are still by your side, will short circuit as they fail to grasp White's long-term positional grip.
13.♗f4! ♗xf4 14.♕xf4

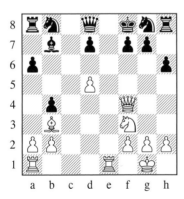

14...a5

14...d6 solves one problem, but leads to

another – now e6 becomes a revolving door for White's rook. 15.♖e6!± g5 16.♕xb4! fxe6 17.♕xb7 ♘d7 18.dxe6 And after White captures on d7, he will have more than enough compensation for the exchange.
15.♕d6†! ♘e7 16.♘e5!

A clever centralizing blow, as Black's rook cannot excavate the white queen from the 6th rank due to a simple yet surprising shot. Meanwhile, the knight has larger plans.
16...♖a6

16...♔g8 17.♘xf7! rips open the black king so that the Italian bishop can do his damage: 17...♔xf7 18.♕f4† ♔g8 19.d6†+– (or first 19.♖xe7+–)
17.♕xb8!+–

12...f6 again critically weakens the squares around the besieged king: 13.♗f4 ♗xf4 14.♕xb4†! A familiar motif – the b4-pawn is always a target once the blockading bishop goes. 14...d6 15.♕xf4 ♗c8 16.♘d4 White's rook or knight dines on e6. 16...♘e7 17.♖e6!+– And once d6 falls, so does the black king.

12...♕f6?

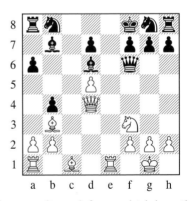

The most direct defense, which happily leads to the most sparkling possibilities as well.
13.♘e5!±

Driving a wedge between the coordinated black queen and bishop. White now threatens ♕b6, and if the queen retreats to d8, then ♘c4 wins. Note that White did not dive in immediately to b6 as ♗xh2† turns the tables.

The less spectacular 13.♕e4± is also promising.

13...♗e7

Black's last desperate attempt to stave off disaster results in an awesome combinational sequence.

The alternatives do not offer salvation:

a) After 13...♗c8 the following line neatly shows how passive defense might fail here: 14.♗f4 a5 15.♕b6 ♖a6 (15...g5 16.♗xg5! ♕xg5 17.♕xd6† ♔g7 18.♖e3+–) 16.♘xd7† ♗xd7 17.♗xd6† ♕xd6 18.♖d8†+–

b) 13...♘e7? simply interferes with the queen's guard of d8: 14.♕b6!+– ♗c8 15.♕d8#

c) 13...♗xe5 14.♕xb4†! reveals the main point of White's 13th move: 14...♗d6 15.♕xb7+–

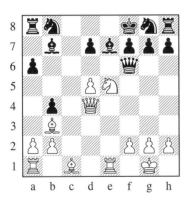

14.♗g5!!

This lights up the dark, though White can also win brutally with: 14.d6 ♗xd6 15.♗g5! ♕xg5 16.♕xd6† ♘e7 17.g3 ♕f6 18.♕c7+–

14...♕d6

Wisely trying to prevent the inevitable fall of b7, which will now occur over ten moves in the future!

14...♕xg5 15.♕b6! is the point of the deflection. White's queen plops on b6 and together with her rook collects Black's

sunken queenside. 15...♗c8 16.♖ac1 The board is cut in two!! 16...♘c6 17.dxc6+– And f7 goes next.

15.♗xe7† ♘xe7

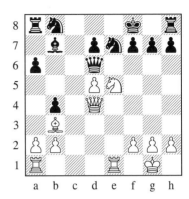

16.♘xf7!

16.♕f4 also wins, albeit more prosaically.

16...♔xf7 17.♖xe7†! ♔xe7 18.♕xg7† ♔d8 19.♕xh8† ♔c7 20.♖c1† ♔b6

20...♘c6 21.♕xh7+–

21.♕d4† ♔b5

21...♔a5 22.♖c5† ♔b6 23.♖c6† ♔a5 24.♕b6#

White can now go for mate, or instead decide to play a practical joke on the black queenside.

22.a4† bxa3 23.♗a4† ♔a5 24.♖c5† ♕xc5 25.♕xc5† ♔xa4 26.♕xa3† ♔b5

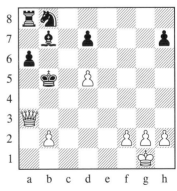

27.♕b3† ♔c5 28.♕xb7

Black's flawed queenside pieces fall like dominoes!

13.♗g5!

This variation requires the utmost accuracy from both players, as you may have already noticed if you are still with me. One slip on either side and the evaluation can change from += to –+ or anywhere in between. White must find a way to disturb Black's effective ...♖a6 defensive ideas, and only 13.♗g5, which seeks to soften the black kingside, succeeds.

13...f6

Most of the alternatives can be quickly dismissed:

13...♘e7? 14.♗xe7† ♗xe7 15.d6 ♗f6 16.♕c4+–

13...♗e7? 14.♕f4 d6 15.♗xe7† ♘xe7 16.♘g5 ♕e8 17.♗a4+–

After 13...♕c7? White can choose between 14.♖ac1+– and 14.♖e8†! ♔xe8 15.♕xg7+–.

13...♘f6!?

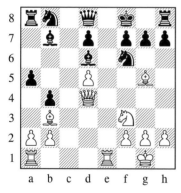

Now White must find the unbelievable 14.♘d2!N, blasting away at the d6-blockade and working the pin, otherwise his attack comes to a standstill. After this deep retreat, the player down a piece still has excellent prospects. For example: 14...h6 15.♗h4 g5 16.♘e4! and White reasserts dominance. 16...gxh4 (16...♗e7 17.d6+– ♗xe4 18.♖xe4

♘xe4 19.♕xh8#) 17.♘xd6 ♗a6 18.♖e8†! ♘xe8 19.♕xh8† ♔e7 20.♘f5#

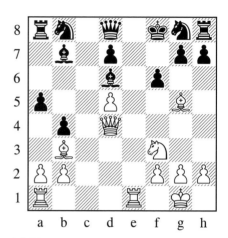

14.♗f4

Black has two paths to try and escape the abyss, but both just descend deeper and deeper.

14...♗xf4

14...♖a6 15.♖e2! It's a bad sign indeed for the defense that White, a piece down, has time for such "calm" maneuvers. Such a move highlights the attacker's complete positional dominance over the opponent. 15...g6 (15...♕b6 16.♕e4+– or 15...♘h6 16.♗xh6 gxh6 17.♕h4 ♔g7 18.♕g4† ♔f8 19.♖ae1 ♖g8 20.♖e8† ♕xe8 21.♖xe8† ♔xe8 22.♕xg8†+–) 16.♖ae1 ♔g7 17.♖e8 ♕b6 18.♕e4!±

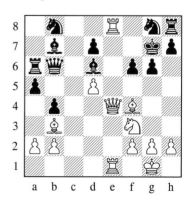

Such a coordinated "triple" barrel will destroy anything in its wake. 18...♗xf4?! 19.♕e7†!!

More treasures! 19...♘xe7 20.♖1xe7† ♔h6 21.♖xh8 g5 22.♖hxh7† ♔g6 23.♖eg7† ♔f5 24.♗c2† ♔g4 25.♖h4# (or 25.h3#)

15.♕xf4± ♕b6

After 15...♖a6 16.♖e3! Black's best efforts will not be enough to contain the boundless attack: 16...d6 17.♘g5 ♗c8 18.♖ae1 ♗d7

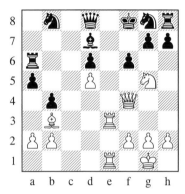

19.♗a4! One deflection... 19...♕c8 20.♕c4! ...and another! 20...fxg5 21.♕xc8† ♗xc8 22.♖e8† ♔f7 23.♖xc8+– Black may have avoided direct mate, but remains completely immobilized.

15...d6 16.♘g5 The virtues of first probing with 13.♗g5 before 14.♗f4 are clearly illuminated in these types of variations. 16...♗c8 17.♗a4 ♘e7 18.♖e6 The threat of ♖xf6† followed by mate cannot be averted, as moving the e7-knight leads to another pitfall. 18...♘g6 (or 18...♘xd5) 19.♕xd6† ♕xd6 20.♖e8#

16.♖ac1!

Black hopes to re-establish dark-squared control, but White shows just how deep the rabbit hole truly goes.[24]

16...♘a6

We're in the darkest of trenches now, and your computers may have already exploded from the pressure below.

16...♘e7 17.d6+–

16...a4 17.♗xa4 ♘e7 (17...♖xa4 18.♕xb8† ♔f7 19.♕e8#) 18.♗b3+–

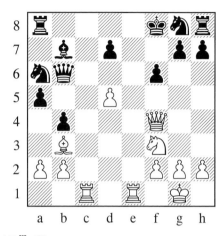

17.♖c6!!+–
Oh my!

17...dxc6

17...♕d8 He can run, but he can't hide. 18.♕d6† ♔f7 19.♖b6! ♗c8 20.♘d4 ♘h6 21.♘e6!

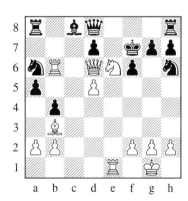

The d5-pawn is everywhere! 21...dxe6 (21...♕e8 22.♕g3 ♘f5 23.♕f3 ♘d4 24.♘g5† ♔g6 25.♕d3† ♔xg5 26.h4†+–) 22.dxe6† ♔g6 23.♕g3†+–

18.♕d6† ♔f7 19.♘e5† fxe5 20.dxc6† ♔e8 21.♖xe5† ♘e7 22.♕xe7#
Silence, sometimes, is best.

Theory II – 10...d6

1.e4 c5 2.d4 cxd4 3.c3 dxc3 4.♘xc3 e6 5.♘f3 a6 6.♗c4 b5 7.♗b3 ♗b7 8.0–0! b4 9.♘d5! exd5 10.exd5 d6!?

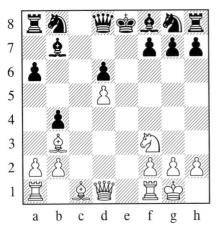

Lastly we take a deeper look at Sarkar's defense 10...d6, and see that the game itself may not tell the final story.

11.♖e1†!

This primitive check, allowing the black king's bishop to develop with ease, may be even stronger than:
11.♕d4!?
    While this proved more than effective in the game, Black can counter with a murky computer defense.
    11...♘d7! 12.♖e1†
        12.♕xb4 ♕b6!
    12...♘e7

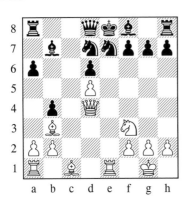

13.♘g5!?
Black's position looks wretched on the surface, but White does not have a clear knockout blow. For example:
a) **13.♗a4 ♕a5!**
b) **13.♕xb4!?** is White's other serious attempt to find an advantage: 13...♘c5∞ (13...♕b6? 14.♕f4± a5 15.♗e3 ♕b4 16.♘d4 0–0–0 17.a3 ♕b6 18.♘e6+–) Feel free to keep searching this dark corner, but be warned, you may suffer from dizziness (I certainly am right now). As a guidepost, I recommend you start with 14.♗f4!?. I have a strong feeling White has an advantage here, but some stones are better left unturned...

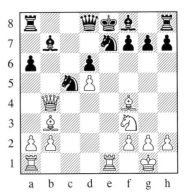

14...♘xb3? (14...f6!? and 14...♕d7!? and 14...a5!? are a few Black responses worthy of investigation) 15.♕xb7 ♘xa1 16.♕c6†!+–
13...♘c5

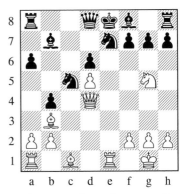

14.♘e4! ♘xb3 15.♕xb4 ♘xa1 16.♕a4†

16.♗f4!? ♕c7! (16...♕d7? 17.♘xd6† ♔d8
18.♕b6†+–) 17.♘xd6† ♔d7! Perhaps you
can find a win for White, a rook and a piece
down, but I have my doubts. 18.♕a4† ♗c6
19.dxc6† ♕xc6 20.♖d1!

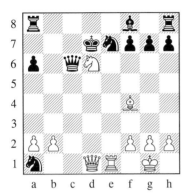

I will leave you alone to investigate this wild
position if you wish, but we are moving
on. White should at least have some sort of
perpetual.
16...♕d7 17.♘xd6† ♔d8 18.♘xf7† ♔c8
19.♕c4† ♕c7 20.♕g4† ♕d7 21.♕c4†=
With perpetual check.

11...♗e7

11...♘e7? simply loses quickly: 12.♗a4†
♘d7 13.♘g5! ♕a5 14.♘e4 ♕xd5 15.♘xd6†
♔d8 16.♘xf7†+–

12.♕d4!?

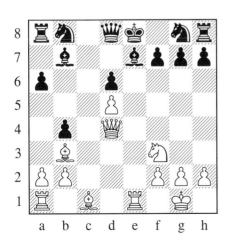

12...♔f8□

12...♘f6?! 13.♕xb4 ♕c7

13...♗c8 14.♗f4 transposes to a line we
analyzed in the Sarkar game, which favors
White after 14...0–0 15.♖xe7 etc.

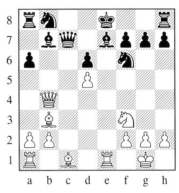

All looks OK for Black – he is about to
castle. But appearances can be deceptive.
14.♗g5!
Even the shocking 14.♗h6!? (Δ♖ac1)
yields White the advantage, an indication
that there is indeed something rotten in
Denmark. Check it out yourself!
The clearer text move, however, with the
same idea in mind but without giving up a
piece, simply wins.
14...0–0
14...♘bd7 15.♖ac1 ♘c5 16.♗xf6 gxf6
17.♗a4† ♔f8 (17...♔d8 18.♕g4! ♗c8
19.♕g7 ♖f8 20.♕xf8† ♗xf8 21.♖e8#)
18.♕f4 with overwhelming threats.
14...a5 15.♖ac1 ♕d7 16.♕b6 ♖a6 17.♕c7+–
15.♖ac1 ♕d7

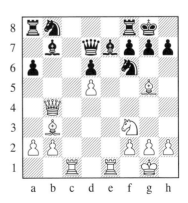

16.♗a4! a5 17.♕h4!

Swinging to the kingside for the final assault.

17...♕d8 18.♗c2+−

Sometimes, it's best to play for the most elementary mates, especially when there is no defense!

18.♘d4!?± is also strong, but less direct.

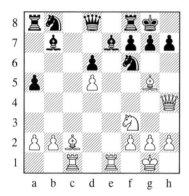

18...h6

There is no defense:

a) 18...g6? 19.♖xe7+−

b) 18...h5 19.♗xf6 ♗xf6 20.♕xh5 g6 21.♗xg6 fxg6 22.♕xg6† ♗g7 (22...♔h8 23.♖c4+− ♗c8 24.♘g5 ♗xg5 25.♖xc8 ♕xc8 26.♕h5† ♔g7 27.♕xg5† ♔h8 28.♖e7+−) 23.♘g5+−

c) 18...♘bd7 Black's pieces finally develop, but one move too late: 19.♖xe7! ♕xe7 20.♗xh7† ♔h8 21.♗d3† ♔g8 22.♖c7+− Renewing the primitive threat on h7 by means of ♗xf6. 22...♖fe8 23.♖xb7+− (23.♗xf6? ♕e1†!) 23...♖ab8 24.♗xf6 ♕xf6 25.♕h7† ♔f8 26.♖xd7+−

19.♗xh6 gxh6

19...g6 20.♗xg6 No mercy! 20...fxg6 21.♕g3 ♔h8 22.♗xf8 ♕xf8 23.♘h4+−

20.♕xh6+− ♖e8 21.♘g5 ♗f8 22.♗h7† ♔h8 23.♘xf7#

It is an important theoretical discovery in this variation that Black cannot respond naturally with 12...♘f6, so his king must concede castling privileges.

13.♕xb4

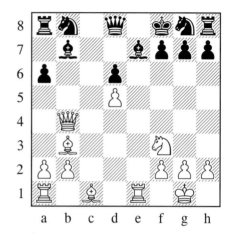

13...♗c8

Black must awkwardly step back with the bishop. More natural moves again fail:

13...♕c7?! 14.♗f4 a5 15.♖ac1 ♕d7 (15...axb4? 16.♖xc7+− as White strikes on e7 next, followed by ♗xd6.) 16.♕b6 ♖a6 17.♕c7 ♕xc7 18.♖xc7 ♖b6 19.♖ec1

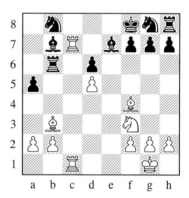

Black's misplaced rook will soon fall. 19...♘f6 (19...♘a6 20.♖xb7+−) 20.♗e3 ♖b4 21.♗d2 ♖b5 22.♖c8†! ♗xc8 23.♖xc8† ♘e8 24.♗a4 As we see time and time again, even after the queens are traded the position remains volcanic.

13...♕d7?! 14.♗a4 a5 15.♕b3 ♕c7 16.♗f4 ♘a6 17.♖ac1 ♕b8 (17...♘c5 18.♖xc5)

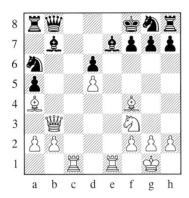

18.♗xd6!+–

14.♗f4! a5 15.♛a3!∞

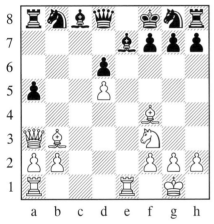

After the natural 15...♘f6? Black is crushed by 16.♖xe7+–. If 15...♗g4, then 16.♘d4 with an everlasting bind. But, of course, Black may have other, more creative defenses. I refuse to give a definitive evaluation to such a rich position. Ending this chapter's analysis with the note "unclear" is far more appropriate, thus celebrating chess's infinite complexity.[25] All I can say is, if you were brave enough to make it this far into the deep, then you will definitely have more knowledge, and nerve, than your opponent. While the moves of this chapter themselves may only apply to a narrow crevasse of chess theory, the conclusions we draw have far greater implications. White sacrifices a whole piece on move 9, yet easily fights for the advantage throughout the struggle. Defensive technique may have risen over the last 100 years, but not to the point where it can deny the purest of attacks. Morphy and the other masters of the old guard would be overjoyed, for the Romantic school clearly has a firm foothold in the 21st century.

Sacrificing with ♘d5 has a rich history in the Open Sicilian, with perhaps no example as famous as Tal's positional sacrifice vs. Larsen.

Mikhail Tal – Bent Larsen

Candidates Match (10), Bled 1965

1.e4 c5 2.♘f3 ♘c6 3.d4 cxd4 4.♘xd4 e6 5.♘c3 d6 6.♗e3 ♘f6 7.f4 ♗e7 8.♛f3 0–0 9.0–0–0 ♛c7 10.♘db5 ♛b8 11.g4 a6 12.♘d4 ♘xd4 13.♗xd4 b5 14.g5 ♘d7 15.♗d3 b4 16.♘d5

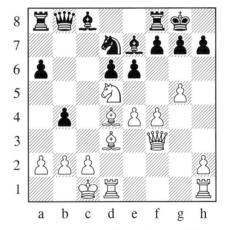

16...exd5 17.exd5 f5 18.♖de1 ♖f7 19.h4 ♗b7 20.♗xf5 ♖xf5 21.♖xe7 ♘e5 22.♛e4 ♛f8 23.fxe5 ♖f4 24.♛e3 ♖f3 25.♛e2 ♛xe7 26.♛xf3 dxe5 27.♖e1 ♖d8 28.♖xe5 ♛d6 29.♛f4 ♖f8 30.♛e4 b3 31.axb3 ♖f1† 32.♔d2 ♛b4† 33.c3 ♛d6 34.♗c5 ♛xc5 35.♖e8† ♖f8 36.♛e6† ♔h8 37.♛f7 1–0

"1...e6? Stronger is 1...c5 which wins a pawn."

– Grandmaster Bent Larsen

Chapter 5

The King in the Windy City – the Chicago Defense

"This is my city."[26] – The Joker

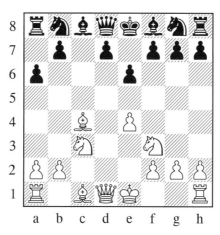

1.e4 c5 2.d4 cxd4 3.c3 dxc3 4.♘xc3 e6 5.♘f3 a6 6.♗c4

We step back on dry land, but danger remains. Enter the Chicago Defense, a highly optimistic system characterized by an early rook maneuver via a7 to d7, which shields the black queen from the menacing pins on the d-file so often swirling in the gambit.

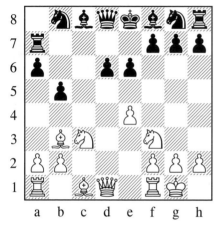

Like so many other schemes, the Chicago has been touted by its zealous adherents as a solution to Morra mayhem. In fact, after I pummeled an expert in 20 moves in the Chicago in 2007, my opponent lamented that this was the first time he had tasted defeat with the ...罝a7-d7 setup in over 30 years! Dejected, he vowed to repair his shattered system.

No doubt, the breezy Chicago contains some positional logic – Black quells the gambiteer's d-file storm, shifting his rook to d7 to subdue White's rook on d1. Such a seductive idea has even attracted such hallowed names as a young Hikaru Nakamura and GM Roman Dzindzichashvili. However, Black's petulant rook just gets pelted by hail, and the Chicago ultimately ranks as one of the flimsiest main line defenses against the gambit. Much in the spirit of Polugaevsky's vaunted defense against the Najdorf (which also contains ...罝a7 as a key motif), Black throws the principles of kingside development first to the wind, and the price he pays is his own tattered king. In fact, only after near perfect defense can Black hope to escape

the first 15 moves alive. Thus, the Chicago can only be recommended to those brave souls who get thrills from chasing down tornados.

Marc Esserman – Vadim Martirosov

Harvard (blitz) 2008

1.e4 c5 2.d4 cxd4 3.c3 dxc3 4.♘xc3 e6 5.♘f3 a6 6.♗c4 d6 7.0–0 b5 8.♗b3 罝a7?!

The Chicago Defense appears in its raw form. As the game continuation will show, Black must first plant his knight on c6 before slipping and sliding with ...罝a7.

9.♗e3!

White races ahead in a blur, twisting the rook to its desired destination.

9...罝d7 10.♘d4!±

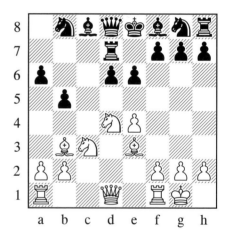

The gambiteer takes advantage of the faulty move order, transforming the game into a Fischer-Sozin attack with many extra tempi of development in return for the sacrificed pawn. Lagging behind, Black cannot escape unscathed. Note that instead of mindlessly continuing ♕e2 and 罝d1, White eyes the sensitive e6-target, which has been critically weakened by the d7-rook interfering with the c8-bishop's guard. Once e6 falls, the black king will sway.

10...♘f6

Black is already busted. Yes, busted! All defensive schemes are resolutely blasted:
10...♗b7 11.f4!

The f1-rook joins the assault. Again play echoes that of the Fischer-Sozin attack.
11...b4 12.f5! e5

12...bxc3 13.fxe6 fxe6 14.♖xf8†!+– is gusty!

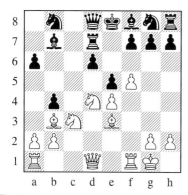

13.♘e6!

Tal's favorite knight sacrifice will appear repeatedly in the Windy City.
13...fxe6 14.♕h5†! g6 15.fxg6 ♘f6 16.g7†+–

The queen disappears, but only for an instant!

11.f4 ♗b7

The only other reasonable try is:
11...b4!?

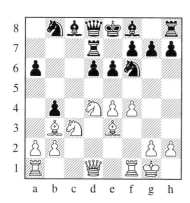

12.e5!±

Another thematic break in Open Sicilian main lines. Although the d-file is pried

open, the rook remains ineffective and Black's defenses are reduced to ruin. The idea combines kingside attack with the possibility of a pin on the weathered d7-rook.

12.♘d5!? Don't become too fixated on this knight thrust. We just left the trenches!
12...exd5 13.e5 dxe5 14.fxe5 ♗e7!∞ Black gives back the piece and flees for cover.
12...dxe5

12...bxc3 13.exf6 gxf6 14.♗a4± The "Chicago" rook best get used to such treatment.
13.fxe5 ♗c5

13...bxc3 14.exf6 cxb2 15.♖b1 gxf6 16.♗a4±
14.exf6 ♗xd4 15.♗xd4 ♖xd4 16.♗a4†

The rook, now on d4, again finds itself stormed, as blocking the check with a minor piece interferes with the queen's guard of the rook. The king, meanwhile, must brave the blizzard.
16...♔f8 17.♕h5!

Threatening carnage on f7.
17...gxf6 18.♘e2

White, a whopping two pawns down, decisively penetrates with ♕h6 followed by ♘f4-h5, forcing catastrophic material losses.
18...♖d5 19.♕h6† ♔g8 20.♘f4+–

12.f5 e5

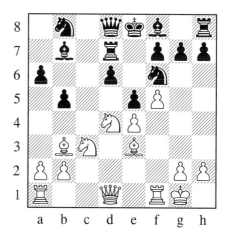

When Tal learned chess, the story goes that he was taught a Latvian variant where the knight was not allowed to move backwards! So often I wish that my students (but not my opponents) had learned this way as well so that they would not consider retreating moves like ♘c2, ♘e2, or ♘f3, when violently streaking forward would devastate.

13.♘e6! fxe6

Refusing the sacrifice is best, but allowing such an invasion to go unpunished cannot end well:
13...♕a5 14.♘xf8!

White destroys Black's castling privileges and obtains a commanding positional grip over the d5-square and the board.
14...♔xf8 15.♘d5 ♗xd5

15...♘xd5 16.♗xd5 ♗xd5 17.♕xd5± yields full domination.
16.♗xd5 ♖c7 17.a3 b4

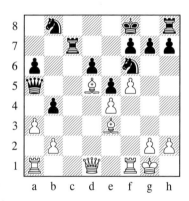

18.♗c4!

The rook has left its post at d7 and is reminded of its duties.
18...♔e7 19.♕b3±

And now with the king interfering, f7 creaks.

14.fxe6

White is down a full piece, but the career of the e6-pawn will be a memorable one. He will be eulogized more than any piece in the Black army, including the queen!

14...♖c7

A move such as 14...♖e7 begs for a speedy conclusion.

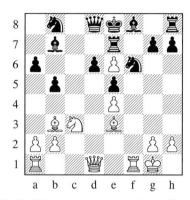

15.♖xf6! What a rush! 15...gxf6 16.♕h5† One star for the e6-pawn. 16...♖f7 17.♕xf7#

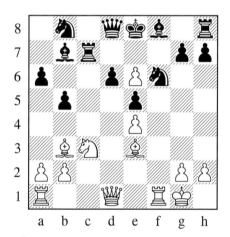

15.♗b6!

The exhausted, poor rook wishes he had stayed grounded on a8 many moons ago.

15...♗e7

15...♕c8 16.♖xf6!+– gxf6 17.♕h5† ♔d8 18.♖c1 ♗e7 19.♘d5 ♗xd5 20.♗xd5

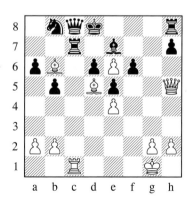

One of the harshest sights I have ever seen in chess!

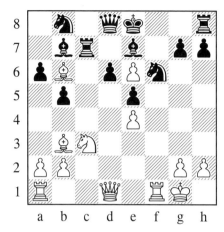

16.罝c1!

I found this novelty during an inspired blitz game in the Capablanca Chess Club in 2000, shortly after my game vs. Nakamura (shown next). My opponent was the dangerous Cuban master Rodelay Medina, winner of the high school national championship that year. Rodelay also loved the gambit, and we would take turns playing both colors in casual games and blitz tournaments throughout those years. Often he would take things to the extreme, playing 1.e4 c5 2.d4 cxd4 3.c3 dxc3 4.奧c4!? (The "Double" Morra Gambit, in the spirit of the Goring Gambit), and then begin his trash talk about how I better not take that second pawn. Naturally I would always indulge my greed.

White misfired with 16.冈d5? 奧xd5 17.exd5 in Weitzer – Lorenz, Germany 1995, when the desperado 17...罝c1! would have given Black the advantage.

16...0–0

Sacrificing the queen is Black's only chance: 16...罝xc3□ 17.奧xd8 罝xc1 18.彎xc1 夾xd8

18...奧xd8 19.彎g5 罝g8 20.e7! Another star for the e-pawn!

19.彎e3!±

However, White's queen is too powerful for Black's disjointed three minor pieces and staggering king. The e6-pawn again sows confusion in the enemy camp.

19...冈c6 20.罝c1 夾c7

20...冈d4 21.彎e1! and the queen has her way: 21...冈c6 22.奧d5+−

21.奧d5+−

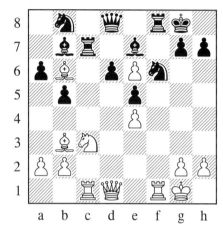

17.奧xc7!

Conventional chess thinking teaches to keep the pin at all costs while building up pressure, but it is the exceptional game which flouts such dogma successfully. If it were not for Rodelay's trash talk, I likely would not have had the fuel to find the refutation to the raw Chicago Defense in a blitz game. Although this combination came from a casual speed encounter played when I was just 16 years old, it still hails as one of my finest achievements in chess.

17...彎xc7 18.冈d5 彎d8 19.冈xe7†!

The monstrous knight gives itself up for Black's buried bishop. Why? To free the e-pawn, of course! There are clearly no hard and fast rules in chess.

19...彎xe7 20.罝c7!!

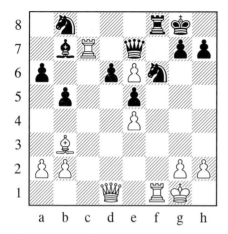

The point behind breaking all the rules – everything is sacrificed so that the e-pawn reaches Olympus.

20...♕xc7 21.e7† d5

21...♖f7 22.♖xf6!+– and the e-pawn threatens to promote to mate.

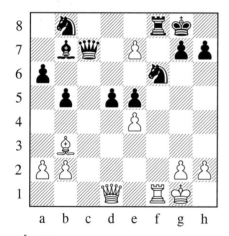

22.♗xd5†

Of course, since both the bishop and queen can work as diagonally checking pieces, this safer capture first is more prudent... Afterwards I explained to Vadim the history behind this scintillating sequence – such is the value of experience. Eight years previously, Esserman – Medina, Miami (blitz) 2000, had concluded: 22.♕xd5†?? At this point, Rodelay's creative verbal tirade off the board finally got the

better of me, and in my excitement I sacked the queen for glory – but quickly lost, never to hear the end of it. 22...♗xd5 23.♗xd5† ♖f7 24.♖xf6 ♕xe7 0–1

22...♗xd5 23.♕xd5†!

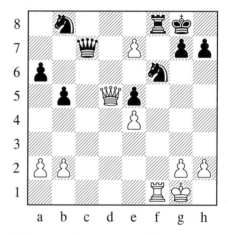

Only now the queen sacrifice, not too soon and not too late.

23...♖f7

23...♘xd5 24.exf8=♖# and the e-pawn taunts its frozen foe.

24.♕d8†

As promised, the e-pawn proved stronger than even the black queen! What a five-star career for the whirlwind foot soldier.

24...♕xd8 25.exd8=♕†
1–0

Marc Esserman – Hikaru Nakamura

US Masters, Chicago(!) 2000

1.e4 c5 2.d4 cxd4 3.c3 dxc3 4.♘xc3 e6 5.♘f3 a6 6.♗c4 d6 7.0–0 b5 8.♗b3 ♖a7 9.♗e3 ♖d7 10.♘d4 ♘f6 11.f4 e5!?

During the game and for many years afterwards, I remained critical of this move, but now I realize that it truly is the only way for Black to reach a semi-playable position. The bestial d4-knight must be driven away, even at the cost of extreme weakening of the light squares.

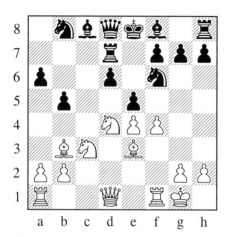

12.♘f3

Just a little earlier I scolded my students for moving their knights backwards during an attacking offensive. Well, there are exceptions to this rule as well! Here of course, a raid into the enemy camp would be premature.

12...♗e7?

Nakamura desperately wishes to castle, but the damage has already been done by 8...♖a7.

12...exf4!? 13.♗xf4 ♗e7 14.♘d4± is probably Black's best continuation as he survives the opening, albeit with a strategically lost game.

12...♘g4!? critically weakens the d5-square and may also allow the possibility of a double check after a subsequent ♗xf7†. For example: 13.♕d2 ♘xe3 14.♕xe3 ♘c6 15.♖ac1± ♗e7 16.fxe5 dxe5 17.♗xf7†+–

13.♗xf7†!+–

The bishop disrupts the rook's guard of f7, and the king is dragged out into the open field. The ruthless attacking sequence now scoops Black's king into the sky.

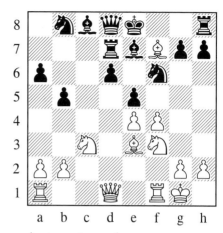

13...♔xf7 14.♘g5† ♔e8

Other king moves fare no better: 14...♔g8 15.fxe5 dxe5 16.♕b3†+– or 14...♔g6 15.f5† ♔h6 16.♘f7# or 14...♔f8 15.♘e6†+–.

15.♘e6

The knight yet again lands on e6 with devastating effect – this time it will roam freely, plundering all in its wake, with the key to the city of Chicago in tow. The masters have long theorized that a knight on the enemy sixth rank is worth at least a rook. This miniature only bolsters their claim.

15...♕a5

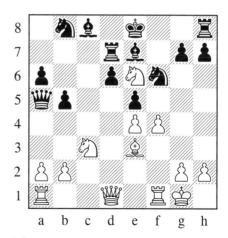

16.fxe5?!

I wanted to break open the f-file before grabbing on g7, but I did not realize that I could have done so afterwards:

16.♘xg7†!

Pulverizing. Black must duck and cover.

16...♔f8

16...♔f7 17.fxe5 will transpose.

16...♔d8 fails spectacularly to an Evans Gambit-like deflectionary tactic: 17.b4!

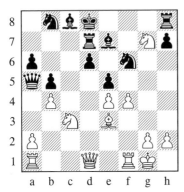

17...♕xb4 (After 17...♕a3 18.fxe5 dxe5 the rook finally gets a threat off, but unfortunately it remains pinned to the king! 19.♗b6#) 18.♘d5! ♘xd5 19.♘e6† The knight triumphantly returns to e6 to announce mate. 19...♔e8 20.♕h5#

17.fxe5

Another way to smash Black is 17.♘h5+–, stripping away the key defender so that the f1-rook can wreak havoc.

17...dxe5

17...♔xg7 18.exf6† ♗xf6 19.♕g4† ♔f7 20.♘d5 (20.♖xf6† also wins, as taking the rook leads directly to mate: 20...♔xf6 21.♖f1† ♔e7 22.♗g5† ♔e8 23.♕e6† ♖e7 24.♕xe7#) 20...♔e8 21.♕e6† ♗e7 22.♗g5+–

18.♕h5!

The key.

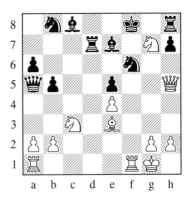

18...♔g8

18...♔xg7 19.♗h6† ♔g8 20.♖xf6!+– and Black falls into the funnel.

19.♕g5 ♔f7 20.♘f5

No lone king can endure such a queen and knight attacking tag team.

20...♕d8

20...♖g8 21.♘h6†+–

21.♘d5 ♖xd5 22.♕g7† ♔e8 23.♕xh8†+–

16...dxe5 17.♘xg7†

Now Black can run his king to d8, and the win becomes more elusive.

17...♔d8□

½–½

The battle ended in repetition, as I already had under 5 minutes, whereas Nakamura had well over an hour. From a very early age, the now super-GM Nakamura knew the importance of putting his opponents in time pressure, and here he once again reaped the rewards for this strategy. I still at that time would take an hour or more on a single move, especially in the rich positions arising from the Morra, when every nuance counts. When just starting out in gambit play, sometimes you must go into such deep meditations if you wish to achieve real attacking chances. Of course this quest for perfection would mar my early career with many such time pressure catastrophes, ruining would-be masterpieces. In this game, I simply did not feel confident that I could pull the win off with an hour disparity on the clock, but if I had known how famous my young opponent would become, maybe I would have pressed forward. And now to the two ways to win:

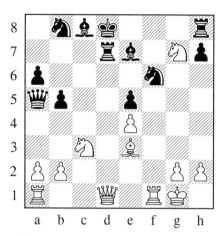

18.b4!+–

The flashier, more difficult shot. The most obvious strike is:

18.♘d5!

Nakamura quickly pointed this out after the game. As 18...♘xd5 again fails to mate in 2 (19.♘e6† and 20.♕h5#), and since ♗b6† wins the queen in many lines, Black is practically forced to give up the Chicago rook.

18...♖xd5 19.exd5

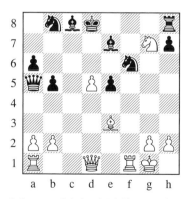

And the painful d5-d6 follows, when Black's position collapses. Glancing at the position now, the wins howl out – I see completely

open lines for all of the white pieces and an exposed black king. But 12 years ago, I did not have the same understanding of the initiative.

19...♘g4

19...♕c7 20.d6+–

19...♘e4 20.♘e6† ♗xe6 21.dxe6† ♘d6 22.♖c1 and White threatens b4+–, or even ♕d5-b7-c8! Black is paralyzed.

20.♘e6†+–

18...♗xb4□

18...♖xd1 19.♖axd1† and White wins prosaically; 18...♕xb4 19.♗b6#

19.♘e6†

Again the knight hops to and fro, flying through the turbulent air.

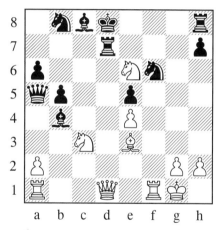

19...♔e8

19...♔e7 20.♕f3! and Black cannot stop the overloading on the f-file: 20...♘e8 21.♖ad1 Weaving the mating net by preventing flight to d6. The chase is on. 21...♖xd1 22.♕f7† ♔d6 23.♖xd1† ♔c6 24.♘d8†! Fittingly, the blustering winds land the knight on the black queen's original square, thus winning her majesty.

20.♘d5

The knight thumps in the center again and the hunt begins anew.

20.♕f3 lacks velocity as Black can respond with 20...♖f7.

20...♖xd5 21.exd5 ♗e7

The b4-diversion has done its damage.

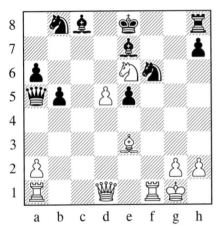

22.♖xf6 ♗xf6 23.♕h5† ♔d7 24.♕f7† ♗e7 25.d6

No mercy for the king. He should have castled many moves ago.

25...♔xd6　26.♖d1†　♔c6　27.♕f3†　e4 28.♕xe4#

Marc Esserman – Renard Anderson

World Open, King of Prussia 2007

1.e4 c5 2.d4 cxd4 3.c3 dxc3 4.♘xc3 e6 5.♘f3 a6 6.♗c4 d6 7.0–0 ♘c6

Now we will examine the Chicago Defense in its only stable form, when the knight comes to c6 first. As shown earlier, with the Chicago structure the white knight cannot be allowed to appear on d4 unopposed.

8.♕e2

The addition of ♕e2 and ...♘c6 in the variation clearly favors Black. But as Black has coolly refused to show his hand, White must continue with the standard plan of ♕e2 and ♖d1 until otherwise notified.

8...b5 9.♗b3 ♗e7 10.♖d1 ♖a7 11.♗e3

I could have taken advantage of Black's unorthodox move order with 11.e5!? here, but I didn't want to give the a7-rook life.

11...♖d7

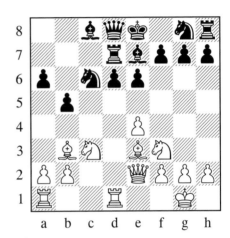

12.♘xb5!

In the next game we will investigate this outrageous idea in great detail. For now, here is a warm up.

12...axb5 13.♕xb5

White has only one pawn for the piece – has he simply lost his mind? For the cynical readers out there, the answer would be yes, because he's already playing the insane Morra Gambit. However, rest assured, the sacrifice not only has a strong positional basis, but is in fact entirely sound! If Black manages to give back some material to blunt the initiative, he still struggles in the endgames due to White's powerful connected queenside passed pawns. And of course, Black will be lucky if he can reach the endgame. The Chicago rook again comes under pressure, this time via the queenside diagonals pinning it to the black king. The mangled rook longs for home as it endures a pounding in the eye of the storm.

13...♗b7 14.♗a4! ♘f6 15.♘d4!

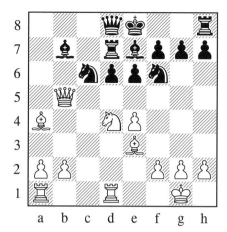

Increasing the volume to a crescendo pitch, and soon the glass will shatter. Here, as is often the case when faced with a shocking sacrifice, the defender does not keep a cool head and fails to put up maximum resistance. This is another psychological advantage you will possess when thrusting gambit play upon your opponents, if you can only manage to conjure up enough real threats. If not, you simply will be down a pawn and watch as they make a queen while scoffing at you.

15...♘e5?

Swapping knights is forced, but still fails to brighten Black's dark day:

15...♘xd4 16.♕xb7 ♘c2

16...e5 17.♗xd4 exd4 18.♖xd4 0–0 19.♗xd7 ♕xd7 20.♕xd7 ♘xd7 21.a4 White easily wins the favorable endgame embedded within the sacrifice.

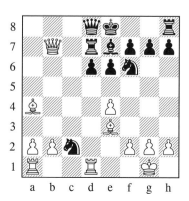

17.♖dc1! ♘xa1

17...0–0 18.♗xd7 ♘xa1 19.♗c6 ♘g4 20.♗b6 ♕b8 21.♗c7 ♕xb7 22.♗xb7± How picturesque! The bishops creatively prevent Black's rook from joining the queenside fight.

18.♗xd7† ♘xd7 19.♖c8 0–0 20.♖xd8 ♖xd8

Black possesses a rook and two knights for the queen. Unfortunately, the a1-knight is trapped and soon to be lost in the corner. Meanwhile, White's connected passed queenside pawns will roll as the queen escorts them to make new queens.

21.♕c7 ♗f6 22.b4+–

16.♕xb7

Anderson, a FIDE master, has simply hung a piece and the game ends. One cannot justly criticize unless one is actually in the arena, present for all its drama, feeling the pounding pressure move by move.

1–0

Theory

1.e4 c5 2.d4 cxd4 3.c3 dxc3 4.♘xc3 e6 5.♘f3 a6 6.♗c4 d6 7.0–0 ♘c6 8.♕e2 b5 9.♗b3 ♖a7

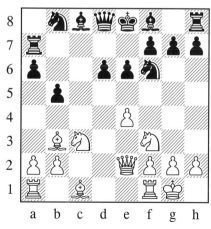

At last we are ready to pronounce the final verdict on the Chicago Defense. As usual, get ready for some dense analysis. For my less experienced readers, rest assured you are already armed with enough themes to successfully combat the Chicago Defense. However, if you dare, come along and find out where the truth really lies!

10.♗e3 ♖d7

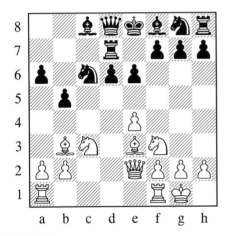

11.♖fd1!!

So far I have just been exposing all the flaws in the ambitious rook maneuver, but in all honesty, if White does not play with extreme precision, Black will get away with the exotic ...♖a7-d7. After all, if strong grandmasters have risked their hides in tournament play trusting the Chicago Defense, it has to have at least some merit. I will now show what can happen if White makes second-best moves:

11.♘d4?!

Logical enough, but too slow, as the gambiteer loses some power and time by exchanging knights.

11...♘xd4 12.♗xd4 ♘f6 13.f4 ♗b7 14.f5 e5 15.♗e3 ♗e7

Black is about to castle, with a pawn to spare. White has already gone wrong – only accurate play can save him.

16.a4

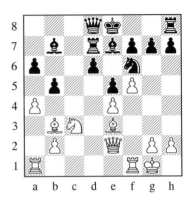

16...d5!

The d7-rook has gone unmolested, and now participates in the central battle.

17.axb5 axb5 18.exd5 b4 19.♘a4 0–0 20.♘c5 ♗xc5 21.♗xc5 ♖e8 22.♗a4 ♖xd5 23.♗xe8 ♖xc5 24.♗a4 ♕b6

Black stands better, with excellent play for the exchange. You can also view Dzindzichashvili's handling of the Black side of the Chicago Defense in the supplemental games to see what happens when White does not play with extreme energy.

11.♘xb5!?

You probably have already asked, why doesn't White just sacrifice on b5 and destroy Black's position, as in the previous game with Anderson? I also pondered this question at least 50 times (the minimum number of blitz games I played here at college with a friend of mine while avoiding schoolwork). I'm proud to say that I won every game (or maybe my memory is just playing tricks on me). As a result, my opponent, the talented mathematician and an ardent proponent of the "materialist" chess school, Danny Goodman, stopped believing in the Chicago Defense. Even better, he started to change his views on the nature of compensation in general! Perhaps other materialists reading will do the same...

11...axb5 12.♕xb5

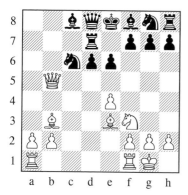

12...♘ge7!

But Danny only continued with 12...♗b7, often transposing back into the positions already analyzed in Esserman – Anderson above. Yet in 2007, against then 11 year-old Robert Perez (who is now 2400+), I discovered that this version of the knight sacrifice is premature due to 12...♘ge7. Note that ...♘ge7 was not available in the Anderson game as Black had already committed his bishop to e7, depriving the c6-knight of an extra defender. The downsides of ...♘ge7 (blocking in further kingside development) are outweighed by its strengths, as the following variations illustrate.

13.♗a4

13.♗b6? fails to win the queen due to 13...♖b7!.

13...♖b7 14.♕a6

14.♕c4 ♗d7! breaks the dangerous pin forever, leaving White a piece down.

14...♖c7 15.♕b5

This is at least equal for Black, so White must find some other way to fight for more. From here I somehow won in Esserman – R. Perez, Miami 2007, although I certainly passed through a losing position at one point before summoning some heavy swindling. Conveniently I have lost the game score!

Following the Perez game I had to accept the reality that the Chicago Defense was yet another serious attempt to refute the Morra Gambit.

After all, if White cannot quickly expose the Chicago rook, then Black, having solved the d-file pressure against his queen, will simply finish development and promote his extra pawn some 50 moves later! But only in the summer of 2008, when I decided to seriously review every main line of the Morra Gambit in the hope of unleashing its fury on top flight competition, did I realize how to exploit the dubious ...♖a7 once and for all. The solution – do nothing! Why, you may ask, does the most thematic move in the Morra Gambit, 11.♖fd1, merit two exclamations? The answer is most certainly not because it pressures the d-file, as Black has gone out of his way to fortify this sector of the board. No, 11.♖fd1 is not forcing – rather, it is simply a waiting move of the highest class. Its power stems from the fact that any logical Black developing move will now allow a ravaging attack impossible before, thus hurling the defender into a state of opening zugzwang. But Black must develop. He is compelled to move, or White will sweep him aside with ♖ac1.

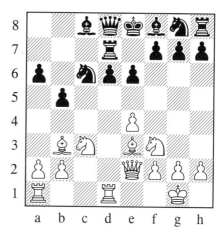

11...♗b7

We first consider the logical kingside developing moves 11...♘f6 and 11...♗e7, hoping to quickly castle. However, both of these defenses have the same drawback...

11...♘f6

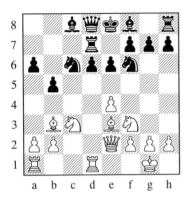

12.♘xb5!

The knight sacrifice reappears with a vengeance, as Black will no longer have the option of ...♘ge7 at his disposal to save the c6-knight as in Esserman – Perez. Ultimately, it is worth the tempo spent on ♖fd1 to deprive Black of this powerful defensive chance. Thus, 11.♖fd1 receives its first "!". The analysis below proves that White retains the better chances in the mayhem.

12...axb5 13.♕xb5 ♗b7 14.♗a4 ♕a8 15.♖ac1!

15.e5?! ♘e4! 16.♖ac1 ♘c5 17.♗xc5 dxc5 18.♖xd7 ♔xd7 19.♘g5 ♗e7! and Black can weather the storm.

15...♗e7

Play transposes to the continuation after 11...♗e7 below.

11...♗e7 12.♘xb5! axb5 13.♕xb5 ♗b7 14.♗a4 ♕a8

14...♘f6?! was seen in Esserman – Anderson: 15.♘d4!±

15.♖ac1

White should avoid 15.♘d4?! ♘b8! and Black somehow coordinates.

However, 15.e5!? could be considered.

15...♘f6

15...♔f8?!, trying to at least break the royal part of the pin, does not lead anywhere as Black remains hounded: 16.♗b6! ♘b8 17.e5! d5 (17...♗a6 18.♕a5! As one pin is removed, yet another appears. The threat of ♖c8 is now decisive. Such is the nature

of bad positions! 18...♕b7 19.exd6 ♗xd6 20.♗xd7 ♕xd7 21.♖xd6 ♕xd6 22.♗c5 Too many pins!) 18.♕b3 ♕a6 19.♗c7!+– Black's position is no paragon of coordination!

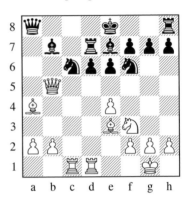

16.♕c4!

White is gearing up for the final blow on c6, but right before striking, wisely gets cold feet! This is the best way to fight for the advantage. White delays capturing on c6 for a move in order to harmonize his forces. Chaos lurks.

16.♖xc6!? 0–0! and Black morphs into the gambiteer. He now has excellent compensation in the form of the fully mobilized a8-b7 queen-bishop battery and the overextended white rook. Explore this turbulent variation at your own peril!

16...0–0!

a) 16...♘b8!? leads to mind-bendign complications. Will you be preferring the blue pill or the red pill?[27] 17.e5! ♘d5 (17...dxe5 18.♘xe5+– or 17...♗xf3? 18.exf6+–) 18.exd6 ♗xd6 (18...♗f6? 19.♘e5! and the d6-pawn sows the necessary confusion... 19...♗xe5 20.♕c8†! ♗xc8 21.♖xc8# A cyclone!) 19.♖xd5! exd5 (19...♗xd5 20.♕c8† ♔e7 21.♕xh8 ♕xa4 22.b3! ♕a6 23.♖c8! Black must forfeit his queen or get mated after the thumping ♗g5†!) 20.♕g4! White is down a rook for a pawn, but he will get back at least an exchange, and eyes the critical g7-pawn as well:

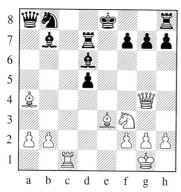

a1) 20...♗c6 21.♕xg7 ♖f8 22.♗b3± The gambiteer creeps closer. Not only does White objectively stand better, but playing Black is a practical disaster. I show one possible highlight. 22...♗a4 23.♘g5! ♗xb3 24.♘xh7 ♘c6 25.♗c5!+– Removing the guard on the f8-rook in an unusual manner. 25...♕b8 26.♗xd6 ♕xd6 27.♖xc6! Mayhem! 27...♕b4 28.♖c8† ♖d8 29.♕e5† ♕e7 30.♘f6#

a2) 20...g6 21.♗xd7† ♘xd7 22.♗d4 The pin evaporates but Black's king remains chained to the center. 22...♖f8 23.♕h4± Black braces for pain as White continues to reap a rapid return on his initial investment.

a3) 20...0–0 21.♗xd7± ♕xa2? 22.♗d4 f6 23.♕e6†+–

b) 16...d5!?

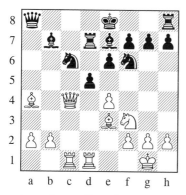

17.exd5 exd5 18.♕c2 ♘b8 Giving up the exchange rather than the whole piece is the lesser of the two evils. 19.♗xd7† ♘bxd7 20.♘d4 0–0 21.♘f5± ♖e8 22.♘xe7† ♖xe7

23.♗d4± White's strong rooks and overall centralized forces, along with his outside connected passed pawns, offer him all the winning chances. Black's minor pieces are a pitiful sight. 23...♕xa2 24.♕c7! White maintains the pressure.

17.♗xc6 ♗xc6

17...♖c7 18.♗xb7 ♖xc4 19.♗xa8 ♖xc1 20.♖xc1 ♖xa8 White would have a clear advantage here even after a calm move like 21.♖a1 (again the two connected outside passers), but he can immediately slice through. 21.e5! dxe5 22.♘xe5 ♖xa2 23.♖c8† ♗f8 24.g4! The pin on f8 decides. 24...♖a5 25.♘c6+–

18.♕xc6 ♕xc6

18...♕xa2 19.e5!+–

19.♖xc6 ♖b7 20.♖c2 ♘xe4 21.♘d4±

White once more can press for the win in this ending, fighting to mobilize his passed pawns.

11...♘a5?!

Apart from developing his other three minor pieces, this is Black's only logical move. The idea of ...♘c6-a5xb3 is a very common defensive motif in the Morra Gambit, and in hardly any cases should White allow his precious bishop to be lopped off. Here he has two very instructive possibilities.

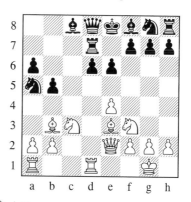

12.♘xb5!

12.♕c2!? ♘c4 (12...♘f6 13.♘xb5! axb5

14.♕xb5 ♗b7 15.♗b6 ♕c8 16.♖ac1±

13.b4! Temporarily giving Black the outpost, which White will soon strip away with a2-a4. As the strongpoint cannot be maintained, the knight seeks the nearest victim. 13...♘xe3 14.♕xe3 ♘f6 15.a4 The queenside is in tatters. 15...♗e7 (15...♖b7 16.axb5 axb5 17.e5+– The Chicago rook forgot its primary purpose – shielding the queen!) 16.axb5 axb5 17.♗d3 0-0! 18.e5 dxe5 19.♘xe5 ♖d6 20.♘xb5±

12...axb5

12...♘xb3 13.axb3 ♗b7 Black must calmly return the material to prolong the agony: 14.♘a7! ♘f6 15.b4 ♗e7 (15...♕a8 16.b5) 16.♘d4!± White roars to an advantage.

13.♕xb5 ♘xb3 14.axb3+–

Pins on the diagonals and back rank beckon!

14...♗b7

14...♘e7 15.♗b6 is a pitiful picture.

15.♗b6 ♕b8

15...♕f6 16.♖a7+–

16.♘e5! ♘f6 17.♘xd7 ♘xd7 18.♖dc1+–

12.♘g5!N

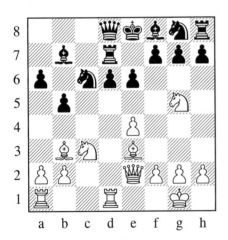

Once the bishop drifts to b7, the entire f7/ e6 complex is irreparably weakened. (It was already compromised with the rook on d7, but not soft enough for an immediate strike with 11.♘g5?! – the ambitious reader can confirm

why this is true.) Thus, the other purpose of 11.♖fd1 is revealed, earning it a second "!".

12...♘f6

12...h6 13.♘xe6±

13.f4!

If Black sits idly, White will bust through with f4-f5.

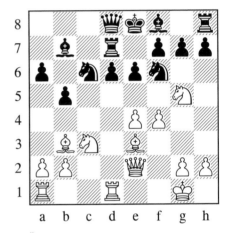

13...♘a5

But if Black forces the issue, White will strike on e6:

13...h6 14.♘xe6 fxe6 15.♗xe6!

We have already witnessed what havoc a knight on e6 can wreak. Now it is the Sozin (or Italian) bishop's time to shine.

15...♖e7 16.♗f5 ♔f7 17.a4!

This preliminary probing move is best, securing the advantage.

17.e5!? looks very tempting.

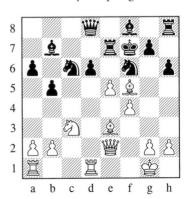

This would be shattering after 17...♕e8? 18.exf6 ♖xe3 19.♕h5† ♔g8 20.♗g6! with an f6-f7† cruncher next. But Black instead has the strong counter: 17...♘xe5! 18.fxe5 ♖xe5∞

17...♗c8

17...g6 18.axb5 axb5 (18...gxf5 19.bxc6 ♗c8 [19...♖xc6 20.♕c4†+−] 20.e5+−) 19.e5! ♘xe5 (19...gxf5 20.♖xd6 ♘d7 21.♖ad1 Although Black has two extra pieces, dark clouds are gathering. 21...♖h7 22.♘d5 ♖e8 23.e6†+−) 20.fxe5 ♖xe5 (20...gxf5 21.♖xd6+−) 21.♗c2† Black's king faces the hailstorm. Now 17.a4! seems even more prophetic as ♖a1-a7! swirls in the air. The gambiteer swarms from all sides! 21...♔g7 22.♖a7 ♖e7 23.♕d3 ♕e8 24.♗d4 Too many pins!

18.♗xc8 ♕xc8 19.axb5 axb5 20.♕xb5

The attack rages on.

20...♖c7 21.♖ac1±

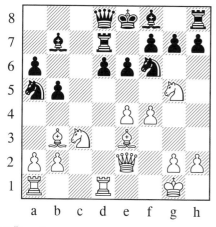

14.♘xe6!

14.♗xe6 is also playable, but it is the bishop's turn to slash on e6.

14...fxe6 15.♗xe6 ♖e7 16.f5

A bishop on e6 will never allow the black king to castle when nothing stands on d7 or f7, and in this case, nothing does! Black is simply choking with the bishop in such an advanced

position – he must remove the obstruction before losing all oxygen.

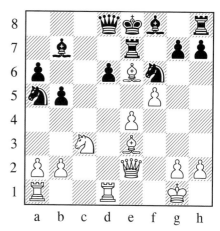

16...♖xe6

16...♗c8 17.e5+−

16...♘c4 17.♗d4 transposes to our main line after 17...♖xe6 18.fxe6.

17.fxe6

Unfortunately for Black, as one obstruction on e6 disappears, another appears.

Although not necessarily as powerful as a bishop, a "lowly" pawn on e6 has already proven its valor in the game Esserman – Martirosov.

17...♘c4 18.♗d4

If there are any Catalan fans out there still reading, please note that White continues to centralize and follow the teachings of Nimzowitsch even while playing the Morra Gambit. You need not fianchetto to play positionally!

18...♗e7 19.♘d5

For all Morra bashers, I must point out that White is by no means winning here yet, but on the other hand, Black is by no means drawing yet, either.

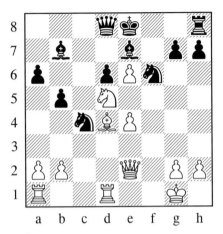

19...♘xd5?!

Best is to remove the steed with the now useless bishop, and finally castle: 19...♗xd5 20.exd5 0–0±

20.exd5 0–0

20...♘e5!? 21.a4±

21.a4!±

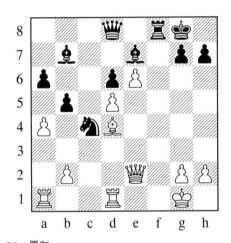

21...♖f5

After 21...♗xd5 22.axb5 axb5 23.b3 ♘e5 24.♗xe5 dxe5 White must be careful to take the right pawn with 25.♕xb5+–. It would all go horribly wrong after: 25.♕xe5? ♕b6†
26.♔h1 ♗xg2†! 27.♔xg2 ♕f2† 28.♔h1 ♕f3† 29.♔g1 ♖f6! My, how the wind blows! 30.♕b8† ♗f8–+

22.axb5 axb5 23.b3 ♘a5 24.♕g4

White now launches a decisive attack, again featuring that stormy foot soldier, the e6-pawn!

24...g6

24...♖g5 25.♕f3 ♗xd5 26.♕f7† ♔h8 27.♖xa5! ♖xg2† 28.♔f1+–

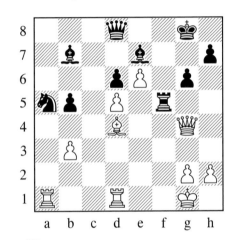

25.♖f1!

Stripping away the key defender. The gambiteer's tornado-like initiative has scattered Black's army across the field. At last, Black's king flies away into oblivion.

25...♖xf1†

25...♖xd5 26.♖f7+–

26.♖xf1 ♗xd5 27.♖f7+–

"Time to quit chess. Your Morra is drawing dead."
Hikaru Nakamura (2008)

Chapter 6

Slaying the Dragon

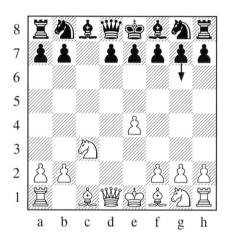

1.e4 c5 2.d4 cxd4 3.c3 dxc3 4.♘xc3

Strap on your armor as we ride off to battle the rare but dangerous Dragon variation of the Morra Gambit. If allowed to grow undisturbed in the early stages of development, a fully formed Dragon will light the board on fire. The Dragon's tail, in the shape of the d6-pawn, will flick any hope of a White e4-e5 advance aside. Meanwhile, the Dragon's head (the g7-bishop) will fly over the a1-h8 diagonal, patrolling key squares in the struggle for central supremacy. Black's king will then become firmly nestled inside the sinister Dragon's lair, and White's army will slowly burn in flames. A terrifying tale, and one that could give any Morra player a nightmare. Yet if you fall into such a position, this nightmare may become a painful reality (and don't say I didn't warn you!).

But do not despair – our history is filled with inspiring tales of a young knight slaying a menacing fire-breathing Dragon. To become the hero, you must ground the Dragon before it soars. In mainline Sicilian Dragon adventures, White lacks the developmental advantage to prevent the Dragon from hatching. Instead, he often unleashes the famous Yugoslav Attack, castling queenside and launching a prolonged assault on the h-file against the Dragon bishop. But castling long in the Morra (especially against the Dragon!) leads to ruin; the open c-file (not to mention the Dragon bishop spitting fire from afar!) makes the c1-square a scorching hot home for a king. Instead, the gambiteer must use his superiority in the early phase of the fight to clip the Dragon's wings. After the black moves ...♞c6, ...g6 and ...♝g7, the aspiring hero thrusts e4-e5!, sacrificing a second pawn and preventing the Dragon's tail from inflicting a serious case of whiplash.

If Black removes the e5-thorn, the Dragon loses his head (the g7-bishop).

If the Dragonmaster insists on preventing e4-e5 with the move order ...♞c6, ...d6, and ...g6,

then he is caught with his tail in between his legs after 7.♕b3!.

After the obligatory 7...e6, the Dragon structure loses its shape – both the d6-tail and the entire kingside dark-squared complex creak, ensuring that the only fires burning in this fairy tale will be those ravaging the black king's palace.

JJRambo (Esserman) – emcf (GM Cordova)

Internet (blitz) 2008

Before moving on to the critical variations, we will first observe why the Dragon's tail (d6) is so vital to forming a robust fianchetto structure against the Morra Gambit (or any other opening). In the following miniature my opponent forgets which central pawn creates a shapely Dragon and pays dearly. I could dismiss this debacle as the product of a mere Internet mouse-slip, but it has occurred several times in my practice! Nevertheless, Black's instructive "fingerfehler" highlights the dangers of mixing systems.

1.e4 c5 2.d4 cxd4 3.c3 dxc3 4.♞xc3 g6 5.♞f3 ♝g7 6.♝c4 e6?

Time after time I have lectured my students on the dangers of playing ...e6 after fianchettoing in a Sicilian! Here Black voluntarily uncorks a move that White would spend a whole tempo to force after 6...d6 7.♛b3!. Perhaps after seeing this game they will learn once and for all!

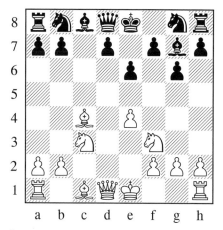

7.♘b5!+–

No Dragon's tail will be forming in this epic. The valiant white knight rides into d6, grazing on the very square that could have harbored a Dragon's tail. Black is already wasted.

7...♘e7

Resigning to fate. Consistently following up with 7...d5 may be Black's best practical hope in a blitz battle, but it still gets bludgeoned: 8.exd5 (or 8.♗f4!?) 8...a6

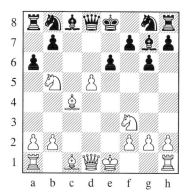

9.dxe6! axb5 10.exf7† The variations resemble checkers, not chess.

8.♘d6† ♚f8 9.♘g5!

Victory day for the white knights.

9...f6 10.♘gf7 ♛a5† 11.♗d2 ♛c5 12.♖c1

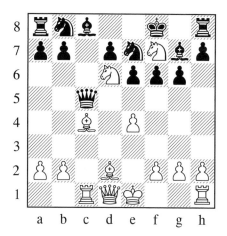

The Morra rook bursts onto the field, and the struggle ends abruptly with Black's resignation. The e7-pawn should have a "Hazardous – Touch with caution!" sign attached to its forehead in the Dragon.
1–0

Black defers taking the e-pawn

1.e4 c5 2.d4 cxd4 3.c3 dxc3 4.♘xc3 ♘c6 5.♘f3 g6 6.♗c4 ♗g7 7.e5!

The Dragon variation's main line against the Morra Gambit. The gambiteer's 7.e5 effectively snips the Dragon's tail, thus wreaking havoc in the Black camp. The defender must make a choice, to grab or not to grab, and in this case he prolongs the decision for a move. The consequences of capturing immediately will be covered in the theoretical section.

7.0–0 lacks vigor and allows Black to mold the Dragon's tail after 7...d6.

Note that 7.♛b3, hoping to force ...e6, fails due to the typical open-game trick: 7...♘a5! 8.♗xf7† ♚f8 9.♛d5 ♘f6 and the bishop falls.

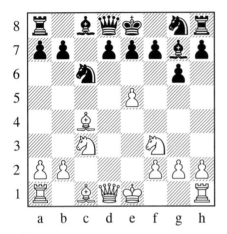

7...♕a5?!

Unwise! When facing a gambit there is no time to lose. Bringing one's queen out early on dubious expeditions is a sure way to become dethroned. Listen closely as King Richard II mutters his ageless advice in Shakespeare's epic tragedy: "I have wasted time, and now time doth waste me."[28]

As the game continuation will show, Black must grab immediately. For now we just note that after 7...♘xe5 8.♘xe5 ♗xe5 9.♗xf7† ♔xf7 10.♕d5† the Dragon's body flounders without a head. If Black tempts fate by rushing his king to the bishop's aid, then he is reminded that kings should not get too adventurous when enemy queens lurk nearby: 10...♔f6 11.♘e4† ♔f5

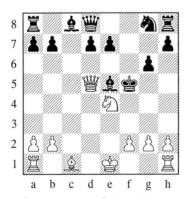

12.g4† ♔xg4 13.♖g1† ♔f5 14.♖g5# The black king should have stayed in his cave. Remember this mating sequence![29]

8.0–0!

White cannot be troubled to defend the brave foot soldier on e5. Upon crossing the Rubicon, the pawn knew he was passing the point of no return.

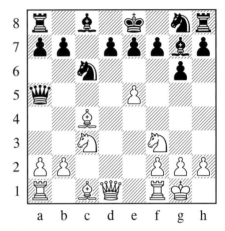

8...♘xe5?!

After Black's indecisive queen sortie, he should admit the error in his ways and keep the game closed at all costs.

8...♘h6□

The only other feasible defense. Observe now how the e5-pawn creates confusion and cacophony in Black's position.

9.♖e1

Just in case Black has any further fantasies of grabbing on e5, White's rook reminds him of reality.

9...0–0 10.♗f4±

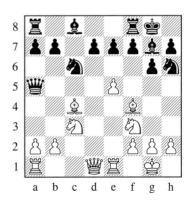

The e5-pawn is now firmly entrenched and unassailable. Sadly the Dragon will never grow a tail, hence Black's queenside must sleep for eternity. But in the present, White aims to win the runt on h6.

10...♔h8

10...♘f5 11.g4 ♘h6 12.h3 only hastens the end. 10...♘g4 11.♕e2 d6 is another pitiful attempt which results in even more carnage: 12.exd6 exd6 13.♗xd6 ♖d8

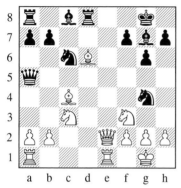

14.♕e8†! ♖xe8 15.♖xe8† ♗f8 16.♖xf8† ♔g7 17.♖xf7† ♔h6 18.♗f8† ♔h5 19.♖xh7† ♘h6 20.♖xh6† ♔g4 21.♖xg6†+– The white rook gorges upon the enemy!

11.♕d2 ♘g4 12.♗b5!

Cutting off the queen from her army ensures that chaos engulfs the board.

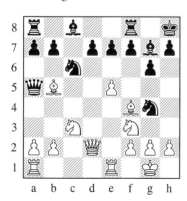

12...a6

12...f6 is a futile half-measure to free the wayward knight. Black must surely regret not taking that pawn when he had the chance. 13.exf6 ♘xf6 14.♗xc6 dxc6 15.♖xe7 The execution will be swift and painless. 15...♗f5 16.♗h6 The Dragon bishop never got to fly in this fairy tale. 16...♖g8 17.♘g5+–

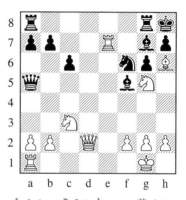

17...♗xh6 18.♘f7† ♔g7 19.♕xh6#

The king is slain where the Dragon bishop once roamed.

13.♗xc6 dxc6 14.h3

The runt finally goes.

14...g5

A last gasp...

15.♗xg5 ♘xe5 16.♘xe5 ♗xe5 17.♗xe7 ♖e8 18.♕h6

Flashier than the prosaic 18.♗f6†+–.

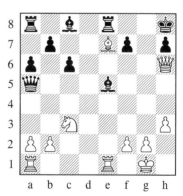

White's threats include ♖xe5, while 18...♖xe7 19.♕f8# would mock the snoring Black queenside.

9.♘xe5 ♗xe5

9...♕xe5 offers no salvation: 10.♖e1 ♕h5 11.♕b3± Black must now budge the e-pawn despite its "Touch with caution!" sign and hope for the best. But as we know, hoping is not a sound chess strategy.

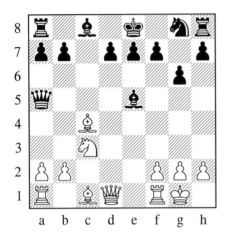

10.♘b5!±

This position has occurred three times in actual tournament practice, and shockingly Black won twice – but he should have been mercilessly smashed every time! White's steed cuts the queen from the action, rendering her fine post useless. Threats on f7 now swirl about.[30]

10...♘f6

10...a6 11.♕d5! axb5 12.♕xf7† ♔d8 13.♕f8† ♔c7 14.♗xg8

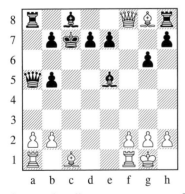

A white rook will soon pay a not-so-friendly visit to the wayward black king.

10...e6

We have seen ...e6 fail Black twice so far, but will a third time be the charm?

11.♖e1! ♗b8

11...f6

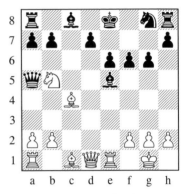

12.♖xe5! No, I'm afraid not. 12...fxe5 13.♘d6† As the knight dominates on d6, White has a number of elegant wins. I will just display a couple. 13...♔d8 14.♗xe6 (Or 14.♗g5† ♘e7 15.♕f3 ♕c5 16.♖d1+– and e7 will fall. Too many wins is a pleasant problem!) 14...♘e7 (On 14...dxe6 15.♘xb7† the knight takes a joyride.) 15.♘xc8† ♔xe6 16.♕d6† ♔f7 17.♕xd7† ♔f6 18.♗d2 ♕a6 19.h4+– By this stage almost any logical move wins.

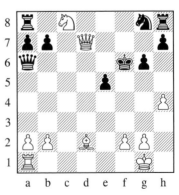

19...h6 20.g4 g5 21.♕f5† ♔g7 22.♖c1 Say goodnight!

12.b4!

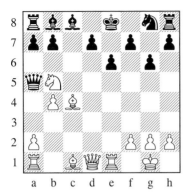

The swashbuckling 19th century seafaring Captain Evans, inventor of the famed Evans gambit, would be proud!

12...♕d8

12...♕xb4 13.♗a3 ♕xc4 14.♘d6† (or 14.♖c1+–) 14...♗xd6 15.♕xd6+–

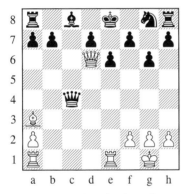

Certainly not the fire-breathing tale of dark-squared domination that Black had imagined upon trumpeting the Dragon!

13.♗b2 f6 14.♖c1

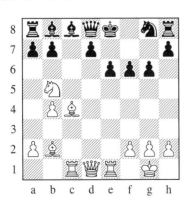

Yet another case where all of White's pieces are ready to strike, whereas Black's – well, they speak for themselves. Whenever you get one of these positions, I recommend taking out your camera for a snapshot. It's the perfect time for a picture, that is if they still allow cameras in chess tournaments. If not, just wait until you get home and set up the photo op yourself.

14...a6 15.♘d6† ♗xd6 16.♕xd6

The dark squares emit foul odors.

16...♕e7 17.♕c7 ♕d8

Tactics will always flow when such glaring developmental inequalities exist.

18.♖xe6† dxe6 19.♕g7!+–

11.♖e1 ♗b8

11...d6 12.f4 (12.♘xd6†?? ♗xd6 13.♕xd6 ♕xe1† would be embarrassing... Safety before brilliance?!) 12...♘g4 13.fxe5 ♕b6† 14.♕d4 ♕xd4† 15.♘xd4 ♘xe5 16.♗b3+– Black has three pawns for the piece but White possesses the two bishops and a massive lead in development.

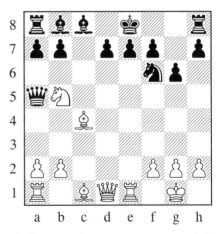

Black crouches in extreme defensive formation, yet the two wins for Black in this line both resulted from this position. Perhaps the bishops nestled side by side on the back rank next to their entombed comrade put the disgraced gambiteers (who fell off their horses with 12.♗h6) under a spell? How else could White lose such a position? Well, I've botched better.

12.♖xe7†!!

A gorgeous blow, pleasing the masters of the old guard.

12.♗h6 is a reasonable move, but too soft, under the circumstances...

12.♗d2 is a stronger option for the bishop, heading to b4 for the finishing blow. But this pales in comparison to the sparkling text.

12...♔xe7

Refusing the rook also leads the king to doom.

13.♕e2† ♔f8

13...♔d8 14.♗g5 ♕b6 15.♖e1 and mate on e7 is unstoppable.

14.♗h6† ♔g8 15.♕e7+−

Black's extra rook cannot silence the king's shouts. Another more sadistic way to win is: 15.♕f3! ♗e5 (15...♕b6 16.♖e1 threatens the decisive blow ♕xf6 followed by ♖e8#.) 16.♘d6!

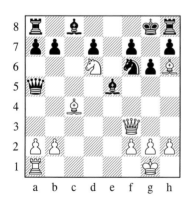

Here the computer gives the comical 16...♕xa2 to defend against mate on f7. Very creative indeed, but some creatures just don't know when to cry for mercy.

Black plays an early ...d6

Before flying into the analytical fire after 7.e5!, we first handle those stubborn souls who insist on flapping the Dragon's tail at all costs.

1.e4 c5 2.d4 cxd4 3.c3 dxc3 4.♘xc3 g6 5.♘f3 ♘c6

5...♗g7 6.♗c4 d6?

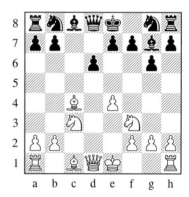

This highly popular move order is simply unplayable. After 7.♕b3! the Dragon's tail will be sliced off. 7...e6 This move again! 8.♗f4! ♘c6 9.♖d1± ♗f8?! The Dragonmaster wails that he won't be mating a queenside-castled white king (as in the Yugoslav attack) anytime soon. 10.♘b5+− Black would need two Dragon bishops to save the d6-pawn now. Unfortunately, this is not bughouse.

6.♗c4 d6

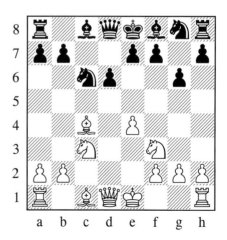

7.♕b3!

Almost all players reaching this position have castled here, including Adams against Nunn in a 1992 blitz game. However, this hackneyed move allows the Dragon to soar high above the sky, and must be harshly rebuked. 7.0–0?! is a byproduct of the routine thinking that plagues amateur gambiteers. Their desire to insipidly continue with 0–0, ♕e2 and ♖d1 has allowed a move like 7.0–0 to propagate more than 70 times here, whereas the creative 7.♕b3 appears only twice in the database.

7...e6

At least Black's bishop is now firmly committed to the d6-tail, but we must ask – why then play ...g6? So that the Dragonmaster could only dream of growing a head on g7?

7...♘h6 fails to 8.♗xh6, after which White regains the pawn with the advantage.

8.♗f4 a6
8...♘a5 9.♗b5† ♗d7

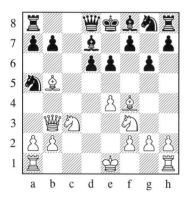

10.♕c2!

10.♕d1!? deserves attention, snipping away even further at the tail: 10...a6 11.♗xd7† ♕xd7 12.♕d4 f6 But after this ugly computer move, Black surprisingly lives. The machine does not know that the Dragon has a head or a tail, and just spits out the wretched but effective ...f6. (12...e5? 13.♘xe5! ♗g7 14.0–0–0±) 13.♖d1∞

10...♗xb5

10...♖c8 11.♗xd7† ♕xd7 12.♖d1± tortures the tail for many moves to come.
11.♘xb5 ♖c8 12.♕a4 ♘c6 13.♖d1±

All is not well in Dragonville!

9.♗e2!

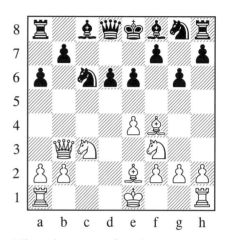

White has time for this unique retreat because the ♗c4/♕b3 raid has created long-lasting structural damage. The Dragon's awe-inspiring features are now no more. Once, I had this position against Fritz 11 in a 3-minute blitz game. As poor Fritz rehashed its opening-book moves, I began to suspect that the programmer may have a fetish for Dragons. I soon built up a decisive advantage in under 15 moves, only to blow the win and flag. Sounds familiar? Although I missed a breathtaking combination, I still cannot remember the game. Which leads me my next question – if a computer falls in a forest and should have broken in half, but nobody witnessed the moment when it should have broken, did it really fall?

9...♘f6

9...♗e7 10.♖d1 and Black cannot finish his development due to the e4-e5 break. If 10...♕c7 to relieve the pin, then 11.♕a3! conveniently redirects the queen.

10.罝d1 ♘h5

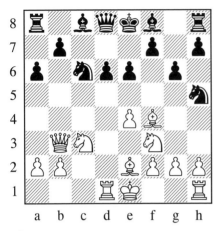

11.♗xd6!

The tail is cut off once and for all.

11.♗e3!? b5 12.e5 d5 13.g4 ♘g7 A pitiful head for a Dragon! The position creeps closer to my battle in the forest with Fritz, but not quite – all I can I recall is a shackled horse on g7. 14.♘e4 ♗e7 Optically Black looks lost, but a chess game is not always a beauty contest.

11...♗xd6 12.e5 ♘xe5

The Dragonmaster makes sure he doesn't also lose his head.

13.♘xe5 ♕c7 14.♘c4 ♗e7 15.♘b6

White's binding knight on b6 buries the black queenside (as is often the case when a knight plops on b6 in the Morra Gambit).

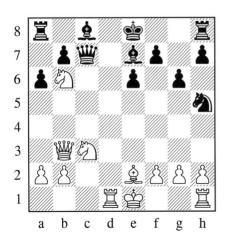

15...罝b8 16.♗xh5 gxh5 17.0–0±

Black has a "spoiled haircut" on h5 (as my old trainer GM Lein used to say), and the c8-bishop can't even move. If 17...e5 to free the imprisoned bishop, then 18.♘cd5 becomes a two knights tango.

Dragon Theory – 7.e5!

At last we will take a deeper look at the 7.e5! second pawn sacrifice. For my less experienced readers, you may still be able to follow along in this theoretical section as the analysis is not quite as dense as in the other advanced sections of the book.

1.e4 c5 2.d4 cxd4 3.c3 dxc3 4.♘xc3 ♘c6 5.♘f3 g6 6.♗c4

For the real swashbuckler who cares more for a rush than objectivity, I recommend you give 6.h4!?!? a shot.[31] I've never believed it, but also never refuted this "coffeehouse" move either. As you'll see below, it contains serious venom.

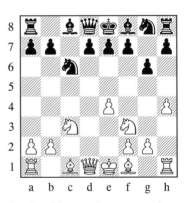

Black should simply ignore the advance and play 6...♘f6. But if instead he gets cautious, he can pay the price: 6...h5?! 7.♗c4 ♗g7 8.♕b3 ♘a5 9.♗xf7† ♔f8 10.♕d5 ♘f6 11.♕d3! White can now sacrifice the bishop with authority, for the inclusion of the moves h4/h5 have softened the g6-square. 11...♔xf7 12.♘g5† ♔g8 (12...♔e8 13.e5+– is crushing, while 12...♔f8 13.♘e6† nets the queen) 13.e5

White's attack is well worth a piece. So 6.h4!? is good for a few thrills and cheap laughs, and just maybe an occasional point.

6...♗g7 7.e5!

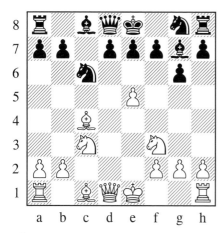

7...♘xe5

Before we analyze the exciting double pawn sacrifice in more depth, I must first discuss Black's only acceptable way to decline the offering:

7...♘h6!?

Other Morra manuals consider Black's chances after this move to be roughly equal,[32] and while I tacitly agree, the gambiteer can still fight for the advantage.

8.0–0 0–0 9.♗f4

Not 9.♖e1, which insipidly allows mass liquidation: 9...d6 10.exd6 ♕xd6 11.♕xd6 exd6 12.♗f4 The gambiteer wins back the pawn, but the position becomes sterile.

9...d6

In the 7...♘h6 variation, Black should not aim to keep the pawn, but instead he must strive to return the material and immediately equalize. This is a difficult concept for the defender to grasp when facing Morra mayhem, since 1.e4 c5! 2.d4 cxd4 3.c3? already drops a pawn in their minds.

10.exd6 exd6

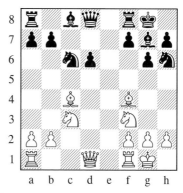

11.♕d2!

While Black may be able to equalize here, White does not ease his burden by resolving the tension on d6 with 11.♗xd6 ♖e8=.

11...♘f5 12.♖ad1

The gambiteer has done everything to inject life into the position and now waits for a misstep.

12...♖e8?

This natural move is resolutely punished, proving that while the scientists in the white coats may say "equal", the gladiators may feel differently in the Colosseum.

Even worse is: 12...♕f6?? 13.♗g5+–

More sensible is 12...♘a5, though 13.♗d5± retains binding energy.

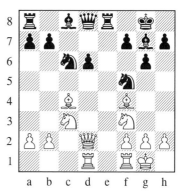

13.♗xf7†! ♔xf7 14.♘g5† ♔f8 15.♕d5 ♖e7 16.♘xh7† ♔e8 17.♖fe1±

And the Dragonmaster's dream of equalizing collapses.

7...♗xe5!?

A rare, tricky move order with independent significance. White cannot lop off the Dragon's head yet as ...♘xe5 will guard f7, so first he sacrifices.

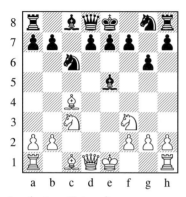

8.♗xf7† ♔xf7 9.♕d5† ♔g7

9...e6? I do not need to repeat myself on the virtues of ...e6 in the Dragon. 10.♘xe5† ♔g7 11.♘xc6! bxc6 12.♕e5† ♕f6 (12...♘f6 13.♘e4 d5

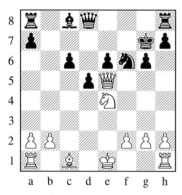

14.♗h6†! ♔xh6 15.♘xf6 The threat of 16.♘g4# silences.) 13.♗f4 ♕xe5† 14.♗xe5† ♘f6 15.♘e4 The pawn's best move here is from e6 to e7, which is illegal.

10.♘xe5

Now 10...♘xe5 transposes to the main continuation below, but Black can create novel positions with the counter-intuitive queen moves to e8 or f8.

10...♕f8!?

10...♕e8!? 11.♘xc6 bxc6 White voluntarily fixes Black's pawn formation and gives him a greater stake in the center. But the gambiteer hopes that his dark-squared domination and centralized queen on d4 will win the day. 12.♕d4† ♘f6 (12...e5?! Please leave the e-pawn in peace! 13.♕d6 ♕e7 14.♘e4±) 13.0–0! ♕f7 14.♘e4→ Black's attempt to liquidate now fails. 14...♕d5 15.♕c3!

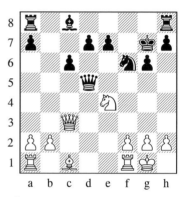

15...♕xe4 16.♖e1± And as the e7-pawn goes, so does the Dragon structure.

11.0–0 ♘f6 12.♕b5 a6 13.♕e2 ♘xe5 14.♕xe5

This has also roughly transposed to the main continuation, except with an awkward queen on f8.

8.♘xe5

Now we will reach the critical position of the Dragon structure against the Morra.

8...♗xe5

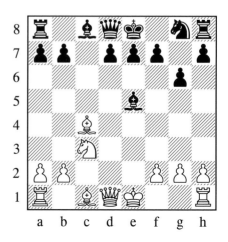

9.♗xf7†!

9.♕d5?! fails to 9...♗xc3† 10.bxc3 e6 11.♕d6 and Black's extra material outweighs his odorous dark squares and lagging development. Of course the Dragonmaster has the advantage here, but the reckless gambiteer can still try to make him crack under pressure.

9...♔xf7 10.♕d5† ♔g7

10...e6? I'm tired of having to give ...e6 a question mark. I'm sure you are too. 11.♕xe5 ♕f6 (11...♘f6 12.♘b5±) 12.♕c7!

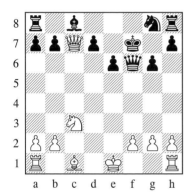

With an analogous, yet more severe dark-squared bind than in the ♕c7-line of the Open Sicilian's Lowenthal variation.

11.♕xe5† ♘f6

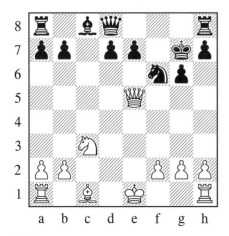

12.0–0

We arrive at the critical position of the Morra-Dragon. While Black retains his extra pawn and possesses two center pawns to boot, the gambiteer must not despair! After all, a headless Dragon cannot fly. Therefore, White should coolly seek long-term positional pressure against the mangled Dragon.

12...d6

I first reached this position in a Miami rapid event in 2007. My opponent, a 1200-rated amateur, informed me in the post mortem that he spawned the Dragon because, as a former Morra gambiteer, the ...g6 lines terribly vexed him. Never trust ratings! And the "3200+" machine also marginally prefers Black – never trust ratings!

Well, in the 2007 playchess.com freestyle event, where humans with computer assistance face off against each other and to the victor goes the spoils, a tense struggle after 13.♕g3!? ended in peace in Supermichi – Granja Velha (see page 320). 13.♕e3!?, aiming for the h6-square, is Rybka's other idea.

13.♕e2!N

My over-the-board inspiration against the "1200" in the game mentioned above. I now deftly control some light squares, while still enabling my dark-squared bishop to develop harmoniously (compare 13.♕e2 to the hindering 13.♕e3). During a bishop of opposite color battle, the masters muse that fortune generally favors the attacker. In the fight to dominate a weakened square color complex, the aggressor has an extra attacking piece at his disposal, while the defender's extra piece stands by idly. And the old adage could not apply more here. The gambiteer ravages on the dark squares, whereas the Dragonmaster drifts listlessly, unable to generate counterplay against White's pristine position. Meanwhile, the gambiteer will entrench his rooks on d1 and e1, where they will act as heavy weights, pressing down on Black's central hanging pawns. A computer programmer would rack his brains trying to quantify such rich strategic ideas into a rigid numerical algorithm.[33]

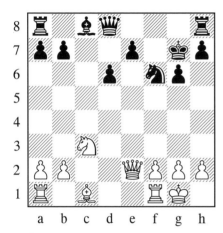

13...♗f5

13...♖e8 14.♗g5! and White's positional pressure begins to wear on the headless Dragon.

14.♗e3

14.♖e1?! is a shade inaccurate, as White needs the queen's rook to be available to press against the d5-square. 14...e5! 15.♗e3 (15.♗g5? h6 16.♗h4 g5! 17.♗g3∓ and Black dramatically turns the tables in the bishop of opposite color battle. White's bishop is a sight for sore eyes.) 15...d5 16.♗g5 d4 17.f4! This thrust still leads to chaos.

14...♖e8

14...e5? Here Black's central pawn mass fails to mobilize in time, as the white queen's rook arrives punctually: 15.♖ad1 d5 16.♗g5!±

15.♖fe1 ♖c8

The gambiteer's centrally charged rooks lie in wait to ambush a premature pawn advance: 15...e5? 16.♖ad1 d5 17.♗g5 d4 18.♕b5! The queen patrols the light squares while the rooks and minor pieces do the rest. The virtues of 13.♕e2! are further illustrated by this

variation. 18...♕d7 19.♗xf6† ♔xf6 20.♘d5† ♔g7 21.♕xd7† ♗xd7 22.♘c7±

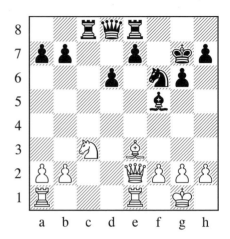

16.♖ad1!

White continues with his simple yet effective plan. Only now does the computer begin to appreciate that Black has no constructive way to improve his position.

16.♗xa7? à la Spassky – Fischer, Reykjavik (1) 1972, when Fischer voluntarily trapped his own bishop, cannot be recommended here: 16...b6 17.♕b5 ♘d7∓

16...♘g4

16...b6 17.♕d2!?± with h2-h3 to follow.

17.♗xa7!

Now the pawn is ripe for the plucking, as ...b6 and ...♘d7 are no longer in the air.

17...♕a5

17...b6 18.♕b5!±

18.h3! ♕xa7 19.hxg4 ♗d7 20.♘d5!

White's centralization is an impressive sight.

20...e6

Oh no! The "Touch at your own risk!" e7-pawn shakes at last.

21.♘c3 ♕b6 22.g5!±

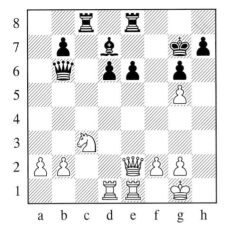

The g-pawn nears the headless Dragon formation. Soon, White's queen and knight will put the lonely black king out of his misery. A glorious image, fittingly concluding our "Morra Gambit Dragon" chronicles.

Fischer's famous miniature against Reshevsky in the Accelerated Dragon neatly summarizes the themes we have just covered in the Morra-Dragon. You will be amazed how Fischer's Open Sicilian masterpiece relates, from the e5(!)-wedge which clips the Dragon's tail, to the sacrifice on f7, even right down to the very mating sequence!

Robert Fischer – Samuel Reshevsky

USA (ch), New York 1958

1.e4 c5 2.♘f3 ♘c6 3.d4 cxd4 4.♘xd4 g6 5.♘c3 ♗g7 6.♗e3 ♘f6 7.♗c4 0-0 8.♗b3 ♘a5?

Reshevsky's greatest strength was his strategic vision. His greatest weakness – his opening preparation. Here, instead of erecting the Dragon's tail with d6, he embarks on an ill-advised hunt for the "Fischer-Sozin" bishop. Always the consummate researcher, the young Fischer already knew the refutation before the game.

9.e5!

Look familiar?

9...♘e8?

Black's only option is to complete the plan he started, even at the expense of the Dragon's head. Of course, White retains a clear advantage. 9...♘xb3☐ 10.exf6 ♘xa1 11.fxg7±

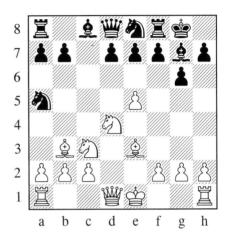

Take a moment to find the decisive blow.

10.♗xf7†!

"Slaying the Dragon" in an Open Sicilian!

10...♔xf7

10...♖xf7 11.♘e6! wins the queen with the same tactic featured after 6.h4!? in the theoretical section!

11.♘e6!

And here Reshevsky should have resigned; but he understandably played on after 11...dxe6 12.♕xd8 for 30 more moves in a hopeless position to avoid losing to the young genius in a mere 11 moves!

The thematic conclusion would have been:

11...♔xe6 12.♕d5†! ♔f5 13.g4†! ♔xg4 14.♖g1† ♔f5

14...♔h3 15.♕g2† ♔h4 16.♕g4#

15.♖g5#

The very same mate can be found on page 142!

"Let me know when you want to learn some real theory."
– Grandmaster Loek van Wely

Chapter 7

The Professional's Choice – ♘ge[00]7

1.e4 c5 2.d4 cxd4 3.c3 dxc3 4.♘xc3 ♘c6 5.♘f3 e6 6.♗c4

For truly passionate players, chess is more than just a mere game. When facing off against the top professionals in the world, chess can have all the intrigue of an international spy thriller. Famous James Bond novelist Ian Fleming certainly thought so when he conjured up super Grandmaster Kronsteen as the chief architect behind the evil organization "SPECTRE" in "From Russia with Love". During the book's film adaptation, the producers even went so far as to feature Kronsteen executing Spassky's finishing combination vs. Bronstein from their legendary 1961 King's Gambit encounter on center stage. Leave it to a Bond film to get things right, for when grandmasters and gambits collide, the already charged atmosphere becomes positively... electrifying.

On ...♘ge7,

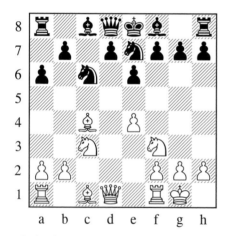

Black plans to mercilessly refute the gambit via a quick ...♘g6, ...♗e7, and castles. With White's e4-e5 shots now misfiring and his d-file targets eliminated, the scheming defender then aims for rapid queenside expansion (...b5/...♗b7/...♖c8/...♘a5), at which point his goal of global chessboard domination would be complete. The gambiteer must throw a wrench with ♗c1-g5!, temporarily halting Black's machinations, but after ...f6 or ...h6,

breaking the pin, the plan is once again set in motion. Naturally, such an aspiring vision has attracted some of the game's top assassins – Kamsky, Nakamura, Gashimov, Shabalov, Van Wely, and even Kasparov, to name a few. Therefore ...♘ge7 is, without a doubt, the professional's choice.

When probed "You are sure this plan is foolproof?", Kronsteen coldly responds, just like his confident grandmaster colleagues must say to themselves after ...♘ge7: "Yes it is, because I have anticipated every possible variation of... countermove."[34] But after a bloody fight, at story's end, regardless of the outcome, the audience will erupt after the iconic line: "The name's Gambit, Morra Gambit."

***Warning! The following spy movies are highly recommended for a greater appreciation of the moves to come.

James Bond:
Goldfinger (1964)
GoldenEye (1995)
Tomorrow Never Dies (1997)
The World is Not Enough (1999)
Die Another Day (2002)
Casino Royale (2006)
Quantum of Solace (2008)

Other:
Austin Powers: International Man of Mystery (1997)

WhYsOSeRiOus – Smallville (Nakamura)

Internet (blitz) 2008

1.e4 c5 2.d4 cxd4 3.c3 dxc3
Grandmaster Nakamura, arguably the world's deadliest blitz chess assassin, boldly accepts the Morra Gambit against me for the first time since 2000. In our other tournament

or blitz clashes, he either stealthily declined the offering, or refused to play the Sicilian altogether. One need not be a hyper-alert secret agent to gather that he had something up his sleeve.

4.♘xc3 ♘c6 5.♘f3 e6 6.♗c4 ♘ge7 7.♗g5!

The only way to attempt to disarm the powerful ...♘ge7 weapon. Black must now waste precious time with the weakening ...h6 or ...f6 to relieve the pin, else he cannot finish his kingside development.

7...h6

Likely trying to follow my defeat vs. Shabalov from a few months prior, Nakamura perhaps chooses the wrong pawn. But I, caught up in the hype of trying to maintain my 3400 ICC provisional rating while facing such a treacherous foe, impulsively responded to his "bullet" speed 7...h6 with the instant 8.♗e3, missing an excellent shot at a quick kill.

8.♗e3

8.♘b5! threatens an immediate smothered mate! Black should either have prevented this via an earlier ...a6, or freed the e7-knight from the pin with 7...f6, allowing 8.♘b5 to be met by 8...♘g6. Now he must run for cover

after the forced 8...d5, when he may hope to survive.

Surely 7...h6 was a mouse-slip and Nakamura did not expect 8.♘b5. Or did he? I will leave an air of mystery.

8...♘g6 9.0–0 ♗e7 10.♘b5?!

Pulling the trigger too late. As is often the case against top players, and especially in gambits, you only get one shot, so you better make it count. Black now effortlessly consolidates, achieving the harmonious pawn-up ...♘ge7 dream position which every Morra player should dread.

10...d6 11.♕e2 a6 12.♘c3 b5 13.♗b3 ♗b7

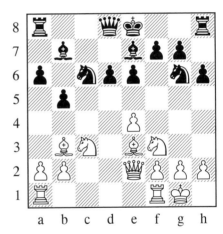

And Nakamura went on to collect one of his many thousands of Internet scalps.

...0–1

I guess a victory in such fashion allowed him to crack the following joke at my expense: "Time to quit chess. Your Morra is drawing dead." Yet a more fitting post-mortem Internet chess exchange, unique for its excessive banter, would be: WhYsOSeRiOus: "Do you expect me to talk?" Smallville: "No, Mr. Bond, I expect you to die! There is nothing that you can talk to me about that I don't already know." (Goldfinger)

Marc Esserman – Alexander Shabalov

Ledyard 2008

1.e4

As a result of this game's seemingly effortless efficiency, others have tried to follow in its path. However, they arrived too late, for the fate of a theoretical chess struggle, much like the spy world, can turn on the edge of a knife.

1...c5 2.d4 cxd4 3.c3 dxc3 4.♘xc3 ♘c6 5.♘f3 e6 6.♗c4 ♘ge7 7.♗g5 f6 8.♗e3 ♘g6 9.0–0 ♗e7!?

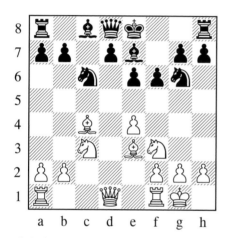

Shabalov introduces a simple scheme which at that time took me by surprise. He avoids ...a6 for now (a move I always thought necessary) and hurries to castle. Off balance, I resorted to the standard shot ♘f3-d4 with a quick f4-f5 thrust vs. the ...♘ge7 lines. But this routine plan allows Black to exchange a pair of knights, reducing White's attacking potential in the process.

10.♘d4 ♘xd4 11.♗xd4

11.♕xd4!? is the other dynamic possibility, but Shabalov could then get his wayward knight into the fray, harassing my queen and bishops while dodging the f2-f4 blow: 11...♘e5 12.♗b3 0–0 13.f4 ♘g4!∓

11...0–0 12.f4?!

Compelled to strike before Black unravels his queenside, I desperately sacrifice another pawn.

The cool 12.♖c1, trusting in the long-term positional pressure of the gambit, may have avoided a shameful defeat. For example: 12...♘e5 13.♗b3 ♘c6 14.♗e3 a6? 15.♘d5!± "And it seems the tables have turned, Dr. Evil" – Austin Powers. But instead of 14...a6? Black may unleash the liquefying 14...f5!, after which, "It seems the tables have turned again, Mr. Powers." – Dr. Evil.

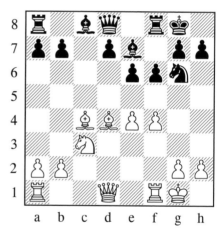

12...♕c7! 13.♗b3 ♘xf4 14.♔h1

I had intended the rapid 14.♖c1, but upon spotting 14...♗c5, I realized I had misfired. Even without the precise 14...♗c5, White never threatens ♘c3-d5, as ...♕xc1 followed by ...♘e2† looms.

14...♘g6 15.♖c1 ♕d8∓

Clearly, I am now completely lost, but why not go down shooting? After all, "There's no point in living, if you can't feel alive." (Bond, The World is Not Enough)

16.♘d5?

Finally, you get a chance to see a ♘d5 "sacrifice" which simply hangs a piece. Don't worry, in this book you won't see many more ♘d5's of this... caliber. "By caliber of course I mean both..." the quality of the move and... "it's a homonym... forget it." (Dr. Evil). Note that 16.♘d5 followed by ♗xd5†, ♕h5, ♖f3, ♕xh7†! and ♖h3# would work if I could take many shots in a row. Unfortunately, chess does not work this way. After such moves, I reserve the right to remain silent.

16...exd5 17.♗xd5† ♔h8 18.♕h5 d6–+ 19.♖c3 ♘e5 20.♖f4

An impressive show of force...

20...g6 21.♕h6 ♖g8 22.♗xg8 ♕xg8 23.♖c7 ♕f7 24.g4 ♔g8 25.g5 f5 26.b3 ♗e6 27.♖xb7 ♗xg5!

Effectively refuting the Morra Gambit?! At least until the next time. M: "Don't make this personal." Bond: "I can't do that. (The World is Not Enough)

0–1

Marc Esserman – Alexander Ivanov

Sturbridge 2008

1.e4 c5 2.d4 cxd4 3.c3 dxc3 4.♘xc3 e6 5.♘f3 ♘c6 6.♗c4 ♘ge7 7.♗g5 f6 8.♗e3 ♘g6 9.0–0 ♗e7

Three months later, Grandmaster Ivanov follows Shabalov's lead. Target acquired.

10.♘b5!N

M: "I thought I could trust you. You said you weren't motivated by revenge." Bond: "I'm motivated by my duty." M: "I think you're so blinded by inconsolable rage you don't care who you hurt." (Quantum of Solace). This is a logical raid into the sensitive d6-square to punish Black's omission of ...a6. Note that Ivanov cannot shield himself with ...d6 as in Esserman – Nakamura, since the inclusion of ...f6 and ...d6 would critically weaken the e6-pawn. I found 10.♘b5 during a summer's

stew after the Shabalov loss, and the results of this game and the next offered a quantum of solace. During the next few moves Ivanov sank into deep thought, soon yielding me a near 1½-hour time advantage. I, meanwhile, passed the minutes prowling about the tournament hall.

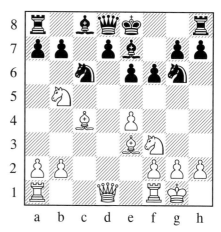

10...0–0 11.♖c1 a6 12.♘d6 ♕c7

Ivanov does not wish to give his bishop, which would leave his dark squares shattered.

13.♘f5!±

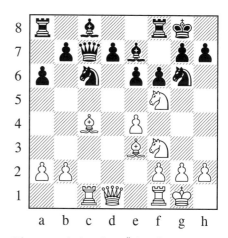

The point behind 10.♘b5, found during my stew. Like it or not, Ivanov must now part with his precious "goldeneye(d)" bishop, and I reap the positional profits.

13...♖f7 14.♘xe7† ♘gxe7

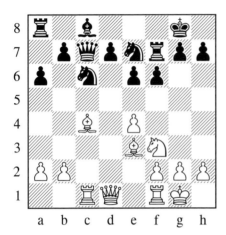

15.a4?!

Preventing the freeing ...b5, but allowing the equalizing 15...d5, as suggested by Ivanov after the game.

White should rush into the tattered d6-square, and trust in the enduring bind:

15.♗c5! d5!?

Giving back the pawn, the defender's classic path to equality or an advantage in gambit play, is of no avail here. 15...b5 16.♗d6 ♕b6 17.♗e2 ♗b7 18.♕d2± with ♖fd1 to come, tightens the screws further.

16.exd5 exd5

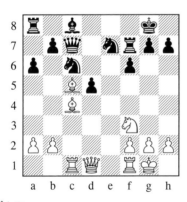

17.♗b3!

Rather than collecting the pawn and making a draw, White should keep the two bishops

and the pressure on.

17...♗e6 18.♖e1 ♕d7 19.♕e2 ♗g4 20.h3 ♗h5 21.g4! ♗g6 22.♖cd1±

And all of White's pieces are ready to strike.

15...b6

Ivanov, already in extreme time pressure, rejects the equalizing 15...d5, preferring to risk living to "die another day." Such is often the dilemma for a professional player vs. the Morra – he scoffs at the gambiteer's hubris for firing the gambit his way, and feels the need to punish his insolent, piratical, opponent. But in seeking chess justice, he often loses his sense of balance, and the joke falls on him. In the remaining moves, Ivanov only barely avoids becoming yet another victim of this psychological snare.

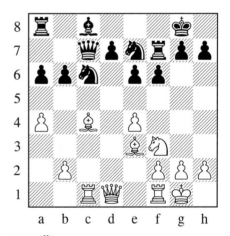

16.b4! ♕b8

Pressing for the loss...

17.♕d2?!

Allowing Black to release the tension, leading to an anticlimactic end.

More ruthless would be 17.♗b3 b5 18.a5 with a crushing grip, which Black cannot break: 18...♘xb4? 19.♗xe6!+–

Or the even harsher 17.b5! axb5 18.axb5 ♘a5 19.♗xe6! dxe6 20.♕d8†±

17...b5 18.axb5 axb5 19.♗b3 ♘g6 20.♗xe6 dxe6 21.♖xc6 ♗b7 22.♖xe6 ♕c8 23.♖b6 ♗xe4 24.♘d4 ♖b7!

One last ruse.

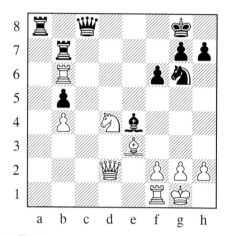

25.♖xb7

25.♖xb5? would reward Ivanov's risky play: 25...♖xb5 26.♘xb5 ♗xg2!–+ 27.♔xg2 ♕g4† 28.♔h1 ♕f3† 29.♔g1 ♘h4 mating, which is definitely not this script's proper dramatic finish.

25...♕xb7 26.f3 ♗d5 27.♘f5 ♗e6 28.♘d6 ♕d7 29.♗c5 ♖a2 30.♕d4 ♘e5 31.♖a1 h6 32.♖xa2 ♗xa2 33.♕e4 ♗e6 34.♕a8† ♔h7 35.♕e4† ♔g8 36.♕a8†

Bond: "Oh dear, do you want to continue?" Graves: "Of course I want to bloody continue! But since we're upping the wager, let's do it the old-fashioned way, first blood drawn from the torso." (Die Another Day)

½–½

Marc Esserman – Jayson Lian

US Chess League, Internet 2008

1.e4 c5 2.d4 cxd4 3.c3 dxc3 4.♘xc3 ♘c6 5.♘f3 e6 6.♗c4 ♘ge7 7.♗g5 f6 8.♗e3 ♘g6 9.0–0 ♗e7

Two months later, young Jayson Lian chooses to play like the pros in the heated US

Chess League team match, Boston vs. New Jersey. Based upon his lightning-like moves in the opening, we can surmise that either he, or the other professionals on his team, helped him prepare to follow Esserman – Shabalov etc. But like a good spy, I only leaked the position and remaining intrigue of Esserman – Ivanov to the national chess website starting after 13.♘f5, in hopes of one day springing 10.♘b5 again. Unfortunately for New Jersey, Lian steps straight into the minefield meant for the top assassins. Surely, somewhere in a distant city, Shabalov was watching...

10.♘b5 0–0 11.♖c1 ♔h8 12.♕d2 ♘ge5

Lian dodges the ♘d6-f5 bomb, but pays the price for leaving the romping knight on b5 for far too long.

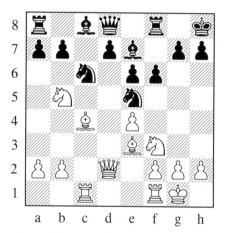

13.♘xe5 ♘xe5 14.♘xa7

Already White gains back his pawn, but there's more fun to come.

14...♘xc4 15.♖xc4

Black's queenside remains hopelessly undeveloped, often the fatal flaw in the ...♘ge7 systems.

15...d5 16.exd5 exd5

16...♕xd5 17.♕c1!+– and Black's bishop suffers from a case of arrested development.

Less convincing is 17.♕c2 ♕f5! and the bishop may live to die another day.

17.♖xc8 ♖xc8 18.♘xc8 ♕xc8 19.♕xd5

White emerges a pawn up (and the extra a-pawn may soon queen), and with a dominating positional advantage to spare. Funny how that works after 3.c3? hung a pawn... The rest is an execution.

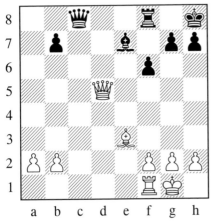

19...♖d8 20.♕b5 ♗d6 21.♖c1 ♕b8 22.g3 ♗e5 23.b4 h6 24.a4 ♗d4 25.♗f4 ♕a7 26.♖c2 ♖a8 27.♔g2

A last, cheap one-liner.

27...♕xa4

Desperate to eliminate the dangerous a-pawn, Lian forgets about his most important piece – the king!

28.♖c8†! ♔h7 29.♕f5† g6 30.♖c7† ♔h8 31.♕xg6

"Let this be a reminder to you all that this organization does not tolerate failure." (Dr Evil)

1–0

After exhausting Black's attempts to play ...♘ge7 without ...a6, we now target the ...a6 variations. While ...a6 stops any immediate ♘b5 raids and prepares for queenside

expansion, the time lost may ultimately cost Black's king his neck. Even the greatest masterminds of all time cannot escape the ruthless law of development. We start with Gata Kamsky, one of chess history's most tenacious defenders.

Borba (Esserman) – Talion (GM Kamsky)

Internet (blitz) 2005

1.e4 c5 2.d4 e6

Kamsky clearly did not expect the Morra, and pre-moves 2...e6 to gain time in this Internet blitz match. Now the solid 3.d5 is best, forming an improved Benoni structure. But against the world's best, my "only goal is chaos." (Bond, The World is Not Enough)

3.♘f3 cxd4 4.c3 dxc3 5.♘xc3 a6 6.♗c4 ♘c6 7.0–0 d6 8.♕e2 ♘ge7!?

A very wily move order, feigning a Scheveningen, then unveiling ...♘ge7 only after White's queen commits to e2.

9.♗g5 h6

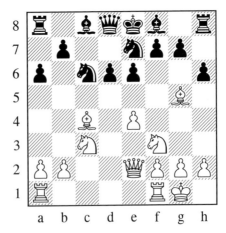

10.♗e3!?

White can consider retreating in the other direction:

10.♗h4!?

Normally I am against dropping the bishop back to h4 when it is inevitably kicked on g5, but against this specific sideline, the idea has some punch. Once on g3, the bishop probes the compromised d6-pawn (as in the Scheveningen structures), and White can then logically follow up with the trusted ♖fd1. A few sample shots:

10...♕a5!?

10...g5?! Such an extreme kingside thrust must bear consequences. 11.♗g3 ♘g6 12.♖fd1! White takes aim to open fire on d6. 12...h5 13.♗xd6! ♗xd6 14.e5 ♘gxe5 15.♘e4± Mayhem erupts.

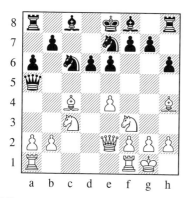

11.♖fd1

A sleek developing move.

11.♗g3 ♘g6 featured in the historic Smith – Byrne, San Antonio 1972, but Smith continued with the slower 12.♕d2 instead of sliding the rook over.

11...♘g6 12.♗g3⇄

Black can certainly block the bullets by lodging a knight on e5, and a long contest ensues. Therefore, the game text comes loaded with even heavier artillery.

10...♘g6 11.♘d4

We have seen this plan before, but now add a new twist.

11...♗d7?!

11...♗e7! is correct, rushing to castle, but

Kamsky believes in the unbreachable integrity of his structure.

12.f4! b5

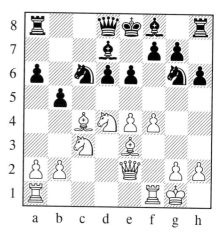

13.♗xe6!?

"James, is it really necessary to drive this fast?" "More often than you'd think." (GoldenEye)

But instead of speeding, in this case driving "slowly" wins the race. After the calm 13.♗b3!± Black cannot untangle: 13...♘xd4 (13...♘a5 14.f5! ♘xb3 15.fxg6 ♘xa1 16.gxf7† ♔e7 17.♘d5† exd5 18.♗g5† hxg5 19.exd5† ♗e6 20.♕xe6# Bond: "Shocking. Positively shocking." [Goldfinger]) 14.♗xd4± Kamsky's kingside is frozen in space. Dr. Evil: "I'm gonna get you Austin Powers! It's frickin' freezing in here, Mr. Bigglesworth."

13...fxe6 14.♕h5

The abstract warning "...h6 weakens the g6-square" now becomes a concrete, flesh-wounding reality.

14...♕f6 15.♘xc6 ♗xc6 16.f5 ♗e7 17.fxg6 ♕h4?!

Black should hide his queen out on the e5-perch. Now she may be nabbed from right under his nose.

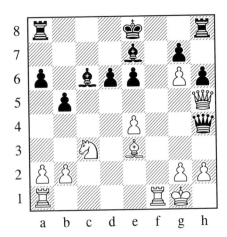

18.♕xh4?!

As Kamsky cannot safely castle, I should keep my queen to create the necessary chaos:

18.♕e2!±

Furthermore, Black's queen is now suddenly short of squares...

18...♗g5

18...♗f6 19.g3 ♕h3 20.♖xf6! shreds the blockade: 20...gxf6 21.♖f1 ♔e7 (21...♖f8 22.♕d2 with unstoppable threats, and if 22...0-0-0 then 23.♖c1 ♔b7 24.♕d4+– silences.) 22.e5! Shattering the king's already battered headquarters. 22...dxe5 23.♗c5† ♔d7 24.♖xf6 ♖hg8 25.♖f7† ♔c8 26.♘e4 ♖b8 27.♘d6† ♔d8 28.♗b4!+–

19.♖ad1 ♖d8 20.♗f2 ♕f4 21.♗b6 ♕e5 22.♗d4!

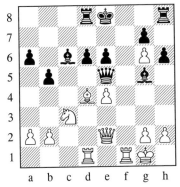

And the black queen fades away. Q: "Aston

Martin called it the Vanquish, we call it the Vanish" (Die Another Day).

18...♗xh4 19.♖f7 ♗f6 20.♖d1 0-0-0?!

20...♖d8! would hang on from the ledge.

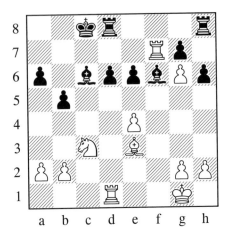

A heavyweight champion like Kamsky does not cut easily in hand-to-hand combat – it takes an exceptional punch to knock him out. He now steers for a clearly favorable, fast-approaching ending, with healthier pawn structure and his golden bishops in tow.

21.♗b6?

Only one last gadget could save me, an old friend:

21.♘d5!+–

Postponing a meat-grinding ending in favor of a flashy, decisive middlegame.

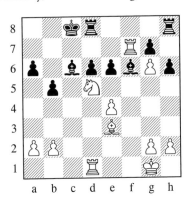

21...♗xd5

21...exd5 22.♖c1!+– is the sharp shot I missed.

22.exd5 exd5 23.♗a7

With an irresistible flurry of threats.

23...♗xb2☐

23...♖d7? 24.♖c1† ♔d8 25.♗b6† ♔e8 26.♖xf6!+–

24.♖d2 ♗c3 25.♖c2 b4 26.a3 ♖hf8 27.axb4 ♖xf7 28.gxf7 ♔b7 29.♖xc3

Only now does White head for a winning endgame! Despite the pawn minus, the f7-thorn proves decisive. I learned from hearing Kamsky lecture once that in the ending, it is not always the quantity, but the quality of one's pawns that ultimately matters.

29...♔xa7 30.♖g3! g5 31.♖e3 ♖f8 32.♖e7† ♔b6 33.♔f2+–

With the black king shut out, White's freely marches to e6.

21...♖d7 22.♖xd7 ♔xd7 23.♗c5 ♗e5

Now I become yet another victim of Kamsky's legendary technique.

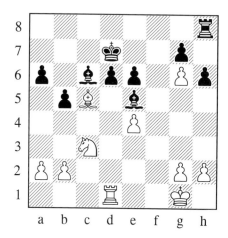

24.♗xd6 ♗xd6 25.e5 ♗d5!

"Closing time James. Last call?" (Trevelyan, GoldenEye)

26.♘xd5 ♗xe5 27.♘b4† ♔c7 28.♘xa6†

♔b6 29.♘b4 ♗xb2 30.♘d3 ♗d4† 31.♔f1 ♖a8 32.♖d2 e5

And fortunately this was blitz, so the torture chamber did not last much longer (time-wise, that is). Kamsky, a hardened professional chess assassin, perfectly follows old Q's advice to Bond upon his retirement. Q: "I always tried to teach you two things. First, never let them see you bleed." Bond: "And the second?" Q: "Always have an escape plan." (The World is Not Enough)

...0–1

Even "The Boss" himself, arguably the greatest player of all time, Garry Kasparov (also known as "The Beast from Baku"), has come to experience the Morra's sharp sword. To his credit, Kasparov only faces the gambit here in a simul against the young and future GM Landa, so he could not give the defensive effort his full power. Too bad no one ever had the nerve to play the Morra against Kasparov in a real tournament! One thing is certain – the legendary World Champion is not a man known to decline a fight.

Konstantin Landa – Garry Kasparov

Moscow Clock Simul 1988

1.e4 c5 2.d4 cxd4 3.c3 dxc3 4.♘xc3 ♘c6 5.♘f3 e6 6.♗c4 a6 7.0–0 ♘ge7 8.♗g5 h6

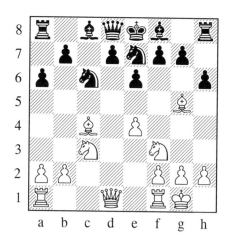

9.♗h4?!

We dissect the superior 9.♗e3 later in the advanced material. Unlike the Kamsky game, here the bishop falling back to g3 makes less sense, as the d-pawn (still on d7) is no longer in the line of fire.

9...d6?!

More in the variation's dynamic style is: 9...g5! 10.♗g3 ♘g6∓

This would also be more in Kasparov's style. Often in his career the champion has won brilliantly in the Open Sicilian, leaving his king in the center and dangerously expanding on the flank (in the 6.♗e3 ♘g4 lines of the English Attack, in particular). Here, with Black's pawn on d7, White's g3-bishop proves to be a greater liability than an asset, while Black's seemingly soft kingside cannot be punctured.

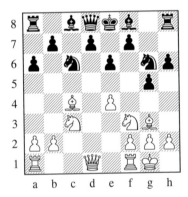

11.♖e1

11.♕d2 g4! 12.♘d4 ♕g5!∓ liquidates the queens and squashes any further hopes of compensation.

11...h5! 12.♘d5?

12.♗d6 g4 13.♗xf8 ♔xf8∓ "I also like to live dangerously." (Austin Powers)

12...d6!∓

Only now ...d6!

10.♕d2

As White's heavy pieces snipe at the d6-pawn, Black's position soon devolves into chaos.

10...g5 11.♗g3 ♘g6 12.♖ad1 ♗e7

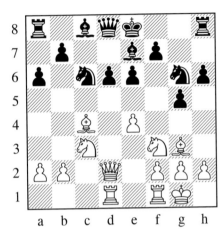

13.♗b3

13.♗xd6, regaining the pawn but heading into a slightly worse ending due to White's dark-squared liabilities, is not in the Romantic style (and likely Kasparov would have been happy with that in a simultaneous exhibition).

13...♘ge5?!

13...♘a5! eliminates the heat-seeking missile/bishop, while still offering the ending after 14.♗xd6, and would have prevented the firestorm to come.

14.♘xe5 dxe5 15.♕e3 ♕a5

As the g3-bishop rots in prison, a certain member of the royal cavalry brings him the keys to bust loose!

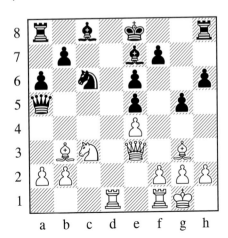

16.♘d5!

It only takes one slip! Even the world champion can succumb to the awesome power of ♘d5! "Let the mayhem begin!" (Elliot Carver, Tomorrow Never Dies)

16...♗d8

16...exd5 17.exd5+–

17.♖c1!± ♗d7 18.♖c5 b5

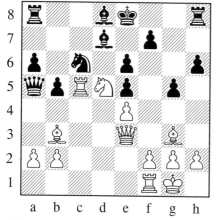

19.♕f3!?

Landa misses his first chance to be immortalized in gambit lore:
19.♖xc6! ♗xc6 20.♗xe5+–

The now freed bishop sprays across the four corners of the board. A few lengthy variations demonstrate what might have been against the deadliest of them all.

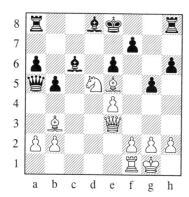

20...♖g8

20...♖h7 21.♕c5 ♖c8 (21...♗xd5 22.exd5 and the bishops spit bullets. 22...♕b6 23.♕c2+–) 22.♘f6† ♗xf6 23.♗xf6 ♕c7 24.♖d1 The once captive bishop is now taking prisoners, including the pitiful h7-rook. 24...e5 25.♖d6 ♗d7 26.♕xe5† ♗e6 27.g3 ♔f8 28.♖xe6 fxe6 29.♕xe6+– Fine swordsmanship indeed.

21.♗d6 b4

21...♗xd5 22.exd5+–

22.♖c1 ♕b5 23.♕d4 ♕b7 24.♘f6† ♗xf6 25.♕xf6 ♖g6 26.♕h8† ♔d7 27.♕d4 ♔e8 28.♗xb4

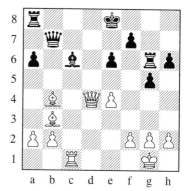

"You should have killed me when you had the chance." (Renard, The World is Not Enough)

19...exd5 20.♗xd5+–

The mayhem continues.

20...0–0

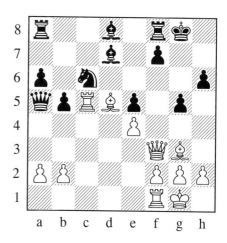

21.♕h5 ♚h7

21...♚g7 22.♗xc6 ♖c8 23.♗xe5† f6 24.♗xd7 ♖xc5 25.♗f5! ♖c7 26.♕g6† ♚h8 27.♕xh6† (or 27.♗xc7+–) 27...♚g8 28.♗e6† ♖cf7 29.♗d6+–

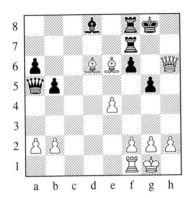

Two bishops are not just positional tools!

22.♗xf7 ♘e7

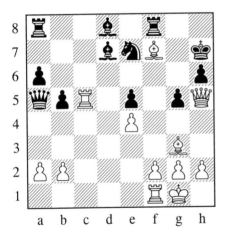

"One... last... screw." (Bond, The World is Not Enough)

23.♖xe5?!

"The man just won't take a hint." (Trevelyan, GoldenEye)

23.♖d5!! is the silencer. As taking the rook allows mate in two, the threat of ♖d6 swiftly decides. 23...♗g4 24.♕xg4 ♖xf7 25.♕e6 ♖f8

26.♖d6 ♘g8 27.♕g6† ♚h8 28.♖d7 ♗e7 29.♖xe7+–

23...♕b6

And we leave this game suspended in midair, along with the players and their pieces, for dramatic effect. I'm already out of breath, and must save myself for the Grand Finale. But if you're dying to know how this thriller ended, just go to page 322.

Marc Esserman – Loek van Wely

US Open, Orlando 2011

Dryden: "Your file shows no kills. But to become a double 0, it takes..." Bond: "Two." Dryden: "Shame, we barely got to know each other." Bond: "I know where you keep your gun." Dryden: "I suppose that's something. How did he die?" Bond: "No contact, not well." Dryden: "You needn't worry. Second is..."(Casino Royale)

1.e4 c5 2.d4 cxd4 3.c3

Before the game, a friend of mine, who happens to be a professional poker player in addition to a strong master, placed a small wager with me on Van Wely's third move. He took "declines", I took "accepts". As I had some sensitive, secret information that he could not possibly have known, I won.

3...dxc3 4.♘xc3 ♘c6 5.♘f3 e6 6.♗c4 a6 7.0–0 ♘ge7 8.♗g5

A few weeks before the US Open, Van Wely visited Boston, where aside from touring he played an informal blitz match vs. a teammate of mine, former World Junior and Dos Hermanas blitz champion Jorge Sammour-Hasbun. Though in Europe at the time, I heard from an undercover agent of mine in the field that Jorge unleashed the Morra in one game, with Van Wely choosing ...♘ge7. But Sammour countered with ♗f4 instead of the testing ♗g5, allowing Van Wely to smoothly finish his kingside development. I realized then that Van Wely might allow me to uncork an outlandish idea I had kept hidden for almost three years, and could barely contain my excitement before the game. But a good spy, rather than broadcasting his emotions, must "become half monk, half hit-man." (Bond, Casino Royale)

8...f6 9.♗e3 ♘g6

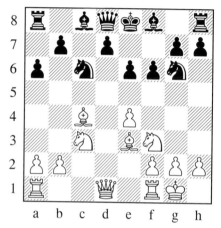

10.♗b3!

I followed the standard plan of 10.♘d4!? (eyeing f4-f5) in tournaments many times during my junior years and in blitz as well. But as explained earlier, while perfectly playable, 10.♘d4 allows Black to exchange a key minor piece en route to neutralizing White's initiative. After the embarrassing Shabalov loss, I subjected the ...♘ge7 lines to exhaustive study, coming up with many sharp improvements which I hoped to unload upon Shabalov himself. However, it is "Lucky Loek" whose luck here runs out, as he unwittingly falls upon one of these ticking time bombs.

I continued cautiously, almost timidly, not wanting to activate Van Wely's highly trained sixth sense of danger. Vesper: "So you're telling me it's all a matter of probability and odds. I

was thinking there was some chance involved." Bond: "Eh, only if you assume that the player with the best hand wins." Vesper: "So there will be what you call bluffing?" Bond: "You've heard the term. So you should know that in poker you never play your hand, but the man across from you." (Casino Royale)

10...b5

Loek desperately wanted to play 10...♗e7 and castle to safety, but after a strained think decided that preventing the unpleasant ♘a4 with 10...b5, while leaving his king in the center, was the lesser of the two evils. However, Black's position may already be critical, and in the theoretical section we will look for earlier improvements.

10...♗e7 11.♘a4! 0–0 (11...b5? 12.♗b6+– Esserman – Fang, Harvard [blitz] 2010.) 12.♘b6 ♖b8 The bind Van Wely feared. White can now either continue sharply with 13.♘d5, threatening to lop off the dark-squared bishop (with resulting middlegame play similar to Esserman – Ivanov), or prophylactically with 13.♕d3, preventing the freeing ...f5 while preparing ♖fd1/♖ac1.

At last, the moment of truth. I almost moved instantly, but restrained myself and seemingly entered into deep, troubled thought.

11.♘d5!!

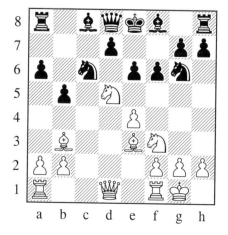

"White rook to white knight. Service the pawns." (Tomorrow Never Dies). After discovering the soundness of ♘d5 in my game vs. Sarkar, I steadily began to appreciate the awesome power of ♘d5 in the Morra. As a result, I would violently toss ♘d5 into the fire in many key positions, no matter how absurd the sacrifice seemed at surface view. And so, after a heated analysis for both myself and the computer, when the evaluations finally switched from ∓ to = and often to ±/+−, I knew I had unlocked my primary weapon.

In late 2009, I first released 11.♘d5 against an unsuspecting young master, and won rather brutally in under an hour. I then quickly cleared the pieces (Shabalov was playing only a few boards down!), ripped up the scoresheet, and threw it in the trash. With all the original evidence destroyed, I then analyzed with my respectful opponent, and he duly agreed not to publish the game. Thus, 11.♘d5 remained a secret...

But the chess world is a vast, unforgiving place, and it's tough to keep up with the hotbed of activity teeming in every locale. So, to my chagrin, I only learned after the Van Wely game that the brilliant 11.♘d5 had already been played by Ukrainian IM Zakharov back in 2001. Not the first time though that I've played the fool – I once ventured 7.g4!? in the Semi-Slav against Shabalov, convincing myself pre-game that he would be intimidated by this volatile gambit. Only in the post-tournament report, penned by just a 2000-rated player, did I read in disbelief: "Esserman plays in his usual swashbuckling style. Shabalov is a well known expert on either side of this position and this is commonly known as the Shabalov Variation."[35] "I've got you now, Dr. Evil." – Austin Powers.

So, while a full novelty in my mind, the theory of the rare 11.♘d5 remained virtually unknown. Well, it shocked a great theoretician

like Van Wely, and I'm sure 99.9% of professionals had no idea of its existence. After all, most grandmasters, still suffering from "1...e6?, 1...c5 wins a pawn" thinking, don't take the Morra very seriously. But after this game, perhaps they will.

11...exd5

Loek grabbed instantly, like Sarkar, refusing to believe in magic. I too began to play instantly, the cat being out of the bag.

11...♕b8

Some analysts suggested this "calm" move as salvation for Van Wely, but perhaps they learned nothing from the game.

12.♖c1!

White simply gains momentum. The fuming knight refuses to budge, and eventually Black must capture.

12...a5

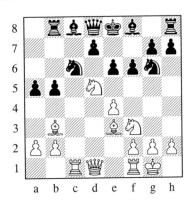

13.a3!

"White Knight, four minutes to impact. Get out of there. You will not wait, now that's an order." (Tomorrow Never Dies)

13.♘f4?! is the machine's top choice. But no, the knight should not get out of there.

13.♖e1!?... Full speed ahead!

13...exd5

13...a4 14.♗a2 exd5 15.exd5±

14.exd5±

12.exd5 ♘ce5 13.d6!

Slicing the board in two. The "Italian" bishop fires at will.

13...♗b7 14.♘xe5 fxe5

14...♘xe5? 15.♖e1 ♕b8 16.♗c5!+– body-slamming Black's position.

15.f4!

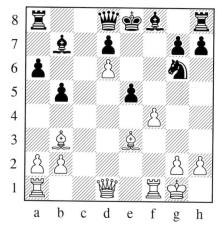

The King's Gambit returns. White rips open the center and the f-file as Black's king becomes target practice. If the f-pawn vanished, ♗f7 would be mate...

15...♕f6?!

Loek plays the most natural move, but he could feel the ship already sinking. It's almost impossible to survive more than a few moves in this position without preparation.

After 15...♘xf4? White can win simply with 16.♖xf4, or spectacularly with 16.♕h5† ♘xh5 17.♗f7#.

15...♕h4? 16.fxe5!
A shredder.
16...♘xe5
16...♕e4 17.♗f7† ♔d8 18.♕d2 ♔c8 19.♖ac1† ♔b8 20.♖fe1 ♕g4 21.♗d5 ♘xe5 22.♗xb7 ♔xb7 23.♖c7† ♔b8 24.♕d5 ♘c6 25.♗a7†+– There is no escape.

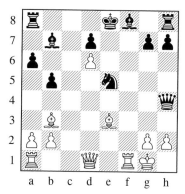

17.♖f4!
Taunting the queen.
17...♕d8
17...♕h6 18.♖xf8†+–
18.♕h5† g6 19.♕xe5† ♕e7
Elektra: You wouldn't kill me, you'd miss me."
20.♖xf8†+–
Bond: "I never miss." (The World is Not Enough)

The equally daring 15...exf4 will be dissected in the advanced material. For starters, the gambiteer laughs at the danger, jettisoning another piece: 16.♖e1 fxe3! 17.♖xe3† ♗e7 18.♕d4!

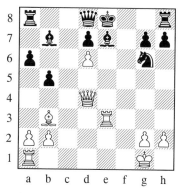

The white queen dominates, as in Esserman – Sarkar. Meanwhile, the black king cries: "Why do I suddenly feel like I'm the one not carrying enough insurance?" (The World is Not Enough)

16.fxe5 ♕xe5

Graves: "Time to face destiny." Bond: "Time to face... gravity."

17.♗g5!!

Preventing the great queenside-castle escape. Black's king now stays buried in the center. Q: "Will you need collision coverage?" Bond: "Yes." Q: "Fire?" Bond: "Probably." Q: "Property destruction?" Bond: "Definitely." Q: "Personal Injury?" Bond: "I hope not, but accidents do happen." Q: "They frequently do with you."

17.♗f7† ♔d8 18.♗b6† ♔c8 19.♖e1 also wins, but not in the Romantic style.

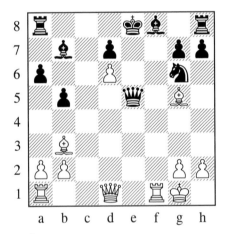

17...♗e7

The only move! Black cannot grab, due to a problem-like finish, showcasing the queen's unique geometry.

17...♕xg5 18.♕e1†! ♔d8 (18...♗e7 19.♗f7† ♔f8 20.♗xg6† ♗f6 21.♕e7† ♔g8 22.♗f7# – No need for the butcher's 22.♕f7#.) 19.♕a5† ♔c8 20.♕c7# Miranda: "My my, you do get around." (Die Another Day)

17...♕c5† is met by 18.♖f2+– and the bishop stays immune. (But not 18.♔h1?? ♗xg2†.)

18.♗f7† ♔d8 19.dxe7† ♘xe7 20.♕d2!

The smoke clears, and the gambiteer remains a pawn down, as on move three. However, with White's two "extra" rooks scorching and bishops blasting away at the exiled black king, it's game over against even the deadliest of opponents.

20...♔c8 21.♖ac1† ♘c6 22.♖fd1

The Morra rooks take their rightful place before the curtain call.

22...♕f5 23.♗f4! ♕xf7 24.♕d6 ♔d8

Alec: "For England, James?" Bond: "No, for me." (GoldenEye)

25.♖xc6! ♗xc6 26.♕xc6

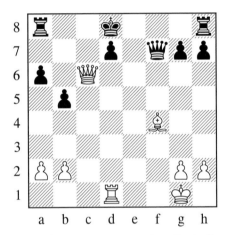

And Black must resign, for if 26...♖a7 or 26...♖c8, the bishop returns to take a bow on g5, delivering mate after 27...♔e8 28.♕(x)c8#. But before conceding, Van Wely, an excellent sportsman, feigned castling kingside, waiting for me to almost fall out of my chair, then resigned!

Frost: "That is enough!" Graves: "Hahaha. It's just a little sport, Miranda. It seems you beat me, Mr. Bond. Settle downstairs, shall we?" (Die Another Day)

1–0

Theory I – Van Wely Improvements

1.e4 c5 2.d4 cxd4 3.c3 dxc3 4.♘xc3 ♘c6 5.♘f3 e6 6.♗c4 a6 7.0–0 ♘ge7 8.♗g5 f6 9.♗e3 ♘g6 10.♗b3 b5 11.♘d5 exd5 12.exd5 ♘ce5 13.d6 ♗b7 14.♘xe5 fxe5 15.f4

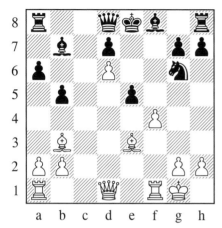

15...exf4! 16.♖e1 fxe3 17.♖xe3† ♗e7 18.♕d4!

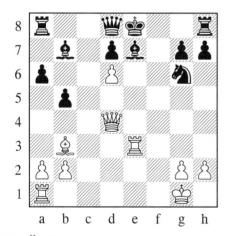

18...♕c8!

A subtle, disturbing computer-like defense. Le Chiffre: "I hope our little game isn't causing you to perspire." (Casino Royale)

18...♕a5?!

This occurred in the aforementioned Esserman – Schoch, Philadelphia 2009, and Black fell hard:

19.dxe7 d5?

19...♘xe7!? 20.♖xe7†! ♔xe7 21.♕xg7† ♔d6 22.♕g3†! The only way to win. The queen again shows off her geometric prowess. 22...♔e7 (22...♔c6 23.♖c1† ♔b6 24.♕f2#) 23.♕e5† ♔d8 24.♕xh8† ♔c7 25.♖c1† ♗c6 26.♕xa8

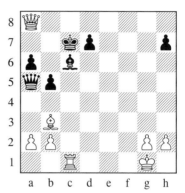

26...♕b6† One last gasp. White must find the accurate 27.♔f1+–, as the plausible 27.♔h1? leads to a stunning perpetual with the white queen shut out on a8: 27...♕e3! 28.♖xc6† dxc6 29.h3 ♕e1† 30.♔h2 ♕e5†= **20.♗xd5 ♕c7 21.♖f1**

Lights out.

21...♘xe7 22.♗f7† ♔f8 23.♗e6† ♔e8 24.♕xg7 1–0

Black resigned, not wishing to allow a rousing finish: 24...♖g8 25.♕f7† ♔d8 26.♕f8†! ♖xf8 27.♖xf8#

18...♕b8 is the most creative try, hoping to pin White's heavy pieces, then castle long: 19.dxe7 ♕a7 Can you find the gorgeous win?

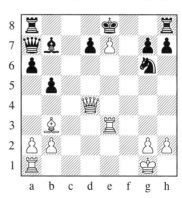

20.♗f7†!! ♔xf7 21.e8=♕†! ♖hxe8 22.♖f1†
♔g8 23.♕xa7+− (or 23.♖xe8†+−) Amazingly, I
discovered this position during an independent
analysis in 2009, only to learn after the Van
Wely game that it had all already been played
in the brilliant game Vl. Zakharov – Gusev,
Tula 2001.

19.♖ae1 ♕c6

Black somehow coordinates for a powerful
battery, and again threatens to castle long.

20.♖f3 ♔d8 21.dxe7† ♘xe7

21...♔c7 22.♖c3+−

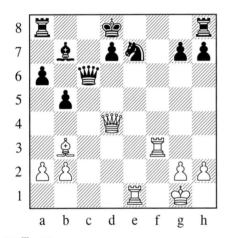

22.♖xe7!

As we saw in the notes to in Esserman –
Schoch.

22...♔xe7 23.♕xg7† ♔d6

Sacrificing the queen for two rooks, and the
computer sees light at the end of the tunnel in
the form of "0.00".

In his notes to the Van Wely game, Grandmaster
Golubev extensively analyzed 23...♔d8 out to
a drawn king and pawn endgame at around
move 50 after several difficult, only moves for
Black. Let me be clear: I have no intention of
draining out the Morra in such a fashion. Even
if this interesting endgame is in fact drawn,

the defender would still have to memorize and
endure 50 moves of pain just to score half a
point. And this makes me more than satisfied! I
doubt such preparation would be acceptable for
aspiring professional players, desperate to win
against the "unsound" Morra! Nevertheless, I
will reproduce up to the starting position of
this sharp king and pawn finale, just so no one
complains that we did not cover Dvoretsky-
like endgame studies in this book! 24.♕xh8†
♔c7 25.♕e5† d6 26.♖f7† ♔b6 27.♕d4† ♕c5
28.♕xc5† dxc5 29.♖xb7† ♔xb7 30.♗d5†
♔a7 31.♗xa8 ♔xa8 32.♔f2 ♔b7 33.♔e3 ♔c6
34.♔e4= It sure doesn't look drawn, does it!?

24.♖f6† ♔c7 25.♖xc6† ♗xc6 26.♗f7!

Putting an end to the drawing dream.
Suddenly Black's rooks are paralyzed.

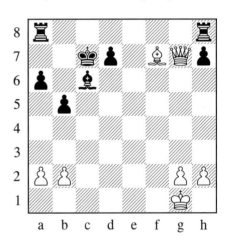

26...♖ac8 27.g4!±

White, meanwhile, just goes to make a
queen after h2-h4. Chess is a very simple game
sometimes. Sorry, computer, better luck next
time! Clearly, the world's greatest assassins
have too much pride to willingly enter such
positions as Black. Van Wely, for one, was
already scouring for earlier improvements
minutes after the game, and so shall we.

Theory II –
Earlier Van Wely Improvements

1.e4 c5 2.d4 cxd4 3.c3 dxc3 4.♘xc3 ♘c6 5.♘f3 e6 6.♗c4 a6 7.0–0 ♘ge7 8.♗g5 f6 9.♗e3 b5!? 10.♗b3

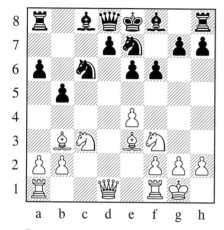

10...♘a5!?

GM Kevin Spraggett suggested this logical improvement (a move he has played with success) after the game.[36] Black's idea is attractive – he aims to lop off the Italian bishop, finish his development, then dominate on the b7-h1 diagonal. But Black wastes precious time in the process – the wily gambiteer must therefore seize the moment.

10...♗b7!?

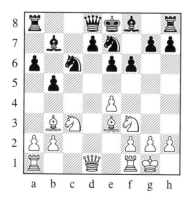

A very risky, counter-intuitive, but serious attempt. Black yet again postpones his kingside development, waiting for White to show his hand. Now White has a few choices which drastically differ in style.
11.♘d2!?
This seems strange to me, but White managed to win in an epic computer vs. computer tournament battle. Unlike 11.♘d4, White refuses to exchange knights, while f4-f5 still beckons.

If 11.♘d4, then 11...♘xd4 12.♗xd4 ♘c6! and Black's pieces instantly spring to life.

11.a3!?∞ is definitely not in the gambit spirit, but remains completely playable! White waits in turn, taking the extra time to preserve his Italian bishop, and in the next few moves simply plans to bring his Morra rooks to c1 and d1. As a result of Black's backwards development, the chances are level.

Lastly, our old friend 11.♘d5 (and the related 11.a4 b4 12.♘d5) must be checked. Surely Van Wely has mined this mayhem, and now I leave you alone to do the same. Spies must keep a secret or two! Please be advised – wear protection in your search, everything is not what it seems.

11...♘a5 12.f4 d5 13.♗f2 ♘xb3 14.♕xb3 ♕d6 15.♖ad1 ♕xf4 16.a4

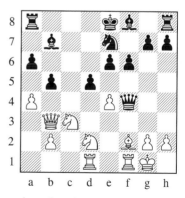

Complete chaos!
16...♗c6 17.axb5 axb5 18.♘f3 ♕d6 19.♖fe1 ♔f7 20.♘d4 ♗d7 21.♘dxb5 ♕c6 22.♘a7±

♕a6 23.♖a1 ♕d6 24.♘ab5 ♕c6 25.exd5
♘xd5 26.♘d4 ♖xa1 27.♘xc6 ♖xe1† 28.♗xe1
♗xc6±

Equidistance – VoidChessICC, Internet
2006, and in this "advanced" humans and
computers death match, White won in 95
moves (see the rest in the supplemental games
section).

I wonder who got more tired, the operators
or the silicon beasts?

11.♘d4!

With 11.♗xe6?! dxe6 12.♕xd8† ♔xd8
13.♗b6† ♔e8 14.♗xa5∓ White regains the
pawn, but Black has all the chances in the
endgame with the bishop pair. Van Wely saw
this possibility during the game, but rejected
it, fearing White's drawing chances. Such is
the dilemma when professionals face lower
rated players – the need to win (to maintain
rating and/or collect a prize) may drive us
to make inferior moves! But true gambiteers
do not seek slightly worse endings out of the
opening!

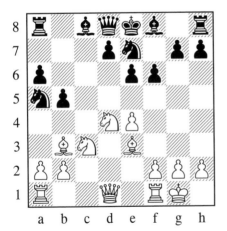

11...♘xb3

Here too, Black can consider:
11...♗b7!? 12.♕h5†! g6
12...♘g6?! can be met by 13.f4→ or by
13.♖ad1 angling for ♘xe6, as in some
variations below.

13.♕h4 g5
The top choice of the "fearless" and often
senseless computer.
Bond: "Who was the insider, who was the
traitor?"
Natalya: "Boris, Boris Grishenko."
Bond: "KGB, or military?"
Natalya: "Computer programmer."
(GoldenEye)
13...♘ec6 14.♘xe6! dxe6 15.♗xe6± ♗c8
16.♖fd1+–
14.♕h5† ♘g6

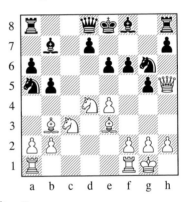

15.♘xe6!
15.f4!?∞ It's hard to resist a King's Gambit.
15...dxe6 16.♗xe6⩲ ♗c8?!
16...♗d6 17.♖ad1! I'd rather not put a
definite evaluation to this position, but
rest assured, White is better. The attacking
themes echo those of 9.♘g5! from the
chapter "Into the Deep".
17.♖ad1 ♗xe6
17...♕e7 18.♘d5+–
18.♖xd8† ♖xd8 19.♗b6+–

12.♕xb3!?

12.♘xb3∞, retaining the possibility of ♕h5†
while allowing the knight to plunder c5, also
unleashes wild complications. But speedily
mobilizing the heavy pieces seems more
powerful.

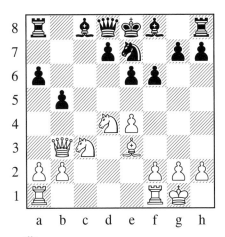

12...♕c7

12...♗b7 13.♖fd1→

12...♘g6 13.♖fd1!
13.f4!? ♗c5 14.♖ac1 0–0 15.♖fd1→ (15.♘cxb5? ♕b6) 15...♕b6? 16.♘d5!
13...♕c7
13...♕e7? hoping to escape with ...♕f7 followed by ...♗e7, is a pipe dream: 14.♘dxb5! axb5 15.♘xb5 ♔f7 16.♘c7 ♖a5 17.♕b8 ♕d8 18.♗b6±
14.♖ac1 ♕b7 15.f4

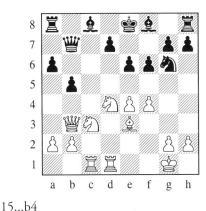

15...b4
15...♗c5 16.♘cxb5+–
16.♘a4 ♕xe4 17.♘xe6! dxe6
17...♕xe6? 18.♘b6 ♕xb3 19.axb3±
18.♖c4! ♕b7 19.♘b6± ♗e7
19...♖b8 20.♕a4† ♔f7 21.♘xc8 ♖xc8 22.♖d7†+–

20.♕c2 0–0 21.♖c1!±

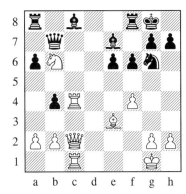

Chess's equivalent of the AK-47, the "triple barrel" on the Morra's favorite firing range – the c-file!

After 12...♘c6!? 13.♘xc6 dxc6 Black possesses the bishop pair, a solid structure, plus a pawn to boot. But his total lack of development still should push the evaluation slightly in White's favor. 14.♖fd1 ♕c7 15.a4 ♖b8 (15...b4 16.♘e2±) 16.axb5 axb5 17.♖a7 ♖b7 18.♖a8 ♖b8 19.♖da1 Black must tread carefully to avoid falling off the cliff.

13.♖ac1 ♘c6

14.♘d5!?

Natalya: "You're like, boys with toys." (GoldenEye)

14.♘ce2!?∞ is also playable, if rather insipid.

14...exd5 15.exd5 ♘xd4?!

15...♘a5!? 16.♖xc7 ♘xb3 17.♘xb3 ♗d6 18.♖c2 ♗b7 (18...0–0 19.♗c5±) 19.♘a5±

16.♗xd4 ♕d6

16...♕b8 17.♖fe1† ♔d8 (17...♔f7 18.d6† ♔g6 19.♕g3† ♔f7 20.♖c7+– 007 heaven!) 18.♕g3 ♕xg3 (18...d6 19.♕e3+–) 19.♗b6† ♕c7 20.♗xc7#

16...♕f4 17.♖fe1† ♔f7 18.d6† ♔g6 19.♕d3† ♔f7 (19...♕f5 20.♖e4! ♔f7 21.♖c5+–) 20.♗e5! fxe5 21.♕d5†+–

17.♖fe1† ♔d8

Boris: "Yessss, I am Invinnncible!" (GoldenEye)

17...♔f7 18.♗c5 ♕xc5 19.d6†+–

18.♕b4!

Sorry, Boris!

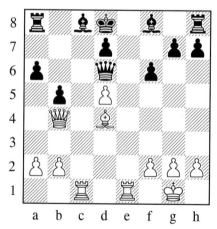

18...♖b8 19.♕a5† ♖b6 20.♕xb6† ♕xb6 21.♗xb6#

Theory III – Lines with ...h6

1.e4 c5 2.d4 cxd4 3.c3 dxc3 4.♘xc3 e6 5.♘f3 ♘c6 6.♗c4 a6 7.0–0 ♘ge7 8.♗g5 h6

Finally we dissect Kasparov's preferred choice against Landa. This is firmer than the creaking 8...f6, however 8...h6 (as well as still softening the g6-square) does not fight for the central e5-square, which can ultimately lead to Black's doom in many key variations.

9.♗e3!

Not 9.♗h4?! as previously discussed. On e3 the bishop exerts a more global influence.

9...♘g6

The alternative is 9...b5!? 10.♗b3.

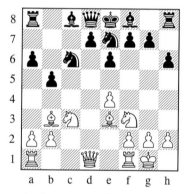

Now we look at A) 10...♘a5 and B) 10...♗b7.

A) 10...♘a5

Forcing matters. Black will gain the two bishops with his pawn advantage to boot, but as in the previous example, the great loss of time behind ...b5/...♘a5xb3 offers White full-blooded compensation.

11.♖e1!N d6

11...♗b7 transposes to 10...♗b7 11.♖e1! ♘a5 below.

11...♘xb3 12.♕xb3 promises White compensation, as raids on d5 loom if the black knight ever leaves its awkward post.

12.♘d4!

Beautiful variations await, combining ♘d4 and ♘d5 motifs with Scheveningen-style themes. Study them well!

12...g6!?

12...♘xb3 13.♕xb3 e5 14.♘c2! ♗e6 15.♘d5⩲̄ f5 16.♘cb4 fxe4 17.♘c7† ♕xc7 18.♕xe6 ♕d7 19.♕b3 ♕b7 20.♖ad1 a5 21.♘d5 ♘xd5 22.♖xd5 a4 23.♕d1 Black labors heavily on the light squares. 23...♗e7 24.♕h5† ♔f8 25.♕f5† ♔g8 26.♕xe4±

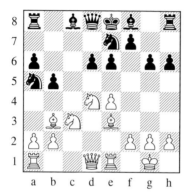

A clever castling attempt, but...

13.♗d5!!

Bond: "You know I've missed your sparkling personality." Zhao: "How's that for a punch line." (Die another Day)

13...exd5

13...♖b8 14.b4⩲̄

14.♘xd5! ♗g7

14...♘xd5 15.exd5 ♗e7 (15...f6 16.♘c6 ♘xc6 17.♗b6† ♕e7 18.dxc6 ♗e6 19.♖e3±) 16.b4±

15.♘f5!

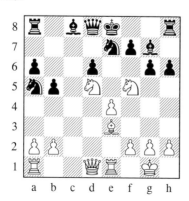

Christmas Jones: "Who are you?" Bond: "I work for the British government." (The World is Not Enough)

15...gxf5

15...♘xd5 16.♘xg7† ♔f8 17.♕xd5 ♗b7 (17...♖b8 18.♗a7 ♖b7 19.♗d4±) 18.♘e6†! fxe6 19.♕xe6±

16.♗b6 ♕d7 17.exf5 ♔f8 18.♖xe7 ♕xf5 19.♗xa5±

B) 10...♗b7 11.♖e1!

Target in range.

11...♘a5

11...♘g6 12.♘d5!⩲̄

11...d6 12.a4 b4 13.♘d5 exd5 14.exd5 ♘a5! (14...♘e5?! 15.a5!+– f6 16.♘xe5 fxe5 17.♕f3! ♕b8 18.♗a4† ♔d8 19.♗b6† ♔c8 20.♕h3†) Bond: "You looked like a man on the edge of losing control." Graves: "It's only by being on the edge that we know who we really are, under the skin." (Die Another Day) 15.♗c2 g6 (15...f6?! 16.♗g6† ♔d7 17.♗f7±) 16.♗d4 ♖g8 17.♗f6 ♖c8 18.♕e2⩲̄

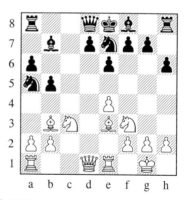

12.♘e5!N

The comment "8...h6 does not fight for the central e5-square" is now taken out of the abstract and into the concrete.

12.♗d5!?N is an adventure for those who wish to live on the edge... 12...exd5 13.exd5 d6 14.♗f4 f5 (14...♘c4?! illustrates the dangers lurking at every corner: 15.b3 ♘b6 16.♘e4+– ♘bc8 17.♖c1 ♔d7 18.♘xd6

♘xd6 19.♗xd6 ♔xd6 20.♘e5 ♕e8 21.♕f3
♖c8 22.♕f4 ♖xc1 23.♘c4† ♔d7 24.♕d6†
♔c8 25.♘b6#) 15.♖e6 ♗f7 16.♖xd6 ♕c8
17.♖d7! It's almost worth sacrificing the
bishop on d5 just for this move alone.
17...♔g8　18.♖c7　♕d8　19.♕e2　♗c8
20.♘h4⩲⩲

12...♕c7

a) 12...♘xb3 13.♗b6! ♕c8 14.♕f3 ♘f5
(14...f6? 15.♕h5† g6 16.♘xg6 ♘xg6
17.♕xg6† ♔e7 18.axb3 ♕e8 19.♗c5†
d6 20.♗xd6† ♔xd6 21.♕xf6+−) 15.axb3
♗d6 16.♕g4 ♗xe5 17.exf5 Perhaps Black
can defend, although in practice, once his
dark-squared bodyguard goes, so should his
king. 17...♗f6 18.♗d4! ♗xd4 19.♕xd4 0–0
20.f6→

b) 12...d6 13.♘xf7! Knights were made to
charge forward, after all. 13...♔xf7 14.♕f3†
♔g8 15.♗xe6† ♔h7 16.♘d5⩲⩲ ♘xd5?
17.exd5+− ♗c8 18.♗d4 ♗xe6 19.dxe6 ♘c4
20.♕f5† ♔g8 21.♕f7† ♔h7 22.e7+− Ouch.

13.♗f4 d6

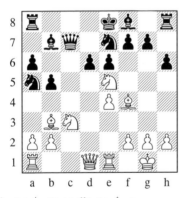

14.♘xf7! ♔xf7 15.♕h5† ♔g8

15...♘g6?? 16.♕f5†+−

15...g6 16.♕f3→

16.♗xe6† ♔h7 17.♖ad1±

17.♗xh6 g6 18.♕f3 ♘f5∞ Christmas Jones:
"Can you put that in English, for those of
us who don't speak spy?" (The World is Not
Enough)

17...♖d8

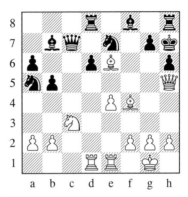

18.♗xh6! g6

18...gxh6 19.♕f7† ♗g7 20.♗f5†+−

19.♕f3 ♘f5

19...♔xh6 20.♕f6+−

19...♔xh6 20.♕f7† ♗g7 21.♖d3+−

20.♗g5!

The point behind the "waiting move"
17.♖ad1 – the bishop now comes to g5 with
a kick.

20...♖e8 21.♗xf5 gxf5 22.♕h5†+−

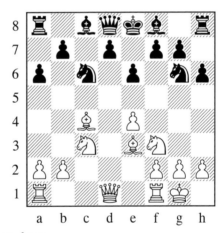

10.♗b3!

As in Esserman – Van Wely. Black must now
play 10...d6 or 10...♗e7, allowing ♘a4-b6
with a bind and full compensation. Tempting
fate, however, leads to annihilation.

10...b5?! 11.♘d5!

A mirror image of the Van Wely game.
This ♘d5, however, is a novelty, unless of

course, there are some hidden correspondence games. But to quote Tal, perhaps the World Champion closest to the Romantic spirit of James Bond: "I smoke, I drink, I gamble, but postal chess is one vice I do not have."

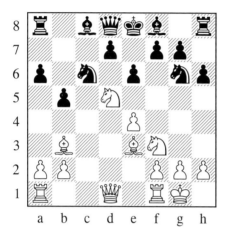

11...exd5

11...♖b8 12.♖c1±[37]

12.exd5 ♘ce5

12...♘a5 13.♖e1 ♗e7 14.d6 ♘xb3 15.axb3 0–0 16.♕d5 ♖b8 17.dxe7 ♘xe7 18.♕d6± Gripping...

13.d6!

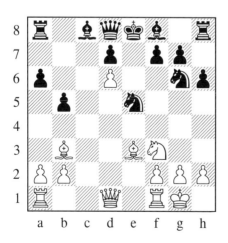

13...♕f6

13...♗b7 14.♘xe5 ♘xe5 15.f4 (or 15.♗f4+–) 15...♘c4 16.♗xc4 bxc4 17.♖e1+–

14.♘xe5 ♘xe5 15.♗d4

15.f4 ♘c4 16.♗xc4 bxc4 17.♖e1±

15...♕xd6

15...♗xd6 16.f4 0–0 17.fxe5+–

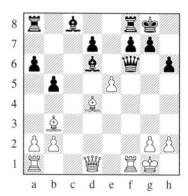

Vesper: "How was your lamb?" Bond: "Skewered. One sympathizes." (Casino Royale)

16.♖e1 ♗e7 17.♗xe5 ♕xd1 18.♖axd1 0–0 19.♗d5

"The name's Bond, James Bond."

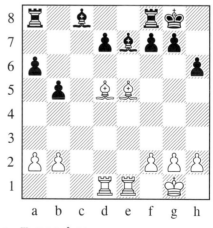

19...♖a7 20.♗d4+–

"I'm going to refute this opening in a week."

– Grandmaster Vadim Milov

Chapter 8

Early Bishop Out –
♘ge[00]7 Reloaded?[38]

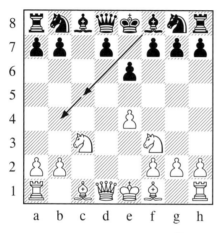

1.e4 c5 2.d4 cxd4 3.c3 dxc3 4.♘xc3 e6 5.♘f3

A sequel rarely lives up to the original, but alas, I shall try. After 6...♗c5 (or 6...♗b4),

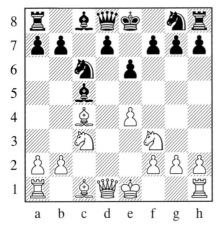

Black solves his dark-squared bishop's troubles once and for all. Only then does he aim for ...♘ge7/...0–0, thus smoothly finishing his development and, at last, "taking over the world". But we've heard that tale before. Yes, Black's setup is more or less bulletproof to the standard shot ♗g5, as the bishop has already escaped f8's orbit, so the knight can simply ignore the empty pin. Therefore, in order to foil the ...♘ge7 henchmen, the gambiteer must pull out a few more creative gadgets from his briefcase.

On 5...♗b4?, the dazzling 6.♕d4!

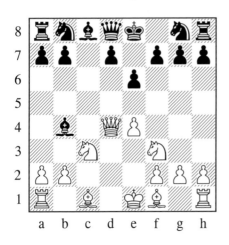

swiftly ends the ...♘ge7 dream after only six moves. And upon 5...♘c6 6.♗c4 ♗b4 7.0–0 ♘ge7, White unveils a subtle queen sortie, revealed only in the final act.

On 5...♘c6 6.♗c4 ♗c5 7.0–0 ♘ge7, White explodes in the center with 8.e5!, threatening the binding ♘e4, and Black's plans go up in smoke.

Marc Esserman – Vijayan

Harvard (blitz) 2011

In blitz and bullet, the Morra Gambit can be even more lethal than in classical chess. Even if Black surgically proves a reckless gambiteer's onslaught to be no more than smoke and mirrors, he may lack the time on the clock to convert his advantage. On the flip side, when I give the insane handicap of 45 seconds or less (in this case 38 seconds) vs. 5 minutes to weaker opponents in money games, the Morra remains my best hope to defuse both the adversary and the ticking clock.

1.e4 c5 2.d4 cxd4 3.c3 dxc3 4.♘xc3 e6 5.♘f3 ♗b4?!

A premature sally. After White's centralizing crusher, the necessity for ...♘c6 before ...♗b4 will become painfully evident.

6.♕d4! ♗xc3†

Black cedes the bishop pair and the dark squares, but this bleak moves still remains the lesser of the two evils.

Casually returning the pawn with 6...♘c6 meets an unpleasant surprise: 7.♕xg7 ♕f6

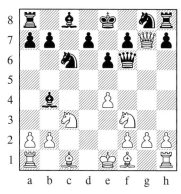

8.♗h6! Lighting a very short fuse! Grabbing the bishop forfeits either rook or queen. Meanwhile, ♕xf6 then ♗g7 burns fast. 8...♗f8?? (8...♗e7!± is Black's only attempt to extinguish the flames, but after 9.e5!, which we analyze later, the position still blows up.) 9.♕xf8# N. Christiansen – Fricker, Boston 2011.

I witnessed this explosive finish live in Boston's Boylston chess club. Afterwards, clearly dazed and confused from the early morning round, Fricker sheepishly explained away the loss to a poor night's sleep. We've all been there before, so may I advise daring Sicilian players out there to get some snooze before taking on c3, or else you will have nightmares for many days to come.

7.♕xc3 ♘f6 8.♗d3!

Loading up to snipe at the naive black king.

8...0–0?! 9.e5 ♘d5

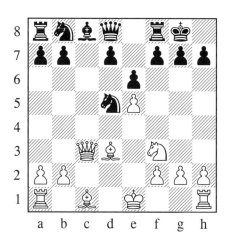

10.♗xh7†!

A rare bolt, the classic "Greek gift" bishop sacrifice in the Morra (the bishop almost always posts on c4).

10...♔xh7 11.♘g5†

Bond: "You can drive this thing, right?" Christmas: "It doesn't exactly take a degree in nuclear physics." (The World is Not Enough)

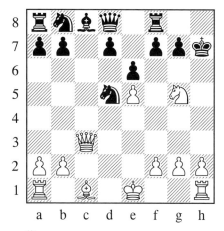

11...♕xg5

11...♔g6 12.♕g3+–

11...♔g8 12.♕h3 ♖e8 13.♕h7† ♔f8 14.♕h5! Precision is always necessary, but even more so in 38-second chess. 14...♔g8 (14...g6 15.♕h7+– Bond: "Sit tight.") White may now announce mate in 5, making sure to deliver the mate with seconds left for pure street chess spectacle: 15.♕xf7† ♔h8 16.♕h5† ♔g8 17.♕h7† ♔f8 18.♕h8† ♔e7 19.♕xg7#

12.♕h3† ♕h6 13.♗xh6 gxh6±

And I went on to win somehow in the ensuing scrum. Bond: "You've defused hundreds of these, right?" Christmas: "Yeah, but they're usually standing still." Bond: "Yeah well, life's full of small challenges. Have a look at this. Someone's stripped the screw heads." Christmas: "Someone's tampered with the

bomb." [Bomb ticks down – 41... 40... 39...]
(The World is Not Enough)
...1–0

Marc Esserman – Yilmer Guzman

Altamonte Springs 2007

**1.e4 c5 2.d4 cxd4 3.c3 dxc3 4.♘xc3 e6
5.♘f3 ♘c6 6.♗c4 ♗c5 7.0–0 ♘ge7 8.e5!**

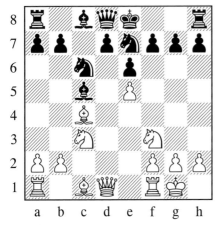

Pinpointing the fatal flaw in the "improved"
...♘ge7 setup. The speedy ♘e4 looms large,
and Black's only hope of preventing a total
bind lies in an immediate 8...d5, featured in
our next illustrative example.

8...0–0 9.♘e4 b6!?

Awkward yet playable. The more natural
9...♗b6 might lead to similar mayhem as in
the game, except that the bishop would take a
less active role in the defensive struggle.

10.♗g5!?

Seeking maximum chaos, but perhaps the
quiet 10.♘xc5 followed by 11.♗e3 with an
easy, stable advantage on the dark squares is
more prudent. But the Morra and prudent
don't really fit in the same sentence.

10...h6

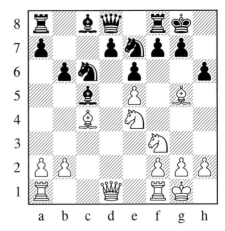

11.♘f6†!?[39] gxf6?!

Guzman must steady his nerves and decline
the sacrifice, but with the knight's nostrils
flaring on f6, he cannot be blamed for giving
into temptation.

11...♔h8! 12.♗d3!

But madness still prevails, and while
objectively Black has enough resources to
force a repetition, only the rare assassin can
summon such reserves in the heat of battle.
12...♘g6 13.♘h7!

M: "Tell me what you know of James Bond."
Frost: "He's a double 0, and a wild one as
I discovered today. He'll light the fuse on
any explosive situation, and be a danger to
himself and others. Kill first, ask questions
later." (Die Another Day)

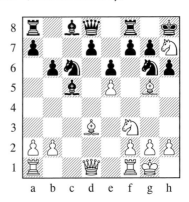

13...hxg5

13...♗e7 14.♗xe7 ♘cxe7 15.♘xf8± 14.♘fxg5 ♘cxe5!?

14...♘gxe5!? 15.♕h5 g6 16.♕h6 ♘g4 17.♕h4 ♔g7 18.♘xf8 ♘ge5! 19.♘xg6!?∞ (19.b4!? Moneypenny: "Don't ask." M: "Don't tell.") 15.♕h5 ♘f4 16.♕h4 ♘fg6=

12.♗xf6

Now the bishop, worth more than the black queen, slices through her king.

12...♕e8

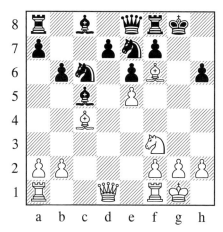

Planning to meet 13.♘h4 with 13...♘g6, and if 14.♕h5, then 14...♔h7, and if then 15.♗d3... then 15...♖g8! Carver: "You see Mr. Bond, I have a backup plan." Bond: "Uh huh. So do I."

13.♘g5!?

Still firing away on h5, but stopping ...♔h7. However, this allows Black an absurd computer defense. Less Romantic, but more... prudent would be: 13.♗d3! ♘g6 14.♕d2 ♔h7 15.♘g5†! Only now. How trite. 15...♔g8 (15...hxg5 16.♕xg5+–) 16.♘e4 ♔h7 17.♕d1+– as ♕h5 reloads.

13...♘f5?!

Black misses a desperado which may allow him to "die another day":

13...♘xe5!

Close your eyes if you do not wish to be disturbed by the next variation.

14.♕h5 ♘f5 15.g4

15.♗xe5 f6!–+

15...♗e7!

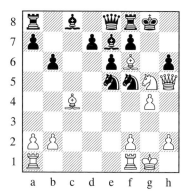

Finally, the bishops meet, tête-à-tête.

16.gxf5 ♗xf6 17.♕xh6 ♗xg5 18.♕xg5† ♔h7

18...♘g6 19.f6!+– Austin Powers: "Ouch baby, very ouch."

19.♕h4†

19.♕h5†= Who plays for a draw, honestly? (Austin Powers: "Who throws a shoe, honestly?")

19...♔g8 20.f4!

Vanessa: "Onward boys." (Austin Powers: International Man of Mystery)

14.♕g4+– ♘e3

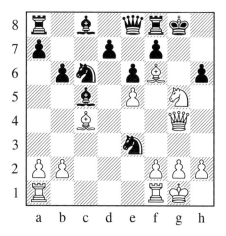

15.♕h5?!

Forcing mate in seven, but shamefully missing mate in three with the immediate queen sacrifice: 15.♗d3! ♘f5 16.♘h7† A first among four equals. 16...♔xh7 17.♕g7#

15...♘f5 16.♗d3 ♕e7

I told you the bishop was more powerful than the black queen.

17.♕xh6 ♘xh6 18.♗h7#

Bond: "You forgot the first rule of mass media Elliot. Give the people what they want [blood]!"[40]

Marc Esserman – Vadim Milov

Philadelphia (blitz) 2008

1.e4 c5 2.d4 cxd4 3.c3

In our first encounter a year earlier, Milov cautiously averted danger, declining with 3...♘f6. But now he flashed a wily, mischievous look, and you just knew what was coming next.

3...dxc3

A Morra Gambit. "Yeah baby!" (Austin Powers)

4.♘xc3

Around this time, not to my knowledge, a "degenerate" student of mine bet on me straight up to win this game. Yes, he ultimately collected, but then couldn't control himself and picked me to win again straight up as Black vs. Milov in the 2nd blitz mini-match. Sadly, I disappointed him, losing badly in the Dutch in 20 moves.

4...e6 5.♘f3 a6 6.♗c4 ♗c5 7.0–0 ♘e7 8.e5![41] d5

Milov refuses to allow the totally suffocating ♘e4, and instead seeks active counterplay.

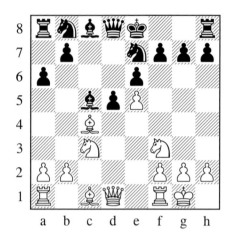

Dr Evil: "The world is mine. The world is mine."

9.exd6!

White rips open the board, hoping to capitalize on his superior development.

9...♗xd6

9...♕xd6?! Attempting simplification only ends in... liquification. Muahaha. 10.♘e4! ♕xd1 11.♖xd1 ♗b6 12.♘d6† ♔f8 13.♘g5+–

10.♕e2 b5?!

Black should evacuate the premises and castle. Now, the door should have slammed shut.

11.♗b3?!

11.♖d1! The classic unstoppable Morra pin decides at once.

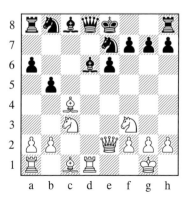

Dr. Evil: "Throw me a freakin' bone here, OK." 11...bxc4 (11...♕c7 12.♗xb5†+–) 12.♗f4 ♘f5 13.♗xd6 ♘xd6 14.♘e4± Dr. Evil: "Not this time, Mr. Powers."

11...♗b7?!

Black misses his last chance to castle.

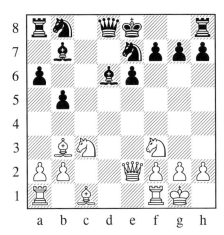

Austin Powers: "I've got you now, Dr. Evil."

12.♖d1±

12.♘g5! also wins shagadelically: 12...0–0 13.♘xf7! ♔xf7 (13...♖xf7 14.♕xe6+–) 14.♗xe6† ♔e8 15.♕h5† ♔g6 16.♖e1 "Yeah baby." 16...♗e7 17.♕xh7+–

12...♕c7

Black runs, but he can't hide. Dr Evil: "Come, Mr. Bigglesworth."

13.♘e4 ♗xe4 14.♕xe4

Notice that Black lags just one move behind.

14...♘bc6 15.♗g5!

The bishop develops with brutal force, shaking the fragile foundations.

15...♖c8

15...0–0 Too late! 16.♖ac1 The Morra rooks arrive just in time. 16...♖ac8 17.♗xe6+–

16.♖ac1 ♕b8 17.♗xe6!

Austin Powers: "Smashing, baby."

17...fxe6 18.♕xe6+– ♖d8

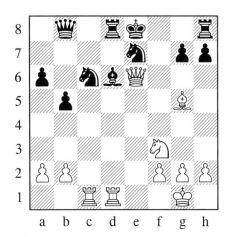

19.♔f1!?

Slipping away from ...♗xh2†, White now threatens 20.♖xc6, and Black must resign. The Morra rooks fire freely. If the c6-knight scatters, then 20.♗xe7 followed by ♖xd8 and ♖c8 looms, or even 20.♘e5 immediately. And if 19...♕b7/c7, then 20.♖xc6 followed by ♗xe7 reaps applause.

1–0

But I could have won with the immediate: 19.♖xc6!

"Oops, I did it again, baby." (Austin Powers, Goldmember)

19...♗xh2† 20.♘xh2 ♖xd1†

Dr. Evil: "You know, we're not so different, you and I."

21.♘f1 ♕b7

21...♖d7 22.♗xe7 ♖xe7 23.♖c8†+–

22.♖b6 ♕c7 23.♗xe7 ♕xe7 24.♕c6†!

Austin Powers: "Show me love."

24...♔f7

24...♖d7 25.♖b8†+–

25.♕f3†+–

After the game, Milov vowed to refute the Morra in a week, but I still haven't heard back! Dr Evil: "I'm going to get you, Austin Powers!"

Sarkar's Revenge

Marc Esserman – Justin Sarkar

Berkeley 2008

1.e4 c5 2.d4 cxd4 3.c3 dxc3 4.♘xc3 ♘c6 5.♘f3 e6 6.♗c4 ♗b4

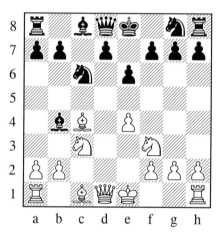

Following his painful defeat a few months earlier, IM Sarkar spent the night before our rematch brewing up a defense. Ultimately, he came across GM Grivas' 2008 *New In Chess* article hailing 6...♗b4 as the elixir to the Morra problem. Justin proceeded tentatively, his expressions seeming to ask if I had an answer. Much to his delight, I simply fired blank shots.

7.0–0 ♘ge7!

Black must not grab on c3 prematurely, but instead reserve the right for later:

7...♗xc3?!

Almost all of my previous games here had involved this hasty exchange, after which White achieves overwhelming dark-squared dominance.

8.bxc3 ♘ge7

8...♕a5?! 9.♕d6! Gambiting the c-pawn yet again! 9...♕xc3?! 10.♗a3 ♘ge7 11.♖ac1± More open lines, please?

9.♗a3±

The bishop heads for a devastating d6-blockade. Black should now passively accept his fate, as trying to avoid it makes matters worse:

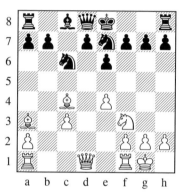

9...d5?! 10.exd5 exd5 11.♗d3 0–0 12.♖e1 ♖e8 13.♘g5 h6

13...g6 14.♕f3±

14.♗h7† ♔f8 15.♕h5! hxg5 16.♗f5! f6 17.♗g6+–

Slicing and dicing.

In hostile territory, I decided to handle 6...♗b4 as if it were 6...♗c5, an ominous sign. Bond: "What's your plan for the bomb?" Renard: "You first, or could it be you don't have a plan?" (*The World is Not Enough*)

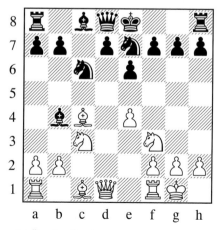

8.e5?! ♘g6 9.♘e4

No longer coming with tempo, but I'm improvising. Sarkar, unimpressed, looked on curiously. Renard: "How sad, to be threatened by a man who believes in nothing." Bond: "And what do you believe in?"

9...♘gxe5!

The Joker: "I believe, whatever doesn't kill you, simply makes you... stranger." (The Dark Knight)

10.♘xe5 ♘xe5 11.♕d4

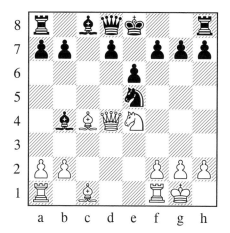

My deep plan, returning to the well of ♕d4 to try and down Sarkar again. If now 11...♘c6, then 12.♕xg7, and if 11...d6 or 11...f6, then 12.♗xe6 and 13.♕xb4... Renard: "A man tires of being executed."

11...f6!

With a wide smile! I slunk back in my chair, absorbing the shock that I had been had, for on 12.♗xe6? Sarkar sticks in the dagger blow: 12...♘c6!–+ Renard: "No hard feelings Mr. Bond, but now, we're even, and soon, you'll feel nothing at all."[42] Depressed and down a full two central pawns, I somehow gathered myself and managed to swindle a draw. But certainly not as a result of the opening. As far as I'm concerned, Justin got his Morra revenge. **...½–½**

Jacek Stopa – Alexandra Kosteniuk

St. Louis (rapid) 2011

Ivana: "Do you know what we do in Russia to keep warm?" Austin Powers: "I can guess, baby." Ivana: "We play chess." Austin: "I guessed wrong."[43]

1.e4 c5 2.d4 cxd4 3.c3 dxc3 4.♘xc3 e6 5.♘f3 ♘c6 6.♗c4 ♗b4 7.0–0 ♘ge7 8.♗g5

8.♘b5?! debuted in a clash of two theoretical titans from the golden age of chess, GMs Igor Zaitsev and Semyon Furman, who curiously enough, were both also loyal seconds to Karpov. In this duel Furman, as Black, got the upper hand, proving the knight raid too optimistic: 8...d5! 9.exd5 exd5 10.♗xd5 ♘xd5 11.♕xd5 0–0∓ Despite giving back the pawn, Furman retained a distinct advantage with his two bishops roaming the open board. The game ended in a draw but remained a clear theoretical victory for Black.

In the "Kings vs. Queens" rapid tournament last fall in St. Louis, five leading male players faced off against top female opponents in a tense round-robin format. Young IM Stopa, already an Evans Gambit disciple, showed up inspired by our European 2011 summer tour, vowing to play the Morra – the sexiest opening in chess – in each and every game he could. He had already defeated IM Fierro in the Morra Declined, but now Women's World Champion GM Kosteniuk was on to his womanizing ways. As Bond speeds in a sleek car, another speeder approaches. Caroline: "I enjoy a spirited ride as much as the next girl but... Who's that?" Bond: "The next girl." (GoldenEye)

8...♕a5?!

Black should ignore the pin and simply castle, exposing 8.♗g5 to be full of hot air.

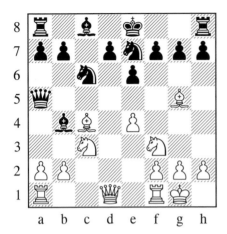

9.♘b5?!

During the interviews, Stopa revealed that never before in his career had he lost to a woman. And had he just found the most vigorous blow, he would have deprived Kosteniuk of the opportunity to sully his pure record:

9.♘d5!N

Ripping the now helpless black queen, as well as the entire position, apart. Bond: "Black queen on the red king, Ms...?" "Solitaire." Bond: "My name's Bond. James Bond." Solitaire: "I know who you are, what you are, and why you have come. You have made a mistake. You will not succeed." (Live and Let Die)

9...exd5 10.exd5

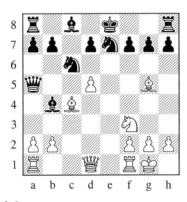

10...h6

As usual with ♘d5, Black has many defenses but all roads lead to mayhem:

a) 10...0–0 11.a3! Exploiting the unusual post of the black bishop as retreating it to c5 leads to b2-b4 forking, but 11...♗d6 also fails to satisfy: 12.dxc6 ♕c7 13.cxb7 ♗xb7 14.♖c1±

b) 10...♘d8 11.d6 ♘f5 12.a3 ♗xd6 13.♕d3! 0–0 14.b4 ♕c7 15.♗xd8! and now:

b1) 15...♖xd8?

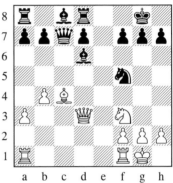

16.♗xf7†! ♔xf7 17.♕xf5† ♔g8 18.♘g5+–
Jinx: "What do predators do when the sun goes down?" Bond: "They feast." 18...♕c4 19.♕xh7† ♔f8 20.♖fe1 ♗e7 21.♖e4 ♕d5 (21...♕g8 22.♕g6 ♗xg5 23.♕xg5+–) 22.♕h8† ♕g8 23.♖f4† ♗f6 24.♖xf6† Miranda: "Mr. Bond here was just explaining his Big Bang theory." Jinx: "Oh, I think I got the thrust of it." (Die Another Day) 24...gxf6 25.♕xf6† ♔e8 26.♖e1†+–

b2) 15...♕xd8! 16.♕xf5⩲ White has clear-cut compensation for the pawn in the form of massive development and soon dominant central rooks, but mating remains a long way off. Miranda: "I'm afraid you'll never have that pleasure, Mr. Bond." (Die Another Day)

11.♗f4! ♘g6

11...♘d8?! 12.a3±

12.♗g3

Black should just give back the piece to minimize the suffering, but stubbornness leads to further friction.

12...♘d8?! 13.♕e2† ♔f8 14.a3 ♗e7

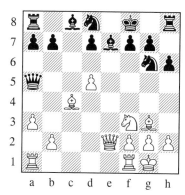

15.h4! h5

15...d6 16.♖fe1→

16.b4 ♕b6 17.♗d3 d6 18.♗xg6 fxg6 19.♖fe1 ♕c7 20.♖ac1 ♕d7 21.♖c3

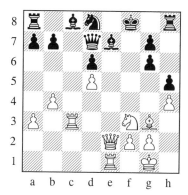

21...♗f6

21...♘f7 22.♖e3+– The triple barrel reloaded! Xenia: "You don't need the gun, Commander."

22.♖c7!+–

Bond: "She always did enjoy a good squeeze." (GoldenEye)

Of course, for the faint of heart, such sensual play is unnecessary, as the simple 9.♗d2!N secures the bishop pair and a dry positional advantage: 9...0–0 10.a3 ♗xc3 11.♗xc3±

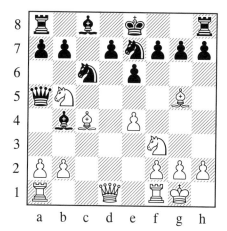

9...d5 10.exd5 exd5 11.♗f4 0–0 12.♗d3 ♕d8 13.♗c7

Xenia: "You think you can hurt me?"

13...♕d7 14.a3 ♗a5 15.♗xa5 ♘xa5 16.♘e5

Xenia: "You think you can break me?"

16...♕d8 17.♖e1 ♘ac6 18.♘f3 ♘g6 19.♕a4 ♗d7 20.♕b3 ♘f4∓

Elektra: "I've always had a power over men."

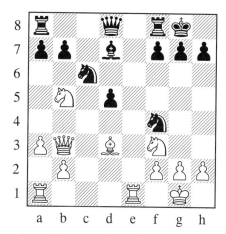

21.♗f1 ♕b6 22.♕a4 ♘g6 23.♕d1 a6 24.♕xd5 ♗e6 25.♖xe6 fxe6 26.♕xe6† ♔h8 27.♘d6 ♕xb2

Elektra: "You should have killed me when you had the chance. But no, you couldn't. Not me."

28.♖d1 ♘ce5 29.♗c4 ♘xf3† 30.gxf3 ♘e5 31.♗d5 ♖f6 32.♕e7 ♕e2

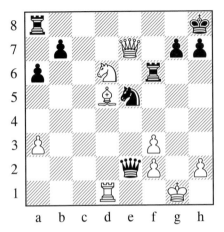

Xenia: "This time, Mr. Bond, the pleasure will be all mine."

0–1

Early Bishop Out Theory I – 6...♗b4

1.e4 c5 2.d4 cxd4 3.c3 dxc3 4.♘xc3 e6 5.♘f3 ♘c6

5...♗b4?! 6.♕d4 ♘c6 7.♕xg7 ♕f6 8.♗h6! ♗e7□ 9.e5! This shatters the fragile Black defenses.

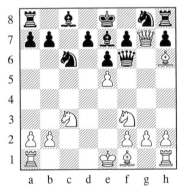

9...♘xe5 10.♘e4 ♘xf3† (10...♗b4† 11.♘fd2±) 11.gxf3 ♕xf3 12.♗g2!+−

6.♗c4 ♗b4!? 7.0–0 ♘ge7

For a long time after the Sarkar game I

searched for the right approach here – many moves came and went into the night, until ultimately I hit upon the right idea. Bond: "There may be one critical element here I may have overlooked." (The World is Not Enough)

8.♕c2!

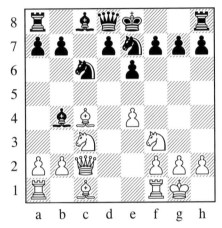

I am convinced this original positional approach is best. The queen slides to c2, when White readies to meet Black's unavoidable ...d5 break with ♗d3, fully coordinating the queen and bishop. On ...♗xc3, White may recapture with ♕xc3, keeping the pawn structure whole, or even bxc3 with the queen's rook sliding to b1, depending on circumstance. Lastly, White's king's rook will take up its natural post on d1. The following variations demonstrate the concrete realities of the subtle 8.♕c2.

8...d5!?

8...0–0!? 9.♖d1 ♘g6 10.♗e3

White brings his pieces to their optimal squares, waiting for Black to show his hand. 10...a6!?

The most optimistic, shooting for rapid queenside expansion.

10...b6!?∞ remains murky.

10...♗xc3? 11.♕xc3 ♕f6 12.♕xf6 gxf6 13.♖d6± is a simple variation showcasing the virtues of 8.♕c2.

11.♗e2!

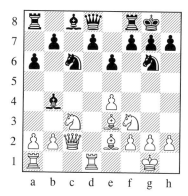

Such deft maneuvers for a "primitive" gambit! White eyes ♘a4-b6, and plots to bust ...b5 with a2-a4. Chang: "Been busy, Mr. Bond?" Bond: "Just surviving, Mr. Chang." (Die Another Day)

11...b5

11...♖b8 12.♘a4⩱̄ ♗a5 (12...b5 13.♘c5∞) 13.♖ac1⩱̄ With full mobilization.

11...♗e7 12.♘a4 b5 13.♘c5∞ d6 14.♘xe6! fxe6 15.♕xc6±

12.a4!

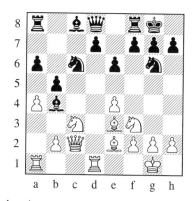

12...bxa4

12...♗b7 13.axb5 axb5 14.♖xa8 ♕xa8 15.♘xb5± (or 15.♕b3±)

13.♘xa4 ♖b8 14.♘c5! a5 15.♖ac1⩱̄

A tense struggle lies ahead.

With 8...d5, Black asks for and receives fireworks.

9.♖d1 ♗xc3 10.bxc3!

Voluntarily wrecking the structure for dynamic factors.

The natural 10.♕xc3?! here fails both strategically and tactically. After ...d5 breaks, she belongs on c2 to form a powerful queen and bishop battery. No surprise then, that Black can force a favorable simplification: 10...♕a5!⩱ 11.♕xa5 (11.♕xg7?! ♖g8!⩱) 11...♘xa5 12.♗b5† ♗d7 13.♗xd7† ♔xd7 14.♘e5† ♔e8⩱

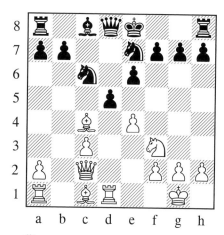

10...♕a5

After 10...0–0!? 11.♗d3! the battery fires away. 11...h6 Now White's potent bishops come into their own. 12.a4!? (or 12.♗b2!? ♕c7 13.c4→) 12...♕c7 13.♗a3 ♖d8 14.c4!∞

11.exd5 exd5

11...♘xd5?! 12.♗xd5 exd5 13.♖e1†±

12.♗d3

Reloading.

12...♗g4

12...g6 13.♗h6→

13.♗f4 ♗xf3

13...♖c8 14.♖ab1 b6 15.♗d6→ Slicing. 15...0–0 16.♖b5±

14.gxf3 ♖c8 15.♖ab1 ♘d4

Trevelyan: "Why can't you just be a good boy and die?"

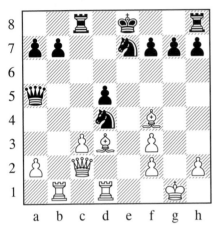

16.♕b2 ♘xf3† 17.♔h1± ♕xc3

17...0–0 18.♕e2±

18.♕xc3 ♖xc3 19.♖xb7

Bond: "You first."

19...♘c6 20.♗d6+–

Theory II – 7...♕c7

1.e4 c5 2.d4 cxd4 3.c3 dxc3 4.♘xc3 e6 5.♘f3 ♘c6 6.♗c4 a6 7.0–0 ♕c7

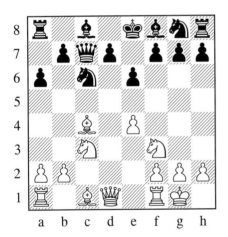

No Morra anthology would be complete

without addressing Larsen's proposed antidote. After all, the famous grandmaster quipped that 3...dxc3 wins a pawn, so we must put his defense to the test. Black now plots to camp his bishop on d6, when his pieces will all converge to grip the central dark squares. He may continue with ...♘ge7-g6, cementing his clamp. However, on the downside, Black's queenside development lags behind, which may lead to his doom. White has a few powerful tries.

8.♖e1!

The most logical response, lining up for a fatal ♘d5 blow.

8.♗b3!?

Primarily designed to clear the road for ♗e3 and ♖c1 and the eventual standard ♘d5 sacrifice.

8...♘f6

8...♗d6 looks best, playing as in the main line. For example: 9.♖e1 ♘ge7 10.♗e3 ♘g6 11.♖c1 transposes to the note to Black's 9th move in the main line.

8...d6?! 9.♗f4 ♘f6 10.♖c1 ♗e7 11.♘d5± gives an improved version of the ...a6/...♕c7 Scheveningen, as White has not wasted time on ♕e2.

9.♘d5!N

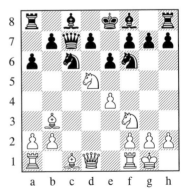

This featured in a home match I ran between Houdini 1.5 vs. Deep Rybka 4. Sicilian players who have bitterly felt the awesome power of ♘d5 should take solace in the knowledge that Rybka herself could not swim through the maze of complications.

9...exd5 10.exd5 ♗b4?!

Rybka should calmly block the e-file with 10...♗e7 and return the piece, but let's not be too harsh – she's only a machine.

11.dxc6 dxc6 12.♗g5! ♕e7 13.a3 ♗a5 14.♗f4

There's no escaping Houdini's torture chamber now.

14...♗g4 15.♗d6 ♕e4 16.♗xf7†! ♔xf7 17.♕b3† ♔g6 18.♘e5† ♔h6 19.♕g3! ♖hg8 20.♕h4† ♔h5 21.f4! ♕f5 22.♗e7! ♗d2 23.g4!

And Houdini went on to tighten the noose. To view this crazy game in its entirety, see the supplemental films.

8...♗d6

Black has a few answers, but Larsen's move seems most promising.

8...♘f6?! 9.e5! ♘g4 10.♗f4

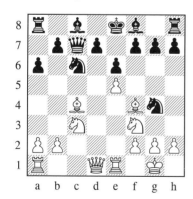

10...b5

10...♗c5 misfires after 11.♘e4→

10...f6?? 11.♘d5!+−

11.♗b3 f6 12.♘d5 ♕a7

#2: "I like to live dangerously."

13.exf6! ♘xf2 14.♕c2

Austin Powers: "I also like to live dangerously."

14...♘d3† 15.♗e3 ♘xe1 16.♖xe1 ♕b7

17.♘g5+−

Mate or catastrophic material loss follows.

8...♘ge7 9.♘d5!

For those who like to live on the wild side. Austin Powers: "Groovy, baby."

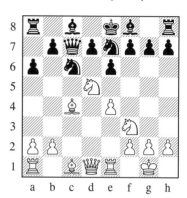

9...exd5 10.exd5

Now Black can gallop to three logical destinations, but for brevity we will only dissect the most active in detail. If you're not convinced, fear not and analyze the mayhem.

10...♘a5!?

10...♘d8 11.♗b3 d6 12.♗f4 ♗d7 13.♖c1

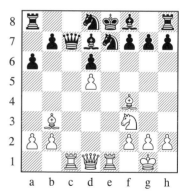

Jinx: "I'm a girl who doesn't like to get tied down." (Die another Day) 13...♕b8 (13...♕b6 14.♘d2+−) 14.♘d2!+− Bond: "No wonder your relationships don't last very long." (Die Another Day) 14...b5 15.♘e4 ♘b7 16.♖c6!+−

11.♗d3!±

Even recklessly gifting the bishop with 11.d6 leads to chaos: 11...♕xc4 12.dxe7 ♗xe7 13.♖xe7† ♔xe7 14.♕e1†! ♔f8 15.♕xa5 b6 16.♕xb6 ♕e6∞ White certainly has enough for the exchange, but perhaps not more.

11...♕d6

11...d6 12.♗d2 b5 13.♖c1 ♕b6 14.♘g5+– is crushing. However, the queen is not the best blockader...

12.b4! ♕xb4 13.♘g5!

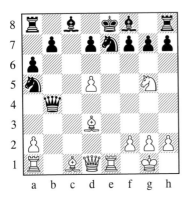

♖b1, ♗d2, ♕f3, ♘e4, and of course, d5-d6, beckon. Yes, it seems all those moves come at once. Austin Powers: "I put the grrr in swinger baby, yeah!"

13.♗d2±

13...♕d4 14.♘xf7 ♔xf7

14...♕xa1 15.♘d6† ♔d8 16.♗e3 ♕b2 17.♕d2 ♕xd2 18.♗b6# Austin Powers: "Yes, yes, yes."

15.♗g6†±

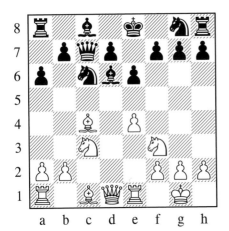

9.♗e3!N

No wasting time! Finally we reach the main line of Larsen's Defense.

Here in my practice I have played 9.♕e2!? (threatening e4-e5) twice with success. Both of my opponents responded with the unnecessary concession 9...f6, and after the standard ♗e3, ♖c1 and ♗b3, I achieved overwhelming positions vs. GM A. Ivanov and future IM Ludwig. But alas, the game scores have been lost in the rubble. However, the correct response is: 9...♘e5! 10.♘xe5 ♗xe5 11.♘d5!? exd5 12.exd5 d6 13.f4 f6 and Black lives to tell the tale.

9...♘e5?!

But now this fails spectacularly.

9...♘ge7!? 10.♖c1 ♘g6 11.♗b3 0–0 (11...♗f4?! 12.♗xf4 ♕xf4 [12...♘xf4 13.e5→] 13.♘d5±) 12.g3!⩱ Restricting Black's minor pieces and bracing for a war of attrition. Black must sit tight, as 12...b5 invites 13.♘d5!.

10.♘xe5 ♗xe5 11.♖c1!

Austin Powers: "Yeah, baby, yeah!"

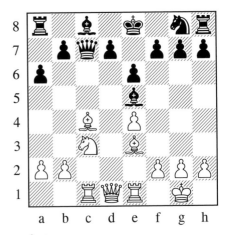

11...♗xh2†

11...♕xc4? 12.♘a4+– ♕b5 13.♘b6 ♖b8 14.a4! ♕a5 15.♖xc8† Austin Powers:

"Smashing, baby." 15...♖xc8 16.♕xd7† ♔f8 17.♕xc8† ♔e7 18.♕d7† ♔f6 19.♕d8† ♔g6 20.♕g5#

12.♔h1 ♗f4
12...♗e5 13.♘a4±

Now, flip a coin to pick your knight sacrifice.

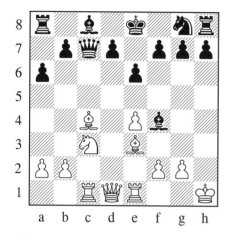

13.♘b5!
13.♘d5!±

13...axb5 14.♗xb5 ♕d6 15.♗xf4 ♕xf4
15...♕xd1 16.♖exd1±

16.♖xc8†+−
Austin Powers: "Name. Austin 'Danger' Powers."

But for the most hardcore swingers/ swashbucklers out there, stay tuned for a ♘d5 sacrifice that will blow your minds. Larsen's Defense, and the entire Morra Gambit, will never be the same.

Theory III – 7...♕c7 8.♘d5!!

1.e4 c5 2.d4 cxd4 3.c3 dxc3 4.♘xc3 e6 5.♘f3 ♘c6 6.♗c4 a6 7.0–0 ♕c7
Larsen's delusion pervades in the present day. As I am writing, I leaf through the December

2011 Christmas edition of *New In Chess* where British superstar GM Nigel Short plays the role of the Grinch who stole the Morra Gambit: "A belief in the existence of Santa Claus is more rational than imagining White has adequate compensation after the unwarranted [3.]c3?" ("Short stories" – *New In Chess* 2011, #8). And this coming from a man who ventures the King's Gambit. Well Nigel – ho, ho, ho, baby.

8.♘d5!!

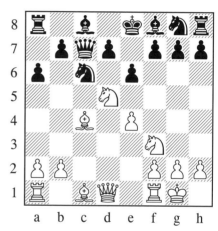

A virtual novelty on move 8 (played only once in a game between unrated players), which stops Larsen's Defense even before it starts. With this dashing knight sacrifice, all the previous ♘d5 themes again apply. Switch on your Rybka and watch as she gyrates wildly from −1 to +1 and beyond! Fembots: "You can't resist us Mr. Powers. You can't resist us Mr. Powers... resist us Mr. Powers." Mr. Powers: "Au contraire baby, I think *you*, can't resist *me*."

8...exd5
Black must accept the sacrifice.

8...♕d8?! 9.♗e3!± exd5 10.exd5 ♘a5 11.♖e1 ♗e7 12.♘d3! ♔f8 (12...d6 13.♗d4± and the knight will fall to b2-b4, a recurring motif.) 13.♕e2!± ♗b4 (13...b6 14.d6! ♗xd6 15.♗xb6+−)

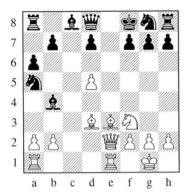

14.♗b6! ♕e7 15.♕c2 ♗xe1 16.♖xe1 ♕f6 17.♕c7+– Austin Powers: "Vanessa, I can explain. See, I was trying to get to Doctor Evil, and then all of a sudden the fembots came by and smoke started coming out of their jumblies. So I thought I'd work my mojo right, to counter their mojo."

9.exd5 ♘ce7

The knight can also head to the queenside: 9...♘a5 10.♖e1† ♗e7

10...♘e7 11.♗d3± transposes to the position that arose after 8...♘ge7 in the *Theory II* analysis.

11.♗d3

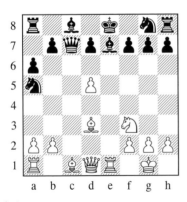

11...b6!?

11...d6!? 12.♗d2→ b5 13.a4 (13.♖c1!? ♕d8) 13...♘c4 14.♗c3 ♘f6 15.axb5 0–0 16.♖xe7 ♕xe7 17.♗xc4 This offers at the very least a slight plus for White, but there may be better lurking earlier.

12.♗d2 ♘b7

12...♔f8!? 13.♖c1 ♕d8 14.♗f4 d6 15.b4 ♘b7 16.♘d4 ♗f6 17.♘c6±

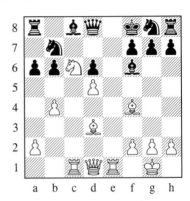

17...♕c7 (17...♕d7 18.♗xa6! "Groovy baby." 18...♖xa6 19.♘b8+–) 18.♕e2 And along with mate, White's threats include 19.♘a7.

13.♖c1 ♕d6

13...♕b8 14.♘g5+– Austin Powers: "We got cross mojoinations going and then..."

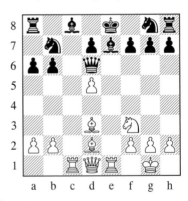

14.♗xa6!±

Austin Powers: "Their heads started exploding, you know, that sort of thing."

14...♖xa6

14...♕xd5 15.♗c4 ♕f5 16.♘h4 ♕f6 17.♗c3 ♕g5 18.♘f3+– and depending where the queen goes, one (or more) of 19.♘e5, 19.♗xf7† or 19.♗xg7 boogies.

15.♖xc8† ♘d8 16.♕b3+– ♔f8

16...f6 17.♗b4 ♕f4 18.d6+–

17.♗b4! ♕xb4 18.♕xb4+–

Vanessa: "OK Austin, I believe you."

10.♗b3 d6 11.♖e1

We reach a freestyle position where White remains a full piece down with seemingly few threats, but Black simply cannot consolidate his material gains. When the smoke clears, White's queen routinely ravages from the a5-square in the key lines.

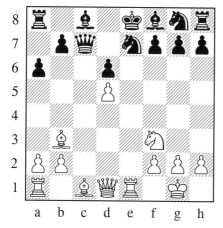

11...♘f6

Black may try making room for the king:
11...f6!? 12.♘d4!

The rook, knight, and pawn take turns frolicking on e6.

12.g6 13.♕f3 ♘f7 14.♗d2 ♘h6 15.♗c3→

White may unload on the e-file next.

15...♗g5 16.♖e5!∞

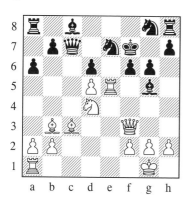

Austin: "No man, what we swingers were rebelling against was uptight squares like you whose bag was money and world domination. It's freedom baby, yeah."

16.♖e6!?

16...♘f5 17.♖xf5! ♗xf5 18.h4 ♗h6 19.g4 ♗d7
20.g5 ♗g7 21.♘e6 ♗xe6 22.dxe6† ♔e7 23.h5

White's only a full rook down, baby.

23...♖f8 24.♖e1→

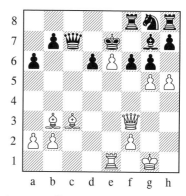

24...fxg5?! 25.♕f7†!±

Austin: "Grrr, baby, very grrrr."[44]

25...♖xf7 26.exf7† ♗e5 27.♖xe5†! dxe5
28.♗b4† ♔d7 29.f8=♕±

Maybe White will sacrifice his queen again!?

11...♗g4 12.♗f4 ♕d7 13.♖c1 ♘h6

13...f6 14.h3 ♗xf3 15.♕xf3 ♔f7? 16.♗xd6!
♕xd6 17.♖e6+–

14.h3 ♗xf3 15.♕xf3 ♘hf5

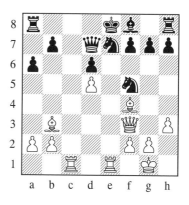

Dr. Evil: "Face it. Freedom failed."

16.♕c3 ♖d8 17.g4 ♘h4 18.♗g3 ♘hg6
19.♕a5±

Austin: "No man, now we have freedom *and* responsibility. It's a very groovy time."

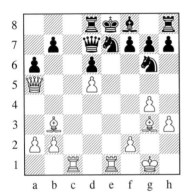

19...♘e5 20.♗xe5 dxe5 21.♖c7 ♕d6

21...b6 22.♕c3 ♕d6 23.♖xe5+–

22.♖xb7 f6 23.♖b6 ♕c7 24.♗a4† ♔f7
25.♖xf6†+–

12.♗f4 ♗g4 13.♖c1 ♕d7 14.h3 ♗h5

14...♗xf3 15.♕xf3± Shockingly, Black finds himself completely handcuffed. Now the white queen swings towards a5. 15...♖d8 16.♕c3 ♕f5 17.♕b4 ♕d7 18.♕a5+–

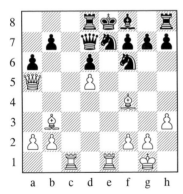

15.♕d3 ♗g6

15...h6 16.♘d2! b5 17.♖c6! +–

16.♕d4+–

Complete domination.

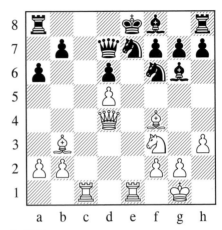

16...♖d8

16...♖c8 17.♖xc8† ♕xc8 18.♗xd6+–

17.♘d2! b5 18.♕b6 ♖c8 19.♖c6!

19.♖xc8†+–

19...♖xc6 20.dxc6 ♕d8 21.c7 ♕c8 22.♘c4!

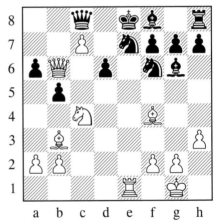

22...bxc4 23.♗a4† ♘d7 24.♗xd7† ♔xd7

Certainly not what Larsen had in mind.

24...♕xd7 25.♕b8† ♕c8 26.♕xc8#

25.♕xd6† ♔e8 26.♕c6† ♕d7

Dr. Kaufman: "Wait, I'm just a professional doing a job." Bond: "Me too." [bang] (Tomorrow Never Dies)

27.c8=♖#

Chapter 9

Taylor's Temple of Doom

1.e4 c5 2.d4 cxd4 3.c3 dxc3 4.♘xc3 ♘c6 5.♘f3 d6 6.♗c4

At last, we enter Taylor's treacherous Temple of Morra Doom.[45] Be sure to clutch your thematic swords at all times, for many a youthful gambiteer has toured the dark bowels of the Morra's underbelly, only to become its eternal guest, ultimately reduced to skull and ash. After ...♘c6, ...d6, ...a6, and ...♘f6,

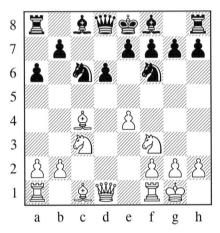

the Taylor's doors pry open. In 1972 the trailblazer Ken Smith stepped inside, but never escaped, leaving behind two bloody losses vs. grandmasters Evans and Mecking. Later, IM Timothy Taylor penned "The Taylor Defense", celebrating these brutal defeats and the demise of the Morra in general. And so, the temple of Morra tombstones grew and grew, until eventually, the defense dominated over the theoretical landscape. Among the Taylor's modern gatekeepers who have all published extensively chanting the virtual death of the Morra: IMs Palliser, Silman, Ginsburg,[46] and GMs Gallagher and Ftacnik. Such loud cries surely have sent chills down any brave buck daring to play the gambit.

In 2003, as a naive lad, I recklessly dove head first into the temple, novelty in tow, challenging Taylor himself in the pit. Alas, I too shared Ken Smith's fate, but now, after many years of languishing, I have found a way out (ironically

with the help of modern computers, the very beasts thought to have destroyed all romance in chess)!

On 7...♘f6, Black threatens to dissolve White's activity with the lava-like liquidating ...♗g4xf3 and ...♘e5xc4. White, with only a move to react, must decide how he wishes to be remembered. On the insipid 8.h3(??), Black responds 8...e6! with a diabolical laugh, transforming into a Scheveningen a tempo up. Instead, I offer three inspiring whip-cracking strikes for varied Morra spirits. For the novice/those who detest thick theory – the simple 8.♗e3!?, sleekly sidestepping the temple of pain. For the hopeless Romantic – the wild Evans-Morra Gambit, 8.b4(?!). While the swashbuckling 8.b4 borders on unsound, that hasn't stopped me from exacting a quick pound of flesh with it from many Morra doomsayers over the years.[47] And for the professionals/truth-seekers – the silicon-laced 8.♗f4, a grenade which finally allows the gambiteer to bust out of the Temple of Doom. Therefore, the theoretically trumpeted Taylor Defense is no refutation, unless of course, by refutation Black wishes to fight for equality as White gallops off into the sunset.

Before we embark on a trip through doom and gloom, Black has some booby-traps of his own to wade through before he can properly set up Taylor's triumph.

Taylor Intro – 6...♘f6?!

1.e4 c5 2.d4 cxd4 3.c3 dxc3 4.♘xc3 d6 5.♘f3 ♘c6 6.♗c4 ♘f6?!

Black makes three logical developing moves, and yet already falls victim to one of the Morra's many snares. In my youth, this position, which showcases the Morra's natural shining compensation throughout the landscape, deeply impressed me; it still does today.

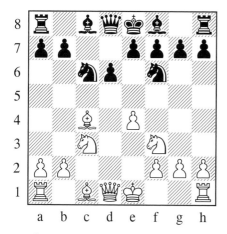

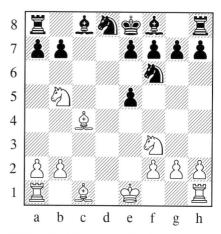

7.e5! dxe5

Black must not venture 7...♘xe5?? as 8.♘xe5 dxe5 9.♗xf7†! rakes in the queen. In a blitz tournament of mine here as a child vs. one of Miami's roughest hustlers, I later decided to toy with my desperate opponent (not a good idea on many levels). Eventually I promoted to a lone bishop and knight to try and execute the tricky mate in under 30 seconds, but failed shamefully, never hearing the end of it in colorful language. My advice now – promote to a queen and spare yourself.

We shall flash through 7...♘g4!, Black's only hope for survival, later on. After 8.exd6! White achieves a lively attack in the open fields.

8.♕xd8†

To be or not to be for Black, but both captures lead to not being.

8...♘xd8

8...♔xd8 9.♘g5! and Black's king must "suffer the slings and arrows of outrageous fortune." (Shakespeare: Hamlet, Act III, Scene I).

9.♘b5!

White's knight grazes freely on b5, eyeing the forking ♘c7†, and soon his comrade joins the fray. In light of the sweeping tactical sequence to follow, Black must first play 6...a6! to prevent such incursions on the b5-square. Only then may he continue ...♘f6 and erect Taylor's Temple.

9...♖b8

9...♗e6   10.♗xe6   ♗xe6   11.♘c7†+–; 9...♔d7?? 10.♘xe5† ♔e8 11.♘c7#

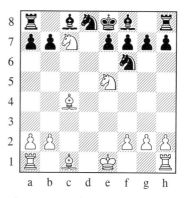

I've lost count how many times I have delivered this comedic finish – I'm sure many of you have as well.

10.♘xe5

After Black finds the only move to save his hide, White menaces mate. Now the king flees his chamber.

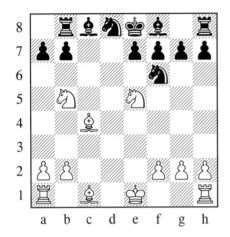

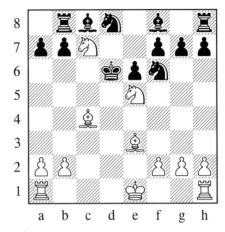

10...e6

10...♘e6 11.♗xe6 ♗xe6 12.♘c7† ♔d8
13.♘xe6† fxe6 14.♘f7†+– No matter which
way the king turns, forks abound!

11.♘c7†

Heedless headhunting! As Black can harness
defensive possibilities on the run, we will
showcase Rybka's murky but powerful 11.♗f4± in the advanced material.

11...♔e7 12.♗e3

Shooting for mate in one yet again.

12...♔d6?!

Tired of daggers flying his way, the foolhardy
Black monarch charges the field, taking
matters into his own hands. Yet in such hostile
territory, he cannot possibly hope to slay one
of White's vigorous knights and live to tell the
tale.

Black may parry the danger with 12...b6,
but after 13.0–0, White's rooks crash into
the center with a clear advantage (although a
forced win remains elusive).

13.♗f4!+–

White plays it "safe", decisively spearing
his majesty to the b8-rook at the end of the
5-piece diagonal shish kebab.

Once upon a time, I believed the bold
13.♘b5†, luring the king to e5, led to a
forced mate or material gain – but the resilient
machine cured me of this delusion. Still, with
the king fighting on e4 amidst a slew of white
pieces, I find the computer's dry assessment of
draw by perpetual check hard to stomach. I
urge you to prove it wrong! 13...♔xe5 14.f4†
♔e4 Charge! 15.♔e2 e5! And with no mate
on the horizon, the lone king chuckles his way
back to e6 and retreats further into his cave to
celebrate his bounty.

13...♘h5

13...♔xc7 14.♘xf7† ♔d7 15.0–0–0† ♔e7
White doesn't go for the rooks, but rather
lashes the king for his misadventures: 16.♘xd8
♖a8 17.♖he1+–

14.♘b5†! ♔c5

14...♔e7 15.♘g6† Neeeeigh! 15...hxg6
16.♗xb8+– Antipova – Lihovid, Nizhnij
Novgorod 1999.

15.♗e3† ♔b4

Run, run, run.

16.a3† ♚a5 17.b4† ♝xb4† 18.axb4† ♚xb4 19.♚d2

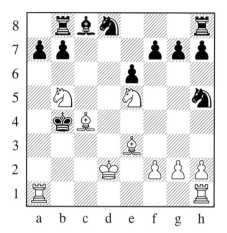

The white king waves farewell to his enemy before 20.♖hb1# delivers the execution.

Before pounding on the temple doors, we rustle in the Taylor's theoretical weeds.

Taylor – 8.♝e3!?

1.e4 c5 2.d4 cxd4 3.c3 dxc3 4.♘xc3 ♘c6 5.♘f3 d6 6.♝c4 a6! 7.0–0

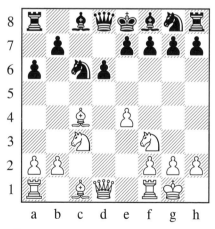

7...♘f6

Black must not prematurely proclaim the Taylor, for 7...♝g4? catches whiplash: 8.♝xf7†! ♚xf7 9.♘g5† ♚e8 10.♕xg4 ♘f6 11.♕e6+– Shattering false idols.

8.♝e3!?

After 8.e5?! dxe5 9.♕xd8† ♘xd8∓ we see that 6...a6! has deprived White of the pivotal attacking point b5, and so he must restrain his attacking lust for later.

With 8.♝e3, the gambiteer responds to Black's flexible strategy with a psychologically challenging waiting move of his own. Black should now calmly head for the beaches of Scheveningen with 8...e6, when White's bishop remains slightly misplaced on e3 as opposed to the more imposing post f4 (see Chapter 3). Nevertheless, not only can White overcome this minor theoretical defect in an unscripted fight, but many hardcore Taylor worshippers may not even have a clue about the Scheveningen structures – they will either handle the resulting positions poorly, or stubbornly insist on their beloved ...♝g4 exchanging motif.

8...♝g4

Extreme dogma! Black lusts after his exchanging fantasy, but White flees the pin, thus coolly regaining his pawn while sidestepping Taylor's Temple.

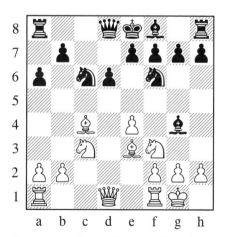

9.♕b3! e6 10.♕xb7 ♘a5! 11.♕b4 ♘xc4

Black may take solace in his trades, but they've cost him that oh so precious pawn!

12.♕xc4 ♗xf3 13.gxf3

Not out of the woods yet, Black must rush to finish developing before he loses his hide.

13...♗e7 14.♕c6† ♘d7 15.♖fd1 ♕c8!

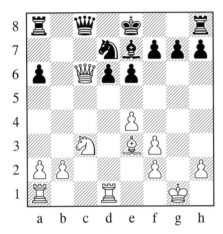

16.♕xc8†

With 16.♖xd6!? White is itching for a tussle. Black must grab the rook, then insist on a queen trade, else his king will remain locked in the center: 16...♗xd6 17.♕xd6 ♕b8 18.♕c6 ♕c8 (18...♔e7 19.♖d1 and mayhem erupts, for example 19...♕c8?? 20.♖xd7†! ♕xd7 21.♗c5†+– reaps the rook.) 19.♕d6 ♕b8= Denying White the fight he seeks.

16...♖xc8 17.♖ac1

White retains an ever-so-slight advantage. Despite his slightly mangled kingside pawn structure, his active rooks and potential outside passed pawn offer him chances to carry on in the endgame. Those who wish to avoid dense theoretical Taylor tomes may always find an ally in 8.♗e3. But don't worry swashbucklers, you're next.

Prepare yourself as we descend into the temple. Watch out for snakes and other harrowing creatures.

Marc Esserman – Michael Goeller

Kenilworth Simul 2010

1.e4 c5 2.d4 cxd4 3.c3 dxc3 4.♘xc3 ♘c6 5.♘f3 d6 6.♗c4 a6 7.0–0 ♘f6 8.b4?!

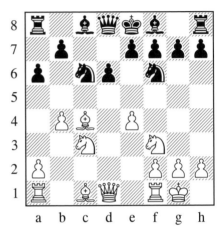

For over ten years I've kept the Romantic Evans Gambit-like thrust 8.b4 in my stash of weapons vs. the Taylor. Objectively, against the most prepared opponents, it should amount to naught. After all, White weakens his queenside while not developing a piece. But enough of 8.b4's negatives, for now.

8...♗g4

Black must not nibble on the poisoned pawn with 8...♘xb4, as 9.♗xf7†! ♔xf7 10.♕b3† leads to a prolonged siege, with his king wasting away in the middle of the board. White may even venture 9.e5!?, as 9.dxe5?? surrenders the queen to 10.♗xf7†.

9.b5

We may summarize b4-b5 as a daring raid to distract Black before he gathers the time to complete his trite liquidating maneuvers. But can Black summarily punish White in time?

9...♘e5?

Black sticks to the plan, but the scenery has changed.

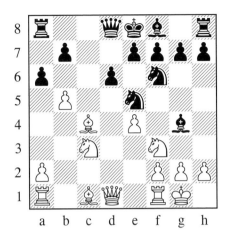

10.♞xe5!

Legal's famous pseudo-sacrifice appears 260 years later in the "Evans-Morra". Of course, Black must not pluck the queen. But his position turns to ash.

10...dxe5

10...♝xd1 11.♝xf7#

11.♛b3!

Hitting f7 while cloaking another threat.

11...e6 12.bxa6 bxa6 13.♝xa6±

I've unleashed this cutting tactic a number of times, and it always sends a chill down the spine of the dazed Taylorphile. Black cannot snap the bishop as ♛b5† snatches the rook, and so, way ahead in development with an outside passed a-pawn to boot, I went on to win rather routinely.

...1–0

Not too scary so far, right? Make sure to light your torches – it's going to get darker.

Marc Esserman – Eric Rodriguez

Internet (bullet) 2009

1.e4 c5 2.d4 cxd4 3.c3 dxc3 4.♞xc3 ♞c6 5.♞f3 d6 6.♝c4 a6 7.0–0 ♞f6 8.b4 ♝g4

Black should not soften the queenside foundations with the ambitious:
8...b5

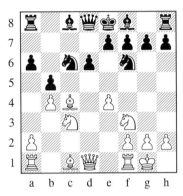

9.♝e2

This original retreat ensures that the Taylor structure breaks. I give one deathly variation pit.

9...e6 10.a4 bxa4 11.♛xa4 ♝d7 12.b5!

Black's b5-pawn has turned to dust. Now White's b5-pawn pounds away at the a-file pin.

12...♞e5 13.♛a5! ♛xa5 14.♜xa5 ♞xf3†
15.♝xf3 ♝e7 16.e5 ♞d5 17.♞xd5 exd5
18.♝xd5 ♜a7

The rook makes a last stand against the swift a-pawn, but still sadly sheds his life.

19.b6+–

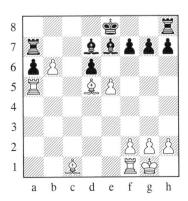

9.b5 &xf3

In the spirit of the Taylor, Black keeps to his exchanging policy. Ironically, almost all of my opponents here from amateurs to grandmasters have made the same choice, except for Taylor himself, who played the icy 9...axb5 first.

10.gxf3

Of course not 10.♕xf3? ♘e5, satisfying Black's trading urges.

10...axb5
10...♘e5!?

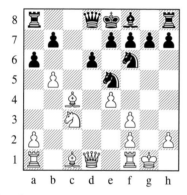

11.bxa6!

I first traversed these breathtaking paths while studying Burgess's 1994 Smith-Morra work, and they inspired me to take up 8.b4 for years to come.

11...♘xc4 12.axb7!

White has jettisoned his bishop, but a dangerous b-pawn looms, and Black must return the material or else face destruction.

12...♖a7

12...♖a5?! 13.♕b3! ♘b6 14.♗e3+− and Black is powerless. Both 14...♘fd7 15.♖ab1 and 14...♘bd7 15.♘b5! followed by 16.♖ac1 are crunching.

13.♘b5!?

The gambiteer may be able to improve with 13.♕b3!N± simply protecting the pawn and heading to queen. If 13...♘b6, then either 14.a4! or 14.♗e3, unleashing a plethora of pins.

13...♖xb7 14.♕a4!

Regaining the material or mating.

14...♖d7!

14...♘b6?? 15.♘xd6#

15.♕xc4 g6

White retained a slight pull thanks to his outside a-pawn in Esserman – Sharma, Internet (blitz) 2010.

We now escape these catacombs and return to the main path.

11.♘xb5!

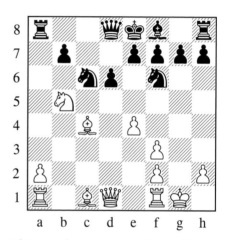

This novel recapture, which I first played against Taylor, injected new life into the chaotic 8.b4. White's knight pressurizes d6 and c7 as Black struggles to castle. If 11...e6, then 12.♗f4 crackles, and if 11...g6, then the bishop may find a new target from b2...

11...g6

11...♖c8 may meet a similar doom as the game after 12.♕b3.

12.♕b3!

Before the king can even think about castling, he gets the whip!

12...♘e5

12...e6? is pulverized by: 13.♗xe6! fxe6 14.♕xe6† ♗e7 (14...♕e7 15.♘c7† ♔d8

16.♕xe7† ♗xe7 17.♘xa8+– and the knight flies out to b6) 15.♖d1!+–

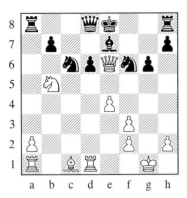

White's queen slashes and burns. The finish with ♘d6 and ♕f7# cannot be stopped. 15...♘f8 (15...d5 16.♗f4+–) 16.♘xd6! ♗xd6 17.♗h6#

13.♗b2!

Properly posting the bishop on the long diagonal where it will cause the greatest mischief. I hurled 13.♗f4 a few years prior: 13...♘xc4 14.♕xc4 ♖c8 15.♕a4 ♕d7? (15...♘d7! 16.♖ac1±) 16.♖ac1 ♖b8 17.♖c7+– Esserman – Gormally, Internet (blitz) 2006.

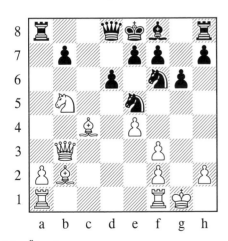

13...♘xc4

White has several options after:
13...♘fd7

I will provide a scintillating variation to light up the darkness.

14.♗xe5!

White must not give up such a radiant bishop unless he has something forcing in mind...

14...♘xe5 15.♖ac1

Threatening 16.♘c7† followed by discoveries.

15...♖c8

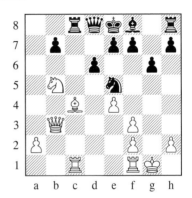

16.♘xd6†!

A bit of foreshadowing.

16...exd6 17.♗xf7†!

Setting the king's residence ablaze.

17...♘xf7 18.♕e6† ♕e7
   18...♗e7 19.♖xc8+–

19.♖xc8† ♘d8 20.♕d5±

White's centralized queen glows. Black, still in chains, cannot properly fend off ♖b1xb7.

14.♕xc4

Ah, Black exhales, having finally exchanged off the two minor pieces. But normal breathing lasts but a move, for now his king falls gravely ill.

14...♖c8

The c-file is creaking, the long diagonal is cracking, the white queen is prying, and the black king is crying.

15.♕a4 ♕d7 16.♖ac1+–

Even in the Temple of Doom, the c-file proves a beacon of hope.

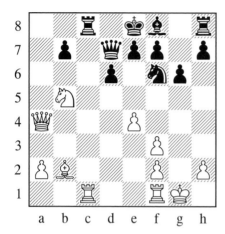

16...Rc6 17.Rxc6 bxc6

17...Wxc6 18.Rc1 crushes brutally: 18...Wd7
19.Nc7† The most accurate amongst many.
19...Kd8 20.Ne6† Wxe6 21.Wa8† Kd7
22.Wc8# May the king rest in peace.

18.Wa8† Wd8 19.Nxd6†!

First 19.Wxc6†, intending 19...Wd7
20.Wa8† Wd8 21.Nxd6† is a shade more
accurate, but that is the only inaccuracy in this
bullet encounter which features some of my
finest preparation.

**19...exd6 20.Wxd8† Kxd8 21.Bxf6†
1–0**

Taylor – 8 b4 e6!

1.e4 c5 2.d4 cxd4 3.c3 dxc3 4.Nxc3 Nc6
5.Nf3 d6 6.Bc4 a6 7.0–0 Nf6 8.b4

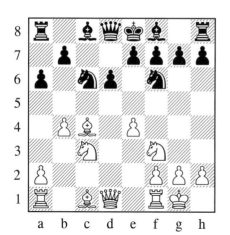

Unfortunately, I must agree with
Grandmaster Ftacnik when he argues in his
2010 tome, *Grandmaster Repertoire 6 – The
Sicilian Defence*, that Black can simply avoid
8...Bg4 altogether and play the resilient:

8...e6

As White cannot provide an explosive
counter (9.b5?! fails), the lunging 8.b4 now
turns out to be nothing more than a positional
weakness, as Black yet again successfully
morphs from a Taylor to a Scheveningen. Of
course, White is worse, but not clearly "lost",
and may hope for a trick or two – so if you
feel the reward of 8.b4 outweighs the risk
(remember, many Taylorphiles lack the feel for
the Scheveningen's waters), then by all means,
unleash.

9.b5?!

9.a3∓

9...axb5 10.Nxb5 Be7

The simplest of Black's options.

11.Bf4

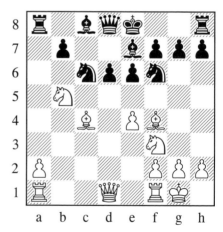

11...Nxe4! 12.Re1 0–0 13.Rxe4 d5∓

However, if you're still ready to gamble your
tournament life on 8.b4, I urge you to study

Esserman – Taylor, Las Vegas 2003, a haunting tale I have buried in the supplemental games section along with my memory of it. If you remain blinded by the darkness of White's prospects after 8...♗g4 9.b5 axb5 10.♘xb5 e6, then move along to the last corridor, as we finally visit the pounding, pulsating heart of Taylor's Temple.

Taylor – 8.♗f4! and 10.g4

1.e4 c5 2.d4 cxd4 3.c3 dxc3 4.♘xc3 d6 5.♘f3 ♘c6 6.♗c4 a6 7.0–0 ♘f6 8.♗f4!

Around 2007-8, still tormented by my 2003 defeat and losing faith in the dashing 8.b4, I began to conclude, along with the help of an early version of Rybka, that this simple bishop moved offered the counter-refutation to the Taylor's enshrined "refutation" of the Morra.

Only in January of 2012 did I realize that I also had another ally attempting to raze the Taylor walls, for in 2007 GM Karsten Mueller published an article hailing 8.♗f4 as the solution to Black's exchanging bloodlust. Well, he didn't quite put it that way!

Later, IM Langrock revised his earlier book's flawed recommendation against the Taylor in favor of 8.♗f4 in his second edition, chiefly following Mueller's analysis.[48] Thus, we have reached a consensus in the strength of 8.♗f4 as the starting point, but from here, our paths diverge in the temple, as I will offer a far more violent approach echoing the chaos of 8.b4. Black can now drift yet again into a Scheveningen, but unlike after 8.h3(?), 8.♗e3!? or 8.b4?!, he will no longer obtain any theoretical advantage from doing so, for 8...e6 9.♕e2 ♗e7 10.♖fd1 ♕c7 11.♖ac1 transposes directly into the ...a6/...♕c7 main line (see Chapter 3).

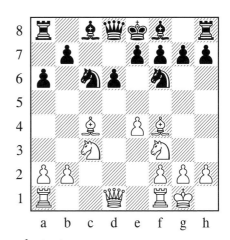

8...♗g4 9.h3!

Each chess move, no matter how similar it may look to another, contains its own life force. A great case in point are the differences between 8.♗e3!? and 8.♗f4!.

8.♗e3 calmly develops the bishop to a healthy square, and while it does not fight for the prime central terrain, it allows White to win back the pawn after 8...♗g4 with 9.♕b3 e6 10.♕xb7.

8.♗f4, on the other hand, drives a firm stake in the center. It stops Black's ...♘e5 liquidating desires in many variations, urges on the devastating possibility e4-e5, and spits fire at the d6-pawn. However, the hyper-active 8.♗f4 fails to regain the gambited pawn on 8...♗g4, unlike its more delicate brother. So White ventures 9.h3, postponing ♕b3 until a more opportune time...

9.♕b3?! e6

Take a moment to try and grasp why White cannot grab on b7 before watching as I send the queen into the lava pit.

10.♕xb7? ♘a5 11.♕b4

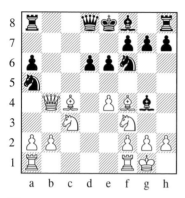

11...e5!!

We're deep inside the temple now. With a simple, single strike, Black resurrects the Taylor bishop, allowing it to return to d7 with a vengeance. If 11...d5, the queen slides to a4, just like after 8.♗e3.

12.♗g3 d5 13.♕a4† ♗d7!–+

And White fries.

9...♗h5!?

9...♗xf3!? Dogmatic exchanging no longer soothes Black's pain, for the bishop beats on e5 and d6. 10.♕xf3

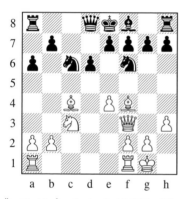

10...♘e5? 11.♗xe5 dxe5 12.♖fd1 The Morra rooks and heavy pieces ravage. 12...♕a5 13.♘d5 ♘xd5 (13...♖c8 14.♖ac1) 14.♗xd5+–

So Black must bend with 10...e6 to flee to safety, but after 11.♖fd1, the d6-pawn wails. I subject this position to exhaustive analysis in a labyrinth of advanced material. Rest assured, White's two bishops and unrelenting pressure

offer more than enough compensation for the pawn, and the Taylor worshippers must try to equalize, if their egos can stomach it.

10.g4!?

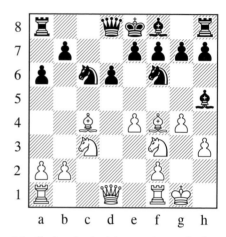

Mueller's principal innovation, which seems sharpest, but in its chief variation leads to balanced endgames.[49] Unfortunately, I don't envision more than equality for White. But the German GM should be praised for his find, for I don't see more than equality for Black, either!

10...♗g6 11.e5!

The thematic break on e5 with the bishop on f4, which you may see again in the thickets of variations to come.

11...dxe5 12.♘xe5 ♘xe5 13.♗xe5 ♕xd1!

If Black stubbornly refuses to exchange, then the white queen jumps to f3, and up against a massive developmental disadvantage, the defender will come to regret his decision. I now briefly reduce 10.g4!? to equal rubble before we move on to sharper, Morra middlegame mayhem.

14.♖fxd1

14.♖axd1 e6 15.♘b5!? ♖d8! 16.♘c7†?! ♔e7 17.♗c3 ♖d6† 18.♗b4 ♔d7 locking the knight in doom.

14...e6 15.♗e2!⩲

The main strategic theme behind 10.g4. White's bishops besiege the queenside. Black must defend tenaciously.

15.♘b5 ♖d8 16.♖xd8† ♔xd8 17.♖d1† ♘d7! 18.♘d6 ♗xd6 19.♗xd6 ♗e4 reaches approximately equality, White's bishops compensating for the pawn.

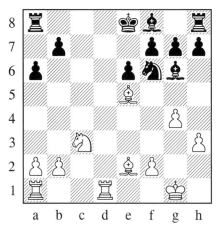

15...♘d7!

Note the accuracy required for Black to keep the balance, a testament to Mueller's idea.

16.♗g3 ♘b8!

Aiming to stop at least one of the slinging bishops.

17.♖ac1 ♘c6 18.♗f3 ♗e7 19.♘b5!? 0–0!

19...axb5 20.♖xc6 0–0 21.♖b6 ♖xa2 22.♖xb5±

20.♘d4 ♘xd4 21.♖xd4 ♗f6 22.♖b4 ♖ad8

Black solves his problems with the incoming ...♖d2. You may investigate any revolving door along the way during these extended lines, but I doubt you will find anything greater than =. Nevertheless, 10.g4 remains an excellent practical gun to carry in your Morra holster.

Taylor – 8.♗f4! and 10.♕b3!

1.e4 c5 2.d4 cxd4 3.c3 dxc3 4.♘xc3 d6 5.♘f3 ♘c6 6.♗c4 a6 7.0–0 ♘f6 8.♗f4! ♗g4 9.h3! ♗h5!?

But let us return to the moment before 10.g4 and try to find the blow that tears out the beating heart of Taylor's defense.

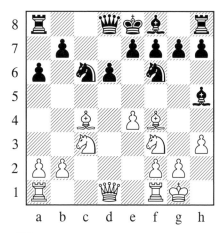

10.♕b3!

IM Langrock brands this the "positional" alternative to 10.g4, but misses 10.♕b3's absurdly savage possibilities in the dim surroundings of theory's end.

First off, White now threatens e4-e5, so that if Black fires a blank such as 10...♖b8, then 11.e5 (or 11.g4 ♗g6 12.e5) whips up a sweltering attack.

But why can't Black simply play 10...e6 as before, you may ask? Then the second, penetrating point of 9.h3! reveals itself – the bishop can no longer return to d7, and so White gallantly collects the b7-pawn with an overwhelming advantage: 11.♕xb7 ♘a5 12.♕b4 ♗xf3 (12...e5?? ♕a4+–) 13.gxf3 ♘xc4 14.♕xc4±. Unlike the line after 8.♗e3!?, Black cannot finish developing with 14...♗e7, as after 15.♕c6†, the d6-pawn and his entire position collapse.

So Black must defend the b7-pawn somehow. Now find a few moments of complete solitude to mimic tournament conditions. Put yourself in the hot seat of a devout Taylorphile, and try to muster a defense. Then compare your work with the blood curdling lines I am about to show. After this exercise, you may fully appreciate the practical power of 10.♕b3.

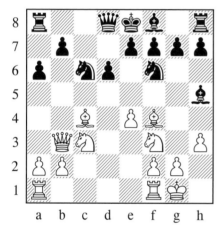

10...♖c8!?

Brace yourself.

10...♘a5?!

Black fires another empty shot.
11.♕a4† ♘d7!

The alternatives are worse:
a) 11...♘c6 12.g4! ♗g6 13.e5 dxe5 14.♘xe5+– ♕a5 (14...♖c8 15.♘xc6 ♖xc6 16.♗xa6!) 15.♕b3! ♘xe5 16.♕xb7 ♖d8 17.b4!+– The b2-b4 thrust returns with a vengeance.
b) 11...b5?

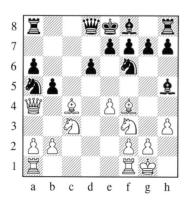

12.♗xb5†! axb5 13.♘xb5!+– ♘d7 (13...♘c6 14.♕xa8! ♕xa8 15.♘c7†+–) 14.♖ac1! Black grovels for mercy... 14...e6 15.♘c7† ♔e7 16.♗xd6† ...but receives none. 16...♔xd6 17.♕b4† ♘c5 18.♕xc5† ♔d7 19.♖fd1†+–
12.♗e2 e6 13.♗g5!→

Black still struggles to develop.

10...♕c7?! places the queen in the line of the Morra rook's fire. 11.♖ac1! e6 12.g4 ♗g6 13.♖fe1 Setting up the irresistible shot e4-e5, while our old friend ♘d5 may also feature. 13...♗e7 14.e5 dxe5 15.♘xe5 ♗d6

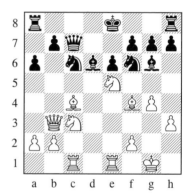

16.♗xe6! 0–0 (16...♗xe5 17.♗xe5 ♘xe5 18.♘b5+–) 17.♘d5 ♘xd5 18.♗xd5± Clearly, the black queen should avoid the c-file.

10...b5?!

For those who opted for Rybka's first instinct, this hyper-active yet obvious move, "[you] choose poorly." (Guardian Knight, Indiana Jones and the Last Crusade)

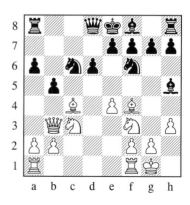

11.♘xb5!!N

You didn't really think we'd play the tame 11.♗e2, did you? Now watch in horror (or delight) as Black's position disintegrates into ashes and dust.

11...♘a5

a) 11...axb5 12.♗xb5 ♖c8 13.♘d4+– À la Chicago Defense pinning themes from Chapter 5. 13...♕b6 14.♖ac1 ♕xd4 15.♖xc6 ♔d8 16.♖xc8† ♔xc8 17.♗a6† ♔d7 18.♕b5† ♔e6 19.♕f5# All but an eerie silence remains.

b) 11...♖b8 12.♘g5! Going for the jugular, à la ♘g5-themes from previous Morra massacres. Black is defenseless:

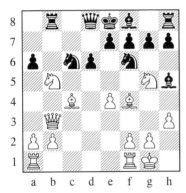

b1) 12...♖xb5 13.♗xf7† (13.♗xb5± also leads to pain, but it's more Romantic to head-hunt.) 13...♗xf7 (13...♔d7 14.♕e6† ♔c7 15.♕c4!+– with c-file rage and ferocious forks.) 14.♕xf7† ♔d7 15.♖fd1+–

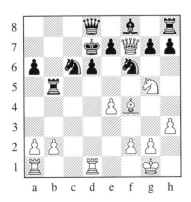

b2) 12...♖xb5 13.♗xf7† also

Now ♖xd6† hangs over the black king, and 15...♔c8 is punished by 16.♖ac1.

b2) 12...e6 13.♗xe6! Naturally! 13...fxe6 14.♕xe6† ♗e7 15.♘xd6†+– White's knights must be fed.

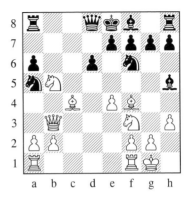

With the queen and knight under attack, of course it's best to sacrifice again!

12.♘xd6†!!

The return of ♘xd6! (see Esserman – Rodriguez, page 209). Buyer beware, this bombshell's not only tactical, but laced with positional venom.

12...♕xd6!?

We teeter on the cliff as the lava pit boils below – knights and queens dangle move after move after move.

12...exd6 13.♕a4† ♘d7 14.♗d5!±

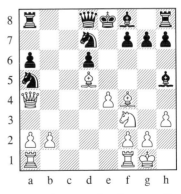

Black's knight, now "under arrest", remains entombed: 14...♖b8 15.♘d4 ♘b7 16.b4+–
13.♕a4† ♕c6

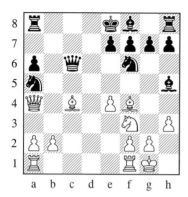

14.♗b3!!

This brilliant rejoinder connects the combination at its seams. Black's knight, under assault, cannot move and so freezes in air. And exchanging queens offers no respite, for the ravenous Morra rooks then put the king out of his misery.

14...♛xa4

14...♛b5 15.♘d4! ♛xa4 16.♗xa4† ♘d7 17.♖ac1+– Eyeing 18.♖c7 or the ridiculous 18.♖c5, hounding loose pieces from the a- to the h-file.

15.♗xa4† ♔d8 16.♖fd1† ♔c8 17.♖ac1† ♔b7 18.♖c7† ♔b6 19.♖dc1+–

And the white queen laughs from up above.

10...♛d7! For those rare breeds who found this controlled move (which we will analyze separately later), "You chose wisely." (Guardian Knight, Indiana Jones and the Last Crusade)

11.♖ac1!?

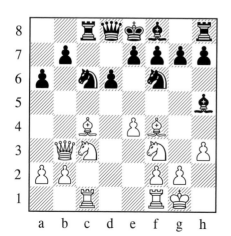

Sweating bullets? I warned you. But don't despair, just imagine how the timid Taylorphiles will feel. Take a breath of fresh air if you must, then another moment of silence, and suffer to find a defense for Black, as before. Then proceed into the abyss.

11...♘a5?!

11...♛d7?! Not this time! 12.♘d5! ♘a5

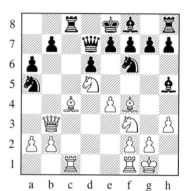

13.♗b5!! Keep your eye on the 5th rank. 13...axb5 14.♖xc8† ♛xc8 15.♛xb5† ♘c6 16.♘xf6†! gxf6 17.♛xh5± The Taylor bishop could never anticipate such a fate.

11...e6?!
Clever, but flawed.
12.♛xb7 ♘a5!?
  12...♗xf3

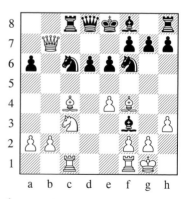

13.♗xa6! White has bigger pieces to capture. 13...♖c7 14.♛b5 ♗h5 15.♘d5!+– (15.♗e3 followed by ♗b6, as in the Chicago Defense,

is also good enough) 15...exd5 16.♖xc6 ♖xc6
17.♕xc6†+– The possibility of exd5 and an
eventual ♗b5 ensures that the black king is
buried alive in the center.

13.♗b5†! axb5 **14.♕xb5† ♘c6**
More Chicago Defense themes.
14...♘d7 15.♕xh5
15.♘a4!±
Pins and needles.

11...♘d7! If you found this subtle retreat, I'll
see you in the advanced material.

12.♕a4† ♕d7
12...♘c6 13.♗xa6! A prelude to the climax.
13...♖a8 (13...bxa6 14.♘d5+–) 14.♗xb7!
♖xa4 15.♗xc6†±

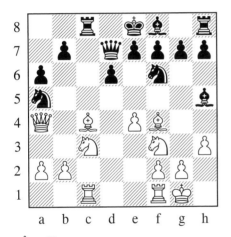

13.♗xa6!!
13.♕xa5? ♖xc4 is less convincing.

13...♕xa4
13...bxa6 14.♘d5! ♕xa4 15.♖xc8† ♔d7
16.♘b6† ♔e6 17.♘g5#

**14.♘xa4 ♖xc1 15.♖xc1 bxa6 16.♖c8† ♔d7
17.♘b6† ♔e6 18.♘d4#**
Shout and listen for the echo, echo, echo!

We proceed to the final theoretical caves,
exploring nuances and improvements for both

sides before escaping Taylor's Temple forever.
I will keep my comments sparse and analysis
intense, so only brave souls should venture
forth.

Theory I – 6...♘f6?!

**1.e4 c5 2.d4 cxd4 3.c3 dxc3 4.♘xc3∞ d6
5.♘f3 ♘c6 6.♗c4 ♘f6?!**
Most opponents who play the careless
6...♘f6?! are too inexperienced to handle the
violence after 7.e5. Nevertheless, I include the
best computer defenses. In all lines, White
retains at least a pull.

7.e5 dxe5
Black best chance of survival is:
7...♘g4!

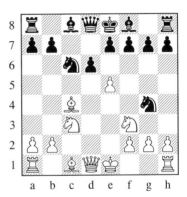

8.exd6!
Ripping open the center for White's pieces
to roam.
8.e6?! This second sacrifice, which Burgess
recommended in the 90's, is narrowly
refuted by Rybka: 8...fxe6! 9.♘g5 ♘ge5
10.♘xe6 ♕a5! 11.♗b3 ♗xe6 12.♗xe6 ♕a6!∓
8...♕xd6
8...exd6 may be Black's most tenacious
defense in all of the 6...♘f6?! variations.
The defender keeps his pawn but White
maintains nagging positional pressure:
9.0–0 ♗e7 (9...♘ge5?! 10.♘xe5 ♘xe5
[10...dxe5 11.♕b3±] 11.♗b5† ♗d7 12.♗xd7†

♕xd7 13.♘d5 ♗e7 14.♖e1± 0–0 15.♘xe7†
♕xe7 16.f4+–) 10.h3 ♘ge5 11.♘xe5 dxe5
(11...♘xe5 12.♗d5 0–0 13.♖e1± with a bind)
12.♕h5 0–0 13.♖d1 ♕a5 14.♗e3± White's
full range of motion more than compensates
for Black's extra e5-pawn.

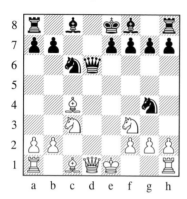

9.0–0!

The b5-square again torments Black.

9...♕xd1

9...e6 10.♘b5 ♕b8 11.h3 ♘f6 12.g3!±
Aiming to trap the "Siberian queen," as in
Chapter 1. 12...♗e7 13.♗f4 e5 14.♘xe5
♘xe5 15.♖e1 ♘fd7 16.♕h5 g6 (16...0–0
17.♖xe5!+–) 17.♕h6 ♗f8 18.♗xe5 ♘xe5
19.♕f4!+–

10.♖xd1 ♗f5 11.♘b5 ♖c8 12.h3 ♘ge5
13.♘xe5 ♘xe5 14.♗d5

White has at the very least a nominal
advantage, and possibly more.

8.♕xd8† ♘xd8

8...♔xd8 9.♘g5 ♘a5!

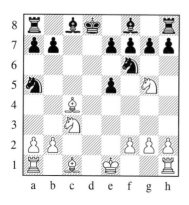

I had always thought 8...♔xd8 lost easily,
until in 2007 a very young child named
Ho shattered me of this delusion when he
creatively found 9...♘a5! over the board.

Struggling to find a "forced" win, I even
misplayed and drew. White should continue:
10.♗b5! (10.♘xf7†? ♔e8 11.♘xh8 ♘xc4
is inadvisable as White's knight languishes.)
10...♗e6 11.♘xe6† fxe6±

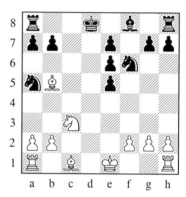

White has an obvious positional advantage
with two bishops, a clear lead in development,
and structural plusses which compensate for
his two pawn minus. Black's tripled pawns are
only envied in an art gallery.

9.♘b5 ♖b8 10.♘xe5 e6 11.♗f4!±

Rather than playing for mate, Rybka's
butcherous 11.♗f4 eventually reaps material
profit. Black's loose b8-rook and a7-pawn are
the chief victims in the crime.

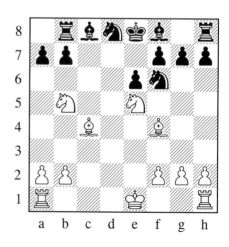

11...♘h5 12.♗e3 ♗b4†

12...♘c6 13.♗e2! ♗b4† (13...♘xe5 14.♗xa7!+–) 14.♔f1 a6 15.♘c7† (15.♘xc6 bxc6 16.♘a7! ♘f6 17.♘xc6 ♖b7 18.♗xa6+–) 15...♔e7 16.♘xa6!

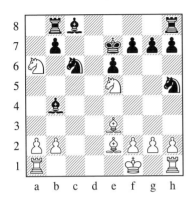

White wins.

13.♔f1 0–0 14.♗e2 a6

14...♘f6 15.♘d3! ♗e7 16.♗f4± and Black's rook falls.

15.a3 ♗e7

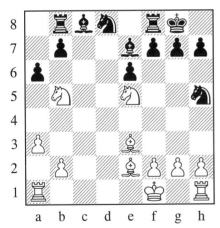

16.♘a7!

Either c8 or h5 must fall.

16...♘f6 17.♖c1 ♗d7

17...♗d6 18.♘c4 ♗e7 19.♗f4 ♖a8 20.♘b6 ♖xa7 21.♘xc8+–

18.♘xd7 ♘xd7 19.♖c7 ♘f6

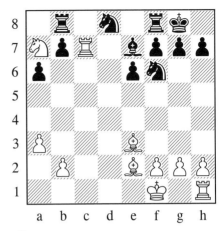

20.♘c8!+–

White amazingly saves his knight while trapping Black's bishop!

We now take an exhausting tour of the main lines, especially 9...♗xf3.

Theory II – 11...♕a5 and Sidelines

1.e4 c5 2.d4 cxd4 3.c3 dxc3 4.♘xc3 d6 5.♘f3 ♘c6 6.♗c4 a6 7.0–0 ♘f6 8.♗f4! ♗g4

The alternatives fail miserably.

8...b5?!

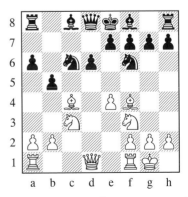

9.♗xf7†! A surprising shot, tossing sand in the king's face while preying on Black's loose pieces. 9...♔xf7 10.e5! Now neither 10...d5 11.exf6→ nor 10...dxe5 11.♘xe5†± is satisfactory for Black, while 10...♘h5? 11.♘g5† ♔g6

12.e6!+– is a disaster, for example 12...♘xf4 13.♘f7 ♕e8 14.♕g4† ♔f6 15.♘e4#.

8...g6?! Black lacks the necessary central control for such extravagance: 9.e5! dxe5 10.♘xe5 ♘xe5 (10...e6 11.♕e2 ♗g7 12.♘xc6 bxc6 13.♖ad1 followed by 14.♗d6±) 11.♕xd8† ♔xd8 12.♗xe5±

9.h3! ♗xf3!? 10.♕xf3 e6!

Under pressure, Black has no choice but to adopt a compromised Scheveningen structure to complete his development (10..g6?! gets squashed by 11.♖fd1). To counter White's two bishop advantage and the heavy incoming fire on the d6-pawn, the defender must trust in a firm control over the d4- and e5-squares.

11.♖fd1

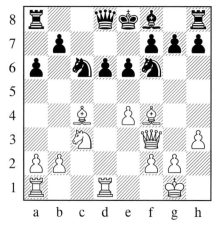

After dismissing the alternatives, we will examine three queen moves (11...♕a5, 11...♕b6, and 11...♕b8) in great detail. Each either directly or indirectly holds the d6-pawn, and each requires a unique handling.

11...♕a5!?

We look quickly at three other options:

11...♗e7? 12.e5±

11...♕c7?!

Landing on the mined c-file naturally leads to doom. A few thematic examples follow.
12.♖ac1 ♗e7
   12...♘e5?? 13.♖xe5 dxe5 14.♘b5+–
13.♗b3! ♖c8
   13...0–0 14.♘d5 À la ♘d5! in the Scheveningens Part II. 14...exd5 15.exd5 ♘xd5 16.♗xd5 ♖ac8 17.b4 ♕b6 18.♕e4 ♖fe8 19.♕f5 ♖f8 (19...♗f6 20.♗e4+–) 20.♗xf7† ♔h8 21.♗xd6 ♗xd6 22.♖xd6 ♕xb4

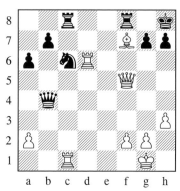

23.♖h6! Bone-chilling.
14.♘d5! exd5 15.exd5 ♘e5 16.♕g3 ♕d7 17.♖xc8† ♕xc8 18.♗xe5 dxe5 19.d6 ♗d8
   19...♗xd6 20.♕xg7+–
20.♕xe5† ♔f8 21.d7 ♕c6 22.♕b8 ♕b6

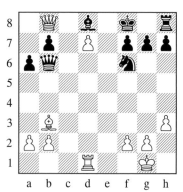

23.♗c4 ♖g8! 24.b4 ♕c7 25.♕xc7 ♗xc7 26.d8♕† ♗xd8 27.♖xd8† ♔e7 28.♖xg8 ♘xg8 29.♔f1±

Black is not out of the woods yet.

11...♘d7

Further clasping at the dark squares fails to impress, so long as White does not prematurely dive for d6.

12.♕g3!

You will see this queen shift over and over in these narrow passageways.

12.♗xd6? ♗xd6 13.♖xd6 ♘ce5 14.♕e2 ♕c7 15.♖d4 0–0 16.♗b3 ♘c5∓

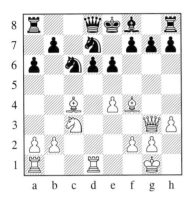

12...♘ce5

12...♘de5?! 13.♗d5 gives White a dangerous attack. For example: 13...exd5 14.exd5 ♘e7 15.♗xe5 dxe5 16.d6 ♘c6 17.d7† ♔e7 18.♘d5† ♔e6 19.♖ac1+−

13.♗e2 h5 14.h4!

Black's bishop and king remain entombed. 14.♖ac1 h4 15.♕e3 ♗e7 would allow Black more freedom.

14...♖c8 15.♖ac1 g6 16.♗g5 ♗e7

16...♕a5 17.b4! ♕xb4 18.♘d5+−

17.♖xd6→

I first faced the clever 11...♕a5 during some 2010 marathon Morra blitz sessions vs. a tenacious Taylor specialist, Arun Sharma. I offer three possible bishop retreats, each posing subtly different problems. If White wishes, he can force Black to steer for sterile equality after 12.♗e2!? or 12.♗f1!?, but in the final analysis, 12.♗b3!? offers the best chance for a full-blooded struggle.

12.♗b3!?∞

Although White now lacks an immediate b2-b4 strike, the slithering ♗a4 ensures that Black cannot meekly return the d6-pawn and equalize.

12.♗xd6?? ♗xd6 13.♖xd6 ♘e5 14.♕e2 ♕c5−+ shows why the bishop must vacate the premises.

12.♗f1!?=

If a Taylorphile wishes to "refute" the Morra here, he must clasp onto his extra d6-pawn. Yet as we shall see, the lurking lunge b2-b4! makes this quest pure fantasy.

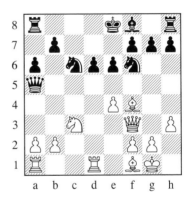

12...♗e7!=

Black maintains objectivity, concedes the pawn, and hopes for a draw (the mentality Sharma adopted in our blitz sessions in this line).

a) 12...♖d8 13.b4! ♘xb4 14.♖ab1 ♖d7 (14...♗e7 15.♗d2± With ♘e2 ideas. 15...♕c5?! 16.♘a4 ♕a5 17.♖xb4 d5 18.♖c4+−) 15.♗d2 ♘c6 (15...♗e7

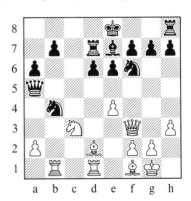

16.♘e2! Note that such a deft retreat would be impossible if White's bishop stood on e2. 16...d5 17.exd5 ♕xd5 18.♗xb4 ♕xf3 19.♖xd7!±) 16.♘d5 ♕d8 17.♘b6 ♖c7 18.♗c3⯹ With a boa constrictor's grip.

b) 12...♘e5 13.♕e3! ♖d8?! (13...♗e7 14.b4!→ or 13...♘fd7 14.♕g3⯹)

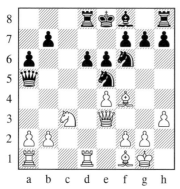

14.♕a7!± A surprising invasion. 14...♖d7 15.♗b5! ♘c6 16.♗xc6 bxc6 17.♕a8†+−

13.♗xd6 ♗xd6 14.♖xd6 0–0 15.♖ad1 ♖ad8=

12.♗e2!?=

Stopping ...♘e5 and allowing the ♕g3 shift plus b2-b4 possibilities.

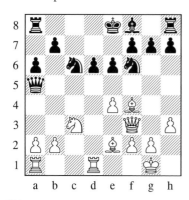

12...♖d8!?

If Black chooses to hold on to the extra pawn delusion, the proper punishment now slightly differs in execution.

a) Again, Black should lack an ego with 12...♗e7, allowing 13.♗xd6=. But you may refuse to regain the pawn (true Romantic

spirit!) and simply expand on the queenside with 13.a3!?⯹, followed by b2-b4 and ♖ac1, at your own risk.

b) After 12...♘e5?! both 13.♕g3 and 13.♕e3 offer White excellent prospects as the e2-bishop keeps the h5-square under lock and key.

13.a3!

This forces the action regardless.

13.b4!? no longer sparkles, as after 13...♘xb4 14.♖ab1 ♖d7 15.♗d2 ♗e7, the move 16.♘e2! is impossible.

13.♖ab1!?⯹ ♗e7 14.b4 ♘xb4 15.♗d2 d5 is also unclear.

13...♗e7 14.b4 ♕b6

14...♕c7 15.b5→

15.♗e3 ♕c7 16.♖ac1 ♕b8

16...0–0 17.♘d5→

17.♕g3 0–0 18.♗h6 ♘e8 19.♗e3 ♘f6

White must either choose to repeat or look for some other way to keep attacking. So overall 12.♗f1!? (allowing an immediate b2-b4) marginally seems the better of these two bishop retreats.

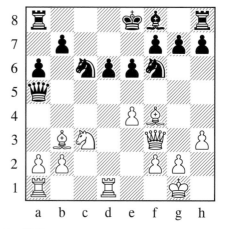

12...♖d8

Here too, Black has several other tries:

12...♗e7 13.♗a4!

13.♗xd6=

13...♕c7

13...0–0 14.♗xc6! bxc6 15.♗xd6 ♗xd6
16.♖xd6±
13...e5 14.b4→

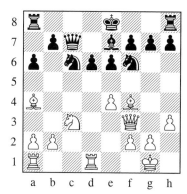

14.♗xc6†!?
    14.e5!?
14...♕xc6
    14...bxc6 15.e5 dxe5 16.♗xe5 ♕b7
17.♕g3→
15.♖ac1 ♕b6 16.♕g3
    16.b4 0–0 17.a3 ♘d7∞
16...0–0
    16...♘h5 17.♗e3→ ♘xg3 (17...♕xb2
18.♕f3 ♘f6 19.♗d4→) 18.♗xb6 ♘h5
19.♘a4!±
17.♗xd6 ♗xd6 18.♕xd6 ♕xd6 19.♖xd6 ♖fd8
20.♖cd1 ♖xd6 21.♖xd6±

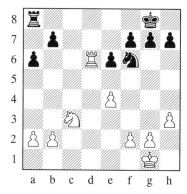

Endgame specialists, rejoice!

12...♕h5?! 13.g4! ♕g6 14.♗a4 e5 (14...♖c8
15.♕e3 ♗e7 16.♗xc6† ♖xc6 17.♕a7±) 15.♗e3

♗e7 16.♕g2 À la Scheveningens from Chapter
2, but with the queens in exotic places.

12...♘e5!? 13.♕e2 ♗e7 14.♗d2!?∞ 0–0
15.♖ac1!
    Black's queen may now fall into the pit.

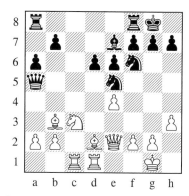

15...♘c6!
    15...♖ac8?? 16.♘d5+−
    15...♖fc8?! 16.♘d5 ♕d8 17.♗a5!→
    15...♕b6 16.♗e3 ♘a5 17.f4 (17.♗d2=)
    17...♘ed7 (17...♘c6 18.♕f2∞) 18.g4→
16.♘d5 ♕d8 17.♘xe7† ♕xe7 18.♗a4∞

13.♗a4!

The tactics now flow violently on the
weakened light squares, ultimately leading to
Black's king.

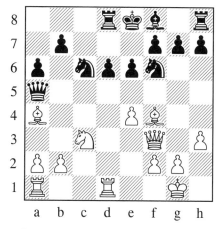

13...b5?

13...♗e7 14.e5!± ♘d5 15.♘xd5 exd5
(15...♕xa4 16.♘c7†+−) 16.♗xc6† bxc6
17.exd6 ♗xd6 18.♕g3 ♗xf4 19.♕xg7 ♖f8
20.♖e1† ♔d7 21.♕g4†±

13...♕b6 14.♘d5!±

13...♖d7 14.b4!→ ♕h5 15.♗xc6 bxc6 16.♕d3±

13...♘d7!? 14.♗xc6 bxc6 15.♗xd6 ♗xd6
16.♖xd6±

14.e5± ♘xe5 15.♗xe5 bxa4
15...dxe5 16.♖xd8† ♔xd8 17.♘xb5 axb5
18.♗xb5† ♔e7 19.♕b7† ♔d6 20.♖c1+−

16.♗xf6 gxf6

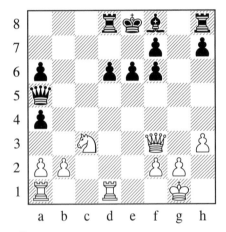

17.♘d5!
Brutality.

**17...exd5 18.♕xf6 ♖g8 19.♖e1† ♔d7
20.♖ac1+−**

Theory III – 11...♕b6

**1.e4 c5 2.d4 cxd4 3.c3 dxc3 4.♘xc3 d6
5.♘f3 ♘c6 6.♗c4 a6 7.0–0 ♘f6 8.♗f4! ♗g4
9.h3! ♗xf3!? 10.♕xf3 e6! 11.♖fd1 ♕b6!?**
Another treacherous path which White must
navigate skillfully.

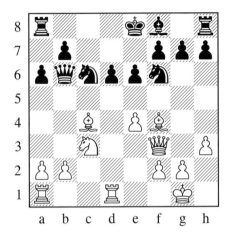

12.♕e2!±
12.♗b3 ♖ad8! 13.♗a4 no longer has the
same sting, as the queen vigilantly guards c6.

12.♗xd6?? ♗xd6 13.♖xd6 ♕b4!∓

12.♖xd6?? ♗xd6 13.♗xd6 ♘a5−+

12...♗e7!?
12...♖c8?! presenting more pitfalls if White
grabs the d-pawn, though it is otherwise
harmless: 13.♗b3! (13.♗xd6?? ♘d4∓) 13...♖d8
(13...♗e7 14.♗xd6 ♗xd6 15.♖xd6 0–0 16.e5
♘e8 17.♖d7±)

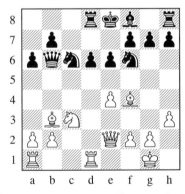

14.♘d5! exd5 15.exd5† ♘e7 16.♗a4† ♘d7
17.♖e1±

12...♘d7!? 13.♗e3 (13.♗xd6? ♗xd6 14.♖xd6
♘d4!−+) 13...♕c7 14.f4!→ b5

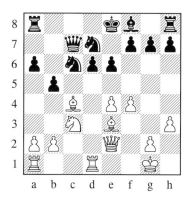

15.♗b3 (Or 15.♘xb5!? with more Chicago themes. 15...axb5 16.♗xb5 ♘a7 17.♖ac1 ♕a5 18.♗xd7† ♔xd7 19.♖c5!±) 15...♘c5 16.f5→

12...♘e5?! 13.♗b3 ♗e7 14.♗a4†± The b6-queen now blocks ...b5 defensive possibilities.

12...♖d8!? 13.♗e3 ♕a5 (13...♕c7 14.♖ac1→) 14.f4 ♗e7 (14...♕h5 15.♕f2!±) 15.a3 0–0 16.♕f2 ♘d7 17.b4 ♕c7 18.♖ac1± White's two bishops, activity, and space offer more than enough compensation for the pawn.

13.♗xd6!?

This time, White can take the pawn.

13.a3!?∞ at your own peril!

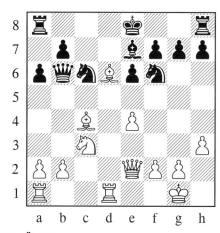

13...♘d4?!

This attempt at the d6-trick backfires. Black must only aim to equalize here:

13...♗xd6 14.♖xd6 0–0! 15.♖ad1
    15.e5!? ♘h5! 16.♘e4 ♘f4 17.♕c2 ♖ad8 18.♘g5 g6 19.♕d2 Black remains under pressure but can hold after: 19...♘xe5! 20.♖xd8 ♕xd8 21.♕xf4 ♘xc4 22.♘xe6 fxe6 23.♕xc4 ♕d5=
13...♖fd8
    15...♖ad8?! 16.e5 ♖xd6 17.♖xd6 ♘e8 18.♖d7→ ♘c7 19.♗d3±
16.e5 ♖xd6 17.♖xd6 ♘e8 18.♖d7 ♖d8

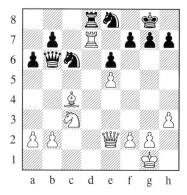

Seemingly coasting to draw-land but...
19.♗xe6! fxe6 20.♕h5
Black still must sweat.

14.♖xd4! ♕xd4

14...♗xd6 15.♖xd6 ♕xd6 16.e5±

15.♖d1 ♕b6 16.♗xe7 ♔xe7 17.e5! ♘d7 18.♕g4!∞

Black's king nears the precipice...

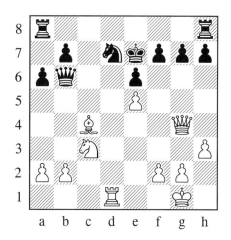

18...♖hg8

18...♘xe5? 19.♕g5† f6 20.♕xg7† ♘f7
21.♖e1+−

19.♖d6!+−

...And now falls into oblivion.

19...♕c7

19...♕c5 20.♘d5† exd5 21.♖xd7† ♔e8
22.♗xd5 ♖f8 23.♕f5+−

**20.♖xe6†! fxe6 21.♕xe6† ♔d8 22.♕xg8†
♔e7 23.♘d5#**

Theory IV – 11...♕b8!?

**1.e4 c5 2.d4 cxd4 3.c3 dxc3 4.♘xc3 d6
5.♘f3 ♘c6 6.♗c4 a6 7.0–0 ♘f6 8.♗f4! ♗g4
9.h3! ♗xf3!? 10.♕xf3 e6! 11.♖fd1 ♕b8!?**

The most direct defense of the d6-pawn,
subsequently leading to the most direct
response.

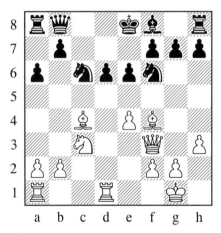

12.♗e2!

Preparing for the shifty ♕g3.

12...♗e7

12...♘e5 13.♕g3→ and Black cannot finish
developing.

13.♕g3! 0–0

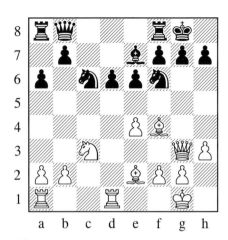

14.♖xd6!?

14.♗xd6 only led to sterility and a draw in
Zelic – Stokke, Pula 2008. If White wishes to
win, he must live dangerously and sacrifice the
exchange for long-term pressure.

14...♗xd6

14...e5?! 15.♗h6!→

15.♗xd6 ♕d8!?

15...♕a7 16.♗xf8 ♖xf8 17.♖d1±

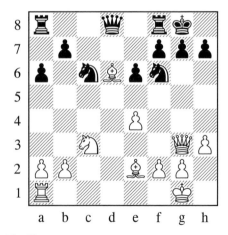

16.e5!

Charge!

With Black's queen more active than on a7,
restoring the material balance with 16.♗xf8
should lead to equality.

16...♘d7 17.♖d1⩲

No doubt, White has more than enough punch for the exchange, as his d6-bishop dominates the board. While Black should have sufficient defensive resources, I'll showcase one inspiring display of attacking firepower.

17...♕b6 18.b4! ♖fd8

18...♘xb4? 19.♖b1+−

19.a3 ♘d4 20.♗g4 ♖ac8 21.♗e7 ♖e8 22.♗g5±

The bishops swoop to the kingside, awaiting decisive action as White's e5-pawn supports the invasion. Black's knights, initially seeking superficial activity, remain paralyzed, whereas White's knight jumps to e4 and beyond.

22...h6 23.♗xh6 gxh6 24.♘e4! ♖f8

24...♔h7 25.♕f4 ♖f8 26.♖xd4+−

25.♘d6 ♖c7 26.♗xe6† ♔h8 27.♗g4± ♘e6 28.♕h4 ♘xe5 29.♕xh6† ♔g8 30.♘e4

30.♗f5!? ♘g6 31.♗xe6 fxe6 32.♕xg6† ♖g7 33.♕xe6† ♔h7 34.♕e4† ♔h8 35.♘f5+−

30...f6

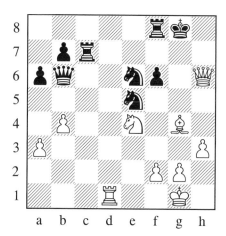

31.♖d6!

The rolling tank razes the Temple of Doom to rubble.

31...♘xg4 32.hxg4 ♖c6 33.♖d7 ♖f7 34.♘xf6† ♖xf6 35.♕h7† ♔f8 36.♕h8#

Theory V – 9...♗h5 10.♕b3

1.e4 c5 2.d4 cxd4 3.c3 dxc3 4.♘xc3 d6 5.♘f3 ♘c6 6.♗c4 a6 7.0-0 ♘f6 8.♗f4! ♗g4 9.h3! ♗h5!?

Lastly, we cover Black's stiffest resistance after retreating the bishop.

10.♕b3

As we saw earlier, you may play Mueller's stable 10.g4!?, but the practical power of the chaotic 10.♕b3!? cannot be denied.

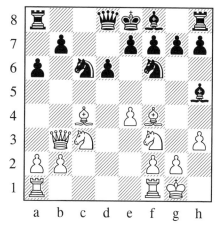

10...♕d7!?

I again mention all of Black's dubious replies – 10...♘a5?! or 10...♕c7?! or 10...b5?! or 10...e6?! or 10...♖b8?! – as a reminder of the slippery terrain ahead.

The other playable option for Black is 10...♖c8!?, after which we look at the volatile A) 11.e5!? and the typical B) 11.♖ac1!?.

A) 11.e5!?

In theory Black can defend here and even assume the advantage, but in practice I can imagine a different outcome. You be the judge.

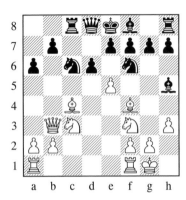

11...♘a5

11...dxe5?! 12.♘xe5→ ♘xe5 13.♗xe5 ♘d7
14.♖fe1± ♘xe5 15.♖xe5 ♗g6 16.♖d1 ♕c7
17.♕a4† ♕c6

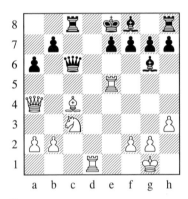

18.♖c5!+−

12.♕a4† ♘d7!

Black survives the first wave, but more
mayhem awaits. 12...♕d7?? 13.♗xf7† ♔xf7
14.e6†+−; 12...b5? 13.♗xb5† axb5 14.♘xb5
♘d7 15.exd6 exd6 16.♖fe1†+−

13.♗d5 ♗xf3!

a) 13...e6?

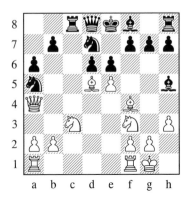

14.exd6! ♗xf3 15.♗xf3 ♖c4 16.b4 ♖xf4
17.♘d5!+−

b) 13...b5? 14.♕d1! dxe5

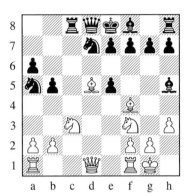

15.♘xe5! Legal's pseudo-sacrifice returns,
this time with double the fun. 15...♘f6
16.♕xh5! ♕xd5 17.♘xd5 ♘xh5 18.♖ac1±

14.♗xf3 ♖c4

14...dxe5! 15.♗g5 h6 16.♕h4∓ is objectively
a touch in Black's favor, but White can still
seek mischief.

15.b4!∞

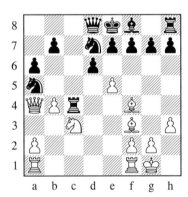

You may analyze this version of b2-b4 for
your own harrowing entertainment.

B) 11.♖ac1!? ♘d7!

Shockingly, this difficult retreat is Black's
only defense. The weaker alternatives
11...e6?!, 11...♕d7?! and 11...♘a5?! featured
earlier in the chapter.

Now White must retreat in turn to keep the
balance.

12.♗e2!?⩲̲

12.♕xb7?? ♘c5–+

12.♘g5?! This Romantic raid narrowly misses the mark: 12...e6 13.♗xe6 fxe6 14.♘xe6 ♘c5!∓

12...♘c5

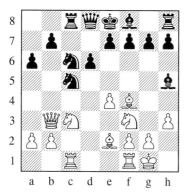

13.♕d1!=

White retracts like a bow and arrow before waiting to rejoin the fray.

13.♕c2?! ♗xf3! leads to liquidations favoring Black: 14.♗xf3 ♘b4! 15.♕d2 ♘bd3 16.♖cd1 ♘xf4 17.♕xf4 e5∓ The knight will head to e6-d4.

13...e6 14.a3 a5

14...♗xf3 15.♗xf3 ♗e7 16.b4 ♘d7 17.♗xd6=

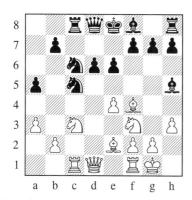

15.♘b5 ♘xe4?!

15...♗e7 16.♗e3 0–0 (16...♘xe4 17.♕a4!→) 17.♘xd6 ♗xd6 18.♗xc5=

16.♕a4!±

The arrow releases.

16...♘c5

16...d5 17.♘a7!±

17.♖xc5 dxc5 18.♖d1 ♕b6 19.♕b3!+–

11.♗e2!

White must again skirt ...♘a5 dangers. The structure should now morph into a Scheveningen (with themes familiar to us from Chapter 2) when a rich struggle looms.

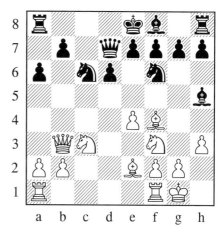

11...♗xf3

11...e6? 12.♖fd1 ♕c7 13.♖ac1±

11...e5!? 12.♗e3 ♗e7 13.♘a4!→

12.♗xf3 ♘d4

The Taylorphile finally achieves his much desired exchanges, but still must suffer.

12...e5?! 13.♗e3 ♘d4 14.♗xd4 exd4 15.♘e2±

13.♕d1 ♘xf3†

13...e5 14.♗g5! ♗e7 (14...♘xf3† 15.♕xf3 ♗e7 16.♖fd1 0–0 17.♗xf6 ♗xf6 18.♘d5⩲̲

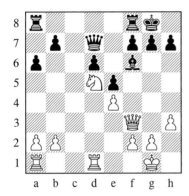

An image of White's strategic dream in the Scheveningens.) 15.♗xf6 ♗xf6 16.♗g4 ♘e6 17.♘d5 ♗d8 18.f4→

14.♕xf3 e5

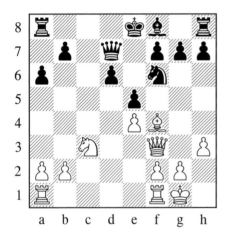

15.♗h6!?

Beating the drums...

15...♕e6   16.♗g5   ♗e7   17.♗xf6   ♗xf6 18.♘d5⯳

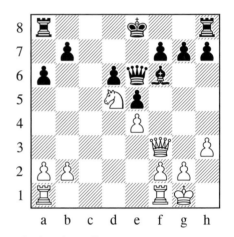

The knight walks on water.

You may stay locked in an eternal analytical battle in Taylor's Temple of Doom if you wish, but I'm jetting loose, straight out through the roof and all the way up to the heavens above.

Chapter 10

Finegold's Final Frontier

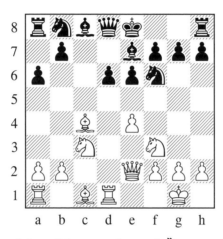

**1.e4 c5 2.d4 cxd4 3.c3 dxc3 4.♘xc3 e6 5.♘f3 d6
6.♗c4 a6 7.0–0 ♗e7 8.♕e2 ♘f6 9.♖d1**

Alas, we have traversed almost all Morra main lines – only one remains. In the year 2000, National Master Bob Ciaffone and IM Ben Finegold launched "The Finegold Defense", an unabashed analysis of the Morra's ultimate destruction. From their very first words, the authors sent a resounding message to any delusional gambiteer who would dare champion the Morra in the face of hard, cold-blooded logic: "If you expect to get a good result with [the Morra] at the higher levels of serious tournament competition, and think the logical outcome of a game after using it is only a draw for Black with perfect play, we express our condolences. It is difficult to have a serious discourse with someone who insists the earth is flat."

After **1.e4 c5 2.d4 cxd4 3.c3 dxc3 4.♘xc3 e6 5.♘f3 d6 6.♗c4 a6 7.0–0 ♗e7 8.♕e2 ♘f6 9.♖d1 b5,**

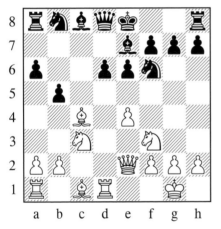

we reach Finegold's Final Frontier. In truth, the Finegold Defense is nothing more than a glorified name for the Najdorf variation of the Open Sicilian vs. the Morra Gambit, but considering the Najdorf's great pedigree, this fact only makes the Finegold even more intimidating. On 10.♗b3, Black ices the fire on the d-file with 10...♘bd7, thus forming the chilling Najdorf structure. In only a few more

moves, he will complete his development with a free pawn to spare, thereby utterly eradicating the Morra Gambit from the chess planet.

For years I fought the Finegold, and although I achieved mating attacks against both the authors, I took no solace, knowing full well that my ideas would not stand the test of time. Finally, one night while stargazing, I found another-worldly novelty that effectively puts an end to the Finegold delusion, once and for all. And so, to the creators of Finegold's Defense, I say this: The sun does not revolve around the earth, the earth is not the only planet in our vast galaxy, and the Milky Way is just one of billions of galaxies. So suit up, and get ready to experience chess's expanding universe.

Marc Esserman – Ben Finegold

Internet (blitz) 2006

1.e4 c5 2.d4 cxd4 3.c3 dxc3 4.♘xc3 d6 5.♘f3 e6 6.♗c4 ♗e7 7.0–0 ♘f6 8.♕e2 a6 9.♖d1 b5

True to name, Finegold uncorks his defense. But I intend to show him that he is in an intergalactic cyber-duel with the wrong creature.

10.♗b3 ♘bd7

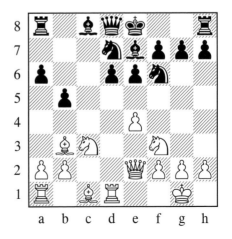

11.♘d4!?

11.e5!? dxe5 12.♘xe5 ♕b6 (12...♗b7??
13.♘xf7!+– ♔xf7 14.♕xe6† ♔g6 15.♗c2†
♔h5 16.♕h3#) 13.♗e3 ♕b7

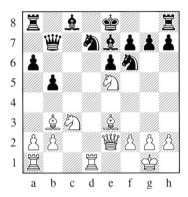

We arrive at Finegold's cherished main line.
Black's queen, though in the nether realms
on b7, has effectively avoided a heavy meteor
shower from White's rooks on c1 and d1.
Although lacking the life-force e4-pawn, all of
White's pieces remain highly charged, yielding
him excellent long-term compensation. Before
leaving this position in the dust for now and
cruising forward, note that the immediate strike
14.♘xf7?! ♔xf7 15.♗xe6† ♔xe6 16.♗c5† fails
as after 16...♘e5!–+ Black weathers the storm.

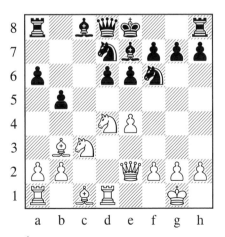

11...♗b7?!

Even as I overtly threaten to turn e6 into
a wasteland, Finegold surprisingly refuses to

adopt the signature maneuver of his defense:
11...♕b6! 12.♗e3

12.♗xe6?! leads to naught: 12...fxe6 13.♘xe6
This now comes without tempo, and after
the incoming ...♘e5 the c8-bishop will
punish White's invading knight. 13...g6∓

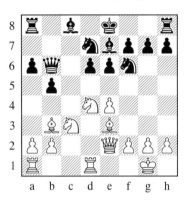

12...♕b7!

As is typically the case in the gambit, if Black
secures his queen he also solves the Morra
problem. But even here, he must watch for
streaking comets!

13.♖ac1 ♘c5!∓

13...0–0 14.♘c6!→ ♕xc6 15.♘d5!± and yet
again the queen burns.

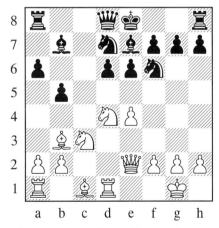

12.♗xe6! fxe6 13.♘xe6 ♕b6 14.♘d5!?

The knights cannot be bothered by meager
pawns, but rather have the king on their mind.
14.♗e3! harassing the queen still further, would

leave Black lost in cold space forever: 14...♕c6 15.♘d5 ♔f7 16.♘g5† ♔f8 17.♖ac1+–

14...♗xd5 15.exd5 ♘e5 16.♗e3 ♕b7 17.f4 ♘c4 18.♗d4±

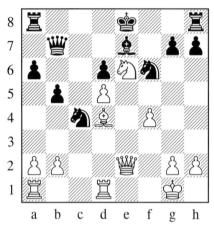

Although a piece down, White's powerful central pieces emit rays of energy. Most importantly, the e6-knight severs the board in two, effectively reducing Black's rooks to spectators in the fight while their rivals wait to destroy the helpless king. Under intense pressure, Finegold collapses.

18...♘xd5 19.♗xg7 ♖g8 20.♖xd5+– ♔d7 21.♘c5† ♔c6 22.♘xb7 ♖xg7 23.♕e4 ♔c7 24.b3 ♘b6 25.♖c1† ♔d7 26.♘c5† ♔e8 27.♖xd6

With "refutations" and egos at stake, Finegold resists until the bitter end, whereas I, savoring the moment, purposely prolong the inevitable, if only to send an encrypted message that he has not heard the last of the Morra Gambit.

27...♖c8 28.♖c6 ♖b8 29.♘e6 ♔f7 30.♘xg7 ♗f6 31.♖c7† ♔g8 32.♘h5 ♘d7 33.♖xd7 ♗e7 34.♕xe7 h6 35.♖cc7 b4 36.♘f6† ♔h8 37.h4 a5 38.♕h7#

I had won the battle, but not the analytical war.

Finegold Refutation

1.e4 c5 2.d4 cxd4 3.c3 dxc3 4.♘xc3 d6 5.♘f3 e6 6.♗c4 a6 7.0–0 ♗e7 8.♕e2 ♘f6 9.♖d1 b5

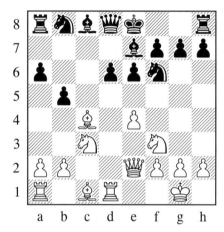

10.e5!

We have liftoff! The gambiteer now sacrifices a second pawn, and the bishop pair, for nebulous compensation...

10...bxc4 11.exf6 gxf6

11...♗xf6? 12.♗f4! ♗e7 13.♗xd6! ♗xd6 14.♘e4±

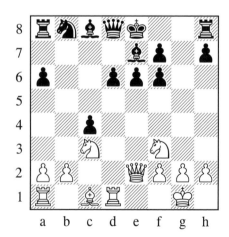

In the "Finegold Defense", the authors dismiss this line, giving only 12.♕xc4?! ♗b7∓. Of course, nothing could prepare them for the dazzling supernova explosion to come.

12.♘d2!!±

Shattering all the principles faster than the speed of light. Despite an ultra-dynamic position, White moves the same piece twice in the opening, in addition to blocking in the rook and bishop! It's the Morra Gambit, not the Benoni, after all. Yet even while possessing extra material and the two bishops, Black still cannot find a defensive salvation. White's knights will soon swarm on c4 and e4, and the seemingly secure black king will suddenly disappear into a black hole. A remarkable find, revealing not only the solution to the Finegold riddle, but also the power of dynamic developmental compensation to dominate over static positional and material factors in even the haziest of attacks.

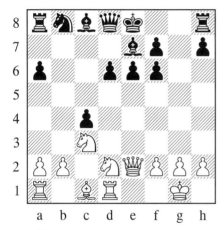

12...a5?!

Black has several other options:

12...♗b7!? 13.♘xc4 ♖g8 14.♘e4! d5 15.♗f4±

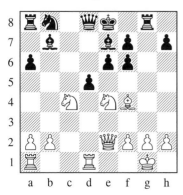

White's minor pieces form a globular cluster in the center. We'll peer into this constellation in the advanced material.

12...♘d7?! 13.♘xc4 ♘e5
13...d5 14.♘xd5! exd5 15.♘d6† ♔f8 16.♗h6† ♔g8 17.♕g4# With the king lacking proper cover, mates of this type light up the sky in the variations to come.
13...♕c7 14.♗f4 ♘e5 15.♘xd6† (15.♗xe5 dxe5 16.♖ac1±) 15...♗xd6 16.♖xd6 ♕xd6 17.♘e4 ♕e7 18.♘xf6† ♕xf6 19.♗xe5±

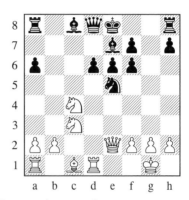

14.♘xd6†! ♗xd6 15.♘e4+–
When such logical developing moves fail, you just know the defender is in for a rough interstellar adventure.

12...♘c6!? 13.♘xc4 d5 14.♗f4 0–0
a) 14...♗b7?

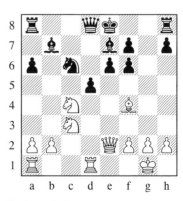

15.♖xd5! Black's king comes crashing out

of orbit. 15...exd5 16.♘d6† ♔f8 (16...♔d7 17.♕g4†+–) 17.♗h6† ♔g8 18.♕g4#

b) 14...d4 15.♕f3 ♗b7 16.♘e4 e5 17.♖e1!±

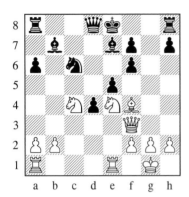

17...♘a5 18.♘xa5 ♕xa5 19.♗xe5! fxe5 (19...♕xe5 20.♘xf6† ♔f8 21.♕xb7+–) 20.♘f6† ♗xf6 21.♕xf6+– Outer space can be a very scary place!

15.♕f3±

Even more powerful than 15.♖d3!? or 15.♗h6!?. Black's airy king now floats about in a zero-gravity environment.

15...♔h8 16.♘xd5! exd5 17.♖xd5 ♕e8

17...♗d7 18.♖ad1+–

18.♘d6 ♗xd6

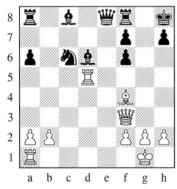

19.♗g5!+–

Or 19.♗xd6+–.

19...fxg5 20.♕f6† ♔g8 21.♖xg5#

12...♕c7!? 13.♘xc4 d5

13...♗b7 14.♗f4 e5 15.♖ac1 exf4 16.♘b5+–

Space's version of a queen out in Siberia with no heat (see Chapter 1).

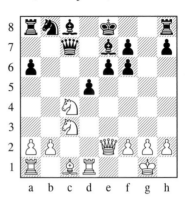

14.♖xd5!

Black's position now teeters upon the event horizon...

14...♗b7!

The rook must not be captured, else Black falls into the zone where light never escapes: 14...exd5? 15.♘xd5 Black must choose between being swiftly mated or shedding massive amounts of material from pulsating knight forks. 15...♕d8 (15...♕b7 16.♘d6†+– or 15...♕d7 ♘xf6†+– or 15...♕a7 16.♘d6† ♔d8 17.♘xf7†+–) 16.♘xf6† ♔f8 17.♗h6# 15.♖d1± ♖g8 16.♘e4

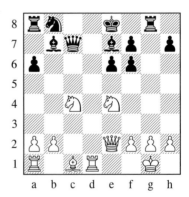

The centralized, charging knight forces Black to part with his raking b7-bishop. When all the dust clears, White smoothly flies to a superior ending, with his Morra rooks and potential outside passed pawn leading the way.

16...♗xe4 17.♕xe4 ♕c6 18.♕xc6† ♘xc6
19.♗e3±

13.♘xc4 ♗a6

13...d5 14.♘b5! Now the knights invade through a different wormhole. 14...♗a6 (14...♗b7 15.♗f4±)

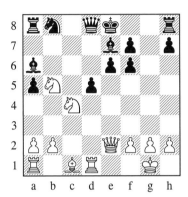

15.♖xd5! exd5 16.♘cd6† ♔d7 17.♗f4 ♗xb5 (17...♗xd6 18.♕g4†±) 18.♖xb5† ♘c6 19.♕xd5+– The queen arrives through the portal to pay the king an up-close personal visit.

14.♕f3! d5

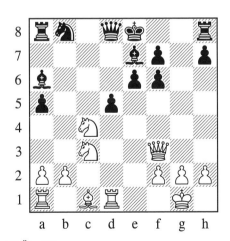

15.♘xd5!

White's encircling pieces form rings around the enemy, ultimately driving the hapless defender into a black hole.

15...exd5 16.♖xd5 ♘d7

16...♕c7 17.♘xa5!+– Gaze upon this quasar and you shall find that although White only has three pawns for the piece, Black simply cannot move and should resign immediately!

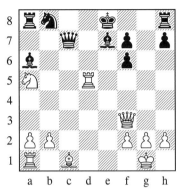

If 17...0–0, then 18.♗h6! followed by ♕g4† bursts forth. If 17...♗b7 then 18.♘xb7 ♕xb7 19.♖d8† beams, while 17...♘d7 is met by 18.♖xd7 ♔xd7 19.♗f4+–. Lastly, if nothing else, ♗f4 followed by ♖e1 may flash in the not too distant future.

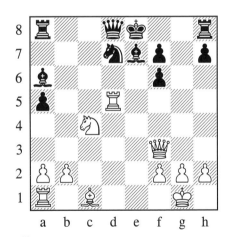

17.♖xd7!

Black spirals into the abyss, past the point of no return.

17...♔xd7 18.♕d5† ♔e8 19.♕c6† ♔f8 20.♗h6† ♔g8 21.♕f3+–

The inevitable ♕g4† or ♕g3† leads to nothingness for the black king.

Theory I – 9...♘bd7

1.e4 c5 2.d4 cxd4 3.c3 dxc3 4.♘xc3 d6 5.♘f3 e6 6.♗c4 a6 7.0–0 ♗e7 8.♕e2 ♘f6 9.♖d1!

9.e5!? was my old weapon vs. Finegold's Defense, and it is also playable, offering White full compensation for the pawn in the form of active piece play after 9...dxe5 10.♘xe5!?∞ (or 10.♖d1!?∞). But of course, it does not allow Black the opportunity to fall into the hole after the awesome 9.♖d1 b5?! 10.e5!.

9...♘bd7!?

Black avoids the pit, but fails to achieve the ambitious queenside expansion that Finegold's Defense aims for.

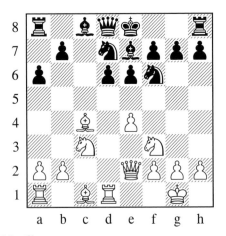

10.e5!

Again, the gambiteer strikes in the center, as usual counting on his pieces to swirl up counterplay once devoid of the clamping e4-pawn.

10...dxe5 11.♘xe5 0–0 12.♗f4⩱ ♕b6

The queen skirts the pin and guards the sensitive e6-grid, but still blocks in the b-pawn, thus freezing Black's queenside.

The claustrophobic 12...♕e8, meanwhile, presents the defender with cramping problems of an altogether different sort after 13.♖ac1.

12...♕a5? is an even worse spot for the queen: 13.♘xf7 ♖xf7 14.♕xe6+–

Black's attempt to drum up the desired queenside activity with 12...b5? fails to: 13.♘c6 ♕e8 14.♘xe7† ♕xe7 15.♗d6±

13.♗b3 ♘xe5 14.♗xe5

Black has done well to exchange off some firepower, but no further easy solutions remain. His queenside remains tied in knots, while White eyes transfers of force to the kingside in the form of ♗c2 followed by ♘e4 and crushing rook lifts.

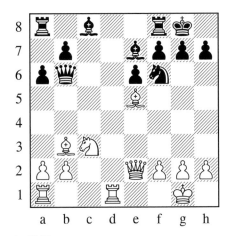

14...♖d8

Chasing the e5-bishop is weaker:
14...♘d7?! 15.♗d4 ♕a5
15...♗c5 16.♘a4 ♕a5 17.♘xc5 ♘xc5 18.♕e5+–

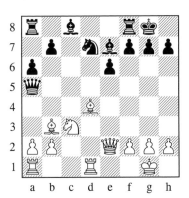

16.♘d5!±
  16.♖d3!?→
16...♗c5
  16...exd5 17.♕xe7±
17.♗xc5 ♕xc5
  17...♘xc5 18.♘e7† ♔h8 19.♗c2 Menacing mayhem with ♗xh7†. 19...h6 20.♕e5±
18.♖ac1 ♕a5 19.♘e7† ♔h8 20.♘xc8+−

15.♖xd8† ♕xd8 16.♖d1⇄
Black's rook remains compressed, and the clock is ticking before the big bang.

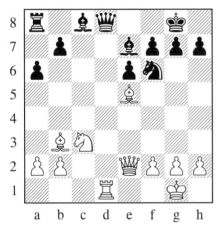

16...♕b6?
  16...♗d7!? 17.♗c2→

16...♕a5 17.h3! Preventing the freeing ...♘g4 thrust. Black stays stifled. 17...b5?! 18.♗xf6 (18.♕f3!? ♖a7 19.♗xf6 ♗xf6 [19...gxf6†] 20.♕c6+−) 18...♗xf6 19.♕e4 ♖b8 20.♘d5!± ♗d8 21.♗c2 g6 22.b4+−

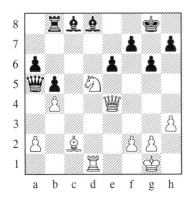

With Black's pieces stranded on the outer rims of the board, he cannot muster a defense. Figure out why for entertainment!

17.♗xf6! ♗xf6 18.♘d5

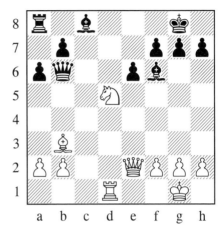

18...♕d8 19.♘xf6† ♕xf6 20.♖d3!
  20.♕e5!? would be a prelude to the climactic explosion.

20...b5
  One last desperate developing attempt...

21.♕e4 ♖b8
  21...♖a7 22.♕c6+−

22.♕e5! ♖a8 23.♕c7+−

Theory II – 9...b5

1.e4 c5 2.d4 cxd4 3.c3 dxc3 4.♘xc3 d6 5.♘f3 e6 6.♗c4 a6 7.0–0 ♗e7 8.♕e2 ♘f6 9.♖d1! b5 10.e5! bxc4 11.exf6 gxf6 12.♘d2!!± ♗b7!?
  Attempting to solve the problems in earthly "Chicago" fashion leads to cosmic annihilation:

12...♖a7?! 13.♘xc4 d5
  13...♖d7 14.♗e3 ♗b7 15.♘a4±
14.♗e3 ♖b7
  14...♖d7 15.♗b6+−
15.♖ac1

The Morra rooks rage.

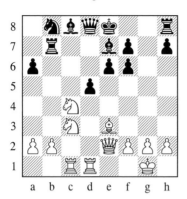

15...♖g8

15...♗d7 16.♕f3 (16.♘xd5!?→) 16...♗c6
(16...♘c6 17.♘xd5 exd5 18.♖xd5 0–0
19.♘b6!±) 17.♕g3 ♘d7 18.♘d6† ♗xd6
19.♕xd6 ♕c7 20.♕a3→ Keeping the king
in firing range.

16.♘b6 ♗d7

16...♖xb6 17.♗xb6 ♕xb6 18.♘xd5+–
17.♘bxd5 exd5 18.♘xd5+– ♗e6 19.♘xe7
♕xe7 20.♗c5 ♕c7 21.♗a3

White's rooks are a sight to behold.

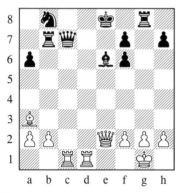

21...♕e5

21...♘c6 22.♕e4 ♖b6 23.♕xh7!+–
22.♕d3 ♕a5 23.♖c5 ♕b6 24.♕c3

Mates abound.

13.♘xc4 ♖g8 14.♘e4!±

Finally, we visit White's globular cluster of
pieces in the center after the critical 12...♗b7.

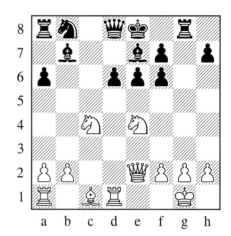

14...d5

14...♗xe4 15.♕xe4 d5 16.♕xh7±

15.♗f4!

15.♕h5!?

15...e5

White's three minor pieces float in air, but as
Tal mused, the defender "can only take them
one at a time".

16.♗e3!

16.♖ac1!?

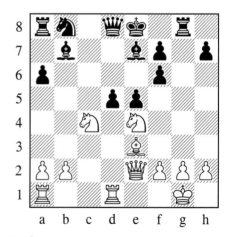

16...f5

16...♘c6 17.♗b6 ♕d7 18.♗c5±

16...d4?! 17.♗xd4! The bishop swarms from all angles. 17...exd4 18.♘xf6† ♔f8 19.♘xg8 ♔xg8 20.♕g4† ♔h8 21.♖xd4±

16...♖g6 17.♖ac1! (17.f4!?) 17...♘c6 (17...d4 18.♗xd4+–) 18.♕f3!→

17.♗b6 ♕d7

The board's spectacular piece distribution is a stargazer's dream. Now White releases a furious combination which lights up Finegold's Defense and the night sky.

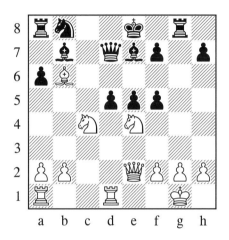

18.♘cd6†! ♔f8 19.♕h5 ♗xd6

19...♕e6!? 20.♘xf5! ♕xb6
   20...dxe4 21.♘xe7+–
   20...♕g6 21.♕xg6 ♖xg6 22.♗c5 ♗xc5 23.♘xc5±
21.♘xe7 ♔xe7 22.♕xe5†
There is no escaping the beaming rays of attacking energy.
22...♕e6
   22...♔f8 23.♘f6+–
23.♕c7† ♕d7 24.♕c5†+–

20.♕h6† ♖g7

20...♔e7 21.♕f6†+–

21.♘f6

The final burst.

21...♕e6 22.♘xh7† ♔g8

22...♔e7 23.♕xg7±

23.♘f6† ♔f8 24.♕h8† ♔e7 25.♗d8#!

"Why did you elect to take up the Smith-Morra Gambit in the first place? The gambit is a good weapon for blitz chess, useful in teaching tactics to a young player, and fun to play. But if you expect to get a good result with it at the higher levels of serious tournament competition, and think the logical outcome of a game after using it is only a draw for Black with perfect play, we express our condolences. It is difficult to have a serious discourse with someone who insists the earth is flat."

– Bob Ciaffone and GM Ben Finegold

Chapter 11

Searching the Stars for a Refutation

There are more possible chess moves than atoms in the universe.

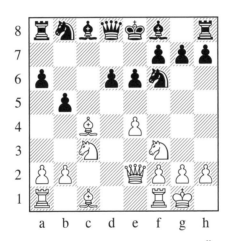

**1.e4 c5 2.d4 cxd4 3.c3 dxc3 4.♘xc3 d6
5.♘f3 e6 6.♗c4 a6 7.0–0 ♘f6 8.♕e2 b5**

We've searched far and wide, and yet a refutation to the Morra Gambit remains light years away. Over time I thought I had found many depressing deaths to the gambit, but upon deeper analytical review, sometimes minutes, sometimes years later, I discovered the Morra not only survived, but thrived. Today, as a result of this painstaking process of endless demise and rebirth, my faith in the total soundness of the Morra Gambit stands as strong as ever. While in my eyes the other classical gambits have all fallen to the brutality of modern computer analysis, the Morra Gambit has and will continue to endure the test of time. If, in the future, a chess authority announces the destruction of the Morra Gambit, I would caution skepticism. Likely the counter-refutation will lie just a move or two beyond the horizon.

To conclude, I will extend the theory of the gambit still further, offering a "refutation" of my own which ultimately fails to suppress the ever-expanding Morra.

Searching the Stars I

1.e4 c5 2.d4 cxd4 3.c3 dxc3 4.♘xc3 d6 5.♘f3 e6 6.♗c4 a6 7.0–0 ♘f6

Black now may aim for an improved version of Finegold's Defense, or the variations from Chapter 4 (Into the Deep) as we shall see.

8.♕e2

Endgame connoisseurs may revel in 8.e5!? when White obtains long-term dynamic equality, but no more, in the Morra's queenless middlegame version of the Berlin Defense: 8...dxe5 9.♕xd8† ♔xd8 10.♘xe5 ♔e8 11.♗e2! ♘c6 (11...♘bd7 12.♘c4! b5 13.♘a5⩲) 12.♘xc6 bxc6=

8...b5!

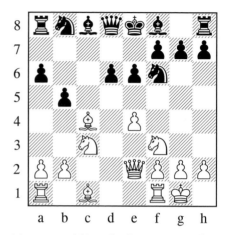

The Finegold/Najdorf structure is forming, but this time the gambiteer does not have the game changing 10.e5! shot.

9.♗b3!? ♘bd7! 10.♖d1!?

But White fears not, trusting in the Morra's natural compensation vs. the dreaded Finegold.

10...♗e7 11.e5!

11.♘d4?!∓

11...dxe5 12.♘xe5 ♕b6 13.♗e3 ♕b7

13...♗c5?! 14.♘d5! exd5 15.♘xd7 ♗xd7 16.♗xc5† ♕e6 17.♕d3+−

14.♗d4

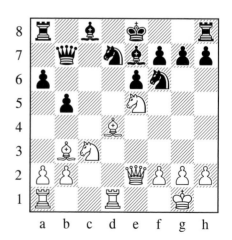

With a nuanced move order, Black avoids the pitfalls and finally achieves Finegold's desired position. Yet even here, White's swelling piece pressure more than compensates for the pawn. Meanwhile, the b7-queen, though out of harm's way, still greatly harms Black's backward queenside.

14...♘xe5

14...♘c5?! 15.♗c2± b4 (15...0-0 16.♖ac1 b4 17.♘a4 ♘xa4 18.♗xa4 ♗d7 19.♘xd7 ♘xd7 20.♗xg7+–) 16.♗xc5 ♗xc5 17.♗a4†+–

15.♗xe5 0-0

15...♗d7!? 16.♗xf6 gxf6 17.♕h5 ♖g8 18.g3⩲ White maintains the positional grip. Black must now avoid tactics such as 18...b4? 19.♖xd7!+–.

16.♗c2⩲

Again White shifts gears, aiming for a menacing kingside assault.

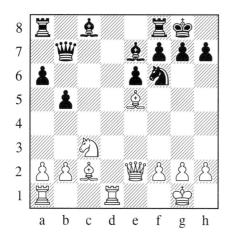

16...b4 17.♘e4 ♘d5 18.♖ac1

Staring across the board and shuddering to see his fully mobilized opponent, Black can only think of surviving, rather than realizing his material advantage. I provide just one flashy continuation.

**18...f6 19.♗d6→ ♗xd6 20.♘xd6 ♕d7
21.♕e4 ♕xd6**

21...g6 22.♖xd5!?⩲

**22.♕xh7† ♔f7 23.♗g6† ♔e7 24.♕xg7†
♔d8**

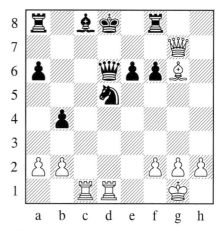

25.♖c7!
Mass mayhem!

25...♕xc7?
25...♖e8 is the only way to fight on.

26.♕xf8† ♔d7 27.♗e8† ♔d8 28.♗a4#

Searching the Stars II

1.e4 c5 2.d4 cxd4 3.c3 dxc3 4.♘xc3 d6 5.♘f3 e6 6.♗c4 a6 7.0-0 ♘f6 8.♕e2 b5 9.♗b3 ♘bd7 10.♖d1!? ♗b7!?

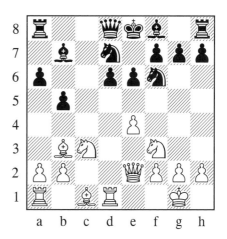

The cunning defender avoids the meteor 9.♘g5! that we saw in Chapter 4 (after 4...a6 5.♘f3 e6 6.♗c4 b5 7.♗b3 ♗b7 8.0–0 d6) and flies towards another Najdorf star system. Yet even in the friendly confines of the Sicilian's most stable structure, the Morra's massive activity wreaks havoc.

11.♗f4 ♕b8

11...♕b6 12.a4! Ideas with ♘d5 lurk here and elsewhere. 12...b4 13.a5 ♕d8 (13...♕c7 14.♘d5 exd5 15.♖ac1 ♘c5 16.♗a4† ♔d8 17.♘g5+− is similar to Esserman – Sarkar, Miami 2008 – see page 103.)

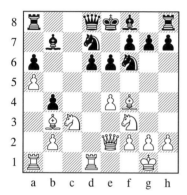

14.♘d5 exd5 (14...♘c5 15.♖ac1!→ ♘xb3?! 16.♘c7† ♔d7 17.♘e5† ♔e7 18.♘c6† ♗xc6 19.♖xc6+−) 15.exd5† ♗e7 16.♗xd6 ♔f8 17.♗g3!⯹ Black pays a heavy price for his extra piece.

11...b4

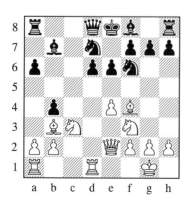

12.♘a4!
Tempting Black to grab a mere extra pawn, and not an extra piece, for a change! Whether or not he takes the plunge, he will feel a solar burn.

12.♘d5?! exd5 13.exd5† ♗e7 14.♗xd6 ♘b6! 15.♘d4 ♕xd6 16.♘f5 0–0!? 17.♘xd6 ♗xd6∓

12...♗xe4
a) 12...♗e7?! 13.e5 ♗xf3 14.♕xf3 dxe5 15.♗xe5 0–0 16.♗xf6 ♗xf6 17.♕b7+−
b) 12...♕a5 13.e5! dxe5 (13...♘h5 14.♗g5∞ Visit this spiraling galaxy at your own risk.) 14.♘xe5 ♘xe5 15.♕xe5 ♕xe5 16.♗xe5±
c) 12...♕b8 13.♘d2!→
d) 12...♘xe4 13.♘d2!∞ ♘ec5 14.♘c4 ♘xb3 15.axb3 d5 16.♘d6† ♗xd6 17.♗xd6→

13.♘g5!
The meteor returns with a vengeance.

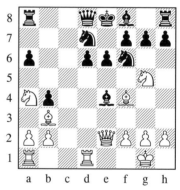

13...♗f5
13...♗b7? 14.♘xf7 ♔xf7 15.♕xe6† ♔g6 16.♗c2† ♔h5 17.♕h3#
13...d5 14.♘xe4 ♘xe4 (14...dxe4 15.♖ac1±) 15.♗xd5! Destruction. 15...exd5 16.♖xd5+−
14.♘xe6! fxe6 15.♗xe6 ♗xe6
15...♕e7 16.♖xd6±
16.♕xe6† ♕e7 17.♕c4→

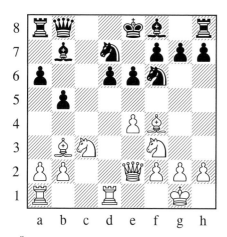

12.♘d5!

12.e5!?⯹ sacrifices a second pawn for wide open expanses,[50] but I prefer to sacrifice pieces. 12...♗xf3 13.♕xf3 dxe5 14.♗g5→

12...exd5

The machine's two other absurd attempts just show that it's lost in space:

12...e5?! 13.♘xf6† ♘xf6 14.♘g5±

12...♘g4 13.♘d4! ♘ge5 14.♖ac1 exd5 15.exd5 ♕d8 (15...♗e7 16.♘c6+−) 16.♗xe5 dxe5 17.♘e6!→

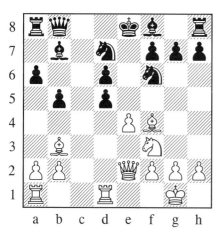

13.e5!

13.exd5†?! ♗e7 14.♖e1 ♘g8!∓ This retreat

enables Black to survive here, but it foreshadows the final Morra explosion...

13...♘xe5 14.♘xe5 dxe5 15.♗xe5 ♕c8!

The only move to avoid an instant loss.

16.♗xf6† ♕e6 17.♖e1 ♕xe2 18.♖xe2† ♔d7 19.♗c3‡

Let the endgame torture phase begin!

Searching the Stars III

1.e4 c5 2.d4 cxd4 3.c3 dxc3 4.♘xc3 d6 5.♘f3 e6 6.♗c4 a6 7.0–0 ♘f6 8.♕e2 b5 9.♗b3 ♘bd7

If you've gotten this far, but still doubt the Morra's raw dynamic power, well then, I save the best for last. Behold, as we open up a new portal in chess theory. I give you, the Fischer-Sozin-Morra attack.

10.♘d4!?

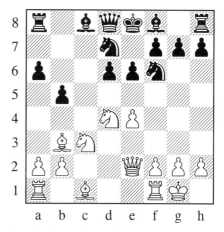

Don't dare play this move unless you're prepared to pitch at least a piece into the fire. Black cannot now castle quickly as 10...♗e7 meets 11.♘c6 or the shattering 11.♗xe6. If 10...♗b7, then 11.♗g5!?, with luminous threats. If ever ...b4, then ♘d5 lurks. But of course, the stultifying computer gives a crystal clear advantage for Black after 10...♘c5.

But can its cold, calculating equations tame infinity?

10...♘c5 11.♗d5!!

The beginning of a superb sacrificial chain culminating in a blinding gamma ray burst.

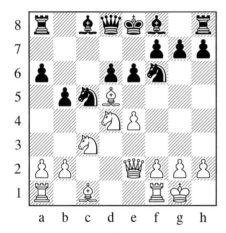

11...exd5 12.exd5† ♗e7

With 12...♕e7!? Black intends to vaporize his queen in exchange for a mass of material: 13.♕d1 b4! 14.♖e1 bxc3 15.♘c6 c2!

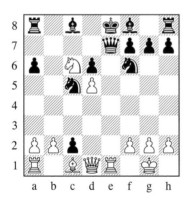

Now 16.♖xe7† is unclear, but I would recommend the less obliging 16.♕d2!!∞. Perhaps not what Nimzowitsch had in mind when he penned his famous maxim: "The threat is stronger than the execution." Peer into your deep field telescopes to unlock the mysteries of the position.

13.♘c6 ♕d7 14.♖e1 ♘g8

In one dimension, Black possesses the two bishops plus an extra piece. However, in a higher dimension, his knight must return to its starting position, while his king braces for cosmic disaster.

15.♗g5

Light speed ahead.

15...f6 16.b4!

16.♗f4!?∞ is possible, but we've travelled this far and wide, so why bother saving dangling bishops now?

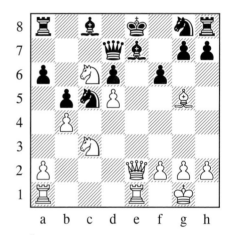

16...♘a4

After 16...fxg5?! 17.bxc5 Black's central blockade implodes: 17...dxc5 (17...♔f8 18.♘e4!→) 18.♘xe7 ♘xe7 19.d6! ♕xd6 20.♖ad1+−

17.♘e4!

The gambiteer's hanging pieces defy all of chess's physical laws.

17...fxg5

17...♔f8?! 18.♘xe7 ♘xe7 (18...♕xe7 19.♗f4+−) 19.♘xf6! Black's kingside will bend before buckling: 19...gxf6 20.♗xf6± ♘g6 21.♕h5 ♖g8 22.♖e6!±

18.♘xg5

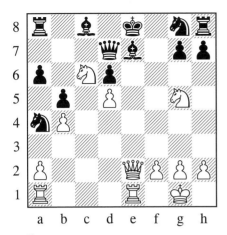

18...♕g4

18...♘c3? 19.♕h5†! g6 20.♕f3 ♕f5 21.♕xc3 ♕f6 22.♕xf6 ♘xf6 23.♖xe7† ♔f8 24.♖f7† ♔e8 25.♖e1†+– leads to mate.

19.♕xe7†!

Not to be outdone, the queen at last chooses to sacrifice herself, rather than meekly trading.

19...♘xe7 20.♖xe7† ♔f8 21.♖f7† ♔e8 22.♖e1† ♗e6

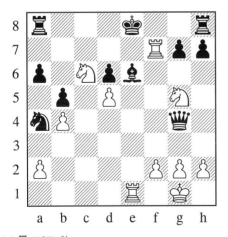

23.♖e7†!!±[51]

23.♖xe6† ♕xe6 24.dxe6 ♖c8! forces White to take perpetual check: 25.♖e7† ♔f8 26.♖f7†= (26.♘xh7†!? ♖xh7 [26...♔g8 27.♘g5! ♔f8 28.♖f7†=] 27.♖f7† ♔e8 28.♖e7†=) 26...♔e8 (26...♔g8 27.♘e7#) 27.♖e7†=

Throughout our tour we have exhaustively searched for an advantage for White in the Morra Gambit in the face of overwhelming odds, so even at journey's end, nearly a full queen down, we fight on!

23...♔f8 24.♘xe6† ♔g8

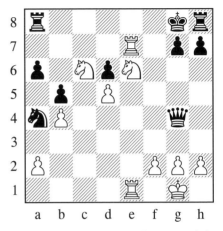

Black's pieces on a4, g4, a8, and h8 are scattered across the four corners of the sky. White's centrally energized forces, meanwhile, hone in on ♖xg7#, thus rendering Black's extra queen inert.

25.h3! ♕g6 26.♖e3! ♖e8

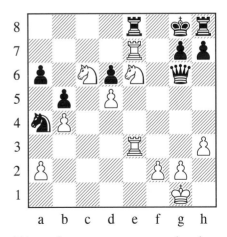

Take a few moments to ponder the spectacular. White longs for a dramatic resolution, but unfortunately, Black eyes a cunning escape with ...♕b1† followed by ...♖xe7.

27.♔h2!!+–

Not all fireballs involve sacrifice. Black is frozen in space, while 28.♘f4! will erupt. Only the afterglow remains. Long live the Morra Gambit!

* * * * *

Related Games

Robert Fischer – Jorge Rubinetti

Palma de Mallorca 1970

1.e4 c5 2.♘f3 d6 3.d4 cxd4 4.♘xd4 ♘f6 5.♘c3 e6 6.♗c4 a6 7.♗b3 b5 8.0–0 ♗b7 9.♖e1 ♘bd7 10.♗g5 h6 11.♗h4 ♘c5

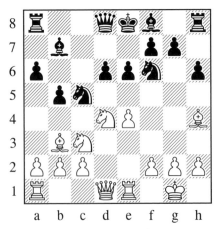

12.♗d5!± exd5 13.exd5† ♔d7 14.b4 ♘a4 15.♘xa4 bxa4 16.c4 ♔c8 17.♕xa4 ♕d7 18.♕b3 g5 19.♗g3 ♘h5 20.c5 dxc5 21.bxc5 ♕xd5 22.♖e8† ♔d7 23.♕a4† ♗c6 24.♘xc6 1–0

Marc Esserman – Eli Vovsha

US Chess League, Internet 2010

1.e4 c5 2.♘f3 d6 3.d4 cxd4 4.♘xd4 ♘f6 5.♘c3 a6 6.♗c4 e6 7.0–0 b5 8.♗b3 b4 9.♘a4 ♗d7 10.c3!

The Morra-Sozin-Fischer Attack!

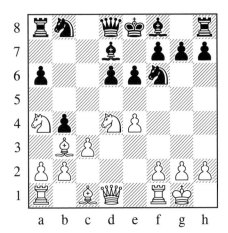

10...♘c6 11.cxb4 ♘xb4 12.♗e3 ♗e7

12...♘xe4 13.♖c1! ♘c5 14.♘xc5 dxc5 15.♘xe6! ♗xe6 (15...fxe6 16.♕h5† g6 17.♕e5+–) 16.♗a4† ♗d7 17.♖e1!+–

13.♖c1 ♘xe4 14.♘b6! 0–0 15.a3 ♕xb6 16.♘xe6 ♕b5 17.♘xf8 ♖xf8 18.axb4 ♕xb4 19.♖c7 ♘f6 20.♗d4 ♗d8 21.♖c3 ♗e6 22.♖e1 ♖e8 23.♖ce3 d5 24.♗c3 ♕b6 25.♗xd5 ♘xd5 26.♕xd5 h6 27.♖g3 f6 28.♕h5 ♔f8 29.♖xg7 ♔xg7 30.♕xe8 ♗f7 31.♕e4 ♕d6 32.♕g4† ♔h7 33.♖d1 ♕e7 34.♕d7 1–0

Chapter 12

Morra Declined Potpourri

1.e4 c5 2.d4 cxd4 (2...e6? 3.d5± 329; 2...d6? 3.dxc5!± 254) **3.c3**

There will always be those schemers who do not wish to test the limits of chess theory, those who yearn to play it safe, to spoil the party – those who choose to decline the Morra Gambit! Shying away from an open fight for the advantage in a chaotic struggle, the decliner instead prefers to minimize risk, quietly equalize, and then calmly outplay the swashbuckling gambiteer. Yet upon passing up 3...dxc3, whether or not he consciously realizes this, the decliner has revealed his fear of Morra mayhem. Therefore, every chance I get, I will recommend the sharpest lines of the Declined variations to disturb the material and psychological balance. When necessary, we will soundly sacrifice pieces and pawns to haunt the decliner with the ghost of the Morra Gambit on every move. And if the position ever gets technical, we will be doing the squeezing, so much so that you may even hear the decliner whisper: "Why didn't I just take that free pawn on c3?"

As you shall see, contrary to popular opinion, Black does not routinely equalize in the Morra Declined – rather, the variations lead to tense middlegames with White pressing for the advantage, as in other classical openings. In this chapter, we deal with miscellaneous Black responses, focusing primarily on 3...g6 and 3...d5. We then move to the two most popular Declined schemes, 3...d3 (Chapter 13) and 3...♘f6 (Chapter 14).

The pretenders

First we dismiss the weakest Declined lines, before moving on to the "contenders".

Morra Declined – 2...e6?!

1.e4 c5 2.d4 e6?!

2...d6?! is a move most often seen in Internet blitz, when Black, anticipating 2.♘f3, pre-

moves with his d-pawn. 3.dxc5 ♕a5† (3...dxc5 4.♕xd8† ♔xd8±) 4.♘c3 ♕xc5 5.♘f3± White has a massive lead in development, and isn't even down a pawn!

3.d5!

The Morra morphs into an improved Benoni for the gambiteer.

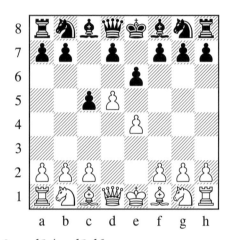

3...exd5 4.exd5 d6

White may now play the solid 5.c4!, securing a dominant space advantage in the shape of his advanced d5-pawn, then follow up with simple development (♘c3, ♗d3, ♘f3, 0–0, etc.). Note that in the Modern Benoni, if White wishes to protect his d5-pawn with another foot soldier, he must eventually venture e2-e4, but then the e-pawn may come under fierce attack on the half-open e-file. However, 5.c4 deprives Black of such classical Benoni counterplay.

But for those who long for a more volatile, piece-heavy fight, you may fire with 5.♘c3, then transfer the king's knight to c4 via f3-d2. To see this traditional plan in action, study the supplemental game Nimzowitsch – Marshall, New York 1927, the debut of the ingenious ♘f3-d2-c4 maneuver into Benoni praxis. Again, Nimzowitsch's idea seems even more effective in the Morra-Benoni version, as the e-file will not come under the same pressure.

Morra Declined – 3...♛a5?!

1.e4 c5 2.d4 cxd4 3.c3 ♛a5?!

3...d6?! 4.cxd4± and White profits from Black's cowardice, obtaining a massive pawn center for free.

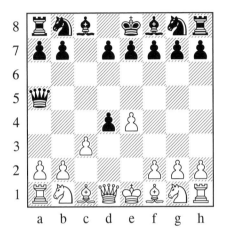

With this ambitious pin, the wily decliner intends to make life miserable for the gambiteer. For example, on the natural 4.♞f3 ♞c6 5.♝c4 ♞f6!, White must now tread carefully around the thorny d4-pawn. If 6.♛e2, then Black may react 6...e6 or 6...d6, threatening ...d5 or ...♝g4 respectively, in either case with at least equality. However, as promised, those who choose to deny the Morra will be in for some cruel surprises.

4.♝d2!

Meeting the pesky queen head on. Like it or not, Black must now satiate the salivating swashbuckler.

c3-Sicilian players take note – if Black meets 2.c3 with 2...♛a5?! then you can reach the current position by 3.d4! cxd4 4.♝d2!.

4...dxc3

4...d3 5.♝xd3± drifts towards the 3...d3 variations of the Morra Declined (which we will study in depth in the next chapter), but

with the insertion of ♝d2 and ...♛a5 clearly favoring White.

4...♞c6?! 5.cxd4 ♛b6 6.d5±

4...♛b6 5.cxd4 ♛xb2 (5...♛xd4 6.♞c3± With ♞f3 coming next, we have a Morra multiple tempi up!) 6.♞c3± ♛b6 7.♜c1 ♞c6 8.d5 ♞e5 9.♞b5+– The wayward queen should have stayed at home.

5.♞xc3

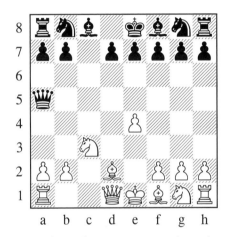

An enhanced Morra Accepted as the d2-bishop smiles at the queen. I give one amusing variation.

5...♞c6 6.♞f3 ♞f6 7.♝c4 e6 8.0-0 ♛c7 9.♞b5! ♛b8 10.e5!

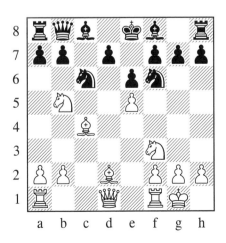

Marking our return to the outlands of the Siberian wilderness (see Chapter 1).

10...♘xe5?! 11.♘xe5 ♕xe5 12.♖e1 ♕b8 13.♗c3+–

The contenders

Morra Declined – 3...e5!?

1.e4 c5 2.d4 cxd4 3.c3 e5!?

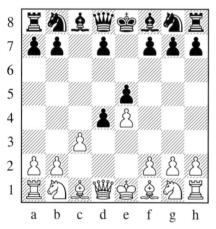

This class of position occurred with regularity in the 19th century, but from slightly different channels. Often the old masters preferred not to enter the Open Sicilian directly with 2.♘f3 followed by 3.d4, but rather 2.d4 first. After 2...cxd4 3.♘f3, they surely intended to tempt their opponents to clasp the extra pawn with 3...e5 (4.♘xe5?? ♕a5†–+). Both Morphy and Adolf Anderssen would then launch into gambit mode with 4.♗c4, reserving c2-c3 for later. But this would be as close as the two greatest Romantics would ever get to touching the Morra Gambit. While I personally have faced 3...e5 just once in my thousands of Morra games, this move of long historical pedigree requires serious attention. The sharpest play will now echo the classic Fried Liver Attack of the Two Knights Defense.

4.♗c4

After 4.♘f3!? ♘c6 White can win back the pawn, but then his lively game may fizzle into only a dry, microscopic edge: 5.cxd4 (5.♗c4 transposes to the main line) 5...exd4 6.♘xd4 ♗b4† 7.♘c3 ♘f6 8.♘xc6 dxc6 9.♕xd8† ♔xd8 10.f3±

4...♘c6

4...♗e7?! 5.♘f3 (with cxd4 or ♕b3 to follow) transposes into Morphy's beautiful rout vs. Journoud – see the supplemental games.

5.♘f3 ♘f6 6.♘g5

Fried Liver-like mayhem ensues, the only differences being that White and Black's c-pawns now stand on c3 and d4 respectively, while the gambiteer's d-pawn is gone! For inspiration, you may wish to study the related game Morphy v. N.N. (featured after this analysis) right now before continuing!

6...d5 7.exd5 ♘xd5

The alternative is:

7...♘a5!?

This is the trusted response in the Two Knights Defense after 4.♘g5 d5 5.exd5, and here too it leads to a rich struggle.

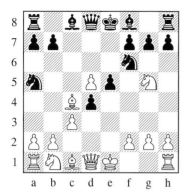

8.♗b5† ♗d7 9.♕e2 ♗d6

Black voluntarily sheds his wayward knight, hoping to receive sufficient compensation for the piece in the form of his superior development and central pawn mass.

9...♘xd5 10.♕xe5† ♕e7 11.♗xd7† ♔xd7 12.♕xe7† ♗xe7 13.♘xf7±

10.b4 h6 11.♘f3 0–0 12.bxa5 ♖c8 13.0–0 dxc3 14.♗xd7 ♕xd7 15.♘a3∞

The resulting position requires further tests. Both sides have their trumps – White, the extra knight, and Black, the far-flung c-pawn and dynamic energy.

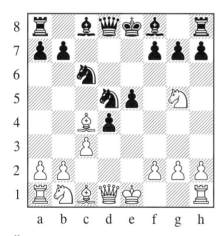

8.♕b3!?

The presence of the extra d4-pawn offers Black's king bolstered central protection against the direct ♘xf7 assault not normally available in the Fried Liver. Thus, I prefer the quieter text move, coolly restoring the

material balance with a slight positional pull. Nevertheless, the creative gambiteer may hazard the piece sacrifice, and while I shall point out Black's defensive resources, perhaps you can find an attacking improvement: 8.0–0 ♗e7

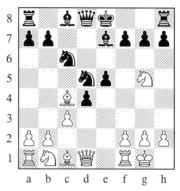

9.♘xf7!? ♔xf7 10.♕f3† ♔e6 11.♖e1!

11.a4!? spends a tempo to preserve the Italian bishop, but after 11...g5!∓ threatening the disturbing ...g4, Black should hold: 12.♖e1 g4 13.♕xg4† ♔d6!∓

11...♘a5

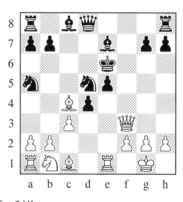

12.♖xe5†!?

shedding everything to expose the king.

12...♔xe5 13.cxd4† ♔e6

13...♔xd4?? 14.♗xd5 ♕xd5 15.♕e3† ♔c4 16.b3† ♔b5 17.♘c3†+−

14.♕e4† ♔f7 15.♗xd5† ♔f8!

Black must tread carefully to endure the barrage.

15...♔e8?! 16.♗f4 ♘c6 17.♘c3→
16.♕f3† ♗f6

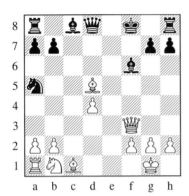

17.b3! g5!
    17...g6? 18.♗h6†+−
18.♗xg5 ♔g7 19.♗xf6† ♕xf6 20.♕g3† ♔h6∓
Surviving and thriving.

8...♗e6
    8...♘a5? 9.♕b5†+−

9.♘xe6 fxe6 10.♕xb7 ♖c8 11.0–0
White's bishops and superior pawn structure
offers him a small edge in the face of Black's
firmly centralized position.

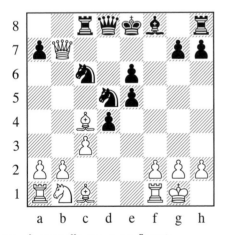

11...♗e7 12.♕a6 0–0 13.♘d2±

New Orleans Simul 1858

**1.e4 e5 2.♘f3 ♘c6 3.♗c4 ♘f6 4.d4 exd4
5.♘g5 d5 6.exd5 ♘xd5 7.0–0 ♗e7 8.♘xf7
♔xf7 9.♕f3† ♔e6**

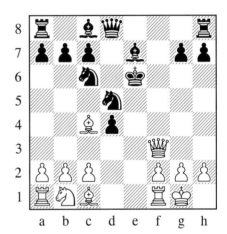

**10.♘c3!! dxc3 11.♖e1† ♘e5 12.♗f4 ♗f6
13.♗xe5 ♗xe5 14.♖xe5†! ♔xe5 15.♖e1†
♔d4 16.♗xd5 ♖e8 17.♕d3† ♔c5 18.b4†
♔xb4 19.♕d4† ♔a5 20.♕xc3† ♔a4
21.♕b3† ♔a5 22.♕a3† ♔b6 23.♖b1#**

Morra Declined – 3...g6 Analysis I

1.e4 c5 2.d4 cxd4 3.c3 g6

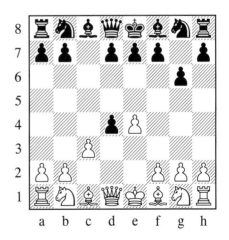

An extremely popular choice for the decliner, who hopes to transpose into either the ...g6 variations of the Panov-Botvinnik Attack or c3-Sicilian after 4.cxd4 d5 5.exd5 (or 5.e5). While I have gleefully played into the Panov throughout my career, I now offer up a continuation which will throw the ...g6 schemers into unfamiliar, boiling-hot water.

4.♘f3!

You can run, but you can't hide, from the Morra Gambit. 4...dxc3 now morphs into an Accepted variation (see "Slaying the Dragon").

4...♗g7

After 4...d5?! 5.exd5 ♕xd5 6.cxd4± White obtains an hyper-active isolated queen pawn formation with the tempo-gaining ♘c3 coming next.

5.♗c4

Developing the bishop in Morra style while preventing Black's freeing break ...d5.

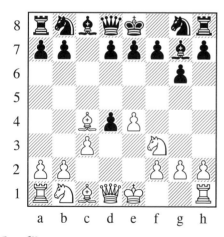

5...e6!?

The decliner faces some tough decisions, none of which will fully solve his problems. Could it be that he must enter the chaos after 5...dxc3? A grim reality for a schemer.

5...d3?!

Another meek refusal to engage which is duly punished.

6.♕b3! e6

Recall the lessons learned from your Morra-Dragon studies – when the Dragon's tail deforms with ...e6 rather than the fluid ...d6, typically the structure collapses around the compromised dark squares, particularly d6.

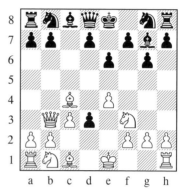

7.♗g5 ♘e7 8.0-0 ♘bc6

8...d6 9.♖d1± collects the d3-pawn and continues the siege on d6.

9.♗xd3 0-0 10.♘a3 a6 11.♘c4 b5 12.♘d6

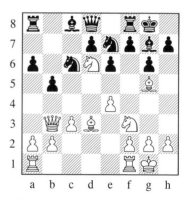

The first of many white pieces ravaging d6 in the variations to come.

12...♕c7 13.♘xc8 ♖axc8 14.a4±

5...d5!?

Black jettisons a pawn in the spirit of the ...g6-Panov, hoping to surround d5 later with his nimble knights. Sadly for him, however,

White should either retain the extra material or drum up nasty threats leading to a clear advantage.

6.exd5 ♘d7

6...♘f6 7.♕xd4!±

7.♘xd4

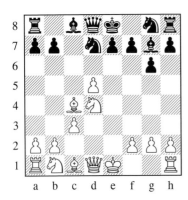

7...♘gf6

7...♘b6 8.♗b3! ♘xd5 9.♘b5!± wreaks havoc, with profit to follow.

8.0–0 0–0 9.♗b3 ♘c5 10.c4 e6 11.♘c3

Black's countergambit keeps falling just a move short.

11...♘xb3 12.♕xb3 ♘xd5 13.cxd5 ♗xd4 14.♗h6±

With an overwhelming initiative as the rooks crash the center.

6.♘xd4!±

The key capture! After 6.cxd4?! d5! Black nears equality.

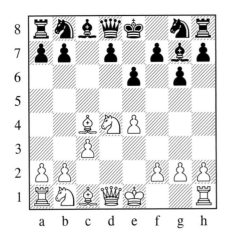

But now if the decliner ever strikes with ...d5, he will be saddled with a blockaded and easily targeted isolated pawn after the exchange on d5. If he prepares ...d5 with ...♘ge7 first, aiming to recapture with the knight, then he will remain behind in development without any clear plan. To add to Black's confusion, the d4-knight keeps lusting after the d6-square.

6...♘e7!?

6...♘c6?! 7.♘b5!±

6...a6!? 7.0–0 ♘c6 8.♗e3 ♘f6 (8...♘ge7 9.♘xc6 ♘xc6 10.♗c5±) 9.♘d2± with a tense struggle ahead. White should consider rerouting his knight to c4 where it can probe the sensitive d6- and b6-squares, if the opportunity arises. 9...d5?! remains premature in view of: 10.exd5 ♘xd5 11.♘xc6 bxc6 12.♗c5!±

7.0–0 0–0

7...d5 8.exd5 ♘xd5 9.♕a4† ♗d7

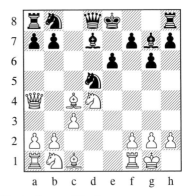

10.♕a3! forces Black to accept positional defects: 10...♕e7 11.♗xd5 exd5 12.♕b3± and the siege continues.

8.♖e1

8.♘b5!? d5 9.exd5 exd5 10.♗b3 a6 11.♘d4∞

8...d5 9.exd5 ♘xd5 10.♘d2

Black cannot easily complete his development with ...♘d7 or ...♗d7 as ♗xd5 strikes. Eventually, he must make some strategic concession.

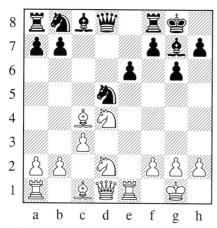

10...♘c6 11.♘xc6 bxc6 12.♘e4±

Enough positional mumbo jumbo. Back to some craziness.

3...g6 Analysis II

1.e4 c5 2.d4 cxd4 3.c3 g6 4.♘f3!? ♗g7 5.♗c4 ♘c6?!

One of Rybka's top choices is:

5...♕c7?!

However, the machine cannot appreciate the psychological pitfall attached to the move, as after the bishop retreats the decliner must finally appease the gambiteer by taking on c3, otherwise 7.cxd4 follows with obvious central supremacy.

6.♗b3!

White may also try to force the action in a heavier manner by 6.♕b3!?, with the main continuation producing stormy complications. 6...e6 7.♘a3 a6 8.cxd4 and now:

a) 8...♘c6?! 9.d5 ♘a5 10.♕b4 b5 11.♗xb5!±
b) 8...b5 9.♗xb5! Again White's steed will graze upon the fertile dark squares. 9...axb5 10.♘xb5 ♕b6 11.♗f4±

c) 8...♘e7! 9.d5 With a cramping effect. 9...b5 The defender refuses to go quietly.

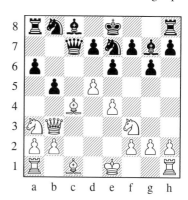

Now 10.♗xb5!? exd5 11.exd5 0–0 12.♗a4 ♕a5† would be level, but instead White can unleashing fantastic fireworks with 10.0–0!∞

6...dxc3

6...♘c6?! 7.cxd4! ♘xd4 8.♘xd4 ♗xd4 9.♕xd4 ♕xc1† 10.♗d1±

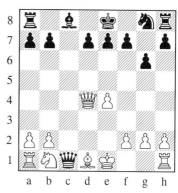

A highly original display, but White's dark-squared dominance remains all the same.

7.♘xc3⇄

A Morra with a frigid queen on c7!

7...♘c6

7...♗xc3† 8.bxc3 ♕xc3† 9.♗d2± Only in his worst nightmare will the decliner be lured into grabbing two pawns by move 9!

8.0–0 ♘f6 9.e5!

We've heard this tale before. Welcome to Siberia!

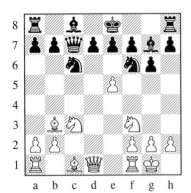

9...♞xe5 10.♞xe5 ♛xe5 11.♖e1 ♛f5 12.♛d6 ♝f8

12...0–0 13.♖xe7→
13.♝h6!+−

6.cxd4!

6.0–0?! dxc3! 7.♞xc3 d6 8.♛b3?! ♞a5∓

6...♛b6

Another hare-brained scheme which you may encounter as it has some popularity via c3-Sicilian move orders. But why go running around with the queen chasing an extra pawn when you can just take one on move 3? Well, the Morra must inspire such madness.

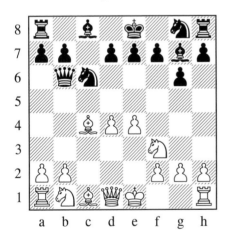

7.0–0!

The gambiteer gives the decliner his death wish.

7...♞xd4 8.♞xd4

8.♞c3!?→

8...♝xd4

8...♛xd4 9.♛b3! e6 10.♞c3 ♛b6 11.♞b5 a6 12.♝e3 ♛c6 13.a4!±

9.♞c3 ♞f6 10.♞b5 ♝c5

10...e5 11.♝e3±

11.b4!±

Evans-Morra chaos!

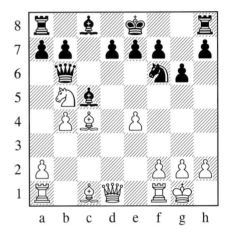

11...♝xb4 12.♖b1 a6

12...♝c5 13.e5+−

13.♝e3

There is no escape.

13...♛d8

13...♛c6 14.♛b3 axb5 15.♝xf7† ♚d8 (15...♚f8 16.♝h6#) 16.♖fc1 ♛d6 17.♛xb4

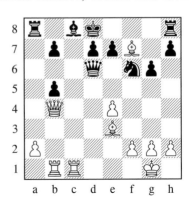

17...♕xb4 18.♗b6#

13...♕a5   14.♖xb4!   ♕xb4   15.♕d4   (or
15.♘c7†+−) 15...♕a5

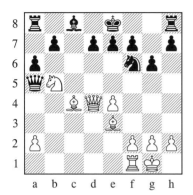

16.♘d6†! ♔d8 (16...exd6 17.♕xf6 ♖f8
18.♗g5+−) 17.♕b6† ♕xb6 18.♗xb6#

14.♖xb4 axb5 15.♗xb5 0–0

16.♗h6 ♖e8 17.e5 ♘h5 18.♕d4 e6 19.g4
Suffocating positional play returns with a
vengeance.

**19...♘g7 20.♕f4 ♕e7 21.♕f6 ♕f8 22.♖f4
♖a5 23.a4+−**

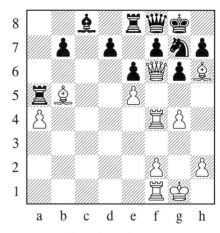

A picture of total paralysis.

We now turn to the last of the contenders –
3...d5.

Milan Matulovic – Dragoljub Janosevic

Yugoslavia (ch), Novi Sad 1955

1.e4 c5 2.d4 cxd4 3.c3 d5
In the spirit of the Scandinavian, the decliner
aims to neutralize White's central advantage
immediately.

4.exd5 ♘f6?!
With this knight move, Black again hopes to
redirect play into the classical variations of the
Panov-Botvinnik Attack after 5.cxd4?! ♘xd5
6.♘c3 ♘c6 7.♘f3. But the alert gambiteer
should have none of this.

We will examine the main line 4...♕xd5 next.

5.♗b5†!
Over half a century ago, GM Matulovic
found the solution. This disruptive check
secures White either an extra pawn or a
dominant space advantage.

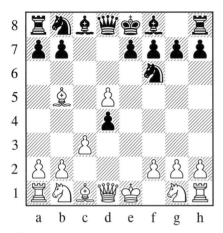

5...♘bd7

After 5...♗d7 6.♗c4 White menaces ♕xd4 and the defender cannot rest: 6...dxc3 (6...b5 7.♗b3 a5 [7...dxc3 8.♘xc3±] 8.♕xd4±) 7.♘xc3± The piece count may be even but the first player's freewheeling game nets Black's 4th move a clear assessment as dubious.

6.♕xd4 a6 7.♗e2 b5

7...♕a5 8.♗f3±

7...♘b6 8.c4 e6 9.♗e3! ♘a4 10.♗d1! No respite! 10...♘c5 11.♘c3±

8.♗f3 ♕b6 9.♕xb6 ♘xb6

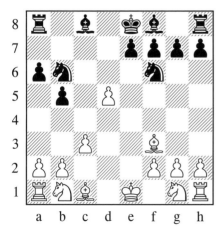

10.d6 ♘fd5 11.dxe7 ♗xe7±

And White converted his extra material into victory (see the supplemental games).
...1–0

Morra Declined – 3...d5 4.exd5 ♕xd5

1.e4 c5 2.d4 cxd4 3.c3 d5

3...♘c6 transposes into the main line after 4.cxd4 d5 5.exd5 ♕xd5 6.♘f3

4.exd5 ♕xd5 5.cxd4!

True to gambit style, White trusts in the dynamic strengths of his position. Before Black can blockade and destroy the isolated pawn, the possessor of the isolani hopes that his superior space and development will produce game-changing threats that will ultimately win the day.

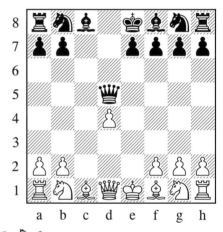

5...♘c6

5...e5!? 6.♘f3 exd4 7.♕xd4 ♕xd4 8.♘xd4±

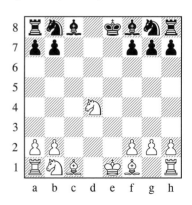

Black's policy of seeking quick, mass exchanges here results in a modest but pronounced advantage for White with no risk moving forward, as his d4-knight dominates the otherwise symmetrical board.

6.♘f3 e5

The decliner cannot expect to fight successfully in a classical isolated queen pawn duel here as the incoming ♘c3 will win White a critical tempo – in isolated pawn positions, it's all a matter of timing. Therefore, Black typically prefers the more radical approaches of the text and the theoretically dubious 6...♗g4, both of which force action in the center in their respective ways.

6...e6 7.♘c3 ♗b4 8.♗d3 ♘f6 9.0–0 ♕d6 10.a3 ♗xc3 11.bxc3 0–0 12.♖e1 b6 13.♗g5±

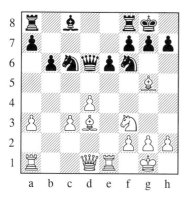

White's raking bishops and superior development more than compensate for his slightly mangled pawn structure. See also Tal – Dzindzichashvili, New York (blitz) 1991, in the supplemental games, for an instructive "isolani" effort from the great world champion.

7.♘c3 ♗b4 8.♗d2 ♗xc3

Black trades the bishop pair for time, while entrenching his queen in the center.

9.♗xc3

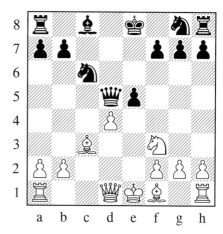

9...e4!

Of course, opening up the board against the powerful prelates would lead to disaster: 9...exd4?! 10.♘xd4 ♘xd4 11.♕xd4±

10.♘e5 ♘xe5 11.dxe5 ♘e7

For now the struggle remains semi-closed and for the next few moves the bishops fail to come into their own. This tabiya has been debated for one hundred years with no clear consensus, but I feel White retains a clear advantage after the counter-intuitive:

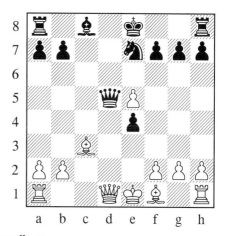

12.♕e2!

Nimzowitsch introduced the creative plan 12.♕a4†!? ♗d7 13.♕a3, which prevents Black from castling for the moment. Although he won brilliantly vs. Chajes, modern analysis shows that the queen sortie leads nowhere: 13...♗c6! 14.♖d1 ♕e6 15.♖d6 ♕f5 and Black's queen weasels out, the king castles, and the knight jumps to d5.

We now pick up the action in the following game, which reached this position via a c3-Sicilian.

Marinus Kuijf – Eelke Wiersma

Leeuwarden 1995

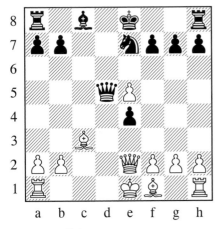

12...0–0 13.♖d1

White puts further pressure on the compromised e4-pawn.

13...♕xa2

The computer-like defense 13...♕c6 14.♖d6 ♕a4 15.b3 ♕a3 may be Black's only salvation. 16.♕d2! White's queen gets out of the king's bishop's way while threatening to trap her counterpart. 16...♕c5 (16...♘c6?? 17.♖xc6 bxc6 18.♗b4+–)17.♗c4! The press is on.

14.♗b4!

The chief idea. Instead 14.♕xe4 ♗f5 15.♕xb7 ♖ad8 16.♕xe7 led to a draw in the battle of the Sveshnikovs and many other games: 16...♖xd1† 17.♔xd1 ♕b1† 18.♔d2 ♕c2† 19.♔e3 ½–½ V. Sveshnikov – E. Sveshnikov, Di Roseto 2010.

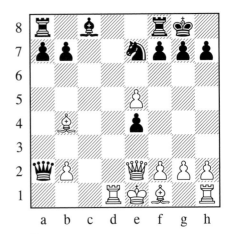

14...♕e6

14...♖e8?? 15.♗xe7+–

14...♘c6!? This daring but desperate exchange sacrifice is the machine's first choice, but it should not suffice – and it just shows how dire the decliner's position has become! 15.♗xf8 ♔xf8 16.♕b5 ♗e6 17.♗e2± a6 18.♕c5† ♔g8 19.0–0! ♕xb2

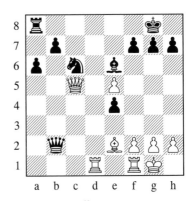

20.♗xa6! ♖xa6 21.♕xc6+–

So the black queen beats a sad retreat as White's bishops now roam free. The rest is a rout.

15.♕xe4 ♖e8

15...♗d7 16.♗c4+–

16.♗b5

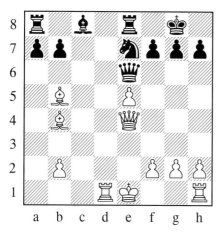

16...♘c6 17.0–0

The tactics begin to flow.

17...♗d7

17...♕xe5? 18.♖xe5 ♖xe5 19.♗xc6+–

18.♖fe1 ♖ad8 19.♗d6 ♘xe5?!

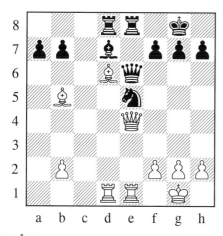

20.♗c7!+–

The "elephants" (Russian for bishops) will not be denied.

20...♗c6

20...♗xb5 21.♖xd8 ♖xd8 22.♗xd8 ♘c6 23.♕b1 ♕d7 24.♕f5!+–

21.♖xd8

Black resigned, as 21...♖xd8 22.♗xc6 ♘xc6 23.♗xd8 ♘xd8 24.♖d1! ♘c6 25.♕xc6 crunches.

1–0

3...d5 with 6...♗g4

1.e4 c5 2.d4 cxd4 3.c3 d5 4.exd5 ♕xd5 5.cxd4 ♘c6 6.♘f3 ♗g4!?

A variation of dubious lineage. Now White once again tosses on his gambit hat.

7.♘c3!

I cannot in my right mind recommend the meek retort 7.♗e2, allowing Black to reach a comfortable isolated queen pawn structure. However, now the decliner's world turns upside down.

7...♗xf3

The schemer must take the bait – otherwise he won't last ten moves:

7...♕d8? 8.d5 ♘e5? 9.♘xe5! ♗xd1 10.♗b5†+–

7...♕a5 8.d5 0–0–0 9.♗d2! ♘e5 10.♘b5 ♗xf3 11.♕c2†+–

7...♕d7?? Believe it or not I've gotten this trap many times against strong players in blitz –

there must be something about that queen and bishop battery! 8.d5 ♘a5 9.♗b5+–

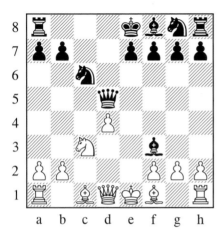

8.gxf3!

The alternative is:

8.♘xd5!?

For a few years I thought this simple capture, which temporarily wins the exchange, closed the door on this suspicious system, and the computer agreed. But Black has a cunning defense, proving that the old maxim "knights on the rim are dim" is true after all, or at least it is in this line...

8...♗xd1 9.♘c7† ♔d7! 10.♘xa8 ♗h5 11.d5 ♘d4 12.♗e3 ♘c2† 13.♔d2

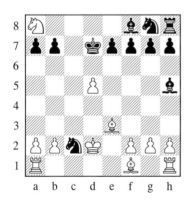

13...♘xe3!

Black's knight wisely refuses to join his counterpart at the end of the earth, even for a "free" rook: 13...♘xa1? 14.♗b5† ♔d8

15.♗xa7+–; Instead, the defense hones in upon the lost creature on a8.

14.fxe3 e5! 15.dxe6† fxe6 16.♗b5† ♔d8 17.♖ac1 ♗b4† 18.♔c2 ♗d6

While White remains "up" an exchange, his position gives off an unfriendly odor.

8...♕xd4

8...♕h5?! 9.d5 0–0–0 10.♕a4 ♘e5 11.♗e3 ♘xf3† 12.♔d1 ♘d4† 13.♔c1±

9.♕xd4 ♘xd4

The decliner emerges up a clear pawn with a far healthier pawn formation. Yet, on the other hand, his kingside lies entombed. Meanwhile, White's blade-like bishops are ready to cut.

10.♘b5!

In the principal variation, both knights will end up buried in the corner. But because of the gambiteer's freedom of movement, he will be first to rescue the cavalry, which ultimately leads to White's enduring advantage.

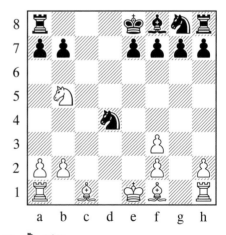

10...♘c2†!?

10...♘e6?! 11.♘xa7!! A fantastic shot, only made possible by Black's total lack of development. 11...♖xa7 12.♗b5† ♔d8 13.♗e3 ♖a8? (13...♖a6 14.♗xa6 bxa6 15.♔e2± ♔e8 16.♖ac1 f5 17.♖hd1 ♔f7 18.♖c6 and the a- and b-pawns should make queens.)

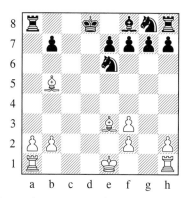

14.♗b6† ♔c8 15.♖c1† ♔b8 16.♗d7+– Slicing and dicing.

10...0-0-0?! 11.♘xd4 ♖xd4 12.♗e3 ♖d6 13.♗xa7 b6 14.♗a6†! ♔d8 15.♗b8! Chop, chop, chop. 15...♖d7 16.♗b5+–

10...e5!? In the 2010 Olympiad, Topalov tried to revitalize 6...♗g4 with this bold exchange sacrifice. Rather than chase the rook, he put all his faith in his centralized knight. While he ultimately struggled and almost lost to GM Stevic (an opponent 200 points his inferior), I nevertheless urge advanced players to study the former world champion's effort in the supplemental games section so you may form your own opinion. 11.♘c7† ♔d7 12.♘xa8 ♗b4† 13.♔d1 ♘e7± is my opinion!

11.♔d1 ♘xa1 12.♘c7† ♔d7 13.♘xa8

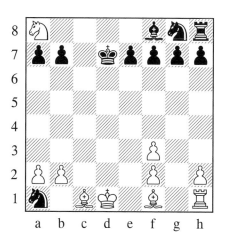

13...♘f6!?

13...e5?! 14.♗e3 White's bishops again save the day. 14...♔c6 (14...b6 15.♗b5† ♔c8 16.♔e2 ♗b7 17.♖c1! ♗d6 [17...♗xa8 18.♖c8†+–] 18.♗c6± White's knight is salvaged whereas Black's steed will fall.) 15.♗h3 b6 16.♔e2 ♗b7 17.♖xa1 ♗xa8 18.f4!± The elephants are just beginning to stomp.

13...g6? is a feeble attempt which meets a similar fate: 14.♗e3 ♗g7 15.♗b5† ♔c8 16.♗xa7+– ♗xb2 17.♔e2 ♘f6 18.♖b1 ♗e5 19.♖c1† ♔d8 20.♗b6† ♗c7 21.♗xc7† ♔c8 22.♘b6#

13...♔c6!?

The luxury behind Black's king travelling to d7, but few humans would be comfortable embarking upon such a journey. Now, by playing only moves, the decliner may live only to reach a tortuous ending.
14.f4 e6
14...♘f6?! 15.♗g2† ♘d5 16.♘c7 ♔xc7 17.♗xd5 e6 18.♗e4+–
15.♗g2† ♔b5 16.♗xb7 ♗d6 17.♗e3 ♘e7 18.♔c1 ♖b8!
18...♘d5 19.♗xa7±
19.♖d1 ♖xb7
19...♘d5 20.♗xd5 exd5 21.♖xd5† ♔c6 22.♖a5 ♖xa8 23.♖a6† ♔d5 24.♔b1 ♘b3 25.axb3± With a long technical phase ahead.
20.♖xd6 ♘d5 21.♖d8!

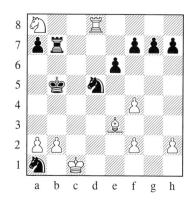

21...♘b4

21...♔c6 22.♔b1 ♘xe3 (22...♖d7?!
23.♖xd7 ♔xd7 24.♗xa7 ♘b3 25.axb3 ♔c6
26.♘b6!+–) 23.fxe3 ♖d7 24.♖xd7 ♔xd7
25.♔xa1 I leave it to the endgame experts to
determine if Black can hold.

22.♖c8!±

An already surreal position reveals yet another
otherworldly move. The rook simultaneously
secures White's knight on a8 while confining
Black's on a1, all while generating mating
threats on c5!

14.♗b5†!

The bishops show no mercy to the weary.

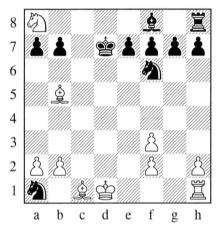

14...♔d6

14...♔d8 15.♗e3 a6 16.♗d3 ♘d5 17.♔d2+–

14...♔c8 15.♗f4 ♘d5 16.♗g3±

15.♗e3 b6?!

15...g6! 16.♗xa7 ♗h6! Fighting tooth and
nail for the corners. 17.♘b6 ♔c7 (17...♖d8
18.♔e2 ♘c2 19.♘c4† ♔e6 20.♖d1±) 18.f4!
(18.♗d3? ♖d8 19.♔e2 ♘h5∓) 18...♗xf4
19.♗d3! e5 20.♔e2 e4 21.♗b1 The corner
siege continues!

16.♔d2± e6 17.♖c1!

Morra mayhem on the c-file.

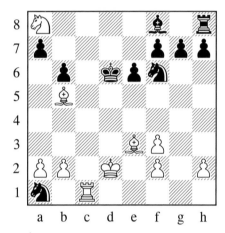

17...♗e7

17...♘d5 18.♗d4 ♗e7 19.♖c6†+–

18.♗f4† e5 19.♖c6† ♔d5

19...♔d7 20.♖xf6†+–

20.♘c7† ♔d4 21.♗e3#

Chapter 13

Crushing 3...d3 with the Morra-Maroczy: squeeze, squeeze, destroy![52]

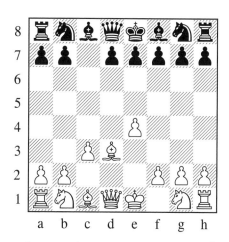

1.e4 c5 2.d4 cxd4 3.c3 d3 4.♗xd3

I'm shocked that the cowardly 3...d3

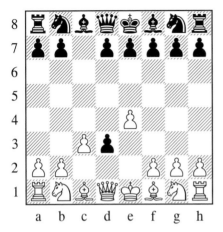

remains so popular at all levels, from amateur to professional. Who knows what motivates the decliner to make this meek pawn push, be it fear, laziness, arrogance, or all of the above. No matter what our scheming antagonist may be feeling, he most certainly dreams of taking the struggle to the quiet backwaters, where despite giving back the pawn and starting out at a clear disadvantage, he hopes to outmaneuver and bore the drifting, listless gambiteer.

However, after 4.♗xd3 and 5.c4! Black's fantasy faces reality in the shape of the concrete positional tower of pain better known as the Maroczy Bind. Soon White's knights flow to f3 and c3, the bishops patrol d3 and e3, and after castles and ♕e2, with the rooks fortifying c1 and d1 (and always throw in a quick h2-h3 to stop any ...♘g4 or ...♗g4 tricks), it's almost as if we have a Morra Gambit with an extra pawn wedging on c4. Of course, the move order matters, but that's easy to master. Gasping for air, the decliner may try to exchange pieces, so remember to avoid all unnecessary liquidation so that the suffering schemer suffocates within the confines of his narrow position. If you think you've squeezed enough, feel free to squeeze some more before finally delivering the fatal blow in dashing style.

The stultifying Scheveningen/Hedgehog

In these structures, the decliner continues with his passive strategy, curling his pieces up into a ball on the first three ranks and lying in wait for White to overstep. But so often in the Hedgehog, it is Black who can't take the squeezing, sticks his head out, and gets stomped.

Marc Esserman – Edward McHugh

Parsippany 2009

1.e4 c5 2.d4 cxd4 3.c3 d3 4.♗xd3 d6
Radical simplification fails brutally after 4...d5?! 5.♗b5† White cleanly wins a pawn.

5.c4!
The squeeze is on.

5...♘f6 6.♘c3 e6 7.♘f3 ♗e7 8.♕e2 ♘bd7 9.0–0 0–0 10.h3!
Preventing any ...♘g4-e5 molestations upon ♗e3.

10...♕c7 11.♗e3 a6 12.♖ac1 b6 13.♗b1!

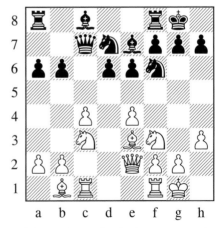

Safely tucking the bishop away where it cannot be swapped for Black's desperate knights. As we shall see repeatedly, b1 is the optimal square for the light-squared bishop in the Morra-Maroczy. Not only does it perform important defensive work in the center, but it aims straight at the heart of the enemy king through the e4-stronghold.

13...♗b7 14.♖fd1 ♖ac8 15.b3

Shoring up all the loose ends. With the foundation cemented, White soon builds a high-rise.

15...♖fe8 16.♘d4 ♗f8 17.♗g5!

So that the bishop stars in the kingside onslaught after the suffocating f2-f4.

17...♕b8 18.f4

The dark side of space is weakness, but White has none. Staring out at the emerging skyscraper, Black rushes to bulldoze, yet only reduces his own position to rubble.

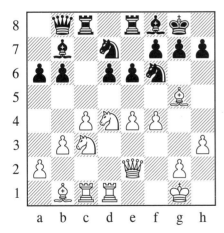

18...e5?! 19.fxe5 ♖xe5 20.♗f4 ♖ee8 21.♘f5 ♘e5 22.♗g5 ♘ed7 23.♗f4

Prolonging the agony.

23...♘e5 24.♗g5 ♘ed7 25.♕f3

Brick by brick.

25...♘e5 26.♕g3 ♖e6 27.♘d5

The cavalry maims.

27...♘g6

27...♘xd5 28.exd5 ♖ee8 29.♗f6± and White's bishops suddenly triumph.

28.♗xf6 gxf6 29.h4

The final nail.

29...♔h8 30.h5 ♘e5 31.♕h4 ♖ce8 32.♖c3 ♕d8 33.♖g3 b5 34.cxb5 axb5 35.♖f1

Completely paralyzed, Black resigned, as mate is inevitable after the merciless ♖f4-g4.
1–0

Marc Esserman – John Fedorowicz

US Chess League, Internet 2011

1.e4 c5 2.♘f3 e6 3.d4 cxd4 4.c3 d3 5.♗xd3 d6

5...d5?! 6.exd5 ♕xd5 7.0–0 ♘c6 8.c4± With a large lead in development.

6.c4 ♘f6 7.♘c3 a6 8.0–0 ♘bd7 9.h3 ♕c7 10.♗e3 ♗e7 11.♖c1 b6 12.♕e2 ♗b7

12...♘e5?! 13.♘xe5 dxe5 14.c5! bxc5 15.♘a4± Chaos on the c-file ensues.

13.♗b1 0–0

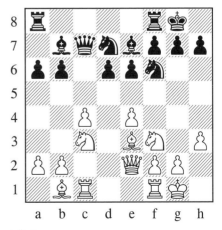

14.♘d2!?

Overprotecting the e-pawn still further,

while leaving the rook on f1 where it will immediately participate in the impending kingside pawn storm. A more refined approach, with two years more gray in my hair.

14...≡fe8 15.a3

With no weaknesses, I'm ready to greedily grab as much space as my heart desires.

15...≜f8 16.b4 ≡ac8 17.f4 ≕b8 18.≜d3!

With great space comes great responsibility!

18...≡c6 19.≕f2 ≜a8 20.g4!±

A great wall of pawns.

20...⍟h8 21.g5 ⍲g8

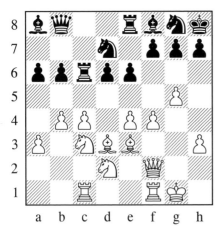

And somehow I misplayed my advantage and almost lost! As Emmanuel Lasker mused, "the hardest game to win is a won game", but surely it's even harder to win a lost position![53]
½–½

The Dragon Returns

Marc Esserman – Zbynek Hracek

New York 2009

1.e4 c5 2.d4 cxd4 3.c3 d3 4.≜xd3 g6

The Dragon returns, but without the fire.

Still, the bishop belongs on g7 after 3...d3, when it will at least exert a powerful grip over the critical h8-a1 diagonal.

5.c4 ≜g7 6.⍲f3 d6

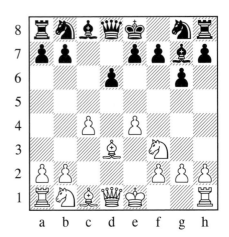

7.h3!

Absolutely vital now. The proud c4 and e4 tag team plans to squeeze, suffocate, and silence, but they leave the d4-square highly compromised in their wake. White must secure this battleground, else Black responds ...≜g4 and eventually ...⍲c6, ...≜xf3 and dominates the board with ...⍲d4.

7...⍲f6 8.0–0 0–0 9.⍲c3 ⍲bd7

The knight belongs on c6 in a pure Dragon, fighting for the prime central real estate. Hracek's Dragon now slowly shapeshifts into what we already know to be a harmless Hedgehog.

10.≜e3 b6 11.≡c1 ≜b7 12.≜b1 a6 13.≕e2 ≡e8 14.≡fd1 ≕b8

The moves require little commentary. Black, although a strong Grandmaster, seemingly shuffles to and fro throughout his tight quarters. White, meanwhile, applies the plaster before expanding.

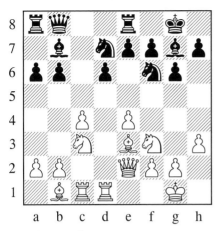

15.b3 ♞c5 16.♞d2
Rock and hammer.

16...e6 17.b4 ♞cd7 18.♞b3 ♜c8 19.f4 ♛c7 20.♛e1
The queen turns her attention towards the ultimate prize, while also tempting a misstep.

20...♜e8
20...♛xc4?! 21.♜xd6 ♛xb4 22.e5± seals the deal.

21.♛f2 ♜ac8 22.♝d3
The bishop dutifully returns to its more active post, no longer fearing exchange.

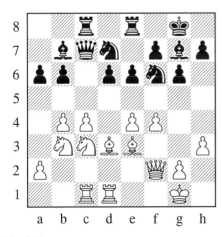

22...h5?±

A chessically shocking, but psychologically understandable error. Hemmed in, Black lashes out, preventing the g2-g4 bulldozer while loudly asserting his presence. Yet he had no choice but to stay small but solid, and brace for White's heavy machinery to try to rip through. Now the b3-knight flies in from the reserves, joining the fray before White's collective forces set the compromised Dragon structure ablaze.

23.♞d2 ♜b8 24.♞f3 ♝a8 25.♜f1
Readying to raze.

25...♛d8 26.f5! exf5 27.exf5 ♝xf3 28.♛xf3 ♞e5 29.♛d1 d5 30.cxd5 ♞xd5 31.♞xd5 ♛xd5

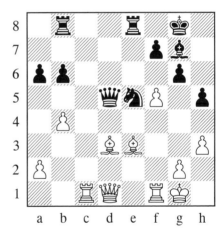

32.fxg6! fxg6
32...♞xd3 33.gxf7†+−

33.♝c4!+−
The game's first tactic, and a devastating one.

33...♛xc4 34.♜xc4 ♞xc4 35.♝f4 ♜bc8 36.♛d7 ♚h7 37.♝g5 ♞e5 38.♛b7 ♜c6 39.♝f6 ♜xf6 40.♜xf6 ♚h6 41.♜d6 h4 42.♛e4 ♚h5 43.♜d5 ♝f6 44.♛f4
Black resigned, as 44...♝g7 45.♛g4† ♚h6 46.♛xh4# leaves no doubt. At the time, Hracek was the highest rated player to fall to

the Morra in classical tournament play... until Van Wely fell in 2011.

1–0

Even world champions cannot escape – correction, should not have escaped – the Morra-Maroczy's death squeeze.

TheDarkKnight (Esserman) – Ruslan Ponomariov

Internet (blitz) 2008

1.e4 c5 2.d4 cxd4 3.c3 d3 4.♗xd3 g6 5.c4 ♗g7 6.♘f3 ♘c6 7.h3 d6

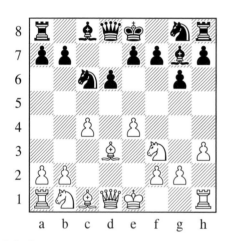

8.0–0

The gambiteer should delay the natural development of the queen's knight until it can no longer be lopped off by the swooping Dragon bishop. 8.♘c3?! is met by 8...♗xc3†! 9.bxc3∞ wrecking the pristine Maroczy structure. From here I suffered a painful defeat in Esserman – Kudrin, Foxwoods 2003, when Black's dark-squared deficiencies were overshadowed by White's mangled formation.

8...♘f6 9.♕e2?!

An imprecise move order. White should continue 9.♘c3, followed by 10.♗e3, 11.♖c1, and only later ♕e2 and ♖fd1.

9...0–0 10.♖d1 ♗d7?!

First and foremost, d7 belongs to the f6-knight, where it may seek an exchange or further positional pressure via c5 or e5. In addition, Ponomariov would have the option to radically alter the nature of the struggle with...♗xc3 should the white knight develop to c3.

11.♘c3 a6 12.♗e3

Those swashbucklers who just can't wait to sacrifice a pawn may play 12.c5!? here, with a serious initiative: 12...dxc5 13.e5 ♘e8 14.♗e4±

12...♖b8 13.♖ac1 ♖e8

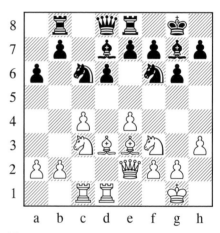

14.b3?!

I play routinely (typical for blitz!), not capitalizing on my great opponent's series of inaccurate moves. After 14.c5!± dxc5 15.♗xc5 White plays a Morra without gambiting a pawn!

14...♕a5 15.♗b1 b5 16.cxb5

Again, thrusting the c-pawn allows the Morra rooks to reap a large advantage: 16.c5! ♘g4 (16...dxc5 17.e5+–) 17.hxg4 ♗xc3 18.cxd6 exd6 (18...♗xg4 19.b4! ♕xb4 20.♕d3+–) 19.♖xd6 ♖ed8 20.♕d3+–

16...axb5 17.♘d5 ♘xd5?!

17...b4!? with mutual chances.

18.exd5± ♘e5 19.♘d4!

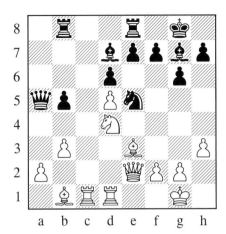

Avoiding exchange, thus allowing Black's lone knight to acutely feel the squeeze. 20.f2-f4 beckons, but the only defense still leads to long-term pain.

19...e6?!

19...f5 20.f4 ♘f7± 21.♘e6 ♗xe6 22.dxe6 ♘d8 23.g4! We will see the conclusion to such a suffocating, sweltering attack in JungleDacha vs. IsamOr next.

20.f4+−

Now, I digress. Groggy in the morning while visiting my family, I logged onto the ICC, sending out an open 3-minute challenge. Low and behold, ex-FIDE World Champion Ponomariov accepts and the game abruptly begins (ah, the joys of Internet chess). Somewhere around the first few seconds, I hear a shout from across the house: "Honey, come downstairs, pancakes are ready..."

20...exd5 21.fxe5

"One moment mom, I'm kind of up a piece against a World Champion..."

21...dxe5 22.♘c6

"I don't care who you're playing, get down here now, the food's getting cold!"

22...♗xc6 23.♖xc6

"Just a second..."

23...b4

"Honey!"

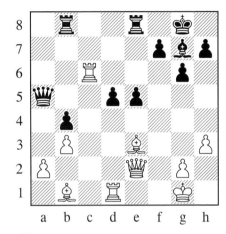

24.♕dc1?

"Arghhhh!" Amidst the chaos, I missed an easy win by 24.♖c5+−, and Ponomariov's mobile pawn mass ultimately pancaked me. As consolation, the pancakes were tasty and still hot. The moral of the story: never give World Champions pancake odds.

...0–1

JungleDacha (Esserman) – IsamOr (IM Ortiz)

Internet (blitz) 2010

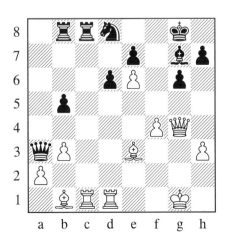

25.f5!

The archer on b1 slings arrows from afar!

25...gxf5 26.♕xf5 ♕b2 27.♕xh7† ♔f8 28.♖f1† ♗f6 29.♕h8#

Borba (Esserman) – Oligarkh (GM Jobava)

Internet (blitz) 2005

1.e4 c5 2.d4 cxd4 3.c3 d3 4.♗xd3 ♘c6 5.c4 g6 6.♘f3 ♗g7 7.h3 d6 8.0–0 ♘f6 9.♘c3 0–0

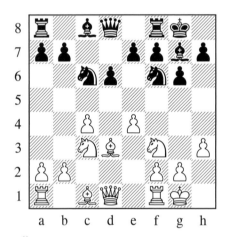

10.♕e2?!

It took me some time to grasp the proper move order, but you will not need to suffer as I did: 10.♗e3! ♘d7 11.♖c1! Preventing the shattering ...♗xc3. 11...♘de5!? 12.♗e2 ♘xf3† (12...♗e6 13.b3 ♕a5 14.♕d2±) 13.♗xf3± Black manages to trade off one pair of minor pieces, but still faces a protracted struggle against the bind.

10...♘d7 11.♗e3 ♘c5

Missing the chance to shake things up: 11...♗xc3! 12.bxc3 ♕a5∞

12.♖ac1 ♘xd3

Jobava wisely exchanges, but even this does not fully solve his problems, as will be evident in the instructive variations to come. While

White now lacks direct kingside attacking prospects without his light-squared bishop, fortunately he still resides within Maroczy's palace, a grand structure which always packs a powerful positional punch.

13.♕xd3±

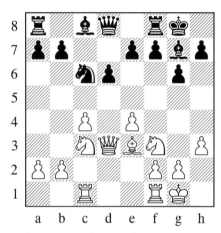

13...♗e6 14.b3 ♕a5 15.♗d2!?

15.a4!?± permanently stifles Black's freeing ...b5 break, at the expense of the b4-square.

15...♖fc8

15...♕h5?! 16.♘d5! cuts the swinging queen's range of motion: 16...♗xd5 (16...♘e5 17.♘xe5 dxe5 18.♘xe7†±) 17.cxd5 ♘e5 18.♘xe5 ♗xe5 19.♖c7±

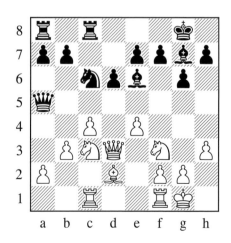

16.♕e2?!

Blitz rubbish, though White still stands superior! However, after 16.a4! the bind sinks its prophylactic teeth in: 16...♖h5 17.♘d5 ♗xd5 18.exd5 ♘e5 19.♘xe5 ♗xe5 20.♗c3 ♗xc3 21.♖xc3

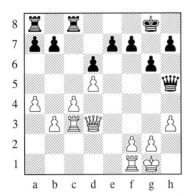

Only the heavy pieces remain, but the decliner still suffers endless strain. As a result of 18.exd5! the gambiteer turned boa-constrictor holds Black's e7-pawn under lock and key. Devoid of any counterplay via the standard ...b5/...f5 anti-Maroczy pawn thrusts, the schemer must return to his passive roots. After harassing the hapless defender on e7 to the point of cries for mercy, only then does White launch a quick and painless mating attack to put the black king out of his misery. An ideal textbook Maroczy bind! 21...a6 22.♖e1 ♖c7 23.♕d4 ♖ac8 24.♖ce3 ♖e8 25.f4 The final phase. 25...♕h4 (25...♕h6 26.f5+–) 26.♖e4 ♕h5 27.♔h2 Now g2-g4 beckons. 27...♕h6 28.f5 gxf5 29.♖h4 ♕g7 30.♕f4+– Next comes ♕xf5 followed by raging rook lifts.

16...♕d8

Even super-grandmasters cannot help but move listlessly when facing the Morra-Maroczy squeeze.

16...♕h5!? 17.♖fe1 The rook targets e7 from its perch. 17...♘e5 18.♘xe5 ♕xe2 19.♖xe2 ♗xe5 20.♘d5 ♗xd5 21.exd5 ♗f6 (21...a6 22.g4 b5 23.c5!±) 22.g4!± Banishing the bishop.

17.♖fd1

17.♘d5 ♗xd5 18.exd5 ♘e5 19.♘xe5 ♗xe5 20.♗c3 ♗xc3 21.♖xc3±

17...a6 18.♗e3 ♕a5 19.♗d2

19.♘d5→

19...♖ab8 20.♘a4 ♕d8 21.c5±

The bishop and queen's little duet ends with a bang.

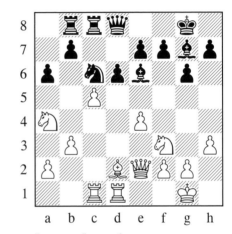

21...♘d4 22.♘xd4 ♗xd4 23.cxd6?!

23.♗f4± works the pin.

23...♕xd6?

23...exd6!

24.♖xc8† ♗xc8 25.♗e3 e5 26.♕d2 b5 27.♘b2 ♗b7 28.♗xd4 exd4 29.♕xd4±

I went on to win in a time scramble.

...1–0

We shall leave 3...d3 in the dust after witnessing two more brutal attacks.

JungleDacha (Esserman) – macia (GM Deepan)

Internet (blitz) 2010

1.e4 c5 2.d4 cxd4 3.c3 d3 4.♗xd3 d6 5.c4 g6 6.h3 ♗g7 7.♘f3 ♘f6 8.0–0 0–0

9.♘c3 ♘c6 10.♗e3!

At last the proper move order.

10...♗e6 11.♖c1 ♘d7 12.b3 a5 13.♗b1 ♘c5 14.♕e2 b6

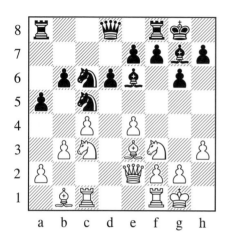

15.♖fd1

15.♘d5! stops any queenside intrigue: 15...a4?! 16.b4 ♘d7 17.a3±

15...♕c8

15...a4!? 16.♗xc5 bxc5 17.♘xa4 ♕a5∞ Black, with a powerful dark-squared presence, gets to showcase his pawn-down skills.

16.♘d5 ♕b7 17.♕d2

Sounding the invasion alarm.

17...♖fc8 18.♗h6

Taking a swipe at the Dragon's head.

18...♗h8 19.♕g5 ♖a7

A typical lifeless move for the besieged defender vs. the Morra-Maroczy.

20.♕h4 f6

The Dragon bishop lives on but it would probably rather be dead.

20...a4?! 21.b4 ♘d7 22.b5+−

20...♗xd5 21.exd5 ♘e5 22.♘d4±

21.♕g3 ♗f7

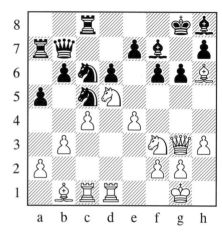

22.h4!?

Either attacking with pieces or the h-pawn first should suffice.

22.♘h4 e6 23.♘c3 a4 24.♘b5+− and the Dragon's tail thrashes no more.

22...b5 23.cxb5 ♕xb5 24.h5

Beating down the gates.

24...♘e5

24...♗g7 25.♗xg7 ♔xg7 26.♘h4 ♕b8 27.hxg6 hxg6 28.e5! ♘xe5 29.f4+− Watch for the b1-bishop out of the corner of your eye in the variations to come.

25.♘d4 ♕d7 26.♘f5+−

Morra maiming. Taking the exchange with 26.♘b6 is also winning, of course.

26...♕e8 27.f4 ♘c6 28.hxg6!?

28.♘dxe7†! Silicon butchery. 28...♘xe7 29.♘xd6 ♕d7 30.♘xc8 ♕xc8 31.f5 g5 32.♕d6+− ♖c7 33.♕d8† ♕xd8 (33...♗e8 34.♖xc5 ♖xc5 35.♕xe7+−) 34.♖xd8† ♗e8 35.♖xe8† ♔f7 36.♖f8#

28...hxg6 29.♘h4 ♔h7

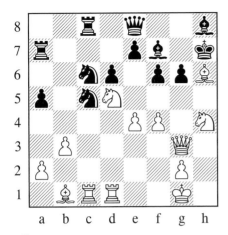

30.♕h2

30.e5!+– The patient bishop finally completes mission "squeeze, squeeze, destroy." 30...fxe5 (30...♔xh6 31.♘xg6 ♗xg6 32.♗xg6 ♕xg6 33.♕h3†!+–) 31.f5! Plowing the road. 31...e4 (31...♔xh6 32.fxg6 ♗e6 33.♘f5† ♗xf5 34.♗xf5 ♔g7 35.♕h3 ♕g8 36.♖xc5 dxc5 37.♗e6+–) 32.fxg6† ♗xg6 33.♗e3 ♗e5 34.♘f4 ♗f7 35.♖xc5 dxc5 36.♗xe4† ♔h8 37.♘hg6† ♗xg6 38.♘xg6†+–

30...♗g7

30...♔xh6?? 31.♘f5#

31.♗xg7 ♔xg7

Only a headless Dragon remains.

32.♕g3 e5

32...♔h7 33.e5+–

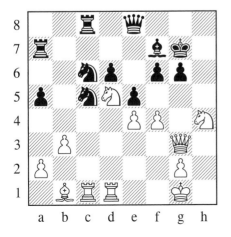

Good enough to induce resignation, but 34.♕h4 is pure barbarism: 34...gxf5 35.♕h6† ♔g8 36.♘xf6#

1–0

Marc Esserman – Igor Sorkin

New York 2009

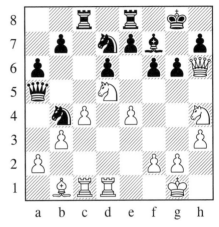

We are forged gambiteers not only in victory but in the flames of defeat. Here, not fully trusting that a headless Dragon is a dead Dragon, I retreated to eventual equality with the insipid 1.♕d2?? and later lost. In the postmortem, after the horrifying discovery of a missed brilliancy, I would vow to frenetically look for blood in such positions until ultimately the variations would paint the black king red. How would you splash the canvas here?

1.♖c3!!

Of course I considered this lift, seemingly drenching the rook, but stopped there. Now White's pieces elegantly combine to slash and burn, with the b1-bishop once again the hidden hero.

1...♘xd5

1...e6 2.♖g3 displays an overwhelming show of force: 2...♘c6 3.♘f4 (Even the unnecessary

3.♘xf6† ♘xf6 4.♘xg6 ♗xg6 5.♖xg6† hxg6
6.♕xg6† ♔h8 7.♕xf6† ♔g8 8.♖d3 crushes.)
3...♘ce5 4.♘h5+−

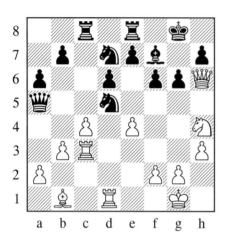

2.♘f5!

The dagger blow. Search and you shall find.

2.♖g3?! misfires: 2...♘f4! 3.♘f5 (3.♕xf4
♕h5!) 3...♘e6!−+

**2...gxf5 3.♖g3† ♗g6 4.exf5 ♘f8 5.fxg6 hxg6
6.♗xg6 ♘xg6 7.♕xg6† ♔h8 8.♕h5#**

Chapter 14

Morra Declined –
The Noxious 3...♘f6

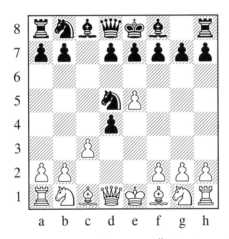

1.e4 c5 2.d4 cxd4 3.c3 ♘f6 4.e5 ♘d5

Alas, we face the schemer's ultimate weapon – after 3...♘f6,

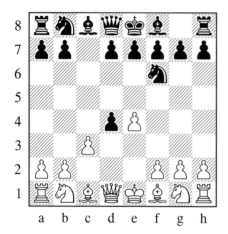

White has no choice but to thrust 4.e5 and directly transpose into the Alapin variation of the Sicilian. A stubborn gambiteer may try and resist fate with 4.♗d3(?!) or 4.♕c2(?!), yearning for chaos, but then he gets his wish after 4...dxc3!(∓) with a superior Morra Accepted for the wily decliner. Thus, many a schemer from amateur to grandmaster has asked me over the years: "What's the difference between the Morra Gambit and the c3-Sicilian if Black plays 3...♘f6?" At first, shocked by such a practical, bordering on putrid approach when juxtaposed to the Romantic ideal, I just coldly responded, "Well, you can always show some courage and take on c3." But no, questioning the valor of the growing legions of schemers worldwide will no longer do.[54] Yes, I understand now: they wish to equalize at *all* costs. Nothing could make them happier than killing a lively game for a sterile draw, or better yet, a long, grinding win after White starts to snore.

So now I have a new answer. The difference is, we're gambiteers, mate. The Morra Gambit is not just an opening, but a lifestyle.[55] Chaos can erupt from anywhere, yes, even the dry c3-Sicilian. Let us finally impose Morra mayhem on 3...♘f6, so that the decliner has nowhere

left to hide. And of course, if the position ever does get "dry", then it is the schemer who will be the one suffering.

Andrei Deviatkin – Vasily Papin

Moscow 2006

1.e4 c5 2.c3 ♘f6 3.e5 ♘d5 4.d4 cxd4 5.♕xd4

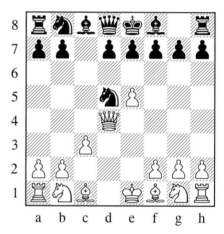

First, for my less experienced gambiteers, I offer the hyper-active freestyling ♕xd4. Of course, tossing the queen out so early to the wolves contains risk, and those interested may study some of the variation's theoretical problems in the supplemental game Esserman – Razuvaev. However, on the plus side, this line contains little to memorize and can be extremely straightforward – White will play a quick ♘f3, g3, ♗g2, 0–0, use his advanced e-pawn as an attacking/restricting wedge, and play chess. I'm sure you can play 5.♕xd4 successfully up to the master level – I even obtained a winning position with it against 2700+ GM Milov in a tough tournament struggle before botching the ending (not the fault of the opening!). And you never know, the position may even get a bit nuts!

5...e6 6.♘f3

The original Morra-man Matulovic preferred 6.♗c4!?, placing the bishop on its natural gambit square in his games, but as it will constantly run up against the e6 roadblock, I advise a more scoping fianchettoed posting.

6...♞c6 7.♕e4 f5 8.♕e2!

Retaining the e5-pawn, even at the cost of temporarily lagging behind in development.

The faster 8.exf6?! keeps the momentum but cedes the center, and after the tactics fail White is left floundering: 8...♞xf6 9.♕h4 d5 10.♗d3 ♗d6 11.♗g6† ♔e7∓

8...♕c7 9.g3

A Catalan-Morra? Not quite.

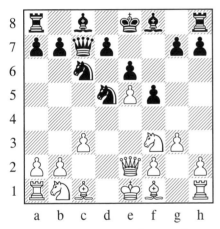

9...b5 10.♗g2 a5 11.0–0 ♗a6 12.♞h4!

White enters chaos mode, striking effectively at the defects in the enemy's camp before his a6-f1 diagonal problems are exposed.

12...g6

Duck and cover.

12...♕xe5? 13.♕xe5 ♞xe5 14.♗xd5 exd5 15.♖e1+– goes splat.

13.♖d1!

The rook glides to d1. Feel familiar? It should.

13...♗g7

I smell a sac.

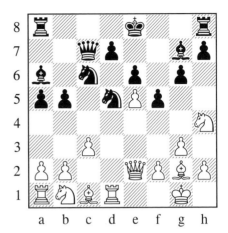

14.♞xf5!

Who knew the c3-Sicilian could be so much fun?

14...gxf5 15.♕h5†

"Run, Forrest, run." (Forrest Gump)

15...♔f8

15...♔e7 16.♖xd5! exd5 17.♗g5† ♔e6 18.♗xd5†! Run! 18...♔xd5 19.♕f7† ♔c5 (19...♔xe5 20.♗f4† ♔e4 21.♞d2† ♔d3 22.♕xf5† ♔e2 Run!! 23.♕e4#) 20.♗e3† ♞d4 21.♗xd4† ♔c6 22.♕xg7+–

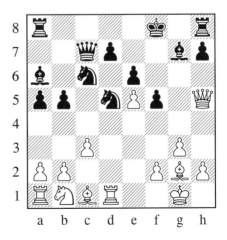

16.♖xd5!

Bang. The rook begs for capture.

16...♘xe5

16...exd5 17.♗xd5 d6 18.♕xf5† ♔e8 19.♕e6† ♔d8 20.♗g5†+−

17.♗h6!±

Eliminating the key defender. And White's not even a pawn down. Full steam ahead!

17...♖c8

17...exd5!? 18.♗xd5→ Well, now he's a rook down, but with a massive attack. Woohoohoo.

18.♖d4!?±

The machine's wild 18.♘a3!, dangling the rook, is more in the gambiteer spirit. But we must forgive Deviatkin for producing one solid but still strong move in a nearly flawless, swashbuckling performance.

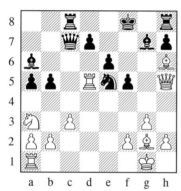

18...exd5 (18...b4 19.♖e1!+− [19.♘b5!?± 19...bxa3 20.♖exe5 axb2 21.♖xf5† exf5 22.♖xf5† ♔e7 23.♕f7† ♔d6 24.♗f4† ♔e5 25.♖f6† ♔c5 26.♕d5#) 19.♕g5!+− d6 (19...♗xh6 20.♕xh6† ♔e8 21.♕xa6+− Total board vision!) 20.♕f6† ♕f7 21.♕xd6† ♔e8 22.♗xg7 ♕xg7 23.♖e1+− Sizzling.

18...♗b7 19.♗xb7 ♕xb7 20.♘d2

Out come the reserves, and what reserves they are!

20...♖g8

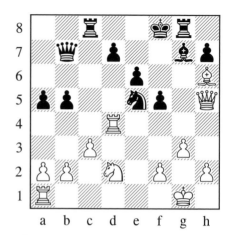

21.♘e4!

Excellent.

21...♘f7

21...fxe4 22.♕xe5 ♗xh6 23.♕f6†+−

22.♘f6!

Neigh!

22...♗xh6

22...♘xh6 23.♖xd7 The last of many crunching blows. 23...♕b6 24.♘xh7#

23.♖xd7
1–0

For those who feel satisfied, congratulations, you may close the book! But for the hardcore searching for more mayhem, keep reading. We'll start "softly" before increasing the volume.

Evgeny Sveshnikov – Sergey Yuferov

Moscow 2006

1.e4 c5 2.d4[56] cxd4 3.c3 ♘f6 4.e5 ♘d5 5.♘f3!

The sharpest move in Morra style. White is in no hurry to take back the pawn. Many Alapin-Morra gambits now lurk, as we shall see, but patience – not yet.

5...d6!?

The decliner demands and receives immediate clarification in the center.

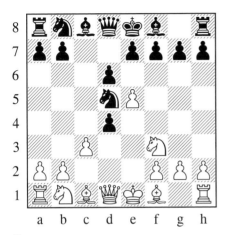

6.♕xd4!?

Our new friend ♕xd4, but with a twist. Now ♗b5† may fire freely, and White keeps on developing speedily while the queen entrenches herself in the center.

6.cxd4!? ♘c6 7.♗c4 ♘b6 8.♗b5 dxe5 9.♘xe5 ♗d7 leads to a much-debated main line of the c3-Sicilian, but I cannot in good conscience recommend such a position, not only because I believe that Black eventually equalizes, but it just fails to inspire my imagination. If you feel differently, by all means give this tabiya a try.

6...e6 7.♘bd2 ♘c6

7...♗d7!? may be met with the natural 8.♘c4, increasing the central tension, or even the violent 8.♕g4!? with enduring kingside pressure. For example: 8.♕g4 dxe5 9.♘xe5 ♘f6 10.♕g3→

7...a6!? prevents ♗b5 at the expense of a tempo. Now White should shift gears to the already familiar g3/♗g2 plan as the bishop has no better home. 8.g3 ♘c6 9.♕e4 ♕c7 (9...dxe5 10.♘xe5 ♘xe5 11.♕xe5 ♕d6 12.♕xd6 ♗xd6

13.♗g2± and it's grinding time!) 10.exd6 ♗xd6 11.♗g2 0–0 12.♘c4 With a balanced battle as the fight rages on.

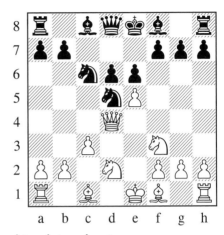

8.♗b5! ♗d7 9.♗xc6

Giving up the bishop pair but gaining time.

9...♗xc6 10.♘c4

The central tension reaches its apex. Here the decliner must show fearlessness with the bold 10...f6, sacrificing a pawn to sap the energy from White's e5-powerhouse while splitting the board open for his bishops. However, almost all grandmasters make the same mistake as in the game and let the knights savagely wreak havoc for many moves to come, after which the theoretical outcome of 6.♕xd4!? is no longer in doubt.

10...dxe5

10...f6! 11.exd6 (11.♘xd6†?! ♗xd6 12.exd6 e5 13.♕c5 ♕b6 14.♕a3 ♗b5∓ and the bishops roamed free in Vysochin – S. Pavlov, Kiev 2010) 11...♘b6!∞

11.♘cxe5 ♕b6 12.0–0 ♕xd4 13.♘xd4 ♖c8 14.c4 ♘b6 15.b3±

White's radiant knights and active queenside majority offer him a lasting advantage, which the great c3-Sicilian expert Sveshnikov brutally converts.

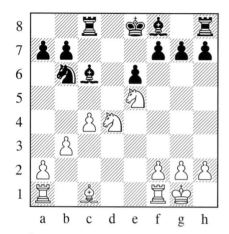

15...♘d7

15...♗d7 16.♖d1±

16.♘dxc6 bxc6 17.♘xd7 ♔xd7

Black neutralizes the cavalry, but not before they shred his pawn structure and rip open his king.

18.♖d1†± ♔e8 19.♗e3 a6 20.♗b6 ♗e7 21.♖d3 ♗d8 22.♗d4 f6 23.♖ad1 ♔f7 24.♗c5 ♗c7 25.♖d7† ♔g6 26.♗d6 ♗d8 27.♖d3 1–0

6.exd6!?

1.e4 c5 2.d4 cxd4 3.c3 ♘f6 4.e5 ♘d5 5.♘f3 d6

With the theoretical state of 6.♕xd4 up in the air, we shall forge a new weapon vs. the direct 5...d6.

6.exd6!?

An obvious but shunned capture. Perhaps a reassessment is in order.

6...♕xd6

6...e6!? hopes for 7.cxd4?! ♗xd6 with at least equality, when the decliner races ahead in his quest to restrain, blockade, and destroy the isolani. But we will not satisfy such fantasies. 7.♘xd4! ♗xd6 8.g3± Catalan players rejoice,

for at last you have your position. The gambiteer turned grinder retains an ever so slight but lasting advantage as the f1-bishop soon scopes the long diagonal.

6...♘c6!? Those decliners that summon the strength to brave this countergambit can no longer be called schemers! 7.♘xd4! But White has the last laugh, giving the decliner a taste of his own medicine. (7.dxe7?! ♗xe7∓ Accept this offering at your own peril!) 7...♕xd6 8.♘a3 e6 9.♘xc6 bxc6± White ensures structural superiority.

7.♘a3!

Woohahaha. Poor little schemer. He had dreamed of sterility. The hackneyed 7.♘xd4 may lead to a similar position as the raw, virtually untested 7.♘a3, but it tragically lacks the necessary mischief. Remember ♘a3, one of the key ingredients for detonating Morra mayhem in the Alapin.

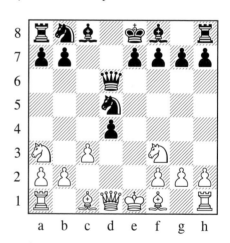

7...a6

7...dxc3?! He should have taken on move 3! 8.♘b5 ♕e6† (8...♕b4 9.bxc3 ♘xc3 10.♘c7#) 9.♗e2 a6 10.♘g5! Swinging freely. 10...♕f6 11.♕xd5 axb5 12.♗xb5† ♘c6 13.0–0±

7...e5 8.♗c4∞ ♘b6 9.♗b3→ You're more than ready to mix it up here by now.

7...♗g4 8.♗e2 e6 (8...a6 9.♘xd4±) 9.♘b5 ♛b6 10.♘bxd4 ♘c6 11.♘xc6 ♛xc6? (11...bxc6±) 12.♛b3+– The tag team threats of ♘d4 and ♗b5 land a devastating knockout.

7...♘c6 8.♘b5 ♛d7 9.♘bxd4 (or 9.♗c4!?→) 9...♘xd4?! (9...e6 10.♘xc6±) 10.♘e5!± Gunpowder and dynamite. 10...♛d6 11.♛xd4 a6 12.♗e2 e6

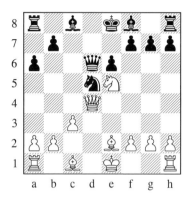

13.♗h5! g6 14.♘c4+–

8.♘c4

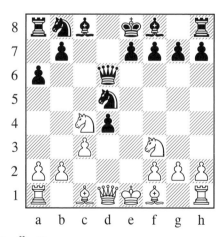

8...♛e6†

Holding on to the pawn regardless of development, naturally the greedy computer's first choice. Now pop the champagne as the machine's evaluation switches from a large edge for Black (∓) to a clear edge for White (±).

8...♛c7 9.♘xd4 Sorry, but there comes a time when you have to take the pawn back! 9...e6 (9...b5? 10.♘xb5 axb5 11.♛xd5+–) 10.a4 g6 (10...♘c6 11.♘xc6±) and now, the gambiteer may venture the solid ♗e2 followed by a4-a5, or, more in the spirit, recklessly thrust 11.h4!?→.

9.♗e2 dxc3 10.0–0± ♛d7

10...cxb2 11.♗xb2± We may brand this... the Danish-Morra-Alapin Gambit!

11...♘f4 12.♗e5! ♘xe2† 13.♛xe2 b5 14.♘d4 ♛xc4 15.♛f3 Disaster engulfs Black's queenside. For example: 15...♖a7 16.♖ac1 ♗b7 17.♛h3 ♛b4 (17...♛d5 18.♗xb8+–) 18.♖c8† ♗xc8 19.♛xc8#

11.♘fe5 ♛d8 12.♘e3! ♗e6

12...e6 13.♗h5! g6 14.♛f3±

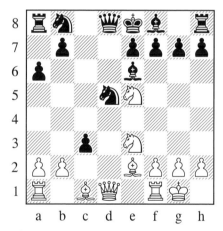

13.♗g4!→

"Get your cameras ready. He's going down." (Apollo Creed, Rocky II)

13...♗xg4 14.♛xd5 ♗e6 15.♛xb7 ♘d7 16.♘xd7 ♗xd7 17.♘d5 ♖c8 18.♗f4±

We continue our tour of schemerville, finding chaos lurking in all corners.

Sergei Tiviakov – Omar Almeida Quintana

Banyoles 2006

1.e4 c5 2.c3 ♘f6 3.e5 ♘d5 4.♘f3 e6 5.d4 cxd4

White now has no better choice but to recapture, postponing hostilities for a finer hour. While the gambiteer floods the center with pawns, the decliner secures and bases his entire operation around the critical d5-square.

6.cxd4 d6

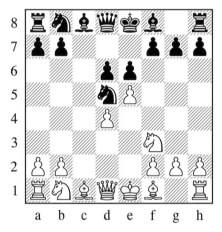

7.a3!?

Tiviakov's favorite prophylactic pawn push, preventing all b4 intrusions. As the position remains in a semi-closed state, White has the liberty to secure the bishop's aggressive d3-post. Then after the straightforward 0–0 followed by ♖e1 (fortifying the powerful e5 foot soldier), a massive kingside assault looms on the horizon. However, it's always good to have options, so while the next few examples will showcase 7.a3, I urge the aspiring gambiteer to carefully study the supplemental games starting with Nisipeanu – Ramirez, Decameron 2003, featuring the natural but analytically dense plan of 7.♗c4 followed by 0–0 and ♕e2. I'll give you a jump-start on the theory, and then those intrepid enough

will be free to cause chaos with both 7.a3 and 7.♗c4.

7.♗c4!? ♘b6

7...♘c6 8.0–0 ♗e7 9.♕e2 0–0 10.♘c3!? ♘xc3 11.bxc3 dxe5 12.dxe5

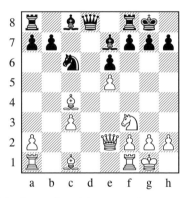

This dynamic tabiya contains many fierce fights. White must seek a quick kingside bloodbath before Black's pristine pawn structure reigns supreme. 12...b6!?∞ (For 12...♕a5!? see Nisipeanu – Ramirez, among others.) 13.♕e4!?→ (13.♗d2!?→) 13...♕c7 14.♗d3→ This line features in Sveshnikov – Oll, Godena – Bruno, and Melekhina – Shabalov. One fantastic variation runs: 14...g6 15.♗g5 ♗b7 16.♗f6 ♘b4! 17.♕h4 ♘d5 18.♘g5 h5

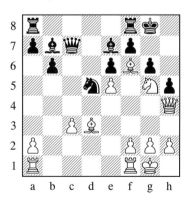

19.♕xh5! ♘xf6! 20.♕h6! ♕xe5 21.♗xg6! fxg6 22.♕xg6† ♔h8 23.♕h6†=! See if you can find an improvement![57]

8.♗d3! ♘c6 9.0–0 dxe5

9...♘b4 10.♗g5!± was highlighted in Jakimov – Rublevsky.

10.dxe5 ♘b4 11.♗e4 ♕xd1 12.♖xd1±

With excellent prospects for White in this rich queenless middlegame (see Timman – Janke).

7...♘d7 8.♗d3 ♗e7 9.0–0 0–0 10.♕c2

Probing for a crucial kingside weakness.

10...g6

White's knights are already dreaming of feasting on f6.

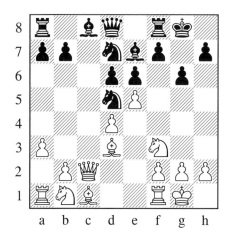

11.♗h6 ♖e8 12.♖e1 dxe5 13.dxe5 ♘c5 14.♗c4 ♘b6 15.♗f1 ♗d7 16.♘c3 ♖c8 17.♕e2 ♘ba4 18.♘xa4 ♗xa4 19.b4 ♘d7 20.♕e3

Creeping closer.

20...♘b6 21.h4

The bayonet spears.

21...a6

21...♗xh4 leads to dark-squared suicide: 22.♘xh4 ♕xh4 23.♗g5 ♕g4 24.♗e2 ♕f5 25.g4 ♕c2 26.♗f6+–

22.♘g5

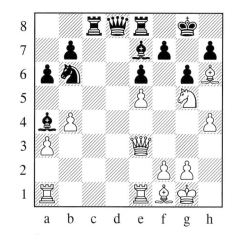

22...♗f8?

A grave positional error, fulfilling the cavalry's f6 lustings.

22...♘d5! 23.♕f3 ♗xg5 24.♗xg5 ♕b6 25.h5 ♖c3!⇄ would launch a feisty counterattack.

23.♗xf8 ♖xf8 24.♘e4

The rest is an execution.

24...♔g7

Fighting off ♕h6 followed by ♘f6/g5, but now the horse grazes other pastures.

24...♕xh4? 25.♕xb6+–

25.♘d6 ♘d5 26.♕e4 ♖c7 27.♖ac1 ♕d7 28.h5 ♘e7 29.♕h4 ♘g8 30.hxg6 hxg6 31.♘e4

Back to f6 at last!

31...♖xc1

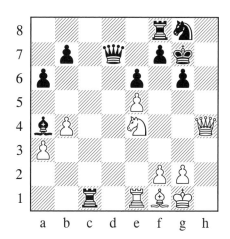

32.♘f6!+– ♘h6

32...♘xf6 33.exf6† ♔g8 34.♕h6 ♖xe1 35.♕g7#

**33.♘xd7 ♖xe1 34.♘xf8 ♗b5 35.♕e7 ♖xf1†
36.♔h2 ♖xf2**

36...♗c4 37.♘d7 ♗d5 38.♕f8† ♔h7
39.♘f6#

**37.♘xe6† ♔h7 38.♘d4 ♗c4 39.♕xb7 ♗f1
40.♔g1 ♗xg2 41.♕xa6 ♖b2 42.e6 ♗e4 43.e7
1–0**

Sergei Tiviakov – Reynaldo Vera

Merida 2006

**1.e4 c5 2.c3 ♘f6 3.e5 ♘d5 4.♘f3 e6 5.d4
cxd4 6.cxd4 d6 7.a3 ♗d7**

The schemer's main response to 7.a3. Seeing
that the b4-square is now off limits for the
horses, Black takes two tempi to post his
bishop on the powerful c6-square, while the
queen's knight will pressure the center from
d7. White adjusts in turn, eventually harassing
the bishop with the space gaining b2-b4,
ultimately waging an assault on both sectors
of the board in a tense struggle. Black must
counterattack vigorously, generally by striking
at White's somewhat compromised queenside,
if he hopes to fight off the squeeze and a brutal
fate of mate.

**8.♗d3 ♗c6 9.0–0 ♘d7 10.♖e1 ♗e7 11.b4 a6
12.♘bd2**

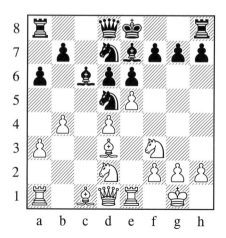

12...♗b5

Aiming for immediate queenside tactics falls
just short:

12...♘c3? 13.♕b3! ♖c8

13...♘b5 14.♗xb5 axb5 15.exd6 ♗f6
(15...♗xd6 16.d5+–) 16.♘e5± Tiviakov –
Kovalyov, Montreal 2009.

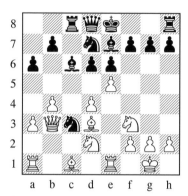

14.exd6!

Throwing a wrench in the decliner's
machinations. Note that had the bishop
stood on f8 (as in the next game), then the
...♘c3 blow would have succeeded.

14.♕xc3?! ♗xf3⇄

14...♗xd6

14...♗d5? 15.dxe7+–

15.♘c4!N ♗e7 16.♕xc3 ♗d5 17.♕d2 ♗xc4
18.♗xc4 ♖xc4 19.d5!±

12...♘f4 is another premature raid: 13.♗e4
♗xe4 14.♘xe4 dxe5 15.♗xf4 exf4 16.d5 0–0
17.dxe6 fxe6 18.♕b3±

12...dxe5!?

The best alternative, depriving the gambiteer
of central pawn ploys.

13.dxe5 ♘c3!?

13...♘f4 14.♗e4 ♗xe4 15.♘xe4± offers a
stable plus with extra space all across the
board.

14.♕c2

14.♕b3? ♘c5! We must not allow such
tricky knight play.

14...♖c8 15.♘e4 ♘xe4 16.♗xe4 ♘b6 17.♗e3

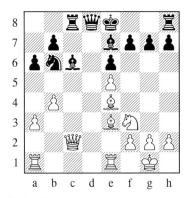

17...♘a4!?N

M. Petrov – Spraggett, San Sebastian 2007, saw 17...♗xe4 18.♕xe4 ♘d5 19.♕g4→ ♔f8 20.♗g5?! ½–½, but instead 20.♘d4!± clearly presses for the win.

18.♕a2! ♘d5 19.♗xd5 ♕xd5 20.♕xd5 exd5 21.♘d4±

The machine proclaims "=", but I sense a long technical squeeze in order.

13.♗xb5 axb5 14.♗b2

14.♕e2!?±N is worth considering. If Black grabs the pawn with 14...♘xb4? White launches a ferocious attack: 15.exd6 ♗xd6 16.♘e4 ♗e7 (16...♕b6 17.♗h6!?±) 17.♗g5 ♗xg5 18.♘d6† ♔f8 19.♘xf7+−

14...♘7b6 15.♕e2 ♕d7 16.exd6

Taking on an isolated pawn, but only for a move.

16...♗xd6 17.♘e5 ♗xe5 18.dxe5

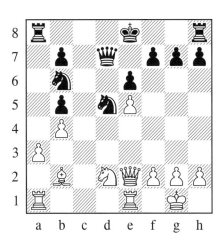

If I said the game will end in only 11 more moves, culminating in a sparkling mating combination, would you believe me? Well, Black remained a skeptic and simply castled into it, trusting in his sturdy centralized knights.

18...0–0?!

Now Tiviakov's e5-pawn will play the starring role as his seemingly dead b2-bishop and downtrodden knight get the prizes for best supporting actors. Beware of getting complacent in seemingly "quiet" positions, for danger always lurks!

Yet via hyper-active defense, Black could have altered his destiny: 18...♘f4!⇄ 19.♕e3 ♘d3 20.♕xb6 ♘xe1 21.♘e4 This is most certainly what Black feared, but after 21...♘c2 22.♘d6† ♔e7 23.♖c1 ♖a6! 24.♕c5 ♖c6 25.♕xb5 ♘d4! 26.♕d3 ♖xc1† 27.♗xc1 ♘f5∓ it is White who must fight for a draw. A superb defensive display.

19.♖ad1 ♖fc8 20.♘e4 ♘c4 21.♕g4!

The first act.

21...♔h8

21...♘xb2 22.♘f6† ♔xf6 23.exf6+−

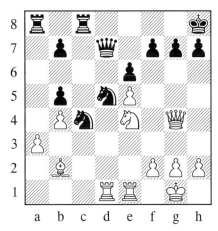

22.♘d6?!

The crescendo.

It is difficult to criticize such a dashing move, but simply retreating the threatened bishop with 22.♗c1 is objectively stronger. Then both 22...♘xa3 and 22...♘xe5 can bet met by 23.♕h5, when the attack remains dangerous.

22...♖c7!

Black is not helped by 22...♘xb2 23.♖xd5± or 22...♘xd6 23.♖xd5+−.

23.♗a1 ♖g8?!

Fearing ♖d3-g3, but again boldness would have saved the day: 23...♘xa3!∓ 24.♖d3 (24.♖xd5 exd5 25.♘f5 [25.e6 fxe6−+] 25...♖g8!−+ Only now!) 24...♘c2! 25.♖g3 g6−+ Great chess requires nerves of steel.

24.♕h3

Now ♖d4-h4 threatens to embarrass the black king, so a repetition is in order.

24...♖a8 25.♕g4 ♖xa3?

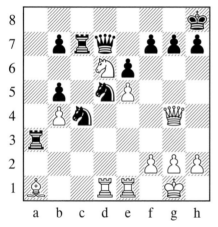

Curses, the wrong capture! Now the bishop makes his presence felt. As we have already seen, 25...♘xa3! is correct.

26.♖xd5!+− f5

26...exd5 27.♘f5! g6 28.e6† ♖xa1 The climax! 29.♕d4† f6 30.♖xa1 (30.♕xf6† ♕g7 31.♖xa1+− provides an echo.) 30...♕xe6

31.♕xf6†! ♕xf6 32.♖a8† ♖c8 33.♖xc8† ♕f8 34.♖xf8#

26...♖xa1 27.♖xa1 exd5 28.♖a8† ♖c8 29.♖xc8† ♕xc8 30.♕xc8#

27.exf6 ♖xa1 28.♖xa1 ♘xd6 29.♕xg7†

If you're ever feeling down, just remember, mayhem is but a move away.
1−0

And now for a ♘g5 appetizer before the main meal.

Patrick Wolff – Alexander Stripunsky

US Chess League, Internet 2011

1.e4 c5 2.♘f3 e6 3.c3

In his youth a swashbuckling Morra gambiteer, GM Wolff, like so many elite players, eventually lost faith in the opening. I hope that this book inspires him to once again raise the Morra's sharp sword.

3...♘f6 4.e5 ♘d5 5.d4 cxd4 6.cxd4 d6 7.a3 ♗d7 8.♗d3 ♗c6 9.0-0 ♘d7 10.b4

Even the slightest move order difference can matter! White may also play it cool, maintaining maximum flexibility with:

10.♖e1!

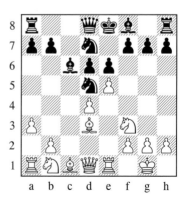

10...♖c8 11.♗d2!?

An ultra-solid approach. The b-pawn bides its time, waiting for the opportune moment to strike.

11.b4 a6 transposes to the game.

11.♘g5?! leads nowhere: 11...dxe5 12.dxe5 g6! 13.♕f3 ♕e7∓ Still to move his b-pawn, White lacks the time to meet the incoming attack on the e5-pawn with ♕g3 followed by ♗b2.

11...dxe5

11...♗e7 12.b4! Now! 12...a6 13.a4→ Play has transposed to the variations after 12.♗d2 ♗e7?! in the note to White's 12th move below.

12.dxe5 ♗e7

12...♘c5 13.♗c2∞ and a tense struggle looms.

13.♘d4!

Once again the knight nestles on d4 (a common theme after dxe5 in these lines), inflicting heavy damage.

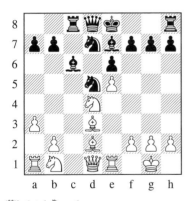

13...♕b6 14.♘xc6

Tactics again will flow towards the decliner's king.

14...bxc6

14...♕xc6 15.♘c3 ♘xc3 16.♗xc3 ♘c5 17.♗c2 0–0 18.♗e3!→ Incoming!

14...♖xc6 15.♘c3± ♘xc3 16.♗xc3 0–0 17.♗xh7†!±

15.♘c3 ♕xb2

15...♘c5 16.♗c4 ♕xb2 17.♘xd5 exd5 18.♗b4! dxc4 19.♖b1 ♕a2 20.♖e2±

16.♘xd5 cxd5

16...exd5 17.e6+–

17.♖b1 ♕d4

17...♕xa3 18.♖b3 ♕a2 19.♖e2 a6 20.♖b7±

18.♗e3 ♕xe5 19.♕a4+–

10...a6 11.♖e1

11.♘bd2?! fails to 11...♘c3! 12.♕c2 ♖c8 13.♕xc3 (13.exd6 ♗d5∓) 13...♗xf3 14.♕b2 ♗c6 15.♘c4 dxe5 16.dxe5 Fenil – Himanshu, New Delhi 2010, and now 16...♘c5!⇄N.

11...♖c8!?

Leaving the king in the fire for an extra move to secure the c-file. Wolff doesn't need any more encouragement to sound the attack drums.

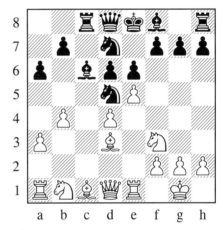

12.♘g5!?

Seeking to capitalize on Black's bishop sleeping on f8 in thematic Morra fashion (Remember our Scheveningen themes – when the c8-bishop ignores e6 defensive duty, ♘xe6 violence may ensue!) But as we shall see, the decliner surprisingly has sufficient defensive resources (if he can find them!), and so I must also point out the calmer alternatives.

Of course, 12.♘bd2?! ♘c3∓ is foolish.

12.♗d2?!

This passive move comes up wanting against accurate play.

12...dxe5!

Preventing a3-a4.

After 12...♗e7?! 13.a4→ the schemer will feel positional pressure: 13...♘7b6?! (Only with hyper-vigilant defense such as 13...♘5b6 or 13...♖a8 can Black hope to hold the balance.) 14.b5 axb5 15.axb5 ♗d7 16.♗a5! 0–0 17.♘bd2±

13.dxe5 ♘7b6 14.♖e4 g6!∓

12.♖a2?!

Taking back the c-file and finishing the developmental process by highly original means, but it ultimately proves defective.

12...♗e7 13.♖c2 0–0!N

13...dxe5 14.dxe5 ♘7b6 15.♘c3! ♘xc3 16.♖xc3 0–0 (16...♘d5 17.♖c4↑ or 16...♗xf3 17.♖xc8 ♗xd1 18.♖xd8† ♗xd8 19.♖xd1±) 17.♘d4± ♗d5 The eccentric rook lift is now crowned with success.

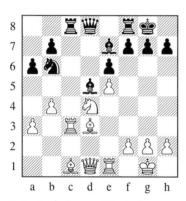

18.♗xh7†! ♔xh7 19.♖h3† ♔g8 20.♕h5 f6 21.♕h7† ♔f7 22.♗h6±

14.♘bd2

White has no better means of completing development other than this lame move:

14.♘c3?! ♘xc3 15.♖xc3 dxe5 16.dxe5 ♗xf3 17.♖xc8 ♗xd1 18.♖xd8 ♖xd8 19.♖xd1 ♘xe5∓

14.♗d2 ♗b5!∓

14...♘f4∓

12.♗g5!? ♗e7! (12...♕c7 led to the following painful miniature: 13.♘bd2 h6 14.♗h4 ♘c3 15.♕c2 ♗d5 16.♖ac1 ♘b6 17.♘b1 ♘ba4 18.♘xc3 ♘xc3 19.♕b2 ♗e7 20.♗g3 1–0 Spasov – Arnaudov, Plovdiv 2008) 13.♗xe7 ♕xe7 Black should hold the balance in this roughly equal position.

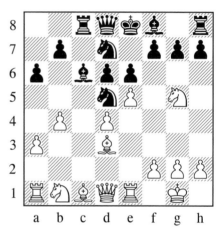

12...g6?

Black buckles under the pressure of the chaos swirling about. But the tenacious machine shows the schemer a possible way out.

12...♗e7!? 13.h4!?N (13.♕h5 g6 14.♕g4 heralds explosions crackling on e6, although 14...dxe5!? 15.♘xe6 fxe6 16.♗xg6† hxg6 17.♕xg6† ♔f8 18.♗h6† ♖xh6 19.♕xh6† only leads to perpetual check.) 13...dxe5! 14.dxe5 We have transposed to the line with 12...dxe5! below.

12...dxe5!

Inviting danger!

13.dxe5

13.♘xe6?! fxe6 14.♕h5† ♔e7!N 15.♗g5† ♘5f6∓ 16.dxe5? ♘xe5–+

13...♗e7 14.h4!?

An ambitious attempt at revival.

14.♕h5?! g6 15.♕h6 ♗f8 16.♕h3 ♗g7∓

14.♕g4?! ♘e3! Pinpoint precision. 15.♗xe3 ♘xe5 16.♕h5 (16.♕g3? ♘xd3–+ Kouvatsou – Nikolov, Agios Kirykos 2010) 16...♕xd3

17.♘xe6 ♕g6!∓

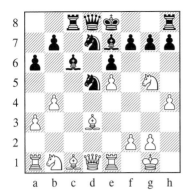

14...♝b5

14...♝xg5?! 15.♝xg5→

14...♕c7 15.♝b2 is unclear. For example: 15...h6 (15...♘f4 16.♝f1 remains unclear, although I might admit to slightly preferring Black.) 16.♘f3 0–0 (16...♘7b6 17.♘d4 ♝xh4 18.♘xc6 ♕xc6 19.♘d2⊼) 17.g3 ♖fd8 18.♕e2 ♘7b6 19.♘d4 ♘a4 20.♘xc6 ♕xc6 21.♕e4∞

15.♝e4 ♘xe5 16.♝b2∞

Purists who remain unconvinced of the merits of 12.♘g5 or in my suggested improvement at move 10 above should pore over the supplemental material covering 7.♝c4 for salvation.

13.♕f3+– ♕e7

13...♘5f6 14.♕f4+–

14.exd6 ♕f6

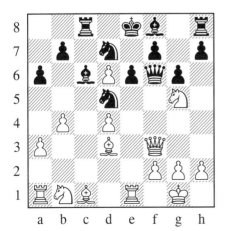

15.♕g4!?

Wolff had a chance for the history books with a fantastic combinational torrent rivaling Morphy's Romantic gems.

15.♕h3! ♝xd6 16.♘xe6+– is a butcher's method.

15.♘xe6!!

The artist's approach.

15...♕xf3

a) 15...♝xd6 16.♕h3+–

b) 15...fxe6 16.♕g4! Black's clumped army can merely huddle around the king and brace for impact. 16...♕f7 (16...♘f7 17.♝g5 h5 [17...♕g7 18.♕xe6#] 18.♝xf6 hxg4 19.♝xh8+–) 17.♖xe6† ♚d8 18.♝g5† ♘7f6 19.♖xf6! ♘xf6 20.♝c4! Wide brushstrokes! 20...♕g7 (20...♝d7 21.♝xf7 ♝xg4 22.♝xf6† ♚d7 23.♘d2+–) 21.♕e6+– The white queen triumphantly lands where the black pawn once stood to deliver the decisive blow.

16.♘g7†

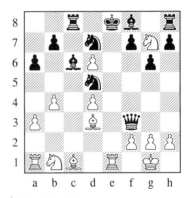

16...♚d8 17.♖e8#

Spectacular!

15...♝h6 16.♝d2?!

Here too, Wolff missed an opportunity with 16.♘xf7! ♝xc1 17.♘xh8 ♕xh8 18.♖xc1+–, eventually winning in a prosaic ending after the text move.

...1–0

We will now see some serious sacrificial mayhem as 12.♘g5 slashes and burns against Black's setup with 5...e6 and 6...b6.

5...e6 and 6...b6 Setup – 12.♘g5 Introduction

1.e4 c5 2.d4 cxd4 3.c3 ♘f6 4.e5 ♘d5 5.♘f3 e6 6.cxd4 b6

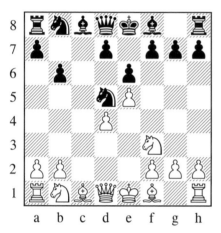

Historically an extremely popular variation of the c3-sicilian. The schemer first aims to secure the h1-a8 diagonal before dissolving White's center with ...d6. However, as he postpones kingside development, Morra mayhem will soon engulf the board.

6...♘c6!? is another viable move order. Now White must again choose between the main line after 7.♗c4 d6 (see the supplemental games), or the Tiviakov style 7.a3 and 8.♗d3 (see Markovic – Zakic, Nis 1997, on page 340).

7.♘c3!

Eliminating Black's best piece at the price of a spoiled pawn structure. But the gambiteer, conditioned to giving the c3-pawn, cannot be daunted by such things as a fragile c3/d4 complex, for he soon plans to sacrifice not just a pawn, but pieces as well!

7...♘xc3 8.bxc3 ♕c7 9.♗d2 ♗b7 10.♗d3 d6

11.0–0 ♘d7
11...dxe5?! 12.♘xe5 ♘d7 13.♗b5+–

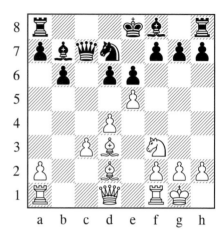

How to cause chaos? Compare this position to the formation after 1.e4 c5 2.d4 cxd4 3.c3 dxc3 4.♘xc3 e6 5.♘f3 a6 6.♗c4 b5 7.♗b3 ♗b7 8.0–0 d6 from the chapter "Into the Deep".

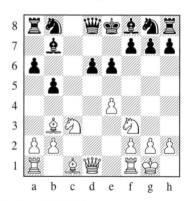

You should find the answer:

12.♘g5!
"WhySoSerious?"[58] – The Joker. As in the Morra Accepted, once the c8-bishop leaves the defense of the e6 Scheveningen structure, ♘g5 followed by ♕h5/♘xe6 violence lurks.

12.♖e1!?
The other main line for those curious. The decliner should be able to endure but the air could get heated.

12...dxe5   13.♘xe5   ♘xe5   14.♖xe5   ♗d6
15.♖h5!?

15.♗b5†!? ♗c6 16.♕f3! ♖c8! (16...0–0–0?!
17.♗xc6 ♗xe5 18.h3 ♔b8 19.a4± when a
brutal attack more than compensates for
the exchange.) 17.♗xc6† ♕xc6 18.d5 ♕b7!
seems to equalize.

15...g6 16.♗b5†!

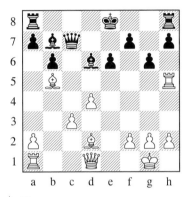

16...♔e7!

16...♗c6 17.♕f3!→

16...♔f8 17.♗h6† ♔g8 18.♕d2!→

17.♖h3

17.♕g4 gxh5 18.♕g5† ♔f8 19.♕h6† ♔e7
20.♕g5†=

17...h5∞

with mutual chances.

12...dxe5

We now pick up the action in Vadja –
Marjanovic, Bucharest 2000, which reached
this position after various earlier transpositions.

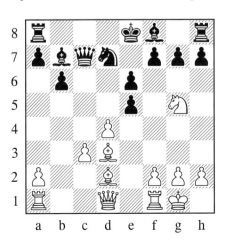

13.♕h5 g6 14.♕h3!

"And I thought my jokes were bad." – The
Joker. ♘xe6 greets the schemer. Instructive
games and dense analysis follow, proving that
even if Black can survive by finding the most
absurdly difficult defenses, the gambiteer will
always be pressing for the win while, most
importantly, having all of the fun!

14...♗e7 15.♖ae1 a6

Stopping the possible menacing pin ♗b5,
but at the expense of a crucial tempo. Now
White unveils the primary weapon in the
attack, the slicing f2-f4 backed by the tanks on
e1 and f1. The decliner's feeble construction
will soon burn.

16.f4! exd4

After   16...♗xg5   17.fxg5⩱   Black's   dark
squares are left to rot, although this was his
only chance. We will showcase the often
necessary ...♗xg5, removing the dangerous g5-
beast at grave positional cost, shortly.

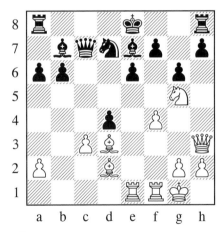

17.♘xf7!

Woohahaha.

17...dxc3

Too late! 3...dxc3, winning a pawn, was best.

17...0–0

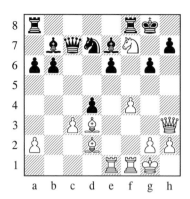

18.f5!+–

Sit back and watch the kingside crumble.

18...♖xf7

18...gxf5 19.♖xf5! exf5 (19...♖xf7 20.♖xf7
♔xf7 21.♕xe6†+–) 20.♖xe7 ♖xf7 21.♖xf7
♔xf7 22.♕xh7† ♔e8 23.♕g6† ♔f8
(23...♔d8 24.♗g5† ♔c8 25.♕e8† ♕d8
26.♕xd8#) 24.♗h6† ♔e7 25.♗g5† ♔f8
26.♕xf5† ♔g8 27.♕h7† ♔f8 28.♗e7† ♔e8
29.♗g6# Mate, mate, always mate.

19.fxg6 ♖xf1† 20.♖xf1 ♘f8 21.g7

21.gxh7† ♔h8 22.♖f7+–

21...♔xg7 22.♕h6† ♔g8 23.♗xh7†! ♘xh7
24.♕g6† ♔h8 25.♖f7+–

Pulverizing.

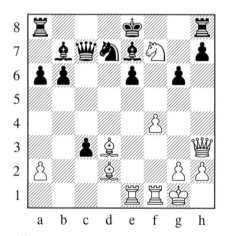

18.♕xe6±

White had the last laugh and went on to win.

Drazen Sermek – Alberto David

Bled 1996

**1.e4 c5 2.d4 cxd4 3.c3 ♘f6 4.e5 ♘d5 5.♘f3
e6 6.cxd4 b6 7.♘c3 ♘xc3 8.bxc3 ♕c7 9.♗d2**

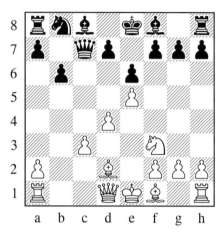

9...♗b7

The alternative move order 9...d6!? fails to alleviate Black's misery as after 10.♗d3 ♘d7 11.♘g5! the schemer must suffer the main line with 11...♗b7 12.0–0, as 11...♗e7?! gets blasted by 12.exd6 ♕xd6 13.♘xf7! ♔xf7 14.♕f3†+–.

**10.♗d3 d6 11.0–0 ♘d7 12.♘g5! dxe5
13.♕h5 g6 14.♕h3**

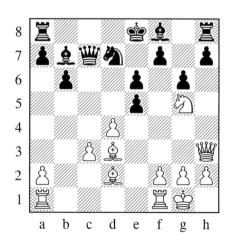

14...♗g7?!

The bishop must stand on e7 as the last line of defense against White's raging attack. But some optimists have simply fianchettoed and turned a blind eye to danger, thus allowing a luminous fireworks display.

15.♖ae1!

15.♘xe6?! is flawed but instructive. 15...fxe6 16.♕xe6† Now Black must choose 16...♔d8∓ rather than: 16...♔f8? 17.♗c4 ♘f6

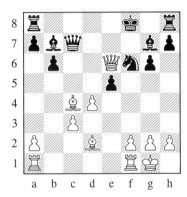

18.♗c1!!+– The ultimate silencer!

15...a6

15...h6? 16.♗xg6±

15...♗d5

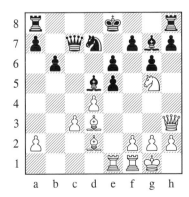

16.c4! ♗xc4 17.♖c1 It's Morra time. 17...b5 18.♗xc4 bxc4 19.♘xe6! fxe6 20.♕xe6† ♔d8 21.♗g5† ♔c8 22.♖xc4+–

15...♗f6 16.♗b5 a6 (16...♗c6 17.♘xe6+–) 17.♘xe6 fxe6 18.♕xe6† ♗e7 19.♗g5±

16.f4! e4 17.♗xe4 ♗xe4 18.♖xe4 ♘f6 19.♖xe6† fxe6 20.♕xe6†

Black resigned, in view of 20...♔f8 21.♗c1!+–. "I like this job, I like it." – The Joker.

1–0

Emre Can – Daniel Ludwig

Vung Tau City 2008

1.e4 c5 2.d4 cxd4 3.c3 ♘f6 4.e5 ♘d5 5.♘f3 e6 6.cxd4 b6 7.♘c3 ♘xc3 8.bxc3 ♕c7 9.♗d2 ♗b7 10.♗d3 d6 11.0-0 ♘d7 12.♘g5! dxe5 13.♕h5 g6 14.♕h3 ♗e7 15.♖ae1

The critical position. Now the decliner has a number of defenses, all leading to mayhem.

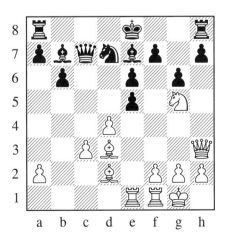

15...♗d5!?

After 15...♗xg5? 16.♗xg5± there are tremors rippling through the dark squares.

15...a6!? 16.f4 ♗xg5 17.fxg5 0–0 18.♖e3→

15...♕d8!?

Just begging to be hit.

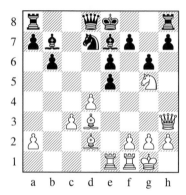

16.♘xe6! fxe6 17.♕xe6

17.♗xg6†?! hxg6 18.♕xh8† ♔f8⇄

17...♕c7

a) 17...♖f8 18.♗g5+– ♘f6 (18...a6 19.f4! is crushing) 19.♗b5† ♘d7 20.♖xe5 ♖f7 21.♗xe7 ♖xe7 22.♕g8# Picturesque.

b) 17...♖c8 18.♗xg6† hxg6 19.♕xg6† ♔f8 20.dxe5 White's down a piece or two, but Black's down a king. 20...♖c6 21.e6 ♕e8 22.♗h6† ♖xh6 23.♕xh6† ♔g8 24.♖e3+–

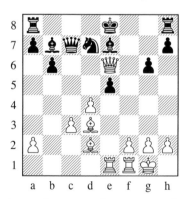

Perhaps the most fascinating of all the variations here. The materialistic machine at first sides with the schemer, but eventually

must admit White's dominance.

18.♗b5! ♔d8 19.c4! ♕d6 20.♕h3! exd4
20...a6 21.♗b4!±
20...♕c7 21.c5→ shreds the c-file.
21.♗f4+–

15...♕d6!?

The computer's top choice – bulking up on e6.

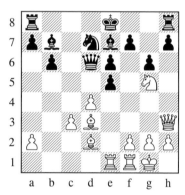

16.♗e4!

So the gambiteer must get creative.

After 16.f4!? Black lives: 16...♗xg5! (16...exd4?! invites entropy down the f-file. For example: 17.f5! exf5 18.♗xf5 gxf5 19.♘xf7 ♔xf7 20.♖xf5† ♘f6 [20...♗f6 21.♕h5† ♔g8 22.♗h6! ♘f8 23.♖ef1! ♕c6 24.♖g5†+–] 21.♗f4! ♕c6 22.♕h5† ♔g8 23.♖g5† ♔f8 24.♕h6† ♔f8 25.♕g7+–) 17.fxg5⩲ 0–0 18.♕h6 ♕e7 19.♖e3 f5!⇄ The typical defensive scheme in action.

16...♗xe4 17.♘xe4 ♕d5 18.dxe5 ♘xe5

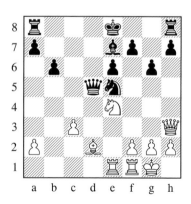

19.c4 ♘xc4 20.♗b4!⩲

20.♗c3 e5∓

20...♖c8 21.♗c3

21.♗xe7 ♔xe7 22.♕h4† ♔f8 23.♕h6†
♔e7=

21...♖f8 22.♘f6† ♗xf6 23.♗xf6→

16.f4!

Ludwig has temporarily averted disaster on e6, but the tanks still plow forward.

16.♕h6?! ♗f8 17.♕h3 ♗e7 18.♕h6=

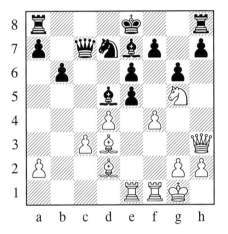

16...exd4

Again, the knight must be snapped off – an unpleasant reality for the decliner:

16...♖xg5 17.fxg5 0–0 18.♕h4 ♕c6 19.♖e3!→
Boldness as always.

19...♗xg2 20.♖f2

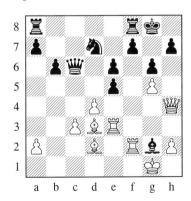

20...e4!

Highlighting the sort of defensive abilities required for the schemer to survive to a middlegame.

20...♗h1?! 21.♖h3 h5 22.gxh6 ♔h8
(22...♔h7 23.♗xg6† fxg6 24.♕e7†+−)
23.dxe5 The thrust h6-h7 △♗g5-f6/e7 hangs over the black king's head.

21.♗e2 ♗f3 22.♗xf3 exf3 23.♖exf3

Black's still a pawn up, but the pain continues.

23...♖ae8!

23...e5 24.♖h3 h5 25.gxh6 ♔h7 26.♖hf3
♕e6 (26...f6 27.dxe5 ♘xe5 28.♖xf6 ♖xf6
29.♕xf6 ♕xf6 30.♖xf6± Let the endgame fun begin.) 27.d5! ♕xd5 28.♕e7 ♔g8 29.c4
♕e6 30.♕xe6 fxe6

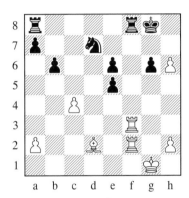

31.h7† ♔h8 (31...♔g7 32.♗h6† ♔xh6
33.♖xf8+−) 32.♖f7! ♖xf7 33.♖xf7 ♘c5
34.♗c3 ♘d3 35.♖d7+− White triumphs after 35 moves of pure precision.

24.♗c1

24.♕h6 ♖e7 25.♖h3? f5!∓ The defensive saving grace reappears.

24...f6 25.gxf6 ♖f7 26.♗a3 e5 27.♗e7→

This may be Black's best, but the battle rages afresh.

17.cxd4 ♕d6

17...♗xg5 18.fxg5 ♕c6 19.♖f4→

18.f5!

It's over. White's overwhelming forces rip through.

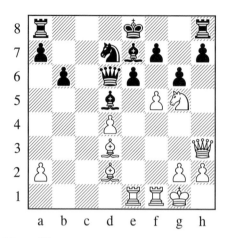

18...gxf5

18...♗xg5 19.♗xg5 0–0 20.♕h6± exf5
21.♗xf5 f6 (21...♖ae8 22.♖xe8 ♖xe8
23.♗xd7+–) 22.♗xg6 hxg6 23.♕xg6† ♔h8
24.♖e3 ♗e6 25.♖e4+–

18...exf5 19.♗xf5 gxf5 20.♕xf5 ♖f8 (20...♖c8;
20...0-0-0 "Run, Forrest, run!" 21.♗f4 ♗e6
22.♕c2†+–) 21.♗b4! ♕xb4 22.♕xd5 0-0-0
23.♕a8† ♘b8 24.♖c1† ♔d7 25.♘xf7 ♖c8
26.♕b7† ♔e6 27.d5# Woohahahaha.

19.♗xf5! ♗xg5

19...♘f6 20.♗d3± and the tanks fire at will.

20.♗xg5 ♖g8 21.♕h5 h6

Children, cover your eyes.

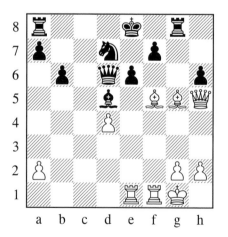

22.♗xe6! ♖xg5

22...♗xe6 23.♕xf7#!

**23.♕xf7† ♔d8 24.♗xd5+– ♕xd5 25.♖e8†
♔c7 26.♕xd5 ♖xe8 27.♖c1†**

Black resigned, in view of: 27...♔d8
28.♕a8† ♔e7 29.♖e1†+– "WhySoSerious?"
1–0

Ogulcan Kanmazalp – Aleksa Strikovic

Istanbul 2010

A parting shot for the Alapin-Morra's ♘g5.

**1.e4 c5 2.♘f3 e6 3.c3 ♘f6 4.e5 ♘d5 5.d4
cxd4 6.cxd4 b6 7.♘c3 ♘xc3 8.bxc3 ♕c7
9.♗d2 d6 10.♗d3 ♘d7 11.♘g5! ♗b7 12.0–0
dxe5 13.♕h5 g6 14.♕h3 ♗e7 15.♖ae1 ♗d5
16.f4 ♗xg5 17.fxg5 ♖c8**

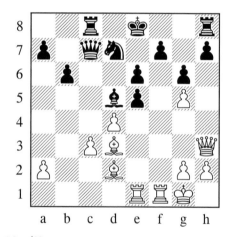

18.c4?!

18.♕h6!± is stronger, and a searing attack
follows. But it is certainly not as spectacular
as the game!

18...♗xc4 19.♗xc4 ♕xc4 20.♖c1 ♕a6?!

The c-file magic hypnotizes the grandmaster.
But only an absurd resource could save him:
20...♕xd4†! 21.♗e3 ♖xc1 22.♖xc1?!
22.♗xd4 ♖xf1† 23.♔xf1 exd4∓

22...♕b4!–+ 23.♗d2!

23.♖c8†?? ♚e7 24.♖xh8 ♕e1#

And now...

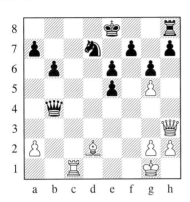

23...♕a4!–+

A miraculous escape! Instead 23...♕xd2? would only draw: 24.♖c8† ♚e7 25.♕a3† ♞c5 26.♕xa7† ♞d7 27.♕a3†!=

21.♗b4!

Razor sharp!

21...exd4

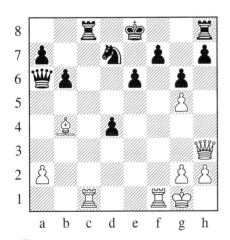

22.♕a3!

22.♕d3!+– When possible, I strongly advise to hang your queen to please the raucous crowd.

22...♕b7 23.♕f3!
1–0

The Morra Returns – Analysis

1.e4 c5 2.d4 cxd4 3.c3 ♞f6 4.e5 ♞d5 5.♞f3 ♞c6

The decliner's last Alapin hideout. But soon he'll be living the nightmare of 3...dxc3 all over again as we unleash chaos with a barrage of Morra themes.

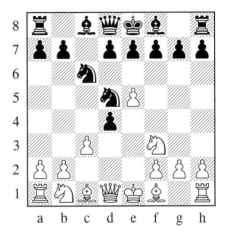

6.♗c4!

Offering up the c-pawn, which the schemer may "win" with ...♞b6.

6...♞b6

6...e6!? is a viable transposition, although I've only seen this move order a few times in the 100+ games I've had here. In my experience, when decliners play 5...♞c6, they overwhelmingly intend to meet 6.♗c4 with the instantaneous 6...♞b6. Nevertheless, so you are not surprised by a schemer, on 6...e6 you may enter the hyper-aggressive variation 7.cxd4 d6 8.0–0 ♗e7 9.♕e2 featured in the supplemental games, or proceed more positionally with 9.a3!? followed by a swift ♗d3 as in the Tiviakov games covered earlier (see Kharlov – Gallagher, Calcutta 2001).

7.♗b3 d6

7...d5 transposes to the main line after 8.exd6.

7...dxc3!?

Almost never ventured! Hardly a shock, for our declining antagonist will scheme until the bitter end. But soon, he will have no choice but to stare down mayhem.

8.♘xc3⇄

Welcome back, Morra Gambit. We've missed you.[59]

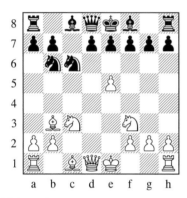

8...d6 9.0–0!→

9.exd6!? ♕xd6 10.♕xd6 exd6 11.♘b5 ♖b8 12.♗f4→ Inflicting damage.

9...dxe5?! 10.♕xd8† ♔xd8

10...♔xd8 11.♘g5+–

11.♘b5+–

We find ourselves in a hologram of Taylor's treacherous Temple, where Black is quickly doomed.

7...g6!?

Attempting to spring a Dragon, but the gambiteer clips its wings.

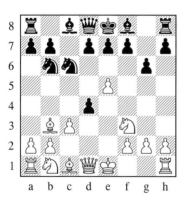

8.♘g5!

"WhySoSerious?" It's Fried Liver time!

8...d5

a) 8...♘xe5? 9.♕xd4± ♗g7?! 10.♗xf7†! ♔f8 11.♘e6†+– illustrates the preliminary tactics which justify the raid.

b) 8...e6?! Remember, ...g6 plus ...e6 just doesn't fly in a Dragon! 9.cxd4 d6 10.♕f3! ♕d7 11.♕f6 ♖g8 12.♘xh7 ♗g7 (12...♗e7 13.♘c3 "Come on, come on, I want you to do it, I want you to do it, come on, hit me." – The Joker. 13...♘xd4 14.♗g5!±) 13.♕xg7!+– Woohahaha.

9.exd6 e6 10.♕f3!

A scholar's mate?

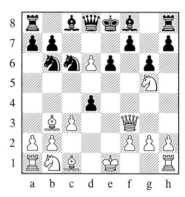

10...♘e5 11.♕g3 ♗xd6 12.♘e4 0–0

12...f6 13.0–0 ♘f7 14.♘xd6† ♘xd6 15.♖d1± The Morra rook and bishops ensure an endless assault.

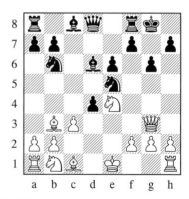

13.♘xd6!

13.♗h6!? ♗c7! (13...♖e8?   14.♗g5!+−)
14.♗xf8 ♔xf8∞
13...♕xd6 14.0–0 ♘ec4 15.♕h4!→
Dining on the dark squares.

8.exd6 ♕xd6 9.0–0!

Once a gambiteer, always a gambiteer,
through thick and thin.

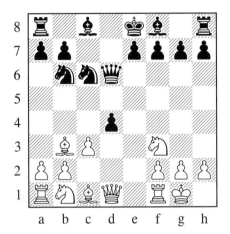

9...♗e6

One of the schemer's most popular attempts
in his search for sterility. But try as he might
to impose order, chaos will come. The rarer
alternatives do not impress.

9...dxc3
Very unschemerly!
10.♕e2!?
The bold swashbuckler's move.
10.♘xc3 ♕xd1 11.♖xd1 ♗g4 12.♘b5 ♖c8
13.♗e3 a6 14.♗xb6 axb5 15.♖d5± with a
permanent press.
10...cxb2
Ah, another Danish-Morra.
10...♕f6?! 11.♘xc3 ♗g4 12.♘e4 ♕g6
13.♗xf7†! ♔xf7 14.♘fg5† ♔e8 15.♕xg4±
Jerez Perez – Matuszewski, Rewal 2007.
11.♗xb2∞

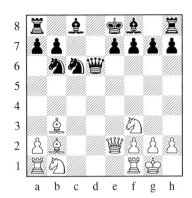

White has compensation for the pawns. A
possible continuation is:
11...♗g4 12.♗xf7† ♔xf7 13.♘g5†→

9...♗f5?! 10.♘xd4 We restore the material
balance, if only for a moment before busting
through the center: 10...♘xd4 11.cxd4 e6
12.♘c3 ♗e7 13.♕f3 0–0 14.d5!±

9...e6!? 10.cxd4 ♗e7 11.♘c3→ Black with
his offside b6-knight struggles to contain the
enormous dynamic energy of the isolated pawn.
The steed has travelled too far from its optimal
post on f6 (where it simultaneously defends
the kingside and eyes the turbulent d5-square).
White swiftly capitalized on such misfortune
with a bruising attack in the supplemental
game Karpatchev – Rauschenbach, Griesheim
2002.

9...d3?! The Morra double-declined (first
...♘f6, then ...d3!). Very soft indeed! Denied
a clear path through the main door (c3), the
knight, nostrils flaring, storms through the side
entrance: 10.♘a3!± ♗f5 (10...a6 11.♗e3 ♘d7
12.♘g5 e6 13.♘e4± and the queen will put
the cowardly pawn out of its misery.) 11.♘b5
♕d7 12.♖e1 a6 13.♘bd4 ♘xd4 14.♗xf7†!+−
"I like this job. I like it." – The Joker.

10.♘a3!

"Good evening, ladies and gentlemen. We
are... tonight's entertainment." – The Joker.

Will the decliner at long last face his worst fears and take on c3?

For years, I believed that the liquidating 10.♗xe6 ♕xe6 11.♘xd4 ♘xd4 12.cxd4!? with rapid development (although such exchanges generally play into the schemer's hands) offered serious chances for a chaotic advantage. But I cannot resist 10.♘a3, both for objective reasons, and because, well, it's just too much fun! However, if you're ever in need of a second bazooka, see Esserman – Sasikiran, Internet (blitz) 2011, for a wild throwdown.

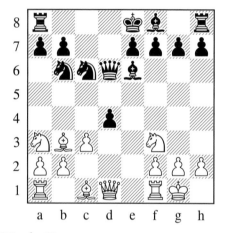

10...dxc3!

The main line of the Morra Accepted – I mean Declined! The schemer feels compelled to take, against his better judgment.

On the other hand, continuing with the policy of "trade, trade, draw" leads to long-term positional pain for Black:
10...♗xb3 11.♕xb3 ♕d5!?
　Tried by such a titan as Kramnik, albeit vs. the c3-Sicilian. I doubt the 14th World Champion would decline the challenge of 3...dxc3!.
　a) For 11...dxc3?! stay tuned...
　b) 11...e6 12.♘b5 Neiiighhh. 12...♕d7 13.♘bxd4 ♘xd4 14.♘xd4 ♗e7 15.♖d1 0–0 16.♘f5! (For 16.♗e3!? see Pavasovic

– Schandorff, Gothenburg 2005, in the supplemental games.) 16...♕e8 17.♘xe7† ♕xe7 18.♗e3 ♘d5 19.♗d4± with c3-c4 to come. The gambiteer, possessing the better bishop and an aggressive queenside pawn majority, must put on his technical torture hat and punish the decliner for such insipid play.

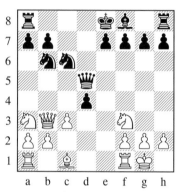

12.♘b5 ♖c8 13.♘fxd4

If Black rushes to exchange on b3, the pressure on the a-file, which at first seems slight, may become unbearable.

13...♘xd4 14.♘xd4 e6 15.♖d1 ♗c5

15...♗e7?! 16.♗e3!± ♘c4? 17.♘b5!+– ♕f5 18.♘xa7 ♘xe3 19.♘xc8 ♘xd1 20.♖xd1 and White coasted to victory in Doncevic – Juhnke, Bundesliga 1985.

15...♕xb3 16.axb3 became a-file annihilation in Zarnicki – Van Wely, Buenos Aires 1995: 16...a6 17.b4!→ ♗e7 18.b5!± axb5 19.♖a7!± Mass trading does not always lead to draws! 19...b4 20.♖xb7 ♘d5 21.♘f5! See page 343 for the finish.

16.♕b5† ♕d7!?

A schemer who has studied the theoretical tomes of the c3-Sicilian may believe that this obvious counter guarantees precious equality after 17.♕e2 ♕e7, but the gambiteer has another vision. The Joker: "We really should stop all this fighting or we'll miss all the fireworks." Batman: "There won't be any fireworks." (The Dark Knight)

16...♔e7?! 17.♕e2± and Black's king roasted in Benjamin – Wolff, New York 1996.

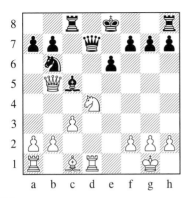

17.♕f1!!

A sublime, game-changing retreat, clearing the e-file for outrageous action.

17...♕c7

17...♕e7 18.♘f5! ♕f6 19.♕b5† ♖c6 20.♘d4 ♗xd4 21.♖xd4 0–0 22.♗g5 ♕f5 23.♕xf5 exf5 24.♖b4± The decliner, euphoric over surviving the opening, now crashes into the reality of a depressing ending.

18.♘b5 ♕b8 19.g3±

And we laugh heartily at the black queen's return to Siberia.

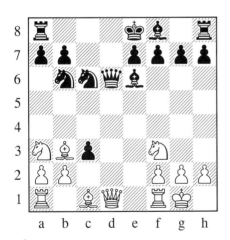

11.♗xe6!

The schemer dares ...dxc3 only because White's common attacking plans are known to fail. However, after this freestyling, super-rare capture, Black won't know where to turn.

11.♘b5?! ♕xd1 12.♖xd1 ♖c8 13.♗xe6 fxe6 14.bxc3 ♘c4∓ Morozevich – Topalov, Monte Carlo (rapid) 2002.

11.♕e2?! is thematic, but flawed: 11...♗xb3 12.♘b5 ♕b8 13.axb3 e6 and the gambiteer slams into a brick wall.

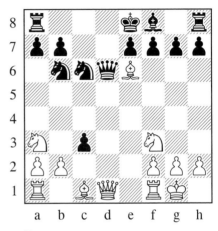

11...♕xd1

11...♕xe6!?N 12.♘b5 ♕d7 13.♕e2 ♖c8 (13...♖d8 14.♗f4→ is promising for White; 13...0–0–0 14.♘xc3⯰ results in a Morra with the black king on the c-file!) 14.bxc3 a6 15.♖d1 ♕e6 16.♕xe6 fxe6 17.♘bd4⯰ With similar mayhem to the main line below.

12.♖xd1 fxe6 13.bxc3⯰

Alas, we're a pawn down. What else is new? Well, the irrepressible Morra rooks now shift from the c- and d- to the b- and d-files, and maybe even the e-file. And, of course, the decliner's extra pawn is now in the form of one of those mangled creatures on e7 and e6 (take your pick), stunting his development. Naturally, we've got compensation for the material, and then some. I'll finish with a bang.

13...♘a4

13...a6? 14.♖b1!± or 13...♖c8 14.♖b1→.

14.♘b5N ♖c8 15.♗f4→

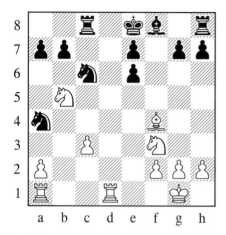

15...e5!?

The schemer squirms to escape the gripping bind in all variations. "A little fight in ya. I like that." – The Joker.

15...h6!? 16.♘c7† ♔f7 17.♘e5† ♘xe5 (17...♔g8? 18.♘xc6 bxc6 19.♘xe6 ♘xc3 20.♖d7±) 18.♗xe5 ♘xc3!? 19.♖d3 ♘d5 20.♖f3† ♘f6 21.♖e1 g5 22.♘xe6!→

15...g6!? 16.♘c7† ♔f7 17.♘g5† ♔g8 18.♘gxe6 ♘xc3 19.♖d2 ♗g7 20.♘xg7 ♔xg7 21.♖e1 Mayhem and maiming awaits but the slightest inaccuracy.

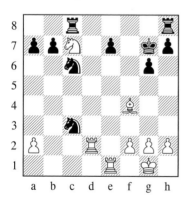

21...e5? (21...♔f7! 22.♘e6→) 22.♖d7†+– ♔f6 23.♗h6! ♖hg8 (23...♖hd8 24.♗g7† Headhunting. 24...♔f5 25.♖f7† ♔g4 26.f3† ♔h5 27.g4† ♔h4 28.♗f6† g5 29.♖xh7#) 24.f4! exf4 25.♖e6† ♔f5 26.♖f7† ♔g4

27.h3† ♔h5 28.♗xf4 h6 29.♖f5† gxf5 30.♖xh6#

16.♘xe5 ♘xe5

16...a6 17.♘xc6 ♖xc6 (17...axb5 18.♘a7!±) 18.♘d4 ♖xc3 (18...♖c4 19.♘e6 ♘xc3 20.♖d8† ♔f7 21.♖e1→) 19.♖ac1! The Morra rooks return with a vengeance! 19...♖xc1 20.♖xc1 ♔f7 21.♖c7 b6 22.♘f3±

17.♗xe5 ♖c5 18.♘c7† ♔f7 19.♖e1 ♘xc3

20.♘e6! ♖c8 21.♔f1!

21.♖ac1?? ♘e2†–+

21...♘d5 22.♖ad1±

The rooks rage. Wooohaha.

We conclude with a battle between two of my close friends, FMs Eric Rodriguez and Charles Riordan. However, in this one, I'll be picking sides. Can you guess which one?

Eric Rodriguez – Charles Riordan

US Chess League, Internet 2011

1.e4 c5 2.d4!

Rodriguez, tired of ten-plus years in the Catalan, unleashes his first ever Morra Gambit. Boy, does he deliver!

2...cxd4 3.c3 ♘f6 4.e5 ♘d5 5.♘f3 ♘c6 6.♗c4! ♘b6 7.♗b3 d5 8.exd6 ♕xd6 9.0–0 ♗e6 10.♘a3! ♗xb3 11.♕xb3 dxc3?!

3...dxc3, winning a pawn, was better.

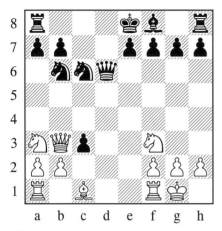

12.♘b5!

"You've changed things. Forever. There's no going back" – The Joker.

12...♕b8

Back to Siberia she goes.

13.♘g5!

"And here... we... go!" – The Joker.

13...e6

Having been on the receiving end of too many maniacal Morra ♘xe6 assaults, Eric knows what to do.

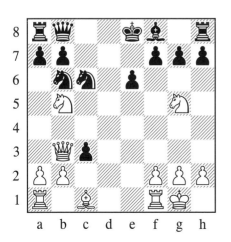

14.♘xe6!

"WhySoSerious?" – The Joker.

14...fxe6 15.♕xe6† ♗e7 16.♖e1!N[60]

16.♗g5? ♕e5!∓

16...♔f8

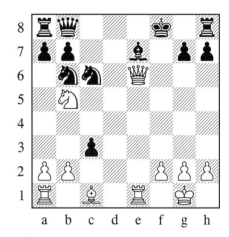

17.♖e3!?

17.♕f5†!? ♔f6 18.♗h6! ♘d5 (18...♔g8? 19.♕e6† ♔f8 20.♕xf6† ♔g8 21.♕xg7# or 18...♔f7 19.♗f4 ♕d8 20.♖ad1+−) 19.♖e6! gxh6 20.♖xf6† ♘xf6 21.♕xf6† ♔g8 22.♘d6 ♕f8 23.♕e6† ♔g7 24.♘f5†+− Woohahahaha.

17...♕c8

17...♕d8 18.♖f3† ♗f6 19.♗f4 ♘c8 20.♗h6! +− "How about a magic trick?" – The Joker.

18.♖f3† ♗f6 19.♖xf6†!

"I just did what I do best. I took your little plan and turned it on itself" – The Joker.

19...gxf6 20.♗h6#!

I leave you with the Joker philosophy, an inspiration for the gambiteer: "Do I really look like a guy with a plan? Do you know what I am? I'm a dog chasing cars. I wouldn't know what to do with one if I caught it. I just doooo things. They're schemers... schemers trying to control their little worlds. I'm not a schemer. I try and show the schemers how... pathetic... their attempts to control things really are. You were a schemer. You had plans. And look where that got ya." – The Joker.

May the Romantic style once again reign supreme in the 21st century.

Appendix

Supplemental Games

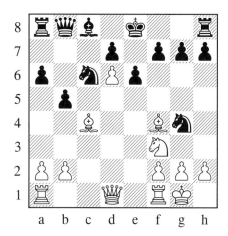

White to play – Morra style!

"I've always considered the Morra a bit of a joke... It's a perfectly reasonable choice for those playing with ratings of 1900 and below. But if we decide to give the Smith-Morra Gambit an honest grade as to its true theoretical worth, we have to throw it on the garbage heap along with other 'toss it out and cross your fingers' systems."[61]
– IM Jeremy Silman

Siberian Wilderness

RawFishStomach (Esserman) – RolMar (IM)

Internet (blitz) 2011

1.e4 c5 2.d4 cxd4 3.c3 dxc3 4.♘xc3 ♘c6
5.♘f3 e6 6.♗c4 ♕c7 7.0–0 ♘f6 8.♘b5 ♕b8
9.e5 ♘g4 10.♗f4 a6 11.♘d6† ♗xd6 12.exd6
b5

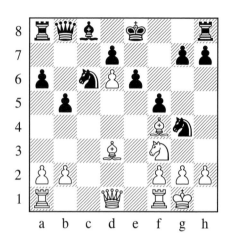

14.♗xf5!+– exf5 15.♖e1† ♔f8 16.♕d5 ♘f6
17.♕xf5 h6 18.♘e5 ♘d4 19.♕g6 ♔g8
20.♘g4
1–0

ClubberLang (Esserman)– Elgransenor (GM Gormally)

Internet (blitz) 2005

1.e4 c5 2.d4 cxd4 3.c3 dxc3 4.♘xc3 ♘c6
5.♘f3 e6 6.♗c4 ♘f6 7.0–0 ♕c7 8.♘b5 ♕b8
9.e5 ♘g4 10.♗f4 a6 11.♘d6† ♗xd6 12.exd6
0–0 13.h3 ♘f6 14.♗b3!?
   14.♘e5!

14...♘h5 15.♗h2 f5?

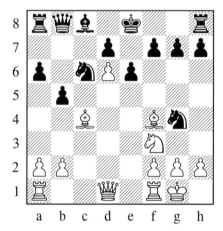

13.♗b3
   13.♗d5!!±

13...f5? 14.♗xe6! dxe6 15.d7† ♗xd7
16.♗xb8+– ♖xb8 17.♕d6 ♖d8 18.♖fe1
♘f6 19.♖xe6† ♗xe6 20.♕xe6† ♘e7 21.♖e1
♘e4 22.♘e5 ♖f8 23.♘c6 ♖d7 24.♘xe7 ♖f6
25.♕g8† ♔xe7 26.f3 ♖f8 27.♕xg7† ♔e8
1–0

Esserman – N.N. (GM)

Internet (blitz) 2010

1.e4 c5 2.d4 cxd4 3.c3 dxc3 4.♘xc3 e6
5.♘f3 ♘c6 6.♗c4 ♕c7 7.0–0 ♘f6 8.♘b5
♕b8 9.e5 ♘g4 10.♗f4 a6 11.♘d6† ♗xd6
12.exd6 b5 13.♗d3
   13.♗d5!!±

13...f5?

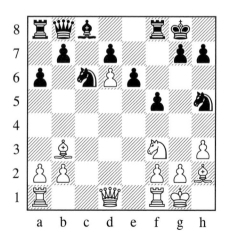

16.&c2

16.&g5! &f6 17.&xe6 dxe6 18.d7 &a7
19.dxc8=&!+–

**16...b5 17.g4 fxg4 18.hxg4 &f6 19.g5 &d5
20.&h4 &cb4**

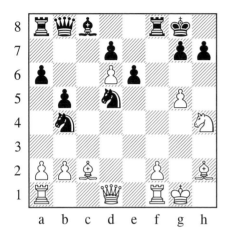

**21.&xh7†! &xh7 22.&h5† &g8 23.&g6
&f5 24.&h8† &f7 25.&e5† &xe5 26.&xe5
&g6 27.&xg7† &f5 28.&ae1 &b7 29.&h7†
&xg5 30.f4† &g4 31.&g6† &h4 32.&e2
1–0**

The Scheveningens

Marc Esserman – Ian Mangion

Kenilworth Simul 2010

**1.e4 c5 2.d4 cxd4 3.c3 dxc3 4.&xc3 &c6
5.&f3 d6 6.&c4 e6 7.0–0 &e7 8.&e2 &f6
9.&d1 e5 10.&e3 0–0 11.&ac1 &e6 12.b4 a6
13.a3 &c8?**

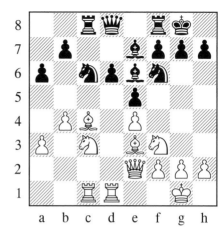

**14.&xe6! fxe6 15.&a2± &d7 16.&a4 &d4
17.&xd4 exd4 18.&xc8 &xc8**

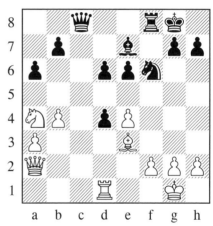

**19.&b6 &e8 20.&xe6† &f7 21.&xf7†
&xf7 22.&xd4 &d8 23.f3 &e8 24.&f2 &c7
25.&d3 &e6 26.&c3 &f6 27.&c4 g6 28.&d5
&g7 29.a4 &d7 30.g3 h5 31.f4 &h6 32.&e2
&g7 33.h3 &f8 34.g4 hxg4 35.hxg4 &g7
36.g5 &d8 37.b5 axb5 38.axb5 &e6 39.b6
&d8 40.&c7 &e8 41.f5
1–0**

Marc Esserman – Mark Kernighan

Kenilworth Simul 2010

**1.e4 c5 2.d4 cxd4 3.c3 dxc3 4.&xc3 d6
5.&f3 e6 6.&c4 &e7 7.0–0 &c6 8.&e2 &f6**

9.♖d1 e5 10.♗e3 0–0 11.♖ac1 ♗g4 12.h3
♗h5 13.g4 ♗g6 14.♘h4! ♔h8 15.♘f5
  15.♘xg6†!?hxg6 16.a3 ♘d7 17.♕d2!±

15...♘e8

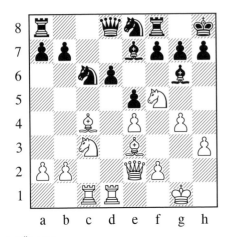

16.♘d5?!
  16.♕d2!±

16...♗g5! 17.b4 ♗xe3 18.fxe3 ♗xf5 19.exf5
♘f6 20.b5 ♘a5 21.♘xf6 ♕xf6 22.♘d5 ♖ac8
23.♕d2 ♖xc1?!
  23...b6!∞

24.♖xc1± ♕d8 25.♕c3 ♕b6 26.♗xf7 g6
27.f6 ♕d8

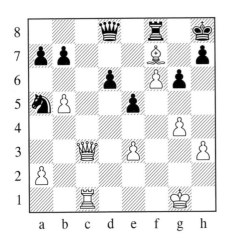

28.♕c7
  28.g5! ♖xf7 29.♕xa5!+−

28...♕xf6 29.♖f1 ♕d8 30.♕xd8 ♖xd8
31.♗d5 ♖d7 32.♖f8† ♔g7 33.♖a8 b6 34.g5
h6 35.h4 hxg5 36.hxg5 ♔h7 37.♔f2 ♔g7
38.♔f3 ♘b7 39.♖xa7 ♘c5 40.♖a8 ♘d3
41.a4 ♘c5 42.a5 bxa5 43.b6 a4 44.♖a7
a3 45.♗e6 ♘b7 46.♗d5 ♖d7 47.♖xa3 ♖d8
48.♖a7† ♔h8 49.b7 ♘d7 50.♖a8 ♘b8
51.♗e6 ♔g7 52.♗c8 ♘c6 53.b8=♕ ♘xb8
54.♖xb8 d5 55.♖b7† ♔h8 56.♗e6 d4
57.♖c7 e4† 58.♔xe4 dxe3 59.♔xe3 ♖b8
  59...♖d3† 60.♔f4 ♖f3† 61.♔g4 ♖g3†
62.♔h4+−

60.♖c8†
1–0

Mladen Zelic – Andrej Grilc

Bled 1994

1.e4 c5 2.d4 cxd4 3.c3 dxc3 4.♘xc3 ♘c6
5.♘f3 d6 6.♗c4 e6 7.0–0 ♘f6 8.♕e2 ♗e7
9.♖d1 e5 10.♗e3 0–0 11.♖ac1 ♗e6 12.b4
♗xc4 13.♕xc4 ♖c8 14.♕b3 ♘g4?!

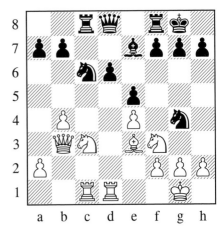

15.♘d5! ♘xe3 16.♕xe3 a6 17.a4± ♖e8
18.b5 ♘d4 19.♘xd4 ♖xc1 20.♖xc1 exd4
21.♕xd4 axb5 22.axb5 ♗f8 23.f3

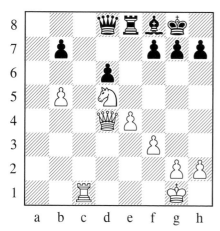

23...f5 24.exf5 ♕g5 25.♕c4 ♔h8 26.g4
h5 27.♕f4 ♕h4 28.♕g3 ♕g5 29.♘f4 h4
30.♕xh4† ♕xh4 31.♘g6† ♔g8 32.♘xh4
♗e7 33.♘g6 ♗f6 34.♖c7 b6 35.♔g2 ♗d4
36.♔g3 ♗c5 37.♖d7 ♖a8 38.g5 ♗e3 39.f6
gxf6 40.gxf6 ♗d4 41.♖g7#
1–0

Into the Deep

kklinheib (Esserman/GM Friedel) – ChessRaptor

Internet (blitz) 2008

1.e4 c5 2.d4 cxd4 3.c3 dxc3 4.♘xc3 e6
5.♘f3 a6 6.♗c4 b5 7.♗b3 ♗b7 8.0–0 b4
9.♘d5 d6?

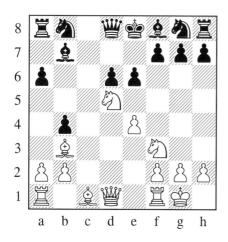

10.♗g5
10.♗a4† ♘d7 11.♗xd7† ♕xd7 12.♘b6±

10...♕a5 11.♖c1+–
11.♗a4†+– ♘d7 12.♗xd7† ♔xd7 13.♘e5†
dxe5 14.♘b6† ♔e8 (14...♔c7 15.♘xa8† ♔b8
16.♗d8! ♕b5 17.♗c7† ♔xa8 18.♕d8†+–)
15.♕d7#

11...exd5 12.exd5
12.♗xd5 ♗xd5 13.♖c8† ♔d7 14.♖xf8+–

12...♗e7 13.♖e1 ♔f8 14.♕e2
14.♗xe7† ♘xe7 15.♘d4 ♘d7 16.♘c6+–

14...♕d8 15.♗f4 ♘f6 16.♘d4+– ♗xd5

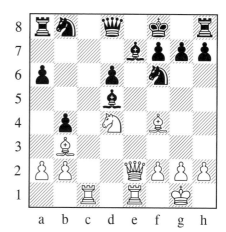

17.♕xe7†! ♕xe7 18.♖c8† ♘e8 19.♗xd6!
♘c6 20.♖xa8 g6 21.♗xe7† ♘xe7 22.♗xd5
1–0

LarryC (GM Christiansen) – BlackSky

Internet (blitz) 2003

1.e4 c5 2.d4 cxd4 3.c3 dxc3 4.♘xc3 e6
5.♘f3 a6 6.♗c4 b5 7.♗b3 ♗b7 8.0–0 b4
9.♘d5 exd5 10.exd5 d6 11.♖e1†!
11.♕d4!?∞

11...♗e7 12.♘d4!?
12.♕d4!?→

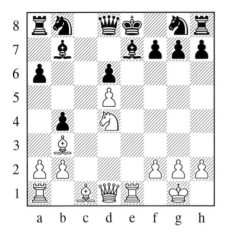

Can Black survive the middlegame?!
Descend deeper...

12...g6?

12...♘d7?!

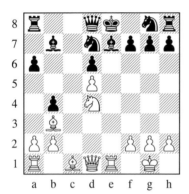

13.♘f5! ♔f8 14.♕g4 ♗f6 (14...g6 15.♘xe7 ♘xe7 16.♕xb4 ♘c5 17.♗g5+–) 15.♕xb4 ♕b6 16.♕xd6† ♕xd6 17.♘xd6±

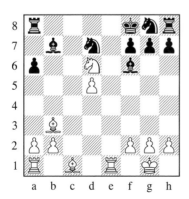

17...♘c5 (17...♖b8 18.♗f4±) 18.♗c4 ♖d8 19.♗e3 ♖xd6 20.♗xc5 ♗e7 21.♗b3 ♖d7 22.d6!+– ♗f6 23.♗a4 ♖d8 24.♖e8†! ♖xe8 25.d7† ♘e7 26.dxe8=♖#

12...♔f8 13.♗f4

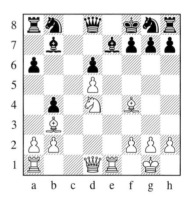

13...♗c8?!

 a) 13...g5? 14.♖xe7!+–

 b) 13...♘d7 14.♘c6! ♕b6 15.♖xe7! ♘xe7 16.♗xd6 ♖e8 (16...♗xc6 17.dxc6 ♕xc6 18.♖c1 ♕b7 19.♗d5+–) 17.♕c2±

 c) 13...a5 Grim... 14.♖c1± ♘a6 (14...♘d7 15.♘f5 ♖a6 16.♖c6!+–) 15.♘f5 ♗c8 16.♖xc8 ♖xc8 (16...♕xc8 17.♘xd6 ♕c7 18.♘xf7 ♕xf4 19.d6!±) 17.♕g4 g6 18.♘xe7 ♘xe7 19.♗h6† ♔g8 (19...♖e8 20.♗a4†) 20.♖xe7±

14.♖c1 g5 15.♖xe7 gxf4 16.♖ec7 ♘d7 17.♕f3 ♘c5 18.♘e6†!+–

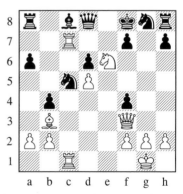

18...♗xe6 19.dxe6 ♕xc7 20.♕xa8† ♔g7 21.exf7 ♘f6 22.♕xh8†!+–

13.♕f3+– ♘d7 14.♗g5
14.♘c6+–

14...♘e5

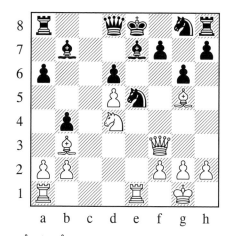

15.♗a4†! ♗c6
15...♔f8 16.♘e6#!

16.♗xc6† ♘xc6 17.♘xc6 ♕d7

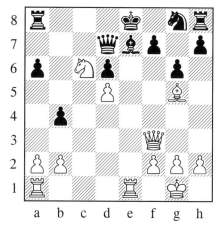

18.♖xe7†! ♘xe7 19.♖e1 0–0 20.♘xe7†
Who said blitz was bad for your chess?!
1–0

Chicago Defense

Marc Esserman – N.N. (GM)

Internet (blitz) 2010

1.e4 c5 2.d4 cxd4 3.c3 dxc3 4.♘xc3 e6 5.♘f3 d6 6.♗c4 a6 7.0–0 b5 8.♗b3 ♖a7 9.♗e3 ♖d7 10.♘d4 ♗b7 11.f4 b4 12.f5! e5

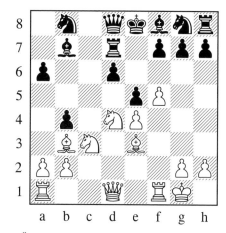

13.♘e6! fxe6 14.fxe6+–
14.♕h5†!+–

14...♖e7 15.♘d5 ♗xd5 16.exd5 ♖b7 17.♗a4† ♖b5 18.♕h5† g6 19.♕f3
Black resigned, as 19...♕e7 can be met by either 20.♖ac1! or 20.♗g5!.
1–0

Edward Friedman – Roman Dzindzichashvili

Chicago 1991

1.e4 c5 2.d4 cxd4 3.c3 dxc3 4.♘xc3 e6 5.♘f3 ♘c6 6.♗c4 d6 7.0–0 a6 8.♕e2 b5 9.♗b3 ♖a7 10.♗e3 ♖d7 11.♖ac1 ♗b7 12.a4 b4 13.♘b1 ♗e7 14.♘bd2 ♘f6 15.♘c4 ♕b8 16.♘fd2 0–0 17.♘b6 ♖dd8 18.♗c4 ♘e5 19.♗xa6 ♘xe4 20.♘xe4 ♗xe4 21.♗b5 d5 22.♗d4 ♗f6 23.♗c5 ♘g6 24.♕d2

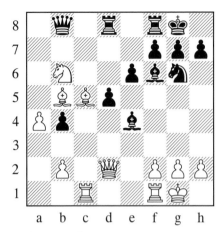

24...♗xg2 25.♕xb4

25.♔xg2 ♘h4†–+

25...♗f3 26.♖c3 ♗xc3 27.♕xc3 ♕f4 28.♖c1 d4 29.♕c2 d3 30.♕c4 ♕g5† 31.♔f1 ♕g2†
0–1

Slaying the Dragon

Supermichi – Granja Velha

Internet (freestyle) 2007

1.e4 c5 2.d4 cxd4 3.c3 dxc3 4.♘xc3 ♘c6 5.♘f3 g6 6.♗c4 ♗g7 7.e5 ♘xe5 8.♘xe5 ♗xe5 9.♗xf7† ♔xf7 10.♕d5† ♔g7 11.♕xe5† ♘f6 12.0–0 d6

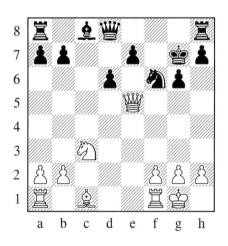

13.♕g3!?

13.♕e2!

13...h6 14.f4 h5 15.h3 b6 16.♗e3 ♗f5 17.♗d4 ♖f8 18.♖ae1 ♔g8 19.♖e3 d5 20.♖d1 ♘e4 21.♘xe4 dxe4 22.♖ee1 ♕d6 23.♕g5 ♕e6 24.♗e5 ♖f7 25.b3 ♖c8 26.♖d4 b5 27.♖ed1 ♕h7 28.♕h4 ♕b6 29.♔h2 ♕a5 30.a4 a6 31.♖d5 ♕b6 32.♗a1 ♖f8 33.axb5 axb5 34.b4 ♖hf7 35.♖c5 ♕e6 36.♖xb5 ♕b3 37.♖bd5 ♕xb4 38.♕g5 ♕b6 39.♗e5 ♕b3 40.♖d7 ♕e6 41.♖d8 ♖h7 42.♖xf8† ♔xf8 43.♕g3 ♔f7 44.h4 e3 45.♖e1 e2 46.♖xe2 ♖h8 47.♕g5 ♖c8 48.♖e3 ♖c2 49.♗d4 ♗e4 50.♗c5 ♖c4 51.♖e2 ♕f6 52.♕g3 ♖xc5 53.♖xe4

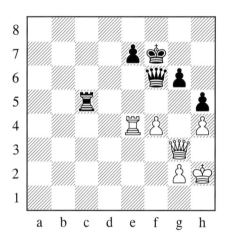

The game was drawn on move 88.
...½–½

The Professional's Choice – ♘ge[00]7

Michael Adams – William Watson

Great Britain (ch), Eastbourne 1990

1.e4 c5 2.d4 cxd4 3.c3 dxc3 4.♘xc3 ♘c6 5.♘f3 e6 6.♗c4 ♘ge7 7.♗g5 f6 8.♗e3 ♘g6 9.0–0 ♗e7

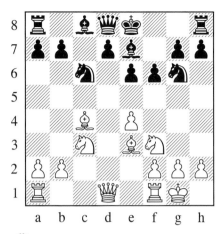

10.♕e2
10.♘b5!

10...a6 11.♘a4 ♕c7 12.♘b6 ♖b8 13.♖ac1 0–0 14.♖fd1 f5 15.exf5 ♖xf5

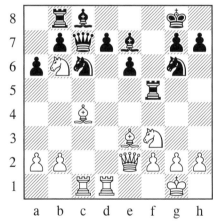

16.♕d3 ♔h8 17.♘xd7 ♗xd7 18.♖xd7 ♕xd7 19.♖xd7 ♘f8 20.♖d2 ♗b4 21.♖e2 ♖d8 22.a3 ♗c5 23.♗xa6 ♗xe3 24.♖xe3 bxa6 25.♖xc6 ♖b5 26.b4 a5 27.bxa5 ♖xa5 28.g3 ♖dd5 29.♖c8 ♔g8 30.♖b3 ♔f7 31.♖b7† ♘d7 32.♘e5†
1–0

Equidistance – VoidChessICC

Internet (freestyle) 2006

1.e4 c5 2.d4 cxd4 3.c3 dxc3 4.♘xc3 ♘c6 5.♘f3 e6 6.♗c4 a6 7.0–0 ♘ge7 8.♗g5 f6 9.♗e3 b5 10.♗b3 ♗b7

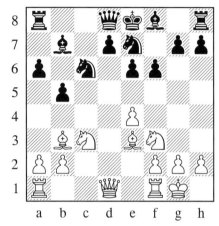

11.♘d2 ♘a5 12.f4 d5 13.♗f2 ♘xb3 14.♕xb3 ♕d6 15.♖ad1 ♕xf4 16.a4 ♗c6 17.axb5 axb5 18.♘f3 ♕d6 19.♖fe1 ♔f7 20.♘d4 ♗d7 21.♘dxb5 ♕c6 22.♘a7 ♕a6 23.♖a1 ♕d6 24.♘ab5 ♕c6 25.exd5 ♘xd5

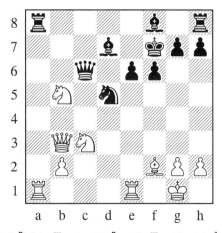

26.♘d4 ♖xa1 27.♘xc6 ♖xe1† 28.♖xe1 ♗xc6 29.♕c4 ♗b7 30.♕b5 ♗a8 31.♕d7† ♗e7 32.♘xd5 ♗xd5 33.♗b4 ♖e8 34.♗c5 ♗b3 35.♗xe7 ♖xe7 36.♕d3 ♗d5 37.♕xh7

♖b7 38.♕c2

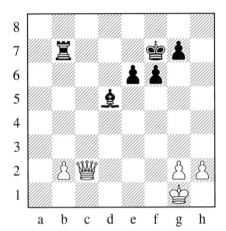

38...♖b4 39.h3 ♖b3 40.h4 ♔g8 41.♔h2 f5
42.g3 ♖f3 43.♕g2 ♔f7 44.♕g1 ♔g6 45.b4
♖d3 46.g4

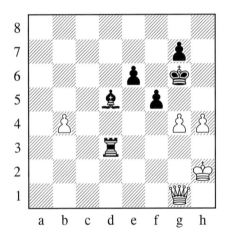

46...f4 47.♕b1 ♗e4 48.♕a2 ♔f6 49.♕c4
♖e3 50.♔g1 ♖g3† 51.♔f2 ♔e5 52.♕c7†
♔d4 53.♕d6† ♔c4 54.♕xe6† ♗d5 55.♕c8†
♔b3 56.♕f5 ♖f3† 57.♔e2 ♖e3† 58.♔d2
♗c4 59.♕xf4

White won on move 95.

1–0

Konstantin Landa – Garry Kasparov

USSR Clock Simul 1988

1.e4 c5 2.d4 cxd4 3.c3 dxc3 4.♘xc3 ♘c6
5.♘f3 e6 6.♗c4 a6 7.0-0 ♘ge7 8.♗g5 h6
9.♗h4 d6 10.♕d2 g5 11.♗g3 ♘g6 12.♖ad1
♗e7 13.♗b3 ♘ge5 14.♘xe5 dxe5 15.♕e3
♕a5 16.♘d5 ♗d8 17.♖c1 ♗d7 18.♖c5 b5
19.♕f3 exd5 20.♗xd5 0-0 21.♕h5 ♔h7
22.♗xf7 ♘e7 23.♖xe5 ♕b6

24.♖xg5 ♕f6 25.♗d5 ♕xg5 26.♕xg5 hxg5
27.♗xa8 ♗b6 28.♗b7 ♗c8 29.♗a8 ♗e6
30.♗b7 a5 31.b3 ♗c8 32.♗a8 ♗a6 33.♗d6
♖xa8 34.♗xe7 g4 35.♖d1 ♖c8 36.♗h4 ♖c2
37.h3 gxh3 38.gxh3 ♗c8 39.♖d5 b4 40.♖b5
♗c7 41.♗e7 ♔g6 42.h4 ♖c1† 43.♔g2 ♖c3
44.h5† ♔f7 45.♗g5 ♗h3† 46.♔g1 ♗g4
47.♗e3 ♗h3 48.♖b7 ♗d7 49.h6 ♔g6 50.♖a7
♖c2 51.♖a6† ♗c6 52.♔g2 ♔h7 53.♔f3 ♖c3
54.♖a7 ♔g6 55.♖a6 ♔h7 56.♖a7
½–½

LarryC (GM Christiansen) – mojo

Internet (blitz) 2010

1.e4 c5 2.d4 cxd4 3.c3 dxc3 4.♘xc3 ♘c6
5.♘f3 e6 6.♗c4 a6 7.0-0 b5 8.♗b3 ♘ge7
9.♗g5 ♗b7 10.a4 h6 11.♗h4 b4 12.♘d5 d6

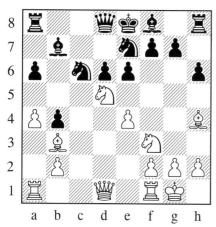

13.a5! exd5 14.exd5 ♘b8 15.♖e1 ♘d7 16.♘d4 ♘c5 17.♘f5 g5 18.♗g3 ♘xb3 19.♕xb3 ♗g7 20.♖xe7†
1–0

Marc Esserman – TitoMC (IM)

Internet (blitz) 2012

1.e4 c5 2.d4 cxd4 3.c3 dxc3 4.♘xc3 ♘c6 5.♘f3 e6 6.♗c4 a6 7.0–0 b5 8.♗b3 ♘ge7 9.♗g5 f6 10.♗e3 ♘g6 11.♘d5 ♖b8 12.♖c1!

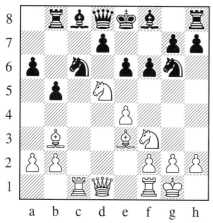

12...♘a5? 13.♘c7† ♔f7 14.♘xe6 ♕e7 15.♘c7† ♘xb3 16.♕d5† ♕e6 17.♘xe6 dxe6 18.♕xb3

And White won smashingly.
...1–0

Mladen Zelic – Sasa Martinovic

Split 2007

1.e4 c5 2.d4 cxd4 3.c3 dxc3 4.♘xc3 ♘c6 5.♘f3 e6 6.♗c4 a6 7.0–0 ♘ge7 8.♗g5 f6 9.♗e3 ♘g6 10.♗b3 b5 11.♘d5 ♖b8 12.♖c1 exd5 13.exd5 ♘ce5 14.♘xe5 ♘xe5 15.d6

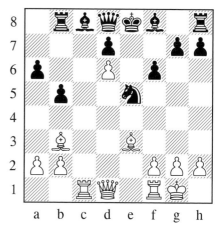

15...♕a5 16.♗a7 ♖a8 17.♕d5 ♘c6

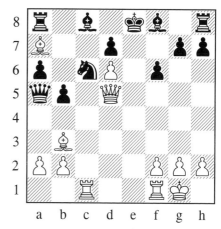

18.♖xc6 ♗b7 19.♕f7† ♔d8 20.♗b6†
1–0

JungleDacha (Esserman) – IsamOr

Internet (blitz) 2010

1.e4 c5 2.d4 cxd4 3.c3 dxc3 4.♘xc3 ♘c6 5.♘f3 e6 6.♗c4 ♘ge7 7.♗g5 h6 8.♗e3

  8.♘b5

8...♘g6 9.0–0 a6 10.♗b3 b5 11.♘d5! exd5 12.exd5 ♘a5 13.♖e1 ♗e7 14.d6 ♘xb3

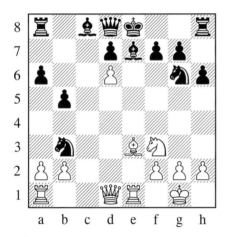

15.dxe7?!

  15.axb3! 0–0 16.♕d5 ♖b8 17.dxe7 ♘xe7 18.♕d6±

15...♘xe7 16.axb3 d6?!

  16...0–0!

17.♗f4 d5 18.♕e2 ♖a7 19.♕e3?

  19.♗e3! ♖d7 20.♗c5!+−

19...♖b7 20.♕c5

  And I went on to flag my opponent in a sloppy effort.

1–0

Marc Esserman – Eric Hansen

Blindfold Bar, Edmonton 2009

1.e4 c5 2.d4 cxd4 3.c3 dxc3 4.♘xc3 e6 5.♘f3 a6 6.♗c4 ♘e7 7.♗g5 ♘bc6 8.0–0 ♕c7 9.♖e1 f6

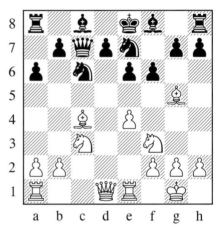

10.♘d5 ♘xd5 11.exd5 ♘e7 12.♗b3

  12.♖c1±

12...fxg5 13.d6 ♕c5 14.♖e5 ♕b6 15.dxe7 ♗xe7 16.♖xg5 ♗f6 17.♗c2 ♕xb2 18.♖b1 ♕c3 19.♖b3 ♕c7 20.♘h4 g6 21.♖g4 d5 22.♖f3

  Game adjourned due to drunkenness.

Early Bishop Out – ♘ge[00]7 Reloaded?

Lionel Kieseritzky – Conrad Vitzthum von Eckstaedt

Paris 1846

The first and only Morra Gambit game – until 101 years later!

1.e4 c5 2.d4 cxd4 3.c3 dxc3 4.♘xc3 ♘c6 5.♘f3 e6 6.♗c4 a6 7.0–0 ♗c5!?

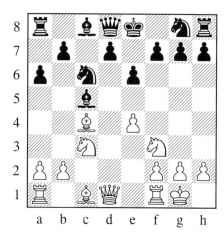

8.罝e1?!

8.e5?! f5!⇄ Note that this defensive resource was unavailable in the games Esserman – Guzman (page 186) and Esserman – Milov (page 188) as the black knight already stood on e7 (when 9.exf6 would then crush).

8.奧f4!

This is the only ...奧c5 move order where we delay the e4-e5 thrust, instead waiting for ...公ge7 before clamping down on the dark squares.

8...d6

8...公ge7 9.e5→

8...b5 9.奧d3! Preparing for a future kingside assault. 9...公ge7 (9...d6 10.e5!±) 10.罝c1 奧b6 11.e5!?→ (or 11.奧d6!?→)

9.a3!→

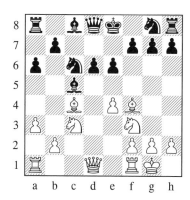

8...b5

8...d6!⇄

9.奧b3 公f6? 10.e5 公g4 11.公e4 奧b4 12.公fg5?

12.奧d2±

12...公cxe5 13.h3 公f6 14.豐d4

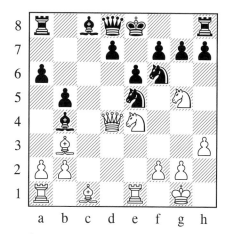

14...奧xe1?

14...公c6∓

15.公d6† 含f8 16.豐xe5+– 豐c7 17.公gxf7 奧b4 18.奧h6! 奧xd6 19.豐xf6 含e8 20.豐xg7 罝f8 21.公g5

21.奧d1!+–

21...豐c5 22.公e4 豐e5 23.罝e1 奧b7 24.奧xe6 dxe6 25.豐xb7 罝b8 26.公xd6† 豐xd6 27.罝xe6† 豐xe6 28.豐xb8† 含d7 29.豐xf8 1–0

Graham Burgess – Jacobsen

Glamsbjerg 1992

1.e4 c5 2.d4 cxd4 3.c3 dxc3 4.公xc3 公c6 5.公f3 e6 6.奧c4 奧c5 7.0–0 公ge7 8.奧f4

8.e5!→ Esserman – Guzman, Altamonte Springs 2007 (see page 186).

8...a6 9.e5 0–0 10.公e4 奧a7 11.奧g5 豐c7

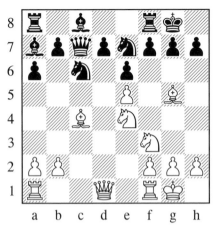

12.♘f6† gxf6 13.♗xf6 ♘f5 14.♘d4 h6
14...♘xe5 15.♘xf5 exf5 16.♕h5+–

**15.♘xf5 ♘xe5 16.♕g4† ♘xg4 17.♘e7†
♔h7 18.♗d3#**

BatsFrightenMe (Esserman) – RiverDolphin

Internet (blitz) 2008

**1.e4 c5 2.d4 cxd4 3.c3 dxc3 4.♘xc3 e6 5.♘f3
a6 6.♗c4 ♘c6 7.0–0 ♕c7 8.♖e1! ♘ge7**

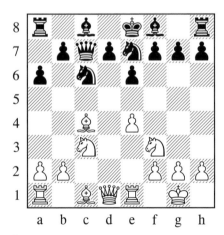

**9.♘d5! exd5 10.exd5 d6 11.dxc6 bxc6
12.♘g5 d5 13.♗xd5 cxd5 14.♕xd5 ♖b8
15.♕xf7† ♔d8 16.♗f4**
1–0

Alex Lenderman – Gregory Braylovsky

New York (rapid) 2005

**1.e4 c5 2.d4 cxd4 3.c3 dxc3 4.♘xc3 ♘c6
5.♘f3 e6 6.♗c4 a6 7.0–0 ♕c7 8.♖e1!**
8.♘d5!!→

8...d6?! 9.♗f4!±
A Scheveningen reloaded!

9...♘f6 10.♖c1! ♗e7

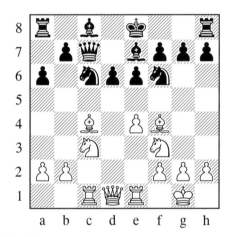

11.e5?!
11.♘d5! Pow! 11...exd5 12.exd5 ♘a7!
(12...0–0 13.dxc6 bxc6 14.♖xe7!±) 13.♗b5†
♘xb5 14.♖xc7 ♘xc7 15.♗xd6 ♘fxd5
(15...♘cxd5 16.♗xe7 ♘xe7 17.♕b3→)
16.♕a4† ♗d7 (16...♔f8 17.♖xe7!) 17.♕e4
♗e6 18.♗xc7 ♘xc7 19.♕xb7 ♗d6 20.♖d1±

11...dxe5 12.♘xe5 ♕d8?!
12...♘xe5!?⇄

**13.♕f3 ♘xe5 14.♗xe5 0–0 15.♖cd1 ♕b6
16.♕g3 ♖d8 17.♖xd8† ♕xd8 18.♖d1 ♕f8
19.♕f3 ♘d7 20.♗g3 ♖a7 21.a4 b6 22.♕c6
♘c5 23.b4 ♗d7 24.♕xb6+– ♖b7 25.♕a5
♘xa4 26.♕xa4 ♖xb4 27.♖xd7 ♖xc4 28.h3 ♕e8
29.♘b6 ♖c5 30.♕d2 h6 31.♗d6 ♗g5 32.♗f4**
1–0

Houdini 1.5x – Deep Rybka 4

Boston 2011

1.e4 c5 2.d4 cxd4 3.c3 dxc3 4.♘xc3 ♘c6
5.♘f3 e6 6.♗c4 a6 7.0-0 ♕c7 8.♗b3!? ♘f6
9.♘d5 exd5 10.exd5 ♗b4 11.dxc6 dxc6
12.♗g5 ♕e7 13.a3 ♗a5 14.♗f4 ♗g4 15.♗d6
♕e4

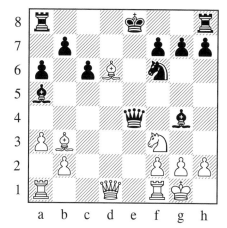

16.♗xf7† ♔xf7 17.♕b3† ♔g6 18.♘e5†
♔h6 19.♕g3 ♖hg8 20.♕h4† ♗h5 21.f4 ♕f5
22.♗e7 ♗d2 23.g4 g5

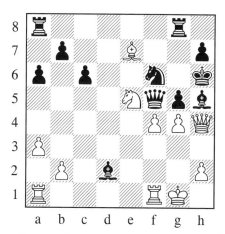

24.♕xh5† ♘xh5 25.gxf5 gxf4† 26.♔h1
♖ge8 27.f6 ♗e3 28.♖g1 ♘xf6 29.♘f7†
♔h5 30.♖g5† ♔h4 31.♗xf6 ♖e6 32.♗c3
♖g6 33.♗e1† ♔h3 34.♖h5† ♔g4 35.♖xh7

♔f5 36.♗c3 b5 37.♘h6† ♔e6 38.h3 ♖g3
39.♘g4 ♖d8 40.♖e1
1–0

Taylor's Temple of Doom

Robert Fischer – Viktor Korchnoi

Buenos Aires 1960

1.e4 c5 2.♘f3 a6 3.d4 cxd4 4.c3 dxc3
5.♘xc3 ♘c6 6.♗c4 d6 7.0-0 ♘f6 8.♗g5
e6 9.♕e2 ♗e7 10.♖fd1 ♕c7 11.♖ac1 0-0
12.♗b3 h6 13.♗f4 e5 14.♗e3 ♕d8 15.♘d5
♘xd5 16.♗xd5 ♗d7 17.♘d2 ♘b4 18.♗b3
♗g5 19.♗xg5 ♕xg5 20.♘f3 ♗g4 21.♖c7
♕d8

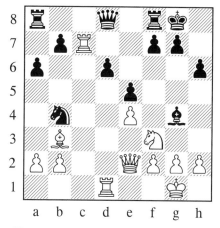

22.♖xb7

22.♖xf7! ♖xf7 23.♗xf7† ♔h8 24.h3 ♗xf3
25.♕xf3 ♘c6 26.♗d5±

22...♖b8 23.♖xb8 ♕xb8 24.h3 ♗xf3
25.♕xf3 ♘c6 26.♕d3 ♘d4 27.♗c4 a5 28.b3
♕b4 29.f4 ♔h7
½–½

wHySoSeRiOoOus (Esserman) – Lalu (Sharma)

Internet (blitz) 2010

1.e4 c5 2.d4 cxd4 3.c3 dxc3 4.♘xc3 ♘c6 5.♘f3 d6 6.♗c4 a6 7.0-0 ♘f6 8.b4 ♗g4 9.b5 axb5 10.♘xb5 ♗xf3 11.gxf3 e6 12.♗f4 ♘e5 13.♖c1 ♖c8 14.♗xe5 dxe5

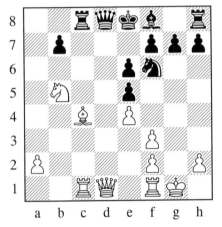

15.♕a4?!

15.♘a7! ♖c7 16.♗b5† ♘d7 17.♖xc7 ♕xc7 18.♕c1!±

15...♘d7 16.♖fd1 ♗e7

16...♗c5!∓ 17.♘d6† ♗xd6 18.♖xd6 ♕g5†!–+

17.♘a7 ♖a8 18.♗b5

18.♖xd7!

1–0

Marc Esserman – Timothy Taylor

Las Vegas 2003

1.e4 c5 2.d4 cxd4 3.c3 dxc3 4.♘xc3 ♘c6 5.♘f3 d6 6.♗c4 a6 7.0-0 ♘f6 8.b4 ♗g4 9.b5 axb5 10.♘xb5 e6 11.♗f4 ♗e7 12.h3 ♗xf3 13.♕xf3 0-0 14.♖fd1 ♖a4 15.♖ac1 ♕a5 16.♘xd6

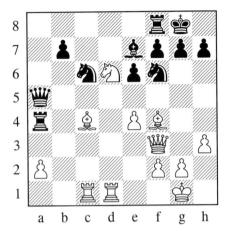

16...♘e5 17.♗xe5 ♕xe5 18.♕b3 ♗xd6 19.♕xa4 ♘xe4 20.♕b3 ♕h2† 21.♔f1 ♕h1† 22.♔e2 ♕xg2 23.♕e3 ♘g3† 24.♘d2 ♘f5 25.♕b6 h5 26.♔c3 ♗e5† 27.♔b4 ♕g5 28.♔b3 ♘d4† 29.♔b4 ♕e7†

0–1

Finegold's Final Frontier

Marc Esserman – Chow

Chicago 2000

1.e4 c5 2.d4 cxd4 3.c3 dxc3 4.♘xc3 d6 5.♘f3 e6 6.♗c4 ♗e7 7.0-0 ♘f6 8.♕e2 a6 9.♖d1 b5 10.♗b3

10.e5! bxc4 11.exf6 gxf6 12.♘d2!!±

10...♘bd7 11.♘d4 ♗b7?!

11...♕b6!

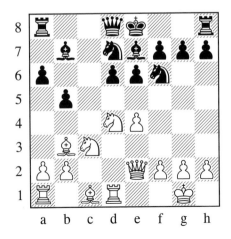

12.♗xe6! fxe6 13.♘xe6 ♕b8 14.♘d5 g6 15.♗f4! ♗xd5 16.exd5 ♘e5 17.♖ac1 ♖a7 18.♗e3 ♖b7 19.f4 ♘ed7 20.♗d4 h6 21.♖c6+–

21.♖e1 ♔f7 (21...♖h7 22.♖c6 ♘xd5 23.♕c2+–) 22.♘g5†+–

21...♔f7

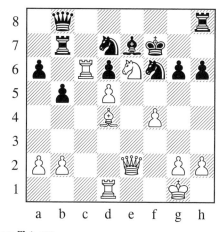

22.♖dc1?!

22.♘g5†! hxg5 23.♕e6† ♔f8 (23...♔e8 24.♗xf6 ♘xf6 25.♖c8†+–) 24.fxg5 ♕e8 25.♖f1 ♕f7 26.♖c8† ♔g7 27.♕xf7† ♔xf7 28.♖xh8+–

22...♖e8 23.♘c7 ♗f8 24.♕d3

24.♘xe8±

24...♖e4⇄ 25.♘e6 ♖xd4 26.♘xd4 ♘c5 27.♕f3 b4

27...♕a7!⇄

28.f5 g5 29.♘e6 ♘fe4? 30.♕h5†
1–0

Morra Declined – Potpourri

Paul Morphy – Alexander Beaufort Meek

New York (blindfold) 1857

1.e4 e6 2.d4 c5 3.d5 e5 4.f4 d6 5.♘f3 ♗g4 6.fxe5 ♗xf3 7.♕xf3 dxe5 8.♗b5† ♘d7 9.♘c3 ♘gf6 10.♗g5 ♗e7

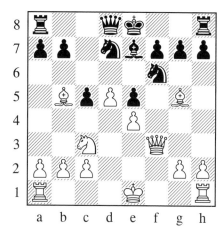

11.d6 ♗xd6 12.0–0–0
1–0

Aron Nimzowitsch – Frank Marshall

New York 1927

1.c4 ♘f6 2.d4 e6 3.♘f3 c5 4.d5 d6 5.♘c3 exd5 6.cxd5 g6

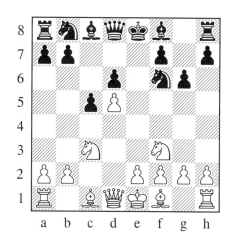

7.♘d2 ♘bd7 8.♘c4 ♘b6 9.e4 ♗g7 10.♘e3
0–0 11.♗d3 ♘h5 12.0–0 ♗e5 13.a4 ♘f4
14.a5 ♘d7 15.♘c4 ♘xd3 16.♕xd3 f5
17.exf5 ♖xf5 18.f4 ♗d4† 19.♔e3 ♗xc3
20.♕xc3 ♘f6 21.♕b3 ♖xd5 22.f5 gxf5
23.♗g5 ♖d4 24.♘b6† c4 25.♕c3 axb6
26.♕xd4 ♔g7 27.♖ae1 bxa5 28.♖e8 ♕xe8
29.♕xf6† ♔g8 30.♗h6
1–0

Paul Morphy – Paul Journoud

Paris 1858

1.e4 c5 2.d4 cxd4 3.♘f3 e5 4.♗c4 ♗e7 5.c3

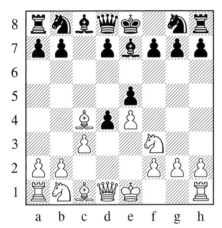

5...d6 6.♕b3 dxc3 7.♗xf7† ♔f8 8.♘xc3
♘c6 9.♗g8 ♖xg8 10.0–0 ♕e8 11.♘g5
♗xg5 12.♗xg5 ♗e6 13.♘d5 h6 14.f4 ♕d7
15.fxe5† ♔e8 16.♘c7† ♕xc7 17.♕xe6†
...1–0

Milan Matulovic – Dragoljub Janosevic

Yugoslavia (ch), Novi Sad 1955

1.e4 c5 2.d4 cxd4 3.c3 d5 4.exd5 ♘f6
5.♗b5† ♘bd7 6.♕xd4 a6 7.♗e2 b5 8.♗f3
♕b6 9.♕xb6 ♘xb6 10.d6 ♘fd5 11.dxe7
♗xe7 12.♘e2 ♗b7 13.♘d2 0–0 14.0–0
♖ad8

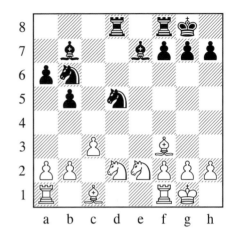

15.a4 ♗g5 16.axb5 axb5 17.♘e4 ♗xc1
18.♖fxc1 ♘c4 19.♘c5 ♗c8 20.♘d4 ♘f4
21.b4 ♘e5 22.♗d1 ♘ed3 23.♘xd3 ♘xd3
24.♖cb1 ♖fe8 25.♗f3 ♗d7 26.♗e2 ♗f5
27.♖d1 ♘b2 28.♖d2 ♘c4 29.♗xc4 bxc4

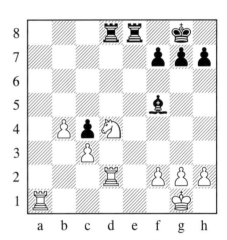

30.f3 ♗d3 31.♔f2 g5 32.♖e1 ♔f8 33.♖a2
♖xe1 34.♔xe1 ♖d6 35.♖a8† ♔e7 36.♖a7†
♔d8 37.♖xf7 ♔c8 38.♖a7 g4 39.fxg4
♖f6 40.♘f3 ♖e6† 41.♔f2 ♖e2† 42.♔g3
♖b2 43.♖a1 ♖c2 44.♖a3 ♗f1 45.♘e1 ♖b2
46.♖a8† ♔b7 47.♖f8 ♗d3 48.♘xd3 cxd3
49.♖d8 d2 50.♔f3 ♖c2 51.♔e3 ♖xc3†
52.♔xd2 ♖b3 53.♖d7† ♔c6 54.♖xh7 ♖xb4
55.h3 ♖b2† 56.♔e3 ♖xg2 57.♔f3 ♖g1
58.♖e7
1–0

Mihail Tal – Roman Dzindzichashvili

New York (blitz) 1991

1.e4 c5 2.♘f3 ♘c6 3.c3 d5 4.exd5 ♕xd5 5.d4 cxd4 6.cxd4 e6 7.♘c3 ♕d6 8.♗d3 ♘f6 9.0–0 ♗e7 10.♖e1 0–0 11.♗g5 ♖d8 12.♕e2 ♘b4 13.♗c4 ♗d7 14.♖ad1 ♗c6 15.♘e5 ♗d5 16.♘xd5 ♘bxd5

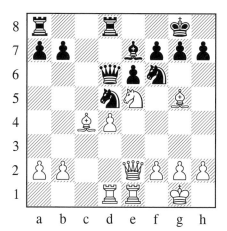

17.♖d3 h6 18.♗c1 ♖ac8 19.♖g3 ♔f8 20.♗b3 ♖c7 21.♕f3 ♖dc8 22.♗d2 a6

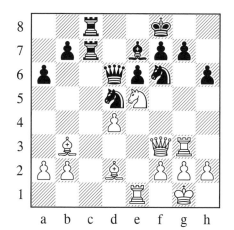

23.♖xg7 ♔xg7 24.♗xh6† ♔h7 25.♕h3 ♘g8 26.♗f8†
1–0

Hrvoje Stevic – Veselin Topalov

Khanty Mansiysk (ol) 2010

1.e4 c5 2.c3 d5 3.exd5 ♕xd5 4.d4 cxd4 5.cxd4 ♘c6 6.♘f3 ♗g4 7.♘c3 ♗xf3 8.gxf3 ♕xd4 9.♕xd4 ♘xd4 10.♘b5 e5!? 11.♘c7† ♔d7 12.♘xa8 ♗b4† 13.♔d1 ♘e7 14.f4
14.♗e3 ♖xa8 15.♗c4!?N

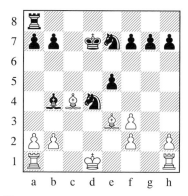

15...♖d8

a) 15...♔e8 16.♗xd4 ♖d8 17.♔e2 exd4 (17...♖xd4 18.♗b5† ♔f8 19.♖hd1±) 18.♖ad1 ♘g6 19.♖hg1 ♘f4† 20.♔f1 g6 21.♖g4+–

b) 15...♘ec6 16.♗xf7 ♔f8 (16...♖d8 17.♗d5 ♔c7 18.♗xc6 bxc6 19.♔c1±) 17.♗d5±

16.♗xf7 ♔c7 17.♖c1† ♔b8 18.♗xd4 ♖xd4† 19.♔e2±

14...♖xa8 15.fxe5 ♖d8⩲ 16.♗h3† ♔e8 17.♗e3

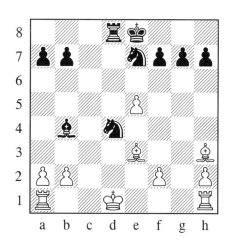

17...♘d5?!

   17...♘b3†=

18.♗xd4 ♘f4 19.♔c2 ♖xd4 20.♗f1 ♘e6 21.♖d1 ♖f4 22.♔b1 ♔e7 23.♗g2 b6 24.♖hf1 ♗c5 25.♖d2 h5 26.♗d5 g5 27.f3 a5 28.♖fd1 ♖f5 29.♗e4 ♖xe5 30.♖d5 ♖xd5 31.♖xd5 f6 32.♔c2 ♗d6 33.♖d2 ♗f4 34.♖f2 f5 35.♗d5 ♘c5 36.♖e2† ♔f6 37.♔c3 b5 38.♔d4 ♗d6 39.♗g8 g4 40.fxg4 hxg4 41.♔d5 ♘e4 42.a4 bxa4 43.♖xe4 fxe4 44.♔xd6 ♔f5 45.♗c4 ♔f4

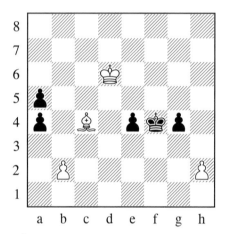

46.♗e2

   46.♔c5! e3 (46...♔f3 47.♗d5! +–) 47.♗e2! +–

46...g3 47.hxg3† ♔xg3 48.♔c5 ♔f2 49.♗h5 ♔e1 50.♔b5 ♔d2 51.♗xa4 ♔c2 52.♗a3 e3 53.♗e2 a4 54.♗a6 ♔c1 55.♔a2 ♔c2 56.♗c4 ♔c1 57.♗b5 ♔d2 58.♔b1 e2 59.♗xe2 ♔xe2 60.♔c2 ♔e1 61.♔c3 ♔d1 62.♔b4 ♔c2 63.♔xa4 ♔xb2

½–½

Morra Declined – 3...d3

Milan Matulovic – Zdravko Vospernik

Yugoslavia (ch), Novi Sad 1955

1.e4 c5 2.d4 cxd4 3.c3 d3 4.♗xd3 g6 5.♘f3 d6 6.0–0 ♗g7 7.h3 ♘f6 8.c4 0–0 9.♘c3 b6 10.♗e3 ♘bd7 11.♖c1 ♗b7 12.♖b1 ♖c8 13.♘d2 ♖e8 14.b4 ♕c7 15.♕b3 ♕b8 16.a3 ♕a8 17.♖fd1 ♗c6 18.f3 ♘f8 19.♗a2 ♘e6

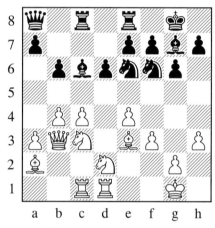

20.♘d5 ♕b7 21.♘f1 b5 22.cxb5 ♗xb5 23.♘f4 ♗d7 24.♕d3 ♘xf4 25.♗xf4 ♗a4 26.♗b3 ♗b5 27.♕d2 ♖f8 28.♕a2 ♘d7 29.♖xc8 ♕xc8 30.♖c1 ♕a6 31.♘e3 ♘b6 32.♖c7 ♗f6 33.♘g4 ♘d7 34.♗xf7† ♔h8 35.♗e3 ♘b6 36.♘xf6 exf6 37.♕e6 ♔g7

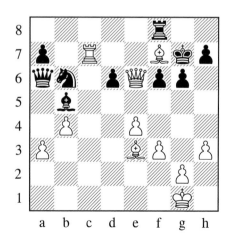

38.h4?!

38.♕e7 mates outright.

38...♗d7 39.♕e7 ♖xf7 40.♗h6†! ♔xh6 41.♕xf7 ♕e2 42.♕f8† ♔h5 43.♕xf6 ♕e1† 44.♔h2 ♕xh4† 45.♕xh4† ♔xh4 46.♖xa7 ♗e6 47.a4 ♗c4 48.a5 ♘a4 49.a6 ♔g5 50.♖a8 d5 51.a7 dxe4 52.♖b8 ♗d5 53.♖b5 1–0

Alex Lenderman – Lubomir Ftacnik

Philadelphia 2006

A crushing positional masterclass by then-IM Lenderman against a reputable Grandmaster.

1.e4 c5 2.d4 cxd4 3.c3 d3 4.c4 g6 5.♗xd3 ♗g7 6.♘f3 ♘c6 7.0–0 d6 8.h3 b6 9.♘c3 ♗b7 10.♗e3 ♘f6 11.♖c1 0–0 12.b3 ♘d7 13.♗b1 a6 14.♕d2 ♖b8 15.♘d4 ♘xd4 16.♗xd4 ♘c5 17.♖fd1

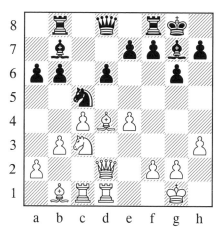

17...a5 18.♕e3 ♗xd4 19.♖xd4 f6 20.f4 ♕d7 21.♖e1 e5 22.♖d2 ♕e7 23.f5 g5 24.♖ed1 ♖fd8 25.♗c2 ♗c6 26.a3 ♘a6 27.♖b1 ♘c7 28.b4 axb4 29.♖xb4 ♘a8 30.♗a4 ♗b7 31.♗b3 ♔h8 32.♘a4 ♕c7 33.♘c3 ♖bc8 34.♔f2 ♕c5 35.♘a4 ♕a5

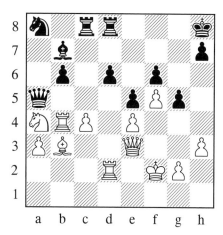

36.♖b5

36.h4! gxh4 (36...h6 37.hxg5 hxg5 38.♕h3† ♔g7 39.♕h5+–) 37.♕h6+–

36...♕a7 37.♘xb6 ♘xb6 38.♖xb6 ♗xe4 39.♖bxd6 ♖xd6 40.♕xa7 ♖xd2† 41.♔e1 ♖dd8 42.c5 ♗xf5 43.♕e7 ♖f8

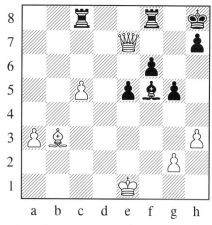

44.♗f7 ♔g7 45.♗e6† ♔g6 46.♗xc8 ♖xc8 47.c6 ♗e4 48.c7 ♗xg2 49.a4 h5 50.♔f2 ♗xh3 51.♕d8 h4 52.a5 g4 53.a6 g3† 54.♔g1 ♗f5 55.a7 h3 56.a8=♕ 1–0

Morra Declined – The Noxious 3...♘f6

ClubberLang (Esserman) – Yuri Razuvaev

Internet (blitz) 2005

1.e4 c5 2.d4 cxd4 3.c3 ♘f6 4.e5 ♘d5
5.♕xd4 e6 6.♘f3 ♘c6 7.♕e4 f5 8.♕e2 ♕c7
9.g3 b6 10.♗g2

10...♗b7

10...♘cb4! 11.c4 ♗a6 (11...b5?! 12.a3!±)
12.b3 b5 13.a3 bxc4 14.axb4 cxb3 15.♖xa6
♕xc1† 16.♔d1∞

11.0–0 h6 12.♖d1 ♘de7

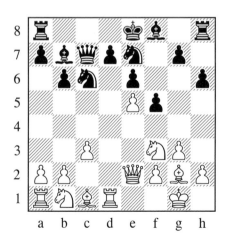

13.h4

13.♘a3!±

13...g6 14.a3?!

14.♘a3±

14...♗g7 15.♗f4 0–0–0 16.c4± g5 17.hxg5
♘g6 18.♘c3 ♘xf4 19.gxf4 a6 20.♘d5! exd5
21.cxd5 ♔b8 22.♖ac1 hxg5 23.♘xg5 ♖h4

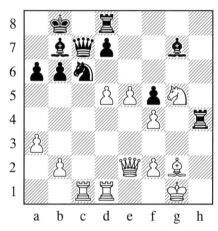

24.♘f7?

24.dxc6! dxc6 (24...♗xc6 25.♘e6 dxe6
26.♖xc6 ♖xd1† 27.♕xd1 ♕e7 28.♖xe6 ♕xe6
29.♕d8† ♕c8 30.♕xb6† ♕b7 31.♕xb7#)
25.♘e6 ♖xd1† 26.♕xd1 ♕e7 27.♘xg7 ♕xg7
28.♕d8† ♔a7 29.♕xh4+–

24...♖g8 25.♘d6 ♗a8?

25...♗xe5! 26.fxe5 ♘d4!–+

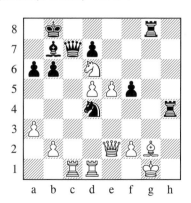

27.♕e3 ♗xd5! 28.♖xc7 ♖xg2† 29.♔f1 ♖h1#

26.♔f1 ♖xf4 27.dxc6
Finally!

**27...dxc6 28.♕e3 ♖g4 29.e6 ♖xg2 30.e7+–
♗h6 31.e8=♕† ♖xe8 32.♕xe8† ♔a7
33.♘c8† ♔b7 34.♖d7**
Black resigns. The finish could be: 34...♗xc1
35.♘d6† ♔a7 36.♖xc7† ♔b7 37.♖xb7#
1–0

Marc Esserman – StepByStep (IM)

Internet (blitz) 2012

**1.e4 c5 2.d4 cxd4 3.c3 ♘f6 4.e5 ♘d5 5.♘f3
d6 6.♕xd4 e6 7.♘bd2 ♘c6 8.♗b5 ♗d7
9.♗xc6 ♗xc6 10.0–0!?**

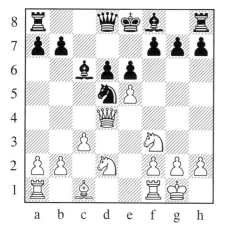

**10...♕b6?! 11.♘c4 ♕xd4 12.♘xd4 ♔d7
13.♖d1 ♔c7 14.exd6†+– ♗xd6 15.♘xd6**
15.♘xc6 ♔xc6 16.♘xd6 ♔xd6 17.c4+–

**15...♔xd6 16.c4 ♘b4 17.♘c2† ♔c5
18.♗e3† ♔xc4 19.b3†**
19.♘a3#!

**19...♔c3 20.♗d4†
1–0**

Liviu-Dieter Nisipeanu – Alejandro Ramirez

Decameron 2003

**1.e4 c5 2.♘f3 ♘c6 3.c3 ♘f6 4.e5 ♘d5 5.d4
cxd4 6.cxd4 d6 7.♗c4 e6 8.0–0 ♗e7 9.♕e2
0–0 10.♘c3 ♘xc3 11.bxc3 dxe5 12.dxe5
♕a5 13.♕e4!?**

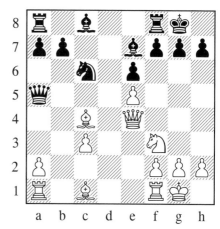

13...♕a4
13...♕xc3!? 14.♗d2 ♕a3 15.♖ab1⩲ Black
must take care, for example: 15...♕a4 16.♖fc1
♖b8 17.♘g5 ♗xg5 18.♗xg5 b6 19.♖b3+–

14.♗g5 h6 15.♗xe7 ♘xe7 16.♖ab1

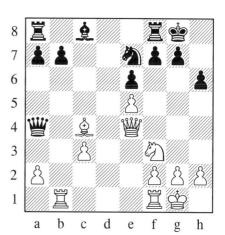

16...♖b8
16...♗d7!?   17.♗d3   (17.♖b4?!   ♗c6!⇄)

17...♕xe4 18.♗xe4 ♗c6 19.♗xc6 bxc6 20.c4 ♖ab8 21.♖fd1 ♖fd8 (21...a5! 22.h3 ♖b4 23.♖xb4 axb4 24.♖d7 ♘g6 25.♖c7 ♖a8 26.♖xc6 ♖xa2=) 22.♖xd8† ♖xd8 23.h4± Mamedyarov – Ramirez, Wijk aan Zee 2005.

17.♖b4! ♕c6 18.♕e3 b6?!

18...a5! 19.♗b5 ♘d5! 20.♕a7 ♕b6 21.♕xb6 ♘xb6 22.♖d4 restricted White to a slight initiative in Can – Saric, Sibenik 2006.

19.♗d3 ♗b7 20.♖g4 ♘f5 21.♗xf5 exf5 22.♘d4 ♕c8 23.♖f4 g6 24.♖h4 h5 25.♖xh5!

Black resigned, faced with: 25...gxh5 26.♕g5† ♔h7 27.♕xh5† ♔g7 28.♕g5† ♔h8 29.♘xf5+–

1–0

Mircea Parligras – Trajce Nedev

Dresden (ol) 2008

1.e4 c5 2.c3 ♘f6 3.e5 ♘d5 4.d4 cxd4 5.♘f3 d6 6.cxd4 ♘c6 7.♗c4 e6 8.0–0 ♗e7 9.♕e2 0–0 10.♘c3 ♘xc3 11.bxc3 dxe5 12.dxe5 ♕a5 13.♗d2!?

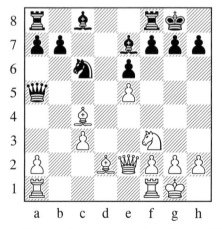

13...♖d8 14.♖fe1 ♗d7 15.♗b3 ♕c5 16.♕e4 ♗e8 17.♖ac1 ♖d7 18.h4 ♘a5 19.♗c2 g6 20.h5 ♘c4 21.♗h6 ♖d5 22.hxg6 hxg6 23.♕f4 ♖ad8 24.♖e2 ♘a3 25.♗b3 ♖d3

26.♗g5 ♗c6 27.♕h4 ♗xg5 28.♘xg5
1–0

Dusko Pavasovic – Viktor Erdos

Rogaska Slatina 2009

1.e4 c5 2.c3 ♘f6 3.e5 ♘d5 4.♘f3 e6 5.♗c4 ♘c6 6.d4 cxd4 7.cxd4 d6 8.♕e2 ♗e7 9.0–0 0–0 10.♘c3 dxe5 11.dxe5 ♘xc3 12.bxc3 ♕a5 13.♗d2 ♖d8 14.♖fe1 ♕a4 15.♗b3 ♕g4 16.♗c2 ♗d7 17.♖ad1 ♕h5 18.h3 ♖ac8 19.♔h2 f5 20.exf6 ♗xf6

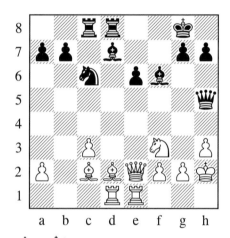

21.♗g5! ♔h8

21...♗xg5 22.♘xg5 ♕xg5 (22...♕xe2 23.♗xh7†±) 23.♖xd7+–

22.♕e4 e5 23.♖d6 ♗xg5 24.♘xg5 ♗e8 25.g4

25.♖xd8!? ♖xd8 26.♖d1! ♖xd1 27.♕f5!+–

25...♕h4 26.♕f3 ♗h5 27.♖h6! ♕xg5

27...♗xg4 28.♖xh7† ♕xh7 29.♘f7† ♔g8 30.♗xh7†+–

27...gxh6 28.♕f6† ♔g8 29.♗xh7#

28.♖xh7† ♔g8 29.♖xh5 ♕f4† 30.♕xf4 exf4 31.♗b3†
1–0

Evgeny Sveshnikov – Lembit Oll

Kuybyshev 1986

1.e4 c5 2.c3 ♘f6 3.e5 ♘d5 4.d4 cxd4 5.♘f3 ♘c6 6.cxd4

6.♗c4!

6...d6 7.♗c4 e6 8.0–0 ♗e7 9.♕e2 0–0 10.♘c3 dxe5 11.dxe5 ♘xc3 12.bxc3 b6!? 13.♕e4

13.♗d3!?∞

13...♕c7

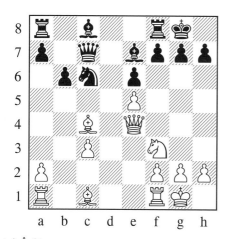

14.♗d3

14.♗g5!? ♗b7 15.♗d3 g6 16.♕h4→ ♗xg5 17.♘xg5 h5 18.♖ae1 ♖ac8 (18...♘xe5? 19.♕g3±) 19.♘e4 ♘xe5 20.♘f6† ♔g7 21.♕g5 ♘xd3 22.♘xh5† ♔h7 23.♘f6†= (23.♖e3?! ♖fd8 24.♖h3 ♕e5! 25.♘f6† ♔g7 26.♖h7† ♔f8 27.♖h8† ♔e7 28.♘d5† ♔d7 29.♕e7† ♔c6 30.♖xd8 ♖xd8∓)

14...g6 15.♗h6 ♖d8 16.♖ad1 ♗b7 17.♕f4 ♖d5

17...♘a5!∓ 18.♘g5 f5!⇄ 19.♘xe6? ♕c6–+

18.♗e4 ♖xd1 19.♖xd1 ♖d8 20.♖xd8† ♕xd8 21.h4 ♕d1† 22.♔h2 ♕a4 23.♘g5 ♘d8 24.f3 ♗d5? 25.♘xh7!
1–0

Michele Godena – Fabio Bruno

Frascati 2006

1.e4 c5 2.♘f3 e6 3.c3 ♘f6 4.e5 ♘d5 5.♗c4 d6 6.d4 cxd4 7.cxd4 ♘c6 8.0–0 ♗e7 9.♕e2 0–0 10.♘c3 ♘xc3 11.bxc3 dxe5 12.dxe5 ♕c7 13.♕e4 b6 14.♗g5 ♗b7 15.♗d3 g6 16.♗f6!?

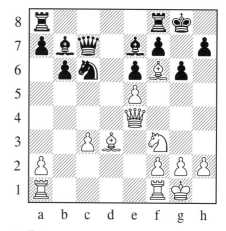

16...♕d8

16...♘b4!? 17.♕h4 ♘d5 18.♘g5 h5 19.♕xh5! ♘xf6 (19...gxh5 20.♗h7#) 20.♕h6 ♕xe5 21.♗xg6 fxg6 22.♕xg6† ♔h8 23.♕h6†=

17.♕h4 ♖e8 18.♘g5 h5 19.♕g3 ♗xf6

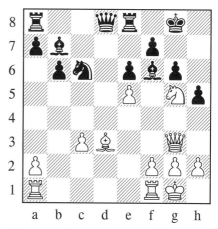

20.♘xf7!+– ♔xf7 21.♕xg6† ♔f8

21...♗e7 22.♕h7† ♔f8 23.exf6 ♕xf6 24.♕xb7+–

22.exf6 ♕c7 23.♖fe1 ♖ed8 24.♕h6† ♔g8 25.♕g6† ♔f8 26.♕h6† ♔g8 27.♖e3 h4 28.♖e4 ♘e5 29.♖xe5 ♖d5 30.♖e4 1–0

Alisa Melekhina – Alex Shabalov

Philadelphia 2011

1.e4 c5 2.c3 ♘f6 3.e5 ♘d5 4.♘f3 e6 5.d4 cxd4 6.cxd4 d6 7.♗c4 ♗e7 8.0–0 0–0 9.♕e2 ♘c6 10.♘c3 ♘xc3 11.bxc3 dxe5 12.dxe5 ♕c7 13.♕e4 b6 14.♗g5 ♗b7 15.♗d3 g6 16.♗f6 ♖fd8?! 17.♕e3→ ♖d7 18.♖ad1

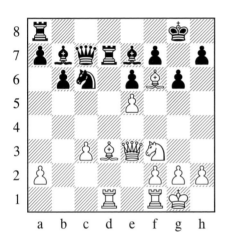

18...♘a5?

18...♕d8 19.♕h6 (19.♗c2! ♗xf6 20.♖xd7 ♕xd7 21.exf6 ♕d8 22.♕f4→) 19...♕f8 20.♕h3 ♗xf6? (20...h6!⇄) 21.♗xg6+– hxg6 22.exf6! ♘d4 23.♖xd4 1–0 Brynell – Nedev, Batumi 1999.

19.♘g5+– ♗xf6 20.exf6 ♖ad8 21.♘e4 1–0

Vladimir Jakimov – Sergei Rublevsky

Plovdiv 2010

1.e4 c5 2.c3 ♘f6 3.e5 ♘d5 4.d4 cxd4 5.♘f3 e6 6.cxd4 d6 7.♗c4 ♘b6 8.♗d3 ♘c6 9.♗g5

9.0–0! ♘b4 10.♗g5 ♗e7 11.♗xe7 ♕xe7 12.♘c3 dxe5 13.dxe5 ♗d7 14.♗e4 transposes to the game.

9...♗e7 10.♗xe7 ♕xe7 11.♘c3 dxe5 12.dxe5 ♗d7 13.0–0 ♘b4 14.♗e4

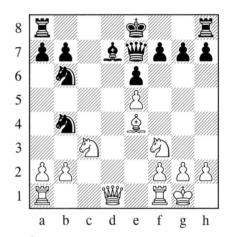

14...♗c6

14...♖d8 15.a3! ♗b5 16.♘xb5 ♖xd1 17.♖fxd1 ♘4d5 18.♘d6† ♔f8 19.a4±

15.a3 ♘4d5 16.♕c2 ♖c8 17.♘d4 ♗a4 18.♕d3 ♘xc3 19.bxc3 ♕c5 20.♗xb7 ♖c7 21.♗e4 ♕xe5 22.♖fe1± ♕g5

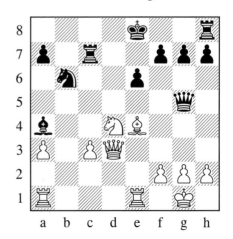

23.♖ab1

23.♗f5! g6 24.♘xe6 fxe6 25.♗xe6 ♖e7 26.♕d6!+–

23...g6 24.h4 ♕c5 25.h5 ♕xh5?

25...♕xc3! 26.♘b5 ♗xb5 27.♕xb5† ♔e7 28.♕g5† ♕f6!∞

26.♘xe6+– fxe6 27.♕d6 ♖c8

27...♖e7 28.♕b8†+–

28.♗f3 ♕g5 29.♕xe6† ♔d8 30.♖xb6! axb6 31.♕xb6† ♔d7

31...♖c7 32.♕d4†+–

32.♕a7† ♔d6 33.♕xa4 ♖he8 34.♕a6† ♔d7 35.♕a7† ♔d6 36.♖d1† ♔e6 37.♕d7† ♔f6 38.♖d6† ♔e5 39.♖d5† ♔f6 40.♕d6† ♖e6 41.♕xe6†
1–0

Jan Timman – Florian Handke

Amsterdam 2001

1.e4 c5 2.♘f3 e6 3.c3 ♘f6 4.e5 ♘d5 5.d4 cxd4 6.cxd4 d6 7.♗c4 ♘b6 8.♗d3 ♘c6 9.0–0 dxe5 10.dxe5 ♘b4 11.♗e4 ♕xd1 12.♖xd1 ♘4d5 13.a4 a5

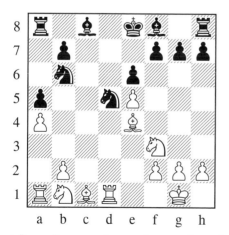

14.♘c3! ♘xc3 15.bxc3± ♗c5 16.♘d4 ♗d7

17.♗xb7 ♖a7 18.♗f3 h6 19.♘b3 ♘xa4

19...♗e7 20.♗e3 ♖a6 21.♗e2+–

20.♘xc5 ♘xc5 21.♗e3 ♖c7 22.♖xa5 ♘b3 23.♖a8† ♗c8

23...♖c8 24.♖xc8† ♗xc8 25.♗c6† ♔e7 26.♗a4 ♘a5 27.♗c5#

24.♗b6 ♖xc3 25.♖d8† ♔e7 26.♖a7†
1–0

Spartak Vysochin – Spas Kozhuharov

Istanbul 2006

1.e4 c5 2.c3 ♘f6 3.e5 ♘d5 4.♘f3 e6 5.d4 cxd4 6.cxd4 d6 7.♗c4 ♘b6 8.♗d3 dxe5 9.dxe5 ♘8d7 10.♕e2 ♘c5 11.♗c2 ♘d5 12.0–0 ♗d7

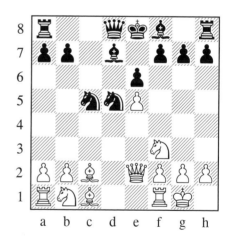

13.♖d1

13.♘c3!? ♘xc3 14.bxc3 ♗e7 15.♖d1± Rublevsky – Topalov, Bastia 2004.

13...♘b4?! 14.♘c3± ♘xc2 15.♕xc2 ♗e7 16.♘e4 ♘xe4 17.♕xe4 ♕c7 18.♕g4 0–0–0

18...0–0 19.♗h6±

19.♗e3 ♗c6 20.♖xd8† ♕xd8 21.♖c1 ♔b8 22.♘d4 ♗d5 23.♘b5 ♕a5 24.♕xg7 ♖f8 25.♗xa7† ♔a8 26.♕xf8†!
1–0

Marc Esserman – Iryna Zenyuk

Philadelphia 2009

1.e4 c5 2.c3 ♘f6 3.e5 ♘d5 4.♘f3 e6 5.d4 cxd4 6.cxd4 d6 7.a3 ♗d7 8.♗d3 ♗c6 9.0–0 ♘d7 10.b4 a6 11.♘bd2

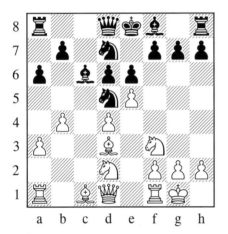

11...♘f4!?

11...♘c3! 12.♕c2 ♖c8 13.♕xc3 ♗xf3 14.♕b2 ♗c6 15.♘c4 dxe5 16.dxe5 ♘c5!

12.♗e4 d5 13.♗c2 ♗b5 14.♖e1

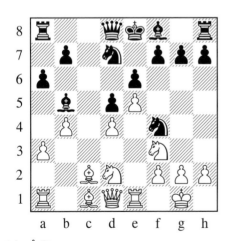

14...♗d3

14...♘d3! would solve the problem of the wayward knight, with a tense game ahead. 15.♖e3 ♘xc1 16.♖xc1∞

15.g3

15.♖a2! ♖c8 16.♘b3!±

15...♗xc2

15...♖c8!±

16.♕xc2 ♖c8 17.♕b3 ♘g6 18.♗b2 ♗e7 19.h4 h5 20.♖ac1 0–0 21.♖xc8 ♕xc8 22.♖c1 ♕b8 23.♘e1 f6?! 24.♕f3 fxe5 25.♕xh5± ♘xh4 26.gxh4 e4 27.♘g2 ♖f5 28.♕g6 ♘f8 29.♕g4 ♖f6 30.♘xe4 dxe4 31.♕xe4 ♖f5 32.d5 ♗f6 33.dxe6 ♗xb2 34.♕xf5 ♗xc1 35.♕f7† ♔h7 36.e7
1–0

Miroslav Markovic – Srdjan Zakic

Nis 1997

1.e4 c5 2.c3 ♘f6 3.e5 ♘d5 4.d4 cxd4 5.♘f3 e6 6.cxd4 d6 7.a3 ♘c6 8.♗d3 ♗e7

8...dxe5 9.dxe5 g6 10.0–0 ♗g7 11.♖e1 0–0 12.♕e2

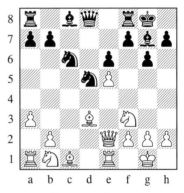

10...b6 (12...♕c7!? 13.♗d2!? [13.h4?! ♘a5∓] 13...♖d8 [13...♘a5 14.♘c3± or 13...b6 14.h4!→] 14.♗g5 ♖d7 15.♗c4∞) 13.h4! ♗b7 14.h5 ♕c7 15.h6 ♗h8 16.♗g5± Jonkman – A. Hunt, West Bromwich 2005.

9.0–0 0–0 10.♕c2 g6 11.♗h6 ♖e8

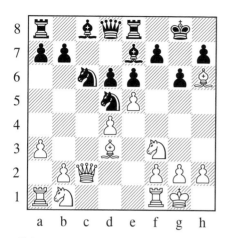

12.罝d1

12.②c3!±

12...奠d7 13.豐e2 豐b6 14.②c3 dxe5 15.dxe5 ②xc3 16.bxc3 罝ed8 17.h4 奠e8 18.h5 罝d7 19.罝db1 豐a5 20.罝b3 罝ad8 21.奠c2 豐c7 22.hxg6 hxg6 23.豐e3 ②a5

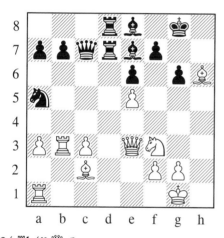

24.罝b4!? 豐c5

24...奠xb4 25.axb4+–

25.②d4 罝d5 26.罝e1 罝c8 27.奠g5 奠xg5 28.豐xg5 豐xc3 29.②f3 ②c4 30.奠xg6 fxg6 31.罝xb7 ②d2? 32.②h4 ②c4 33.②xg6 豐xe1† 34.含h2 罝d7 35.②e7† 含f8 36.豐h6† 1–0

Andrei Kharlov – Joseph Gallagher

Calcutta 2001

1.e4 c5 2.c3 ②f6 3.e5 ②d5 4.d4 cxd4 5.cxd4 d6 6.②f3 ②c6 7.奠c4 e6 8.0–0 奠e7 9.a3!?

9...0–0 10.罝e1 豐c7 11.奠d3 dxe5 12.dxe5 罝d8 13.豐e2 g6 14.奠d2 b6 15.②c3 ②xc3 16.奠xc3 奠b7 17.h4→ 罝d7 18.h5 罝ad8 19.奠b5 豐c8 20.豐e3 a6 21.奠f1 奠c5 22.豐f4 ②e7 23.hxg6 hxg6 24.②g5 ②f5 25.g4 ②h6

25...豐c6!⇄

26.奠g2± 罝d3 27.②e4 奠xe4 28.奠xe4 罝h3 29.罝ad1

29.奠g2 罝h4 30.豐g5 ②xg4 31.罝e2!+–

29...罝h4 30.奠f3 奠e7 31.含g2 罝xd1 32.罝xd1 豐c7 1–0

Aleksandr Karpatchev – Rainer Rauschenbach

Griesheim 2002

1.e4 c5 2.c3 ②f6 3.e5 ②d5 4.②f3 ②c6 5.d4 cxd4 6.奠c4 ②b6 7.奠b3 d5 8.exd6 豐xd6 9.0–0 e6 10.cxd4 奠e7 11.②c3 0–0 12.罝e1 ②d5 13.a3 ②xc3 14.bxc3 b6 15.豐d3 奠f6

16.♗g5 ♕d8 17.h4 ♘a5 18.♗c2 g6 19.♗h6
♗g7 20.♗xg7 ♔xg7

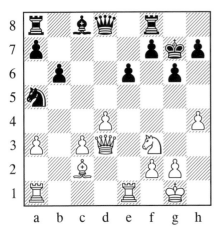

21.♘g5

21.h5±

**21...♕f6 22.♕g3 ♗b7 23.h5 ♖ac8 24.♖e5
♖fd8**

24...♘c4 25.hxg6 hxg6 26.♘xe6†! fxe6
27.♖g5+−

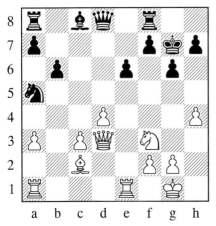

25.♖ae1?!

25.hxg6! hxg6 26.♘xe6† fxe6 27.♖g5+−

25...♘c4

25...♗d5!± 26.♖1e3→ (26.♘xh7!? ♔xh7
27.hxg6† ♔g7 28.♖h5 ♖h8 29.♖ee5→)

26.♘xe6† fxe6 27.♖xe6
1–0

Eros (Esserman) – babloo (GM Sasikiran)

Internet (blitz) 2011

1.e4 c5 2.d4 cxd4 3.c3 ♘f6 4.e5 ♘d5 5.♘f3
♘c6 6.♗c4 ♘b6 7.♗b3 d5 8.exd6 ♕xd6
9.0–0 ♗e6 10.♗xe6 ♕xe6 11.♘xd4!?

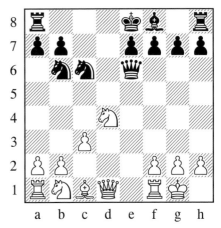

11...♘xd4

11...♕d5!?=

**12.cxd4 ♕d7 13.♘c3 e6 14.♖e1 ♖d8
15.♕g4 h5 16.♕g3 h4 17.♕g4 h3 18.gxh3
♕xd4 19.♖xe6†?!**

19.♖e4!?

**19...fxe6 20.♕g6† ♔d7 21.♗g5 ♔c8
22.♘b5 ♕xb2**

22...♕d5! 23.♖c1† ♗c5! 24.♕xg7 ♖h7!−+

23.♖c1† ♔b8 24.♖b1 ♕xa2

24...♖d1†! 25.♖xd1 ♗c5−+

**25.♗xd8+− ♗c5 26.♕g3† ♔a8 27.♘c7†
♔b8 28.♘a6†**
1–0

Dusko Pavasovic – Lars Schandorff

Gothenburg 2005

1.e4 c5 2.c3 ♘f6 3.e5 ♘d5 4.♘f3 ♘c6
5.♗c4 ♘b6 6.♗b3 d6 7.exd6 ♕xd6 8.♘a3
♗e6 9.d4 cxd4 10.♘b5 ♕d7 11.♘bxd4
♗xb3 12.♕xb3 e6 13.0-0 ♘xd4 14.♘xd4
♗e7 15.♖d1 0-0 16.♗e3

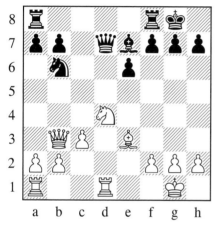

16...♘c8 17.♗f4 a6 18.♘f3 ♗d6 19.♗xd6
♘xd6 20.♕b6 ♖fd8 21.♖d4 ♕c6 22.♕xc6
bxc6 23.♖ad1 ♘b7 24.♔f1 ♔f8 25.♘e5
♖xd4 26.♖xd4 ♘d8

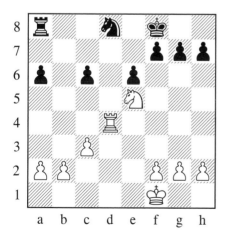

27.♖d7 ♔e8 28.♖c7 ♖b8 29.♘c4 ♔f8
30.♖a7 ♖b5 31.♖xa6 ♖c5 32.♘b6 ♔e8 33.a4
1–0

Pablo Zarnicki – Loek van Wely

Buenos Aires 1995

1.e4 c5 2.c3 ♘f6 3.e5 ♘d5 4.♘f3 ♘c6 5.d4
cxd4 6.♗c4 ♘b6 7.♗b3 d6 8.exd6 ♕xd6
9.0-0 ♗e6 10.♘a3 ♗xb3 11.♕xb3 ♕d5
12.♘b5 ♖c8 13.♘fxd4 ♘xd4 14.♘xd4 e6
15.♖d1 ♕xb3 16.axb3 a6 17.b4 ♗e7

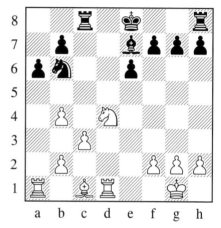

18.b5! axb5 19.♖a7 b4 20.♖xb7 ♘d5
21.♘f5 ♗f8 22.c4! ♖xc4 23.♘e3 ♘xe3
23...♖c5

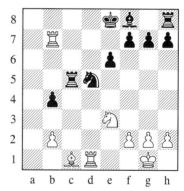

24.♘xd5 ♖xd5 25.♖xd5 exd5 26.♗d2 ♗e7
27.♗xb4 ♔g5 28.♖b8† ♗d8 29.♗a5 ♔d7
30.♗xd8 ♖xd8 31.♖xd8† ♔xd8 32.♔f1+–

24.♖b8† ♔e7 25.♗xe3 f5 26.b3 ♖c7
27.♖xb4 g6 28.♗b6 ♔f6 29.♖b5+– ♖e7

30.♗d8 ♔f7 31.♗xe7 ♗xe7 32.g3 g5 33.♖d7
h5 34.♖bb7 ♖e8 35.b4 e5 36.♖b6 f4 37.♔f1
♖a8 38.♖bb7 ♖e8 39.♔e2 ♔e6 40.♖xe7†
♖xe7 41.♖xe7† ♔xe7 42.♔d3 ♔d6 43.♔e4
f3 44.♔xf3
1–0

The Morra Reversed!

Rolf Wetzell – Vadim Martirosov

Boston 2011

Tired of being on the losing side of history
(see Esserman – Martirosov and Esserman –
"Unnamed teammate" from Chapter 1), FM
Martirosov takes my advice and switches sides,
but not colors! Behold the Morra Reversed vs.
the g3-English.

1.c4 e5 2.g3 d5 3.cxd5 c6!

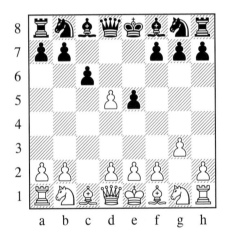

4.dxc6 ♘xc6 5.♗g2 ♘f6 6.♘c3 ♗c5 7.♘h3
0–0 8.0–0 h6 9.♔h1 ♕e7 10.f4 e4 11.♘f2
♗f5 12.♘a4 ♗xf2 13.♖xf2 ♖fd8 14.e3

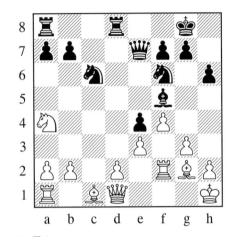

14...♖d3
14...♘b4!∓

15.a3 ♘a5 16.♘c3 b5
16...♕e6!?

17.♕c2
17.♘xb5 ♘b3→

17...♕e6
17...♖c8 18.♗f1 ♕e6 19.♗xd3 exd3 20.♕d1
♘b3 21.♖b1 a5!–+

**18.♗f1 ♘b3 19.♖b1 a6 20.♗e2 ♖ad8
21.♗d1 ♘d4! 22.exd4 e3 23.dxe3 ♖xc3!
24.♕xc3 ♘e4 25.♕e1 ♘xf2† 26.♕xf2 ♕e4†
27.♗f3 ♕xb1**
0–1

Endnotes

---

[1] *Smith-Morra Gambit, Finegold Defense*, page 128.

[2] A reference to Tal's famous quote: "I like to take my opponents into a dark forest when two plus two equals five."

[3] Kieseritzky as you may know was a famous player of the Romantic era, probably most well known for his immortal defeat at the hands of Anderssen in the Immortal Game.

[4] Cynics could argue that Morphy knew the gambit to be rubbish, but as this book will show, Morphy would have swum freely in its waters. It is safe to say that the Morra's disappearance in the Romantic era can be dismissed as an historical oddity.

[5] *Zurich 1953 International Chess Tournament*, Bronstein

[6] After 22.♖xf7! instead of 22.♖xb7, White is pressing for the win in Fischer – Korchnoi 1960 (see the supplemental games)

[7] The Smith-Morra Gambit's other namesake is the obscure chess player Pierre Morra, who published a series of articles in 1950 on the gambit.

[8] http://main.uschess.org/obituaries/smith.php

[9] http://en.wikipedia.org/wiki/Sicilian_Defence,_Smith%E2%80%93Morra_Gambit

[10] Sorry, Wing Gambit fans, but despite Bronstein's admiration for this opening in his last work *David vs. Goliath: Fighting the Computer*, I do not think modern analysis backs up the soundness of the winged gambit!

[11] "Rajlich: Busting the King's Gambit, this time for sure." http://www.chessbase.com/newsdetail.asp?newsid=8047

[12] The a2-g8 diagonal is often nicknamed the "Italian" diagonal as the bishop posts to c4 in the famous Italian Opening.

[13] 11...♗d7 12.♘xe5 dxe5 13.♗xe6 ♗xb5 14.♗xf7† ♔xf7 15.♕b3† ♔g6 16.♕c2† ♔f7 17.♕b3†= with perpetual check, and therefore White must do better than 10.♗f4?!.

[14] I only found this shocking "novelty" in the summer of 2011 while preparing for my opponent in the bathroom of my motel room in the Spanish Alps well after 3 a.m. Not ideal artistic conditions, but sometimes one must make do, for my roommate, IM Stopa, was sound asleep in the main chamber. As a result of our European adventure, IM Stopa, already an Evans Gambit disciple, is now a Morra convert, with one of his games featured later. Throughout the tour, he desperately wanted to see just one of my Morra Gambits appear on the board for pure entertainment value. But alas, it was not to be, and my grandmaster opponent greeted me bright and early the next morning with 1...e5 and a wry smile. Later, much to my chagrin, I learned that my "novelty" had been flushed down the proverbial toilet, as 13.♗d5!! had also been independently analyzed in IM Trent's 2010 Smith-Morra Gambit DVD (oops, I only watch movies on DVD). My Morra version of the famed Topalov vs. Kramnik "toiletgate" scandal. May you all have better Morra Gambit bathroom experiences!

[15] Those in the 7.♘gf3 Tarrasch and in the Milner-Barry Gambit in the Advanced variation, in particular!

[16] I first learned of this great zwischenzug from Burgess and Nunn's sparkling analysis of the position in Winning with the Smith-Morra Gambit.

[17] http://equotes.wetpaint.com/page/Bruce+Lee+Quotes

[18] http://www.nytimes.com/2009/10/25/crosswords/chess/25chess.html

[19] http://en.wikipedia.org/wiki/Mikhail_Tal

[20] *The Dark Knight*, 2008

[21] *Fighting the Anti-Sicilians,* pages 218-9.

[22] *My System* and *Chess Praxis*

[23] More references to Nimzowitsch's famous "lust to expand" quote in *My System.*

[24] Inspired by Morpheus' words to Neo in *The Matrix*: "You take the red pill, you stay in Wonderland, and I show you how deep the rabbit hole goes."

[25] But this may just be wishful thinking for Black!! Delve into the analysis of the supplemental game LarryC (GM Christiansen) – BlackSky, Internet (blitz) 2003, featuring 11.♘d4!?, for the ultimate truth. Unclear may in fact drift towards ±!

[26] *The Dark Knight*, 2008.

[27] A reference to the 1999 Sci-Fi thriller *The Matrix*.

[28] *Richard II*, Act V, Scene V.

[29] In fact, it is more accurate to play 11.♗g5†! after 10...♔f6, as the black king should retreat to g7 on both 11.♘e4† and 11.♗g5†, when the bishop move then offers more attacking chances in the resulting variation.

[30] I found this powerful improvement to Langrock's analysis in his *Modern Morra Gambit* 2006, but he later corrected his error and also gives 10.♘b5! in his 2011 edition. Just one case of two analysts independently arriving at similar conclusions!

[31] I first learned of this move and the subsequent ideas from Burgess's excellent 1994 Morra Gambit book.

[32] Langrock, for one, makes such a sober assessment in his *Modern Morra Gambit*, 2006.

[33] The awkward 13.♕e3!?, as recommended in Langrock's 2006 work, is perfectly playable. The queen then repositions to h4 via h6 and the bishop posts on g5. But I prefer the deeper 13.♕e2.

[34] *From Russia with Love*, 1963.

[35] http://www.uschess.org/content/view/9184/520

[36] http://kevinspraggett.blogspot.co.uk/2011/08/upset-at-us-open.html

[37] In fact, we at Quality Chess did find a hidden correspondence game here... Eilmes – K. Jones, e-mail 2006. Oh that vice that is correspondence!

[38] Title inspired from the blockbuster sequel *The Matrix Reloaded*.

[39] On my birthday, I received the inspiration to play these daring sacrifices from a very similar effort of FM Burgess which I read in his Morra book as a kid (see the supplemental games).

[40] *Tomorrow Never Dies*

[41] Upon the rare line 7...♘c6!? it becomes premature to play 8.e5?! as Black has the defensive resource 8...f5!. Instead the gambiteer should hurl 8.♗f4! first, and only then thrust e4-e5. See analysis of the supplemental game Kieseritzky – Vitzthum von Eckstaedt, Paris 1846(!), for more details.

[42] *The World is Not Enough*

[43] *Austin Powers: The Spy Who Shagged Me*

[44] *Austin Powers: The Spy Who Shagged Me*

45 Title inspired by the blockbuster *Indiana Jones and the Temple of Doom*.

46 Mr. Ginsburg has even gone as far to dub the Taylor Defense "Old Faithful" after Evans' and Mecking's historic wins (http://nezhmet.wordpress.com/2008/10/16/uscl_week_8/).

47 Though not Taylor's!

48 Even Tartakower trumpeted the move way back in 1950, but certainly without knowing 8.♗f4's implications for 21st century Morra theory.

49 Endgames – the German GM Mueller's specialty!

50 Langrock's main variation in *Modern Morra Gambit*, 2011.

51 Credit to Senior Master Matthew Herman for finding this spectacular finish to the combination. Before showing him this variation, I had missed 23.♖e7†!, only concluding that 23.♖xe6† draws.

52 A variation of Nimzowitsch's famous maxim "restrain, blockade, destroy" from his classic *My System*.

53 No doubt many commentators have tried to make light of Lasker's maxim in a similar manner – one such variation including "the hardest game to win is a lost game" (http://www.chessville. com/Quotes/ misc_trivia_quotes_point_and_counterpoint.htm).

54 In a 2011 US Chess League article, while annotating my game vs. Van Wely, I questioned the valor of those who decline with 3...♘f6 in the following fashion: "This move is VERY NECESSARY. Grandmaster Loek Van Wely is a man of principle, a man who never shies away from a challenge, from a duel. Thus, even though many view him as a strictly positional player, you can also argue that he is also a man from the 19th century's Romantic era, and for this I have the utmost respect for him. However, when GM Alejandro Ramirez annotated this game in this month's Chess Life, he argued that "this move [3...dxc3] is unnecessary", that 3...♘f6! is best, and mused, "Why do people take on c3? It will remain a mystery to me." Alejandro, my friend, I must now poke some more fun at you in good humor while answering your question. When Lady Gaga calls your name in her famous hit single ALELLELELLEALLELELELEjandro, she is singing to the Alejandro who takes on c3, not the Alejandro who meekly declines with 3...♘f6. I believe this answers the question to the best of my abilities."

55 GM Jesse Kraai loves to say this about the Morra and my games. In fact, we may give him credit for coining this one-liner that I knew from living but never put into words.

56 Of course Sveshnikov, the great c3-Sicilian expert, did not play the Morra to start. I merely show the Morra move order for instructional value.

57 Also independently analyzed on GM Spraggett's blog in July 2011 (http://kevinspraggett. blogspot.com/2011/07/upset-in-phily.html).

58 *The Dark Knight*

59 Inspired by Agent Smith's comment to Neo in *The Matrix Revolutions*: "Mr. Anderson, welcome back. We've missed you."

60 After 16.♖d1?! ♔f8 17.♕f5† ♗f6 Black survived and later won in Alsop – Lange, e-mail 1997. Note that here the 18.♗h6? lunge is simply refuted by 18...♕e5.

61 http://www.jeremysilman.com/book_reviews_js/Modern_Mora_Gambit.html

Works Cited

Books

Aagaard & Shaw: *Experts on the Anti-Sicilian,* Quality Chess 2011

Bronstein: *Zurich 1953, International Chess Tournament,* Translated by Jim Marfia, Dover Publications 1979

Bronstein & Voronkov: *David Against Goliath: Fighting the Computer*, Olms 2006

Burgess: *Winning with the Smith-Morra Gambit*, Batsford 1994

Ciaffone & Finegold: *Smith-Morra Gambit, Finegold Defense*, Bob Ciaffone 2000

Ftacnik: *Grandmaster Repertoire 6: The Sicilian Defence*, Quality Chess 2010

Langrock: *The Modern Morra Gambit, First Edition*, Russell Enterprises, Inc. 2006

Langrock: *The Modern Morra Gambit, Second Edition*, Russell Enterprises, Inc. 2011

Nimzowitsch: *Chess Praxis*, Quality Chess 2007

Nimzowitsch: *My System*, Quality Chess 2007

Palliser: *Fighting the Anti-Sicilians*, Everyman Chess 2007

Sergeant: *Morphy's Games of Chess*, Dover Publications 1957

Shakespeare: *Hamlet,* Simon & Schuster 2003

Shakespeare: *Richard II,* Empire Books 2012

Articles

Bird: *Esserman and Sadvakasov Thrill in Sturbridge*, Chess Life Online 2009
   http://www.uschess.org/content/view/9184/520

Golubev: *Esserman – Van Wely*, Chess-news.ru 2011
   http://chess-news.ru/sites/default/files/u5/Games/Obzory/essevanvelyg0.htm

Grivas: *A Black Repertoire against the Morra*, Yearbook 88, New In Chess 2008

Short: *Short stories*, New In Chess #8 2011

Harding: *Has the Morra Gambit been Revived?,* Chess Café 2007
   http://www.chesscafe.com/text/kibitz134.pdf

Hays: *In Memoriam – Kenneth Ray Smith*, uschess.org 1999
   http://main.uschess.org/obituaries/smith.php

Rajlich: *Busting the King's Gambit, this time for sure*, ChessBase 2012
   http://www.chessbase.com/newsdetail.asp?newsid=8047

McClain: *An Often-Shunned Opening, for Good Reason*, New York Times 2009
   http://www.nytimes.com/2009/10/25/crosswords/chess/25chess.html

Spraggett: *Upset at US Open*, Blogspot 2011
   http://kevinspraggett.blogspot.com/2011/08/upset-at-us-open.html

Spraggett, Kevin: *Upset in Phily*, Blogspot 2011
   http://kevinspraggett.blogspot.com/2011/07/upset-in-phily.html

Films

From Russia with Love, Dir. Terence Young, Eon Productions 1963
Goldfinger, Dir. Guy Hamilton, Eon Productions 1964
Live and Let Die, Dir. Guy Hamilton, Eon Productions 1973
GoldenEye, Dir. Martin Campbell, Eon Productions 1995
Tomorrow Never Dies, Dir. Roger Spottiswoode, Eon Productions 1997
The World is Not Enough, Dir. Michael Apted, Eon Productions 1999
Die Another Day, Dir. Lee Tamahorj, Eon Productions 2002
Casino Royale, Dir. Martin Campbell, Eon Productions 2006
Quantum of Solace, Dir. Marc Forster, Eon Productions 2008
Austin Powers: International Man of Mystery, Dir. Jay Roach, New Line Cinema 1997
Austin Powers: The Spy Who Shagged Me, Dir. Jay Roach, New Line Cinema 1999
Austin Powers in Goldmember, Dir. Jay Roach, New Line Cinema 2002
The Matrix. Dir. Andy Wachowski & Larry Wachowski. Warner Bros. 1999
The Matrix Reloaded. Dir. Andy Wachowski & Larry Wachowski. Warner Bros. 2003
The Matrix Revolutions. Dir. Andy Wachowski & Larry Wachowski. Warner Bros. 2003
Forrest Gump, Dir. Robert Zemeckis, Paramount Pictures 1994
Gladiator, Dir. Ridley Scott, DreamWorks Pictures 2000
Indiana Jones and the Temple of Doom, Dir. Steven Spielberg, Lucasfilm 1984
Rocky II, Dir. Sylvester Stallone, United Artists 1979
The Dark Knight, Dir. Christopher Nolan, Warner Bros. Pictures 2008
Wall Street, Dir. Oliver Stone, 20th Century Fox 1987

Game Index

Variation Index

Chapter 3

1.e4 c5 2.d4 cxd4 3.c3 dxc3 4.♘xc3 ♘c6 5.♘f3 d6 6.♗c4 e6 7.0–0
7...♗e7 8.♕e2 a6 9.♖d1 ♕c7 10.♗f4! ♘e5?! 11.♗xe5! dxe5 12.♖ac1± *83*
7...♘f6 8.♕e2 a6 9.♖d1 ♕c7 10.♗f4! *85*
    10...♘e5?! 11.♗b5†!± *78, 85*
    10...♗e7 *79*
        11.e5!?(?!) ♘h5! 12.♗g5!∓ *82, 88*
            11...dxe5? 12.♘xe5 ♘xe5 13.♗xe5± *82*
        11.♖ac1! 0–0 12.♗b3 *79*
            12...♖d8/♖e8/♗d7 13.♘d5!→ *80*
            12...♕b8 13.e5! ♘h5 *91*
                14.♗g5 dxe5 15.♗xe7 ♘xe7 16.♘xe5⩱ *92*
                14.♗e3!? dxe5 15.♗b6!∞ *94*

Chapter 4

1.e4 c5 2.d4 cxd4 3.c3 dxc3 4.♘xc3 e6 5.♘f3 a6 6.♗c4 b5 7.♗b3 ♗b7 8.0–0!
8...d6 9.♘g5!→ *99*
8...b4 9.♘d5! exd5 10.exd5 *104*
    10...♗d6 11.♖e1† *107*
        11...♘e7 12.♘g5! 0–0 13.♕h5!+– *108*
        11...♔f8 12.♕d4!± *109, 111*
    10...d6 *105*
        11.♕d4!?∞ *105*
            11...♘f6 12.♕xb4!± *105*
            11...♘d7 12.♖e1† ♘e7 13.♕xb4 ♘c5 14.♗f4∞ *116*
        11.♖e1†! ♗e7 *117*
            12.♕d4!? *117*
                12...♘f6?! 13.♕xb4!± *105, 117*
                    13...♗c8 14.♗f4 0–0 15.♖xe7± *105, 117*
                    13...♕c7 14.♗g5!± *117*
                12...♔f8 13.♕xb4 ♗c8 14.♗f4∞ *119*
            12.♘d4!?→ *317*

Chapter 5

1.e4 c5 2.d4 cxd4 3.c3 dxc3 4.♘xc3 e6 5.♘f3 a6 6.♗c4
6...b5 7.♗b3 d6 8.0–0 ♖a7?! 9.♗e3 ♖d7 10.♘d4!± *122, 319*
6...d6 7.0–0 ♘c6 8.♕e2 b5 9.♗b3 ♖a7 10.♗e3 ♖d7 11.♖fd1!!→ *132*
    11...♗b7 12.♘g5!→ *136*
    11...♗e7 12.♘xb5!→ *130, 134*
    11...♘f6 12.♘xb5!→ *134*

Chapter 6

1.e4 c5 2.d4 cxd4 3.c3 dxc3 4.♘xc3

Chapter 7

1.e4 c5 2.d4 cxd4 3.c3 dxc3 4.♘xc3 e6 5.♘f3 ♘c6 6.♗c4

Chapter 8

1.e4 c5 2.d4 cxd4 3.c3 dxc3 4.♘xc3 e6 5.♘f3

Chapter 9

1.e4 c5 2.d4 cxd4 3.c3 dxc3 4.♘xc3 ♘c6 5.♘f3 d6 6.♗c4
6...♘f6 7.e5! *205*
    7...dxe5 8.♕xd8† *205*
        8...♘xd8 9.♘b5! ♖b8 10.♘xe5± *205, 220*
        8...♔xd8 9.♘g5 ♘a5! 10.♗b5!± *220*
    7...♘g4! 8.exd6!± *219*
6...a6 7.0–0 ♘f6 *207*
    8.♗e3!? *207*
        8...♗g4 9.♕b3!→ *207*
        8...e6!= *212*
    8.b4!? *208*
        8...♗g4 9.b5 axb5 10.♘xb5! *328*
            10...♗xf3 11.gxf3 g6 12.♕b3!± *210*
            10...e6! 11.♗f4 ♗e7!∓ *328*
        8...e6!∓
    8.♗f4! e6 9.♕e2∞̄ *327*
        8...♗g4 9.h3! *213*
            9...♗xf3 10.♕xf3 e6 11.♖fd1 *222*
                11...♕a5!? *222*
                    12.♗b3!?→ *223*
                    12.♗e2!?= *224*
                    12.♗f1!?= *223*
                11...♕b6!? 12.♕e2!→ *226*
                11...♕b8!? 12.♗e2! ♗e7 13.♕g3! 0–0 14.♖xd6!?→ *228*
            9...♗h5 *214*
                10.g4!?→ *214*
                10.♕b3!?→ *215, 229*

Chapter 10

1.e4 c5 2.d4 cxd4 3.c3 dxc3 4.♘xc3 d6 5.♘f3 e6 6.♗c4 a6 7.0–0 ♗e7 8.♕e2 ♘f6 9.♖d1
9...b5 *234*
    10.♗b3!? ♘bd7 *234*
        11.e5!? dxe5 12.♘xe5 ♕b6!⇄ *235*
        11.♘d4!? *235*
            11...♗b7?! 12.♗xe6!± *235, 329*
            11...♕b6!⇄ *235*
    10.e5! bxc4 11.exf6 gxf6 12.♘d2!!± *237, 241*
9...♘bd7!? 10.e5! dxe5 11.♘xe5 0–0 12.♗f4!∞̄ *240*

Chapter 11

Chapter 12

Chapter 13

Chapter 14

1.e4 c5 2.d4 cxd4 3.c3 ♘f6 4.e5 ♘d5
5.♕xd4!? e6 6.♘f3 ♘c6 7.♕e4 f5!? 8.♕e2 ♕c7 9.g3 *285*
    9...b5 10.♗g2 a5 11.0–0 ♗a6 12.♘h4!→ *285*
    9...b6 10.♗g2 ♘cb4! 11.c4 ♗a6 12.b3 b5!→ *334*
5.♘f3! d6
    6.♕xd4!? e6 7.♘bd2 ♘c6 8.♗b5 ♗d7 9.♗xc6 ♗xc6 10.♘c4 *287*
        10...dxe5 11.♘cxe5± *287*
        10...f6!∞ *287*
    6.exd6!?
        6...e6 7.♘xd4 ♗xd6 8.g3± *288*
        6...♕xd6 7.♘a3!→ *288*
5...e6 6.cxd4 *290*
    6...d6 *290*
        7.a3!? *290*
            7...♘d7 8.♗d3± *291*
            7...♗d7 8.♗d3 ♗c6 9.0–0 ♘d7 *292*
                10.b4!? a6 11.♖e1 ♖c8!? 12.♘g5!?∞ *295*
                10.♖e1!? ♖c8!? 11.♗d2!?±
        7.♗c4!? ♘c6 8.0–0 ♗e7 9.♕e2 0–0 10.♘c3!? ♘xc3 11.bxc3 dxe5 12.dxe5 *335*
            12...♕a5!? *335*
                13.♗d2!?→ *336*
                13.♕e4!? ♕xc3 14.♗d2⯮ *335*
            12...♕c7 13.♕e4 b6 14.♗d3 g6 15.♗g5 ♗b7 16.♗f6!? ♘b4! 17.♕h4 ♘d5
            18.♘g5 h5 19.♕xh5 ♘xf6! 20.♕h6 ♕xe5 21.♗xg6!= *337*
    6...b6 7.♘c3 ♘xc3 8.bxc3 ♕c7 9.♗d2 ♗b7 10.♗d3 d6 11.0–0 ♘d7 12.♘g5! dxe5
    13.♕h5 g6 14.♕h3→ *299*
5...♘c6 6.♗c4! ♘b6 7.♗b3 *305*
    7...g6 8.♘g5!→ *306*
    7...d6 8.exd6 ♕xd6 9.0–0 ♗e6 10.♘a3!→ *307, 343*

The Morra Reversed!

1.c4 e5 2.g3 d5 3.cxd5 c6!⯮ *344*

Transpositions

2.♘f3!?

1.e4 c5 2.♘f3

Advantage: Limits the defender's options, especially after 2...e6/g6 3.d4 cxd4 4.c3!?.

Disadvantage: 2...d6! stops the gambiteer in his tracks and forces the Open Sicilian or other sidelines, in view of 3.d4 cxd4 4.c3?! ♘f6!∓. White can now no longer enter the Alapin (5.e5 is impossible), while 5.♗d3 or 5.♕c2 leads to a dubious Morra.

Comical transpositions

1.d4!? c5 2.e4!? springs the Morra on the Czech Benoni player!

1.♘f3 c5 2.d4 cxd4 3.c3!?

3...dxc3 4.♘xc3 leads to Morra mayhem after 5.e4, but 3...d5 and the gambiteer must snore after 4.cxd4!. Who knew the Morra and Exchange Slav were so related?!

The Morra Reversed!?

Upset the Morra only works for White? Don't be. Just play the Morra Reversed, a novel approach against the g3-English (see Wetzell – Martirosov, Boston 2011, on page 344)!
1.c4 e5 2.g3 d5 3.cxd5 c6!

Don't say I never taught you how to play the Black pieces!

Opening books

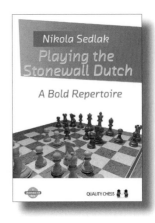

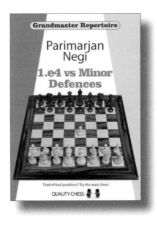